MW00564708

The Stormy Present

CIVIL WAR AMERICA

Peter S. Carmichael, Caroline E. Janney, and Aaron Sheehan-Dean, *editors*

This landmark series interprets broadly the history and culture of the Civil War era through the long nineteenth century and beyond. Drawing on diverse approaches and methods, the series publishes historical works that explore all aspects of the war, biographies of leading commanders, and tactical and campaign studies, along with select editions of primary sources. Together, these books shed new light on an era that remains central to our understanding of American and world history.

ADAM I. P. SMITH

The Stormy Present

Conservatism and the Problem of Slavery
in Northern Politics, 1846–1865

The University of North Carolina Press *Chapel Hill*

© 2017 Adam I. P. Smith
All rights reserved
Set in Arno Pro by Westchester Publishing Services

The University of North Carolina Press has been a member of the
Green Press Initiative since 2003.

Library of Congress Cataloging-in-Publication Data
Names: Smith, Adam I. P., author.
Title: The stormy present : conservatism and the problem of slavery
   in Northern politics, 1846–1865 / Adam I. P. Smith.
Other titles: Civil War America (Series)
Description: Chapel Hill : University of North Carolina Press, [2017] |
   Series: Civil War America | Includes bibliographical references and index.
Identifiers: LCCN 2016055625 | ISBN 9781469633893 (cloth : alk. paper) |
   ISBN 9781469659084 (pbk. : alk. paper) | ISBN 9781469633909 (ebook)
Subjects: LCSH: Northeastern States—Politics and government—19th century. |
   Conservatism—Northeastern States—History—19th century. | Slavery—
   United States. | United States—History—Civil War, 1861–1865—Causes.
Classification: LCC F106 .S598 2017 | DDC 973.7/11—dc23
   LC record available at https://lccn.loc.gov/2016055625

Cover illustration: © istockphoto.com/BCWH.

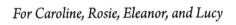

For Caroline, Rosie, Eleanor, and Lucy

The dogmas of the quiet past are inadequate to the stormy present.

—Abraham Lincoln, 1862

Contents

Preface

Imagine you lived in a small town in upstate New York, or Ohio, or Pennsylvania in 1848. It is a town like many others, with a main street that is dusty in the summer and a quagmire in winter. Its principal features are a courthouse, a tavern, and several churches, one with a striking spire. Most of the houses have two or three rooms on a single floor and are built of wood, but there are some brick houses too, some three stories high. You or a member of your family might run a dry-goods store or work as a bookkeeper for a local merchant; or perhaps you are a teacher in a one-room schoolhouse, your salary paid by local taxpayers under the terms of a recent state law establishing a public education system.

You and your neighbors are prospering, on the whole. It has been more than a decade since the last major economic downturn. True, one of your relatives lost his farm when he failed to keep up the mortgage repayments, but he has recently borrowed the money for a steamship passage to California and new opportunity. Indeed, your town has grown rapidly in the last few years and some of the newcomers have arrived from Germany, England, or Ireland, founding new churches, speaking in accents you don't at first understand. You weren't born in the county yourself, but you feel like a well-established presence now: your children were born here—one is buried in the local cemetery—and you like to feel you know what's going on.

Now imagine: recently, a pugnacious young man with some college education and political ambitions has established a new daily newspaper to rival the longer-established organ. You don't always agree with the editor's fiery editorials, but the new paper seems to have better and quicker access to reprinted articles from other states and even—via reprinting stories in the *New York Tribune*—from Europe, which is gripped by political turmoil. The news sparks interesting conversation among neighbors. One of the newcomers speaks personally of having witnessed the army opening fire on protestors in a German town. Another is a Chartist from Yorkshire, who claims to have been thrown out of his job in a textile mill for political organizing and who speaks eloquently and at length about the rapaciousness of the landed classes back home. There are landed gentry here, of a kind, but at least they don't have titles.

Everyone in your town is white, but occasionally there are rumors that a family of fugitive slaves from south of the Ohio River is being hidden in the home of one of the local pastors, an outspoken abolitionist. Sometimes your own minister talks of the universal desire that the institution of slavery should utterly cease in this land of freedom and you nod in agreement. But you nod also when he adds that slavery has law on its side and that any abrupt legislation ending it would bring evils to the country scarcely less palatable than slavery itself. More often his Sunday sermons focus on the need for a religious patriotism as the foundation of a virtuous republic. The love of country, your minister is fond of saying, is required by Holy Religion, but even more so since we have a country so preeminently deserving of affection, so blessed by Divine favor.

Apart from the Sabbath, your life is filled with work and largely bounded within the ten miles or so around your town. The journey to Philadelphia or New York used to take a couple of weeks on pitted roads or by lake and canal, but now the cuttings and embankments for railroads are being built—mainly by the Irish laborers who sometimes cause drunken scenes. You sense that your world is undergoing a transformation never seen by any generation. You feel blessed to live in the freest country on earth. You want to keep it that way.

If you lived in that small town in 1848, the next decade and a half would force you to make difficult political choices, all the while worrying that your prosperous, free society was under threat. In the days to come, your town will be convulsed by politics: some of your friends join secret anti-Catholic and anti-immigrant lodges run by the Know-Nothings. There will be violent attacks on a visiting abolitionist speaker and emotional meetings opposing the extension of slavery into Kansas. Old parties will collapse and with them old certainties. In 1850, it would have seemed impossible to imagine having to make the decisions, commitments, and sacrifices that will be pressed on you in the coming years. In those days, at times you will feel never more alive, and never more determined to do your religious and patriotic duty for your forefathers and for the generations to come. At other times, you will feel despairing of the future. And often you are simply unsure and confused by the choices before you.

Politicians sometimes seem too mired in corruption to be trusted. The stump speakers you hear—some of them the leading men of the county, others who say they're fresh from the people and untainted by office holding—almost all describe themselves as conservatives. They all say they're Unionists and offer solutions that they claim will avoid the nightmare of disunion. Yet the politicians, the newspaper editors, and even some of the preachers you hear also castigate their opponents for having abandoned the principles of liberty. You worry about agitators who use violent language, and the blind partisanship and fanaticism that prevent compromise. You had grown up believing—like all your family and neighbors—that the Constitution's genius was that it mitigated conflicts by acknowledging the different interests of the far-flung republic. And the political institutions of the country, the rituals of national remembrance such as July Fourth speeches, together with churches and schools, had always—up until now—been sources of authority establishing the boundaries within which your free society could flourish. Now those institutions seem at war with one another, exaggerating differences rather than easing them. The sensibility of your society seems to shift around you. There is, you have come to feel, a far tougher, less tolerant, more confrontational pitch to public life; compromise had once been a virtue, but now self-described conservatives are decrying it as submission. And when—eventually—the South launches a rebellion to break up the government and opens fire on the national flag, the question you will face is what price is worth paying to restore the Union.

This book is my effort to imagine what those years were like, to reconstruct how people navigated their way through those stormy times, crisis by crisis and decision by decision.

Introduction
The Dogmas of the Quiet Past

"The dogmas of the quiet past are inadequate to the stormy present," wrote Abraham Lincoln in 1862. "The occasion is piled high with difficulty, and we must rise with the occasion. As our case is new, so we must think anew, and act anew."[1] The president had a specific aim in mind: he wanted the leaders of the slave states that remained in the Union to accept his plan for compensated, gradual emancipation. But, in a larger sense (to use a Lincolnian phrase), his words also captured a question at the heart of the politics of his era. What role could and should the past—whether quiet or not—play in helping people navigate through the tumultuous transformations of the mid-Victorian age? After all, it was one thing to exhort people to think and act anew and quite another for it to happen. The Border States did not, in spite of his pleas, accept Lincoln's plan, although, in less than three years, freedom for enslaved people all across the Union came anyway. The quiet past retained its hold, and its dogmas did not yield so easily to circumstance.

The destruction of slavery through a terrible war was the most dramatic of many interlinked revolutionary changes that threatened to sever the present and the future from the past in the mid-nineteenth century. Civil War–era Americans of all political inclinations regarded themselves as in the vanguard of providential progress. But if this was an age of progress it was also an age of anxiety.[2] As in the melodrama that dominated popular taste on the stage, mid-Victorian society seemed, to those who lived through it, to exist in a state of perpetual tension, suspended between the promise of redemption and greatness and the abyss of violence and immorality. A Presbyterian minister warned in the 1840s that a "general fermentation and excitement of matter and mind" and "sweeping floods of faction [and] passion" threatened "our great political and civil institutions and the social and moral principles upon which they depend for their existence and perpetuity."[3] On the one hand, dizzying population growth seemed to validate the experiment in popular government; on the other, immigration of Catholics from Ireland who seemed so culturally and politically alien raised uncomfortable questions about whether all Americans were capable of self-rule. As the nation doubled in geographical size, and then, after the invasion of Mexico, doubled again, was it now too big and too diverse, too filled with clashing interests to hold together? From the growth of cities and the new railroads to the rising numbers of lawyers and clerks, the evidence of economic growth was everywhere, but was it bringing to America the Old World problems of a clash between rich and poor? Could a mobile, modernizing society remain ordered and free? Ministers wrote anxious sermons about the spread of divorce, old men sighed at the rebelliousness of youth, and editors sternly warned that mob violence was bringing to America the nightmares of Jacobinical terror.[4] Sensational murder cases titillated, horrified, and captivated a newspaper-reading public and touched dark fears about social atomization and the breakdown of moral restraint.[5] Mid-century Americans also lamented the state of their politics—the corruption, the demagoguery, the self-serving character of politicians. And hanging over it all was the threat, and eventually the reality, of disunion: the nightmarish prospect of an end to the great experiment in popular government endangered by what some saw as the wicked fairy's primal curse on the Republic—human slavery.[6] In all these areas, the problem was one of instability in comparison with an imagined past of moral order and high-minded politics.[7]

They talked all the time about the consequences of living in an age of transformation, yet mid-Victorian Americans were still taken aback by the pace of change. Feeling insignificant in the face of onrushing forces that were beyond human comprehension, they told themselves that their nation's destiny was in the hands of an all-controlling Providence: even Lincoln ruminated that he had not "controlled events" but that "events have controlled me."[8] Yet such Providentialism did not usually lead to fatalism; Americans had far too much faith in human ingenuity (albeit through God's grace) for that. The men and women of the Civil War era had projects and dreams: as a conscious undertaking, they faced up to the complexity of modernity as best they could.[9]

The Stormy Present tells the story of how the majority of white Northerners made the political choices that led to war and the destruction of slavery—objectives that few sought but that most, in the end, supported. These were years during which Northerners were forced to confront issues that most would rather not have had to deal with, not least the implications of the existential confrontation over the legitimacy of slavery. How did Northern voters and politicians understand the problems they confronted and how did they prioritize competing values? How, when faced with difficult challenges, did they balance where they had come from against where they wanted to go?[10]

Consciously trying to build institutions and to make choices that would guarantee their freedoms, they stumbled, eventually, into a situation where they felt compelled to use immense force to preserve the Union, not just for themselves but, to quote Lincoln again, for the "whole family of man."

In the chapters that follow, I have sought to recapture the sometimes-confused sense of purpose of Northerners as they navigated these treacherous waters. As they did so, their guiding star, it often seemed, was a conviction that their choices were "conservative." This was an era in U.S. history in which self-described conservatives dominated public life. The newspapers, books, letters, and speeches of Northerners in these years provide ample evidence that the invocation of conservative men or conservative principles was talismanic. Even those who sought radical changes in American society often felt the need to argue that they embodied true conservatism while their opponents traded in false or pretended conservatism. Calling something conservative was a way of legitimizing it: whether opposition to the Fugitive Slave Act or mob violence, whether support for war or for peace. The meanings of conservatism, and the identities of those most likely to be seen and to see themselves as conservative, shifted under the pressure of events. But Northerners' desire to find the conservative path never faltered. By identifying themselves or their positions as conservative, a remarkably broad range of mid-nineteenth-century politicians revealed something very important about their political assumptions.[11]

We know much about those who wanted to transform the United States in these years. Understandably, historians have been drawn to write about the most vocal abolitionists, the most forward-thinking social reformers, or the Southerners who declared their independence in an ultimately self-defeating, vainglorious effort to preserve slavery.[12] We also know much about the five million or so enslaved people in North America and how they sought to transform their desperate situation despite their position of apparent powerlessness. So far, so good: but to understand the crises of the mid-nineteenth century United States—what people thought, how they made decisions, how they acted—we also need to pay attention to the many millions who were not the change-makers but who saw change as something that happened to them, or around them.[13] One newspaper observed on the eve of Civil War that there was a "conservative but silent" majority in the free states.[14] Whether they were the forgotten Americans or not, these people were, to extend the Nixonian paraphrase, the nonabolitionists, the nonradicals. What did they think? What did they want? *The Stormy Present* seeks to answer these questions, and argues that partly because they were very much *in* the majority, this

Northern Civil War–era "silent majority" shaped the way in which political choices were framed. They sought, in essence, less to change their world than to save it.

The principal players in this book are individuals and groups who were most likely to think of themselves or their politics as conservative—and who tended to be thought of in that way by others. That is a very large group, encompassing the broad middle ground of Northern politics ranging from some who were among the first to join the new Republican Party to others who ended up being attacked as "copperhead" opponents of the Union war effort. It is not a book focusing on abolitionists, who rarely called themselves conservative (although they sometimes did) but otherwise my cast is a deliberately wide one. One of my aims is to trace the sometimes-agonizing political journey of Northerners who did not think of themselves as ideologues, to divine how they made political choices, and to trace the consequences of those choices for their nation. It turns out that a good way of doing that is to trace the changing ways they invoked conservatism. But precisely because practically everyone claimed to be a conservative, just as practically everyone claimed to be a patriotic defender of the Union, political language often came down to a contest over what policy, or style, or approach most fitted the conservative label. And so, more broadly, this book is not just a study of a particular set of individuals but about how the gravitational pull of conservatism in political culture helps us comprehend how all politicians and voters in the nonslave states responded to slavery: a moral and political problem that posed an existential challenge to the Republic.[15]

The standard narrative of the coming of the Civil War and emancipation dismisses the moderate majority as bystanders, hapless as the center collapsed in the face of surging political polarization. A narrative that focuses only on the political margins cannot explain why Northerners from all parties and backgrounds were so willing to fight for the Union in 1861 and then to destroy slavery. Of course, radical antislavery politicians, including free blacks, helped define the parameters of the politics of this period in ways that belie their small numbers—although their influence was not always a constructive one, as moderate Northerners recoiled from association with Jacobinical excess. This book makes the case that the conservative majority were not pushed or hoodwinked into supporting radical causes but made choices that in the end led them to programmatic conclusions they could never have envisaged at the start. In the end, the paradox this book explains is of essentially conservative people being drawn to act in fundamentally revolutionary ways.

The Meanings of Conservatism

Histories of American political thought usually stress the relative weakness of a conservative tradition in the antebellum North, while scholars wanting to trace the pre-New Deal ancestors of the modern conservative movement have generally found more to say about the South.[16] Yet if anything, the language of conservatism was more prominent in the mid-nineteenth century than either before or since—in the North as well as the South. Such was the ubiquity of the term, it is folly to try to understand the politics of this period without reckoning with what political actors and observers meant by it. The terms "conservatives" and "conservatism," noted a writer for a religious journal in 1848, were used so frequently that it "becomes a matter of some surprise, how our predecessors managed to dispense with them so generally."[17] In the presidential election of that year, both parties vied to control the language of conservatism. One Whig public meeting adopted resolutions stating, "Whig principles are conservative in their nature, and cultivate a reverence for established customs, laws, [and] constitutions."[18] Whig newspapers were full of appeals to "conservative men" and approving descriptions of Taylor as a "true conservative." Supporters of the Democratic candidate Lewis Cass countered that he was the "true conservative" and Taylor's election would be "destructive."[19] Conservatism was "the middle term of politics," explained one Whig writer: the space that everyone wanted to control in order to win elections.[20] A Democratic journal, meanwhile, argued that conservatism was the desirable state of balancing opposing forces, not least the pull of the future and the past: "Conservatism [is] the make-weight in times of extreme outbursts of passion or popular excitement, placing the weight of reason in each scale of the balance, and thus producing a counterpoise."[21]

As this last quote indicates, conservatism in the sense it was invoked in the mid-nineteenth century was not a political program or an elaborated ideology; still less was it a "movement." It is better understood as a disposition, a way of signaling a measured, mature approach to the problems of the world.[22] "Conservatism" implied an ethic of self-discipline and self-restraint. Self-described conservative men thought of themselves as innately anti-ideological; yet that did that not mean they did not have their own ideological commitments—above all, to the Union as the symbol and guarantor of their freedoms as white men and thus, as Lincoln famously put it, as the "last, best hope of earth." As a political language conservatism rested on the assumption that the freedoms mid-century white Americans enjoyed were hard won and easily lost. It was a language emanating from a postrevolutionary political culture, convinced of the superiority of its existing institutions. As the New England writer James Fenimore Cooper put it, "Here [in America], the democrat is the conservative, and thank God he has something worth preserving."[23]

The adjectives contemporaries attached to conservative—just, sturdy, sound, principled, reasoned, honest—testify to a deeply ingrained sense that conservatism was a positive virtue. It was an ethical claim about the nature and validity of a political posture or about the integrity, manliness, and wisdom of an individual. Therefore it was used to validate a range of different positions. Sharing a consensus about the need to preserve what they thought of as their unique free labor society, Americans living in the most populous section of the country—the Northern free states—diverged over political strategy and priorities, often intensely and violently. The people I write about in this book believed themselves to be consistent in their beliefs and loyal to an idea of what the Republic was intended to be, but that did not stop them from changing their minds about particular issues or switching from one party allegiance to another—and then sometimes to another, and another after that.

Given the slipperiness of political language, and the inherently relational meaning of conservatism, attempting to reduce it to a stable set of meanings—even within the time and place I cover in this book—is a perilous and perhaps distracting exercise. Rather than identify those historical actors who seem to me to fit most satisfactorily into a conservative frame, I have tried to delineate whatever a speaker intended conservatism to mean, and whatever his listeners understood by it, conscious that the adaptability of the language is one key to its power. In other words, I take a decidedly "nonessentialist" approach to understanding conservatism (and indeed liberalism and other ideological concepts I discuss). I do not believe there was such a thing as the "true essence" of conservatism. My concern is with how political actors and observers saw their world, and in that context why they found the language of conservatism helpful. Some of them may have believed that they had captured conservatism's essence, but my aim is to explain how and why they did that, and what political consequences resulted.[24] Insofar as generalizations can be made, it is easier to define conservatism in terms of what it was not. So a self-description as a conservative in nineteenth-century America did not (of course) mean defense of formal aristocracy (though it could mean a defense of hierarchy) nor of an established church (though it may well involve defense of, or reassertion of, the authority of clergymen as well as being based on a theocratic understanding of society and change).[25] Conservatism was not the same as reaction.[26] Nor was it identical with traditionalism, which "just is." As one Whig newspaper put it emphatically, true conservatism should never be mistaken for the "stupid old drone, with about as much sense as an oyster and less activity than a sunfish."[27]

In the twenty-first century we have become used to thinking about conservatism as a political tradition that stands in opposition to liberalism or progressivism. And in much of Europe in the mid-nineteenth century, conservatives and liberals were distinct movements, clashing violently over the legitimacy of constitutional arrangements. But such a distinction makes no sense in the free states of mid-nineteenth-century America. In general the advocates of a conservative course, or of conservative principles, also regarded themselves as the advocates of progress. The sensationally popular evangelist Henry Ward Beecher had a stock lecture on the need to unite progressivism and conservatism.[28] The Whig Party, claimed a supporter, was "in all things essentially conservative, and at the same time [it] is the real party of progress and improvement."[29] The Boston *Daily Atlas* declared itself to be in favor of "progressive conservatism, or which is the same thing, conservative progress."[30] Democrats joined the chorus. "The Democratic Party has become the great conservative as well as the great progressive party of the country," boasted a Pennsylvania Jacksonian paper, while another predicted that the Buchanan administration would pursue a "conservative, progressive, satisfactory and eminently successful" course.[31] Sometimes the terms were even hyphenated, as when a Boston newspaper earnestly explained the importance of having rulers that moved neither "too fast" nor "too slow" to "suit the great mass of the conservative-progressive people."[32] In their pursuit of progress, Victorian Americans were acutely conscious of the risk that advances would be accompanied by instability. Only a conservative temperament might maintain the correct balance

Having said that I take a nonessentialist approach to the political concepts I discuss, there are three very broad generalizations that might be made about self-described conservatives in the Civil War–era North (and given the ubiquity of the term these are generalizations that may therefore be taken to form some of the fundamental contours of political life). First, conservatives generally put faith in institutions—whether (with varying emphasis) they meant the law, churches, the Constitution, local government, schools, or political parties—and saw their authority deriving from their historical continuity, dating back to the Revolution and perhaps further back into British history. Self-described Northern conservatives believed, or hoped, that such institutions provided their Republic with the resilience it may otherwise lack.

Second, conservatism implied a willingness to see politics as a process of compromise. The people conservatives disliked were the dogmatists. And in their civics lessons antebellum Americans learned to celebrate the compromises that had forged the Constitution and kept sectional peace. The problem, of course, was that to accept the legitimacy of compromise you have first to accept the moral legitimacy of each side. So compromise was not necessarily the conservative choice if it conceded too much to evil. Divining at what moment a particular compromise implied a loss of moral integrity—and thus ceased to be, in fact, conservative—was one of the constant challenges for Northerners.[33]

A third and final generalization is that (as often today) to say that one was conservative was to claim to be in touch with the "real" people or the "backbone" of the country. Jacksonian politics was founded on the conceit that it spoke for the "great body of the people," but Whigs also invoked the common sense of "the body of the American people" as their lodestar: "The *conservatism* of the great public . . . has saved it from social anarchy," argued one Whiggish religious journal; "the mass of the people are generally more conservative than their rulers," explained another.[34] A contributor to the *New York Observer and Chronicle* in 1852 put the point this way: "From the noise made by a few . . . editors-errant . . . fifth-rate writers [and] broken-down preachers, one might think that the world was coming to an end . . . and that universal equality . . . and polygamy . . . was about to dawn. But the fool's paradise is still delayed. . . . Church-towers show no tendency to totter. . . . It is a pity to disturb the pleasant dream of drunken zealots, but let us tell them the truth, the American people is conservative after all. . . . The millions of American people are in favor of property, of law, of wedlock, of the Sabbath, of the church, of Christianity. . . . Agitation towards social ruin is, thank God, un-American."[35]

This confidence that fanaticism was "in its very visage foreign" was one respect in which mid-nineteenth-century American political culture resembled that of Britain in the same period. The preoccupation with past precedent, the reverence for the Constitution, the valorization of continuity, the privileged status of pragmatic rather than "ideological" approaches to politics, the conviction that they were in the vanguard of Providential progress, the tensions between middle-class Protestant reformist cultures and anti-elitist working-class cultures: all these characteristics were shared by British and American politics in this period, and all were represented in America as conservative.[36] Furthermore, for all their conviction of the Union's exceptional status in world history, Americans were also deeply aware of their Revolution's place in a long tradition of English liberty; Thomas Paine's concept of America having the power to begin the world anew coexisted with Edmund

Burke's sense that everything—even American freedom—grew from some-thing else.

Continuity, thought the much-admired Whig spokesman Daniel Webster, was the touchstone of the American experience.[37] Webster was the most ad-mired orator of his age, and his every speech—delivered in baritone, rolling cadences, his dark eyes flashing from beneath heavy brows—was regarded as a major public event. "From 1776 to the latest period the whole course of American public acts," Webster declaimed in 1848, in words that, like every-thing he said, sounded as if they were intended to be chiseled in granite, "the whole progress of the American system, was marked by a peculiar conserva-tism."[38] Webster's Massachusetts protégé Edward Everett—more debonair and almost as famous for his oratory as his mentor—devoted enormous en-ergy over many decades to the project of shaping a national consciousness that was rooted in this sense of stability, order, and past precedent, appealing to his listeners to nurture their "just and natural . . . conservative feelings."[39] The New England novelist Nathaniel Hawthorne did not share Webster and Ever-ett's party politics—his most public political service was probably writing his friend Franklin Pierce's campaign biography in 1852 (of which even the au-thor observed that "though the story is true, yet it took a romancer to do it.")[40] Yet in Websterian language, Hawthorne proclaimed in his Pierce bio-graphy that "all the greatest statesmen of America stand in the attitude of a conservative."[41] There was, he believed, something inherently conservative in the mindset of a post-revolutionary society, in which all sides shared a common constitutionalism, even while they fought over its meaning.[42]

The historical continuities binding the English past and the American present and future were one reason for the phenomenal influence of Edmund Burke in nineteenth-century America. Twentieth-century conservatives have returned to Burke as an intellectual godfather. But he had a far broader, less ideological appeal in the nineteenth century as a touchstone for moderate, principled defense of established rights. Intellectuals quoted Burke, but so too did rural newspaper editors and one-term congressmen. In an age that exalted great orators as romantic heroes, Burke's speeches, especially those in the House of Commons defending the rights of colonists in the run-up to the Revolution, were admired and reprinted. Burke, the philosopher-statesman, was pragmatic but principled; accepting of progress, he was cautious about the need to preserve a precious heritage of freedom.[43] In what was at the time conventional boiler-plate rhetoric, *Harper's Weekly*, a new-fangled illustrated newspaper founded in 1857, approvingly defined American conservatism as "a

common-sense estimate of political society as organized in our institutions"—
and cited Burke to prove the point.[44]

The embrace of Burke was emblematic of a political culture that was suspicious of ideology in general and "one-ideaism" in particular. "One-ideaism" was the pejorative term for those who, as their opponents saw it, pursued a single cause with no sense of context or understanding of its practical application.[45] It was the complete antithesis of Burkean pragmatism. The pursuit of supposedly faddish and quixotic one-idea causes like ending capital punishment, temperance, or abolitionism seemed politically dangerous if the argument could be portrayed as based on abstractions, not the reality of the world in all its messy complexity. Ezekiel Bacon, a Whiggish Presbyterian minister, made this case when he told a meeting of a Young Men's Lyceum in upstate New York that the greatest challenge to the stability of the Union came "when an ardent, self-opinionated, perhaps ambitious man has strongly imbibed *one idea*, or enlisted himself to effect *one* particular *object*." Such a man, Bacon warned, then tended to "think and act as though he believed *that* the only one in the world worthy of pursuit" and would say to others who disagreed "like the Pharisee of old, 'stand you by, I am holier than thou.'"[46]

Attacks on one-ideaism betrayed a suspicion that ideology was an inherently foreign and subversive concept, that those who bought into such theories were thereby rejecting some objective moral order, which was assumed to be embodied in American institutions. Even some moral reform campaigners used this language, thereby implying that their own crusade was simply clear-sighted or common sense, while others' was fanatical. A good example is Dorothea Dix, a well-connected and determined campaigner for the establishment of mental hospitals, who was nevertheless deeply anxious about the "wild schemes" pursued by some of her fellow reformers. The gravest threat facing the country, she wrote in 1856, was from "that class of agitators who seem to live for no good, and look never beyond their own interests, which are mostly conflicting with the best interests of every community."[47]

At its most extreme, opposition to one-ideaism extended to a wholesale rejection of the universalism of Enlightenment thought. The best-known (in fact, notorious) advocate for this position was the president of Dartmouth College, Reverend Nathan Lord, a man reared in a strict Calvinist tradition. Thomas Jefferson, wrote Lord, "was caught by the illuminism and cosmopolitanism of his times, and embodied his chimera in the '*glittering generalities*' of the Declaration of Independence." Reformers, he warned his students in 1852, were trying to subvert society not according to the word of God but to socialistic ideas. By "socialistic" he meant notions that substituted a "man-God for a God-man," ideas that were "visionary and impractical in a fallen state" in place of the "everlasting word of natural and revealed religion."[48] Yet even though they venerated Jefferson and lauded his enlightenment "generalities," Democrats also railed against one-ideaism because moral absolutism made the compromises and pragmatism of real-life politics impossible. A "great and conservative party in politics . . . cannot be formed and perpetuated upon one idea," explained a Democratic-supporting Pennsylvania newspaper. "The reason for this is . . . obvious when we consider that . . . politics [is] compounded of many calculations and considerations, and comprehend[s] a variety of subjects, though in theory [it] may be held to contemplate but a single result."[49] Walt Whitman—in his days as a Jacksonian newspaper editor—had no truck with reformers, tinkerers, "wild communistic theories, [or] red-republican ravings." So he mocked utopian socialism as "utterly chimerical . . . to attempt remodeling the world on an unalloyed basis of purity and perfection." Since God had not done so, he did not see why Robert Owen would be able to manage it.[50]

The two broad political persuasions that influenced political thinking in these years, Jacksonianism and Whiggery, shaped what Northerners meant by conservatism. Jacksonianism, so called because of its close association with the public image of President Andrew Jackson, was populist and antielit-ist in spirit. Jackson left office in 1837 and died in 1845, but his influence on American politics lived on. People continued to call themselves Jacksonians into the 1870s—and indeed beyond.[51] The term denoted a style as much as a set of policy prescriptions: Jacksonians privileged an egalitarian, masculine ideal of straightforward "plain dealing" among democratic citizens.[52] In its self-conception, Jacksonianism was restless and radical, the advance guard of human progress. It embraced Romantic ideas about human transformation, fueling some of the reform movements of the age, especially antislavery.[53] But at the same time, there was a deeply conservative strain to Jacksonianism—a defense of ordinary white men's privileges, against not just racial or gender revolution but more broadly against elites, ideologues, and illegitimate con-centrations of power.[54]

The Whig persuasion could be liberal and reformist, while also more likely to appeal to notions of an objective moral order. Sometimes dismissed by histo-rians and contemporaries, as if they were bloodless pragmatists, Whiggish conservatives were often the passionate advocates of the Founders' legacy as they saw it—including to the moral superiority of the practice and principle of compromise in politics. These persuasions helped determine what threats to freedom or the political order seemed most potent. Substantively different conceptions of the nation underlay them. Jacksonians thought that white masculine equality encompassed both the universal "natural rights" of the Declaration of Independence and the political right to self-government. Whigs were more likely to be sympathetic to the view that the "natural" right to life and liberty did not mean an unfettered right to self-government. As a writer for the *North American Review* put it in 1865, "To make society possible the nature of liberty . . . has to be fixed by some authority higher than the will of the individual citizen."[55] Jacksonianism and Whiggery led Northerners to positions they defined as conservative but for different reasons and at different times.

We should be wary of the danger of reifying Jacksonianism and Whiggery, yet as ideal types they are helpful in understanding the political imagination of Northerners. There were many ways in which these two persuasions could be synthesized in particular circumstances. And crucially, neither Jacksonianism nor Whiggery, though each in origin identified with a party, mapped neatly onto party politics into this period; electoral choices were far more complex than that. Jacksonianism and Whiggery did not just persist as political persuasions but also as political identities for many people—thus helping to explain why so many Northerners moved from one party to another without imagining themselves to be altering their core belief system. Consequently, Jacksonianism influenced both the Republican and the Democratic parties by the time of the Civil War, while Whiggery helped shaped the political imagination not only of those who supported the Republicans, but also various conservative, nativist, or Constitutional Union movements—and even, after 1854, the Democrats. Consequently, notwithstanding the demise of the Whig party, Whiggish conservatives exerted great political influence in these years, forming a crucial bloc of voters in key swing states and influencing the tenor of political discussion profoundly. Porous and overlapping, these categories together encompassed the great majority of white Northerners in these years. In itself that suggests that they—and the language of conservatism they deployed—require sustained attention if we want to understand the Northern path to war and victory.

There was also an anticonservative discourse in the antebellum and Civil War North, mainly found in the speeches and writings of abolitionists who associated conservatism with any hint of compromise with the slave interest (a similarly limited usage has been adopted by most historians). As Elizabeth Cady Stanton assured Susan B. Anthony, her fellow campaigner in the cause of women's suffrage, "Fear not that I shall falter. I shall not grow conservative with age!"[56] By the late 1850s, some old Jacksonians bemoaned that the Democracy, which had once been "the radical, progressive, *revolutionary* party opposed to the 'law and order' of conservatism" had now lost its soul. "Conservatism [has] entered the body of the Democratic Party," lamented one former Democrat.[57] So not everyone in Civil War America wanted to be known as a conservative, but that so many did—even while disagreeing with each other about so much—tells us something important about the way in which men sought to anchor themselves and their politics in a most revolutionary and tumultuous age. In a liberal and republican, nonfeudal society, Louis Hartz famously argued, there could be no "genuine" conservative tradition in the European sense.[58] Maybe not; but that did not mean there was no use for the language of conservatism—and during the 1850s more and more Northerners came to embrace it, including some of those Democrats who had once thought of themselves as opposing conservatism in all its forms.

Elizabeth Cady Stanton thought "the great fault of mankind is that it will not think," a deficiency that explained the wall of conservative resistance she faced.[59] One can understand why she thought like that and what she meant—after all she was championing a cause that even many abolitionists refused to take seriously—but lack of thought was not, in general, what made so many Northerners respond positively to the word "conservative." Ultimately, understanding what people meant by this pervasive term (even if what they meant was inherently slippery or negative or relational) helps us see the world through their eyes; it was a world in which the Union was both precious and vulnerable and in which the challenge of modernity was to balance progress with stability. In such conditions, appealing to imagined past certainties was more than just a historical or nostalgic tendency—it was fundamental to planning a path to the future. "They love change but they dread revolutions," observed the perceptive French liberal Alexis de Tocqueville of his chosen specimens, the Americans. While "men are in motion"—a ceaseless, relentless motion—"the mind of man appears almost unmoved."[60] I would not go so far as to say that the minds of Americans remained unmoved in the two decades from the mid-1840s to the mid-1860s, but I do think that, like most people in most times and places, they tried hard to maintain as much intellectual and political continuity as they could in a world they often feared was spinning out of control.

The Politics of Crisis

In a Victorian culture highly attuned to sentiment and affect, mid-century Americans understood only too well the inescapable emotionalism of their politics.[61] Cool heads and dispassionate reason were still, many hoped, the bedrock of political choice, yet public sentiment was shaped by thoughts and feelings too. This was not always regarded as a good thing; some of the political tension of these years was generated by arguments over the place of passion in politics. As the Civil War loomed, Northern Democrats assailed Republicans for irresponsibly stirring up popular anger against the South: anger, a sign of indiscipline, was rarely seen as a positive emotion. Democrats were, in turn, attacked for making crude demagogic appeals to the base feelings of voters. And politicians and editors of all parties routinely traded accusations that their opponents were suffering "gross delusion."[62] Ecclesiastical guardians of the nation's Puritan heritage like the Princeton theologian Charles Hodge noted sadly that in the present "age of passion" a lack of restraint undermined the institution of the family and respect for the Sabbath.[63] As Dorothea Dix put it during the secession crisis, the cause of the trouble was "hot-headed excitement."[64] If negative emotions could undermine the Union, positive feelings were essential for the Republic to survive. When the "sentiment" of "affection" is gone, warned a typical editorial, the Union "is in fact dissolved, or is so enfeebled as to be powerless for the great object for which it was established."[65]

The emotionalism of politics was heightened by the perpetual sense of "crisis," a word widely used at the time, and a key, I believe, to understanding the context in which people made political choices. In mid-nineteenth-century general usage, the term "crisis" was often reserved for "that change which indicates either recovery or death," as the 1828 edition of *Webster's American English Dictionary* put it. The political experience of the United States in these years reinforces the argument of the philosophical anthropologist Janet Roitman that the dichotomy between normalcy and crisis is so entrenched in our political thinking that it is difficult to think outside of it.[66] A yearning for a (possibly imaginary) ideal of noncrisis was the corollary of a gnawing sense that at stake was the life or death of the Union or—which amounted to the same thing—of freedom, self-rule, and stability. The medical origins of the word "crisis" gave sharpness and specificity to the use of the term in the mid-nineteenth century that has since been eroded by overuse. In 1856, a New York newspaper offered the following elucidation of the way in which the term was then being used: "The turning point in a disease is a crisis: so is a journey on a railroad or a steamboat in a man's history, for he is then placed in so critical a position that he scarcely knows whether he ought to hope for life or prepare for death. At present the nation, considered politically, has reached this turning point, this critical moment; it will soon arrive safely at the end of its pleasant excursion, or be blown into fragments by an explosion, or be crushed by a collision; it will shortly recover from its convulsions, or die under the disease of politics. Crisis is the proper and the best word to express the existing state of the country."[67] Above all, "crisis" was a description of experience. People used the term because they had no more dramatic word to indicate the scale of the choices they had to make. In a crisis, action (or at least urgent prayer) is an imperative. For radicals, crisis and convulsion was to be welcomed if it led to revolutionary change. A crisis, noted the abolitionist Lydia Maria Child approvingly, was "so well adapted to call out all the manhood there is in souls."[68] But the dominant crisis metaphor was of the "ship of state" in the "midst of a storm" with a "tempest howling around us." Would a "deliverance from danger" come from the "signal hand of God"? Or would the ship be "tossed onto the rocks" by the "breakers" surrounding it?[69]

The pervasive sense of crisis, of a perpetually stormy present, created one of the most powerful motivating forces in politics—*anxiety*. Fear can be compelling—even Edmund Burke wrote about the "delightful horror" of imagining "pain and terror."[70] Exactly how anxiety changes the nature of political choices, however, is complex. For some, the anxiety prompted by the sense of crisis pushes them to hunker down, comforted by familiar slogans. At the same time, as the psychologist George E. Marcus has argued, when voters are at their most anxious, they may also be jolted out of habitual patterns of thought. The dogmas of the quiet past, as it were, are questioned simply because rival claims have to be assessed according to first principles. "If circumstances generate many anxious voters, they can readily upset the normal expectations," Marcus has written. How individual voters respond— whether by reaffirming previous positions or shifting to new ones—depends on how convincing they find politicians' proposed solutions to their worries.[71] This analysis applies with force to the middle decades of the nineteenth century in the United States. The vast majority of Northern voters in the Civil War era, whatever political labels they responded to, were conditioned by culture and circumstance to see the world in terms of threats that had to be countered.

Crisis-ridden mid-nineteenth-century Americans were the knowing inheritors of a long civic republican tradition that had its origins in the upheavals of seventeenth-century Britain.[72] When they spoke of liberty, tyranny, corruption, power, the threat of centralization, or partisanship, those words had deep historical resonance. So familiar were mid-nineteenth-century Americans with the religious and constitutional struggles of Charles I and the

Parliamentarians that politicians and newspaper editors referred to them readily and without explanation. Republicanism offered a satisfying narrative structure for nineteenth-century Americans. In an era in which politics was a cultural project and culture a political one, republicanism was mirrored by popular melodramas that depicted the world in terms of the threat of subversion and the promise of revenge and catharsis.[73] It encouraged a view of U.S. history since 1776 as one long series of crises in which the manly, honest people had to fight back against crypto-aristocratic, would-be despots or in which the sturdy, upright citizenry had to defeat sinister, hidden conspiracies. Republicanism gave Americans their Revolution: the baptismal moment in which they were reborn, free. It gave them the challenge of preserving that precious heritage against sinister challenges. And after secession, with the enemies of the Republic apparently on the brink of victory, it offered the narrative prospect of catharsis and redemption. Republicanism, one might say, practically *required* a crisis since the enemies of freedom were always plotting.[74]

The Antislavery Consensus

The story of the Civil War I tell here is one in which the common ground shared by Northerners was more striking than their (admittedly very fierce and sometimes violent) disagreements. Southerners also shared many of the values on which Northern politics was founded, but slavery was a wedge that ultimately overshadowed everything else. The free states encompassed everywhere from the Puritan-flecked fishing villages of Maine to the river-bound startup towns of the Midwest, and from the streetcars and stink pits of New York City to the remote logging communities of western Pennsylvania or the even more remote gold rush towns, a three-month steamship voyage away on the distant Pacific shore. On the surface, it may seem absurd to venture any kind of generalization about people so far flung, so differently oriented toward the globalizing, industrializing economy, so variously rooted in different styles of worship and different forms of community organization. Human slavery, however—or rather the formal, legal absence of it—created common ground among these people and divided them from otherwise similar communities in the slave states.

By the mid-1840s, there was a perceptibly different, more open tone to politics in the North than in the South, and the parameters of what was politically sayable were far broader. There has been a great deal of fine historical scholarship that has complicated any simplistic contrasts between North and South before the war.[75] Even so, in political terms sectional identities were pretty well formed by the 1840s if not earlier. Party lines did not yet reflect those differences, and on many issues there were cross-sectional alliances. Yet, as Sidney George Fisher, a Philadelphia Whig, recognized in 1848, the fissure over slavery reflected a difference between North and South that manifested itself "in everything which forms the life of a people—in institutions, laws, opinions, manners, feelings, education, pursuits, climate & soil." Different cultures, moreover, were, Fisher argued, a reflection of antagonistic interests. Describing himself as a "conservative man in spirit and inclination," Fisher had no truck with abolitionism, though he was occasionally moved by stories of the inhumanity of slavery. As early as 1848 it was clear to him, from his vantage point in his well-appointed study, that the nature of slavery required Southern control of the federal government. Only by having the assurance that their conception of property would be protected and respected by the national government—not least through judicial decisions—could they have security. "The South want[s] to rule," Fisher observed in his diary, "but if the North was shut out, civil war would result."[76]

Fisher's privilege and innate discomfort with democracy set him apart in many ways, but he was perceptive about the nature of the political crisis through which he lived. While some—especially Democrats—tried to deny it, everyone in the North knew that slavery formed a sectional interest that was somehow always present. Consequently, when it came to slavery and related questions there was more that united Northerners of all parties than divided them. Northerners shared a commitment to defend a free labor society in which white men could govern themselves, build communities, and make their way in the world. As one astute observer put it in 1854, "The antislavery sentiment is inborn and is almost universal at the North."[77] The common ground over slavery did not—crucially—extend to a consensus about how to deal with it, but had there been an opinion poll conducted in the Northern states in which respondents were asked, "Do you agree that the right to property ownership in human beings is, on balance, a bad thing?" a large majority would have said yes, with most of the rest probably opting for an agonized "don't know."[78]

The antislavery consensus encompassed the overwhelming majority of Whigs, Free-Soilers, Know-Nothings, Constitutional Unionists, and Republicans.[79] But it also included the majority of Democratic Party voters in the free states, who are sometimes (mistakenly, in my judgment) dismissed by historians, as they were by their political opponents, as mere "doughfaces" or defenders of slavery.[80] A Maine Whig newspaper, ruminating on the "general antislavery disposition" of the free states in 1852, observed that there were two classes of antislavery people: the "agitators" and the "conservative" men. The latter—the great majority in both main parties—regarded slavery with a "strong and sincere aversion" and would "do anything they could constitutionally do to effect a gradual emancipation—and yet believe that all hostile action at the North, especially of a political character, tends only to mischief."[81] Evidence for the breadth of the antislavery consensus can be found even in the pages of firmly Democratic newspapers. For example, in 1854, the Cleveland *Plain Dealer* sneered that only "philanthropists" (not a term of praise) believed that slavery was detrimental to black people, and yet on the very same page, in a swipe at Mormon polygamists, the editors of that newspaper acknowledged almost in passing that slavery was "cramping to Anglo-Saxon destiny" and "repulsive" to Anglo-Saxon sentiment (albeit not so repulsive, allegedly, as polygamy).[82]

As this quote indicates, the general assumption that slavery was, in the abstract, wrong coexisted with a profound antiblack racism. For all the well-documented impact of *Uncle Tom's Cabin*, the majority of Northerners were not especially moved by the human plight of enslaved black people, who they assumed to be inferior.[83] Indeed, Northerners were more likely to object to slavery when they began to fear (for good reason) that slavery was not based on race, as the plentiful advertisements in the Southern press for runaway slaves with a "fair complexion" made clear.[84] Until well into the Civil War, most Americans assumed they lived—and always would live—in a whites-only democracy for the simple reason that the black population in the free states was so small that a biracial democracy was unimaginable other than as an occasional Gothic nightmare used by politicians as a scare tactic.[85] More troubling to Northerners in their everyday lives was the influx of 1.5 million Irish Catholic immigrants. Unlike the largely abstract issue of black rights, the status and political influence of Catholic incomers was a real and pressing, and, to some, deeply troubling, problem.[86] In short, the overriding issue in Northern politics was not whether slavery was right or wrong but in what respects it was a threat. Recognizing this general disposition to regard slavery as wrong, politicians competed to make the case that they were the best defenders of Northern free white labor.

In making the case for an underlying antislavery consensus, I am not overlooking the differences among Northerners about such fundamental questions as, for example, whether black people could ever be included in the polity, whether liberty was compromised by free white Northerners being required to acknowledge the legitimacy of human property and even collaborate in its maintenance, or whether a government based on the principle of popular sovereignty could demand loyalty from its citizens: all these differences I discuss at length, but I am struck by how often, in practice, they could be compromised, fudged, or simply ignored. Most people were perfectly capable of holding contradictory opinions simultaneously and they rarely looked for philosophical consistency in their political leaders. And so, while a counterfactual exercise in retrospective polling might tell us that Northerners saw slavery as a distasteful if largely distant institution, it would not tell us why and how the issue of slavery mattered. Ideally, our hypothetical 1850s pollster would not just have asked whether respondents were for or against slavery, but also how important slavery was, on a scale of values, compared to other moral and material goals, not least the preservation of the Union. Needless to say, the task of our imaginary pollster is in truth the task of the historian, but unfortunately scholars of the Civil War era too often rely on dividing people according to whether they were pro- or antislavery. Unless deployed with a battery of caveats, these categories impose a binary on a far more nuanced and shifting politics and fail to capture the human reality that values are always relative.[87]

Above all, coming to terms with how mid-nineteenth-century white Northerners saw slavery is impossible unless we recognize the moral power of the nation—or the Union, as Northerners referred to it. A generation of school children learned by rote the final peroration to the famous 1830 speech of Daniel Webster's that ended "Liberty *and* Union, now and forever, one and inseparable" and that phrase so perfectly captured the nationalist heart of the vast majority of Northern white people that it was embraced by Democrats every bit as much as by Webster's Whigs.[88] The term "Union" carried a huge emotional power in mid-nineteenth-century politics as the living embodiment of the legacy of the revered Founders, a republican system of government built and sustained by the willing and active participation of the citizens and not by the exercise of force by a centralized power as Americans thought was the case in the Old World. The Union was Northerners' guarantor of freedom and a beacon of hope for those abroad still toiling under monarchies and despotisms.[89]

The implications of Northerners' devotion to the Union for the future of slavery were ambiguous. In 1848, most inhabitants of the free states had a general sense that while they did not want slavery in their own society, it was not an institution that was inherently antagonistic to the survival of the Union. Gradually, through the crises of the coming years, more and more Northerners started to question that view. Even so, for most white people in the free states, slavery was a perplexing, emotionally charged issue that could not be entirely separated from everything else they were worrying about at the time. If they feared social disorder, class conflict, or moral decline, or if they were anxious about the growing centralization of government, did slavery, and the politics it created, not compound the problem? Yet if "agitating" the slavery question destroyed the Republic, how would the global struggle of democracy against autocracy be advanced? Slavery was, at the very least, a troubling institution to the vast majority of Northerners, but did that justify disrupting a long-established means of enforcing labor discipline and social order on a race of people most presumed to be inferior?

Through the Storm to Appomattox

The premise of this book is that the coming of war and emancipation are incomprehensible without an understanding of the political mind of mainstream Northerners who made those things happen. Viewed from below the Mason-Dixon line, the sectional crisis looked very different. The antebellum South was totally in the sway of slavery, its leading politicians and economic elite completely dependent on it, and white society as a whole trapped by the fear that they would face total destruction if the enslaved people they lived among were freed. By 1861, the Southern states had carved out a grisly form of exceptionalism; although they were not the only remaining society in the world to still recognize human property, they were by far the most economically advanced of those societies, with the most sophisticated systems for buying and selling enslaved people. As we now know, there is nothing to prevent repressive societies with systems of highly exploitative labor achieving success in the global economy, and there is no reason why slavery could not have survived for many years to come in an independent slave-based South. Although slavery had been given multiple protections under the federal constitution of 1787, Southerners were entirely rational to be nervous about their long-term future if they stayed in a Union with the antislavery North. That was not because Northerners were all abolitionists but because successfully maintaining a slave society requires that virtually everyone in positions of authority in the polity (and in a mass electoral system that meant everyone with a vote) were willing to enforce the legal claim to human property that is the essence of a slave system. If the courts and the government were not willing or able to maintain property rights, ultimately using force to do so, the basis of any economy and society would collapse. That is especially true if the property in question has legs and voices and humanity, and that was why slaveholders worked so hard and so successfully to keep control of the levers of federal power until, in the election of 1860, they lost the presidency. It was natural that slaveholders should feel threatened living in a nation in which a majority of the citizens basically did not accept that one could or should own human beings. It was natural then that a majority of them should want to take back control of their own affairs by seceding and, having done so, entirely to be expected that the vast majority of white people, most of whom were not slaveholders, would be willing to fight against an invading army.

But natural as their desire for independence may have been, it backfired in the most spectacular fashion from their point of view, and as a result the world saw one of the great advances in human freedom of the modern age. The subject of *The Stormy Present* is the reason Southerners' gamble backfired: Northerners' astonishing determination to prevent it. Given the material and manpower advantages of the free states, the Union was always likely to prevail in a military confrontation with the South, *so long as* they were willing to pay any price and bear any burden in pursuit of that objective. Since all the South wanted was to be left alone, it followed that victory would come whenever the North lost the will to continue the war. That might have happened, but it never did. And so, the Union was restored—and slavery, the cause of all the trouble, was destroyed with it. To understand how this happened, we need to revisit, stage by stage, the series of crisis moments that compelled Northerners to make the decisions that led them in the direction we know, in retrospect, they traveled.

The Northern consensus about the use of force after the firing on Fort Sumter in April 1861 did not emerge from nowhere. The preceding decade and a half of political argument had prepared the way for Northerners in all parties to see the South as potentially hostile to the liberty and stability of the Union; we cannot understand the path to Sumter and Appomattox if all we focus on are the roughly half of the electorate who voted Republican.[90] But, as Northerners at the time were acutely aware, the challenges they faced were also those of other modern societies. So the story I tell here is of a politics that revolved around both the specifically American problem of the expansion of slavery in a federal republic and the more general problems faced by other industrializing nations in the mid-nineteenth century, all of which were also struggling with questions about maintaining political legitimacy and social order in the face of revolutionary new ideas, rapid technological change, urbanization, and mass migration. It does not diminish the fatal centrality of slavery to the mid-century crisis to argue that we can only properly understand its political impact if we contextualize it in a world of competing and conflicting pressures. The stresses of modernity formed the prism through which the mid-century politics of slavery played out.

It is salutary to remember that politics, especially in the midst of traumatic crisis, is always, in the end, about individual people struggling to make sense of complexity, drawing—as most of us do—on the past as a guide. Viewed from the Olympian heights that a historian can choose to command, it is clear that in 1861, the constitutional order that had existed since 1789 collapsed. Northerners did not know—and for the most part they did not expect—that their efforts to resolve deep moral and material conflicts would end in the catastrophe of war. Nor did they know how high a price they would have to pay for being unwilling to recognize the nationalization of the principle of human slavery, as the South by the late 1850s was demanding. Even those whose support for the Lincoln administration was generally robust worried, like Democrats, about the cost. "I want the rebellion put down," declared a Vermont woman in 1862, but "I cannot bear the thought that my friends must have a hand in it, and especially my brothers. There is not much of the spirit of '76 in me."[91]

Storm-tossed, a majority of Northerners, in the end, summoned up enough of the "spirit of '76" to preserve their Union—to them, the indispensable guarantor of freedom. As they celebrated the news of General Lee's surrender at Appomattox, most Northerners did not cheer a nation transformed but a Union they had saved from the forces of destruction. Twenty years of national tumult, they hoped, had come to an end; the ship of state that had emerged from the battering of the storm was stronger and more capable of surviving the breakers of modernity as it sailed forward into the future.

CHAPTER ONE

Barricades on Broadway

Mobs and the Problem of Revolution in American Politics

On the night of May 10, 1849, uniformed, well-armed U.S. militiamen killed at least twenty-five people and wounded dozens more. The victims were not plains Indians or Mexican soldiers but working-class white Americans, and the scene took place not on the frontier but in New York City, in the street outside the Astor Place Opera House at the intersection of Lafayette and Broadway. Some of the dead were bystanders; most were rioters who had been hurling stones and trying to set fire to the theater in an attempt to stop a visiting British actor, William Charles Macready, from performing *Macbeth*.[1] This was not so surprising a cause as it may seem: theaters provided celebrity, glamor, scandal, politics, and sex, but they were also sites of violence. One reason was that they were the primary space, other than churches, where people gathered—and not passively to consume culture (as may be the case today) but to participate, vigorously and noisily. In a theater, as in the Republic as a whole, the people assumed they were the sovereign arbiters of what, or who, went on stage.[2]

That New York spring night saw the tragic denouement of a popular campaign against Macready that had lasted ever since he stepped ashore in Boston the previous fall. There was a long tradition of American audiences baiting visiting British actors, but Macready attracted more antagonism than most because he had become embroiled in a high-profile personal feud with Edwin Forrest, the great hero of the popular theater-going audience and the personification of bombastic American nationalism.[3] Forrest, "the American Tragedian" as the press called him, turned Shakespearean characters into American frontier heroes, wrapping himself in the stars and stripes often literally as well as figuratively, performing as an unrestrained volcano of feeling. Whether it was a death scene (head lolling, eyes bulging, body writhing), or an angry declaration of his determination to fight for freedom (muscled arms raised, calves and thighs flexed) the climactic moments of Forrest's performances were met with storms of applause. "If a bull could act," observed one literary New Yorker tartly, "he would act like Forrest."[4] Macready, meanwhile, was so determined to be restrained in his display of emotion that he rehearsed with his hands tied behind his back and a book balanced on his head.

Having made an enemy of Forrest, Macready may as well have declared war on America, or, more precisely, the vision of America championed by populist Jacksonians. "The Eminent Tragedian," as he was fondly known in the British press, had plenty of admirers, but wherever he appeared, he was the target for egg-pelting Forrest partisans in the cheap seats. In Cincinnati, Macready even had to dodge "half the carcass of a dead sheep" which was hurled from the balcony during act 2 of *Hamlet*.[5] A self-important, cerebral actor who counted the antislavery senator Charles Sumner among his elite American friends, Macready was all too easy to caricature.[6] Enterprising theater managers staged burlesques with titles like *Mister McGreedy* in which an effete snob was rude about Americans before meeting a sticky end.[7] When Macready arrived in New York City, a dashing, piratical leader of a Democratic Party political gang, Isaiah Rynders, took the lead in organizing the anti-Macready protests.[8] Possibly subsidized by Edwin Forrest himself, Rynders acquired tickets for Macready's first performance at the Astor Place Opera House, an upscale theater catering to the city's elite with a dress code of white kid gloves, and distributed them for free in taverns and on street corners. Installed in the top tier of the theater and primed with whiskey, Rynders's men then duly subjected Macready to such a barrage of missiles and barracking that the performance had to be abandoned during act 3.[9]

And there the matter would have remained—with some damage to property, a few bruises, and a dent in Macready's considerable pride, but no deaths—were it not for the response of the city's elite. "This cannot end here," fumed the venerable old Whig and former mayor Philip Hone, "The respectable part of our citizens will never consent to be put down by a mob raised to serve the purpose of such a fellow as Forrest. Recriminations will be resorted to."[10] Determined that the "outrage" of Monday night should not be allowed to stand, a group of prominent New York citizens published an open letter to Macready in the *New York Courier and Enquirer* asking him to reconsider his decision to cancel his remaining engagements and pledging that "the friends of order" in the city would protect him.[11] The forty-nine signers of the petition included literary men like Herman Melville and Washington Irving, politician-editors like Henry J. Raymond (the future editor of the *New York Times*) as well as an assortment of lawyers and merchants.[12] This, combined with private assurances from the mayor that he would provide all necessary force, was the critical intervention that transformed Macready's unhappy American tour into a tragic confrontation between the militia and an angry crowd.[13]

To Rynders and his men, who thought they'd won a great victory against Macready and his upper-class supporters, the friends of order petition, with its threat to use force to enforce Macready's right to perform, was a serious provocation. Rynders immediately organized the printing and distribution of hundreds of handbills addressed to workingmen asking whether Americans or English should "rule in this city." The handbills even claimed that the crew of an English steamer, which had berthed in New Jersey the previous week, has "threatened all Americans who dare to express their opinion this night at the English Aristocratic Opera House!"[14] As a result of this mobilization, a crowd of between ten and twenty thousand gathered in Astor Place. Many had clearly come prepared for violence and they soon began throwing stones and attempting to set fire to the theater. At one point a missile smashed through a window and shattered the vast chandelier that hung in the center of the auditorium, and when, in act 5, Macready declaimed the line "our castle's strength will laugh a siege to scorn," it prompted a tumult of applause from the embattled audience.[15]

The state's Seventh Regiment had been standing in readiness in nearby Washington Square Park. When it was clear that the nonuniformed city police could not control the crowd, the mayor ordered the militia to restore order.[16] They "tried to disperse the mob by threats and other means" according to one eyewitness, a visiting Presbyterian minister from Delaware, "but were attacked with showers of paving stones."[17] According to several reports, rioters put their chests in front of the soldiers' muskets daring them to shoot a freeborn American.[18] The soldiers fired three volleys of live ammunition. More people were killed than U.S. troops had died at the battle of New Orleans, Andrew Jackson's famous victory against the British in 1815.[19]

The Astor Place Riot does not usually feature among the familiar stories of the coming of the American Civil War. Yet the reactions to the events of May 10, 1849 illuminate like a lightning flash in the night the assumptions and, to some extent, the alliances and imagined enemies that conditioned Northerners' political choices over the coming decade and a half. This strange and violent episode uncannily anticipated the arguments, and even the political alliances, that shaped Northern politics into the Civil War. The feud between two actors and the roles played by the anti-Macready and pro-Macready forces raised in an especially troubling form some constitutional questions about majoritarianism (should the majority rule—even if it meant preventing an actor who was the minority's favorite from performing?), about political legitimacy (did the state, in a republic, have the right to use force, even to protect property and order?), and about citizenship (what special obligations did living in a republic impose on citizens and government alike?). As Northerners struggled with the problem of slavery, they ran, again and again, into exactly these fundamental issues, made more acute, as the events at Astor Place also illustrated, by the feeling that the world was at a crisis moment.

The Problem of Violence in an Age of Revolutions

The following morning, Friday, May 11, 1849, the workshops and docks of New York City were silent; what one newspaper described as "surly groups" of men gathered on street corners. Dead bodies still lay unclaimed in a police station.[20] Merchants and bankers locked up their valuables. Rumors abounded: that hundreds of people had been killed, that martial law was to be declared, that a nearby British naval vessel was poised to invade, or that armed ruffians were marching from Philadelphia to reinforce the rioters in an effort to take control of the city. Barricades were erected on the narrow streets of the working-class Bowery neighborhood in lower Manhattan. Around midmorning, word spread of a public meeting. Thousands gathered outside City Hall to hear Democratic politicians denounce the "aristocrats" of the city who had chosen to "shoot down their brethren and fellow citizens" purely for the pleasure of being "amused" by Macready. Mike Walsh, leader of the "Shirtless Democrats" (lower Manhattan's answer to the *sanscullottes*) told the crowd that America had succumbed to tyranny.[21] "Even the Emperor of Russia, who holds the lives of the people in little better estimation than that of dogs," Walsh fired out, "has always required three rounds of blank cartridges to be fired by the troops before they fire with ball upon the people."[22] Another speaker warned that "this massacre of the people is but one step, and a long one, too, toward the social and political supremacy of the rich and aristocratic over the working and poorer classes."[23] In the coming days, the press amplified these charges. Were citizens to live under a daily regime of martial law, liable to be shot down in their daily pursuits "if distant rioters provoke militia-men to fire through crowded streets?" asked the *Democratic Review*, a monthly magazine that combined cultural and political commentary in a distinctively Jacksonian style. The "massacre" at Astor Place suggested that Americans' "boasted institutions are, after all, dependent on the bloody means that have cemented the reeking thrones of European despots."[24] Meanwhile, invoking the spirit of the patriots who had died fighting similar tyranny in Ireland, the *Irish-American* called for armed resistance against the authorities.[25]

This was "the age of revolutions" wrote the *Evening Post*'s poet-editor William Cullen Bryant. "To whatever part of the world the attention is directed, the political and social fabric is crumbling to pieces."[26] The urban reformer

Charles Loring Brace reflected on this transatlantic revolutionary instability when he wrote, "There are just the same explosive social elements beneath the surface of New York as of Paris."[27] The rioters and the authorities, and those who interpreted the riot in the hours and days afterward, were on some level consciously playing roles in an age of revolution—the crowd imitating their idea of Parisian martyrs, the authorities the stern guardians of the republic against Jacobins, just as Americans, more broadly, were enacting the rite, as well as the right, of self-government with the rest of the world as an audience. Without events in Europe, the anti-Macready movement would not have generated the same sense of crisis—or the willingness to use lethal violence to combat it.

The European revolutions of 1848 were as cataclysmic and transfixing as the French Revolution of 1789 and its aftermath had been to an earlier generation.[28] Americans of all political persuasions followed the revolts in France, Belgium, Italy, Hungary, Germany, Poland, Austria, and Ireland with careful, almost obsessive, interest. The very notion of an important European country like France becoming a republic again was utterly intoxicating to many. The *New York Herald*, confirming the news of the overthrow of the July Monarchy in Paris in March 1848, thought "this wonderful event has astonished all classes, and created a tumult of excitement beyond parallel in New York. It will extend from one end of this republic to the other—from the shores of the Atlantic to the foot of the Rocky Mountains, and across the continent, wherever an American citizen is to be found, to the billows which wash the sands of California and Oregon."[29] Sidney George Fisher described the excitement in his neighborhood when the word went out that the newspapers had fresh news from Europe. "Each arrival," he wrote, "is like the rising of the curtain at a theater for a new act in some interesting drama."[30] Throughout the summer and fall of 1848, European events were reimagined in American popular culture in highly melodramatic terms. The June Days uprising was restaged as tableaux, songs, and plays in popular theaters and conjured up by orators, ministers, and politicians. It was not a simple matter of celebration or condemnation but of a Gothic fascination with a clash of such magnitude. The Philadelphia novelist and pamphleteer George G. Foster told the story of France in 1848 as high Gothic melodrama, describing the leading politicians as actors playing out scenes.[31] Although the 1848 revolutions largely failed in their immediate aims and were followed by two decades of relative political stability in the center of Western Europe, no one at the time expected the ideas and the movements they had spawned to go into retreat.[32] Americans remained transfixed during the 1850s as the Risorgimento pursued a goal of

Italian unification that perfectly expressed (at least to foreign observers) the ideal of the nation-state as a moral entity and a vehicle for liberation.[33]

At least at the beginning, the European revolutions seemed evidence of the inexorable spread of the American democratic example: the "great idea of the world's future" that was "sweeping all before it," as an antislavery journal enthused.[34] Foster's book stretched the credulity of his readers by asserting that the reading of the annual message of the president of the United States by the French people helped to push them toward republicanism. President Polk's disquisitions on the state of the public finances, Foster mused in a triumph of nationalist faith over evidence, had demonstrated "that a government might be constituted which while it secured popular right, should be cheap and efficient."[35]

For many Americans, however, events in Europe soon rekindled the horror of undisciplined violence that had stalked the American imagination since the twin Reigns of Terror in the 1790s—in Jacobin France and the racial apocalypse (as it was imagined) of Haiti. For Herman Melville, the "red year Forty Eight" was a story of "terror that into hate subsides."[36] Anti-Catholic riots in Philadelphia, St. Louis, Cincinnati, and other cities were routinely described in numerous press accounts as a "reign of terror." Reports of violence in San Francisco—where the homicide rate was ten times that in the East—followed similar patterns. There, in 1856, the Committee of Vigilance—made up of businessmen and anti-Catholic leaders—staged a coup d'état, killed their opponents after a quasijudicial hearing, and even interned for a while the chief justice of the state supreme court.[37] Press reports of these events drew on the same set of images: of "infuriated masses" who "moved swiftly" while fire bells rang (the ringing fire bell being a recurrent literary device conjuring terrified night awakenings, was famously evoked by Thomas Jefferson in his alarmed reaction to the sectional fight over whether slavery should be allowed in the new state of Missouri in 1819–20). Anti-Catholic riots and violence prompted by opponents of the Fugitive Slave Act or by slave-catchers trying to seize African Americans were made up of similar images, characteristically described as a "most exciting and terrifying scene."[38] To Karl Reemelin, a German immigrant who had come to the United States in the 1830s and went on to play a leading role in the Ohio Republican Party, the revolutions of 1848 brought "mischief untold" because the "furor for liberty" it created was "little understood."[39] As one Maine newspaper summed up such feelings, "We live in an age of alarm and terror, as well as progress."[40]

And if the revolutions spread the wrong sort of ideas, some feared they also stimulated the migration of the wrong sort of people. The *Philadelphia*

Inquirer issued a typical warning in 1851 about "the wild and impracticable theories of socialism, which are inculcated at the present time by the visionaries, the ultras, and the enthusiasts of the Old World." Such "heresies and delusions," transplanted "to our own soil" would "sooner or later" lead to "rapine, bloodshed, and civil war."[41] The New England novelist Catharine Maria Sedgwick, born in 1789, the year that Washington became president, thought the European uprisings threatened the American republic with "swarms of Irish, and Irish priests and German radicals."[42] Sedgwick was certainly not against progress: she moved in Boston antislavery circles and was a passionate advocate of numerous social reform movements—but her words echo those of a prominent nativist politician in New York, Thomas R. Whitney, who warned that the revolutions brought to America the "malcontents of the Old World." What was imagined to be dangerous about such people was that, in Whitney's words, they were the sort of people "who hate monarchy not because it is monarchy, but because it is *restraint*."[43] Such undisciplined intruders were a threat to what the Whig *North American Review* called the "conservative influence that springs from general virtue and uncompromising integrity," without which the Republic could not survive.[44]

Three and a half years after a working-class New York crowd gathered to drive William Charles Macready from the American stage, thousands of German immigrants in Cincinnati armed themselves to drive off—or worse—an unwanted European visitor. The episode—in some ways very reminiscent of the Astor Place Riot and in others very different—illustrates the divergent ways in which violence was given political meaning. Playing the role of foreign lightning rod that Macready had performed in New York was Gaetano Bedini, archbishop of Thebes and a papal nuncio to the United States, dubbed the "butcher of Bologna" in the British and American press after his time as bishop in that city during the tumultuous years of 1848–50. The accusation was that—tacitly or otherwise—Bedini had allowed the execution of Ugo Bassi, a charismatic Italian nationalist priest, by the Austrian authorities who were using draconian force to quash rebellion. "There is blood on his hands—human blood!" exclaimed the German language newspaper the *Hochwachter* when it was announced that Bedini would be visiting Cincinnati in December 1853—"He is the hyena of Italy!"[45]

A coalition of anti-Catholic nativists, German immigrants, and a few Italian exiles was mobilized using some of the same tactics that had been used to mobilize the anti-Macready movement: handbills were printed, sensational claims were published in newspapers, and the visitor's presence in the city was dramatized as a sign that the republic was being corrupted. Macready had symbolized the pretensions of an Anglophile aristocratic class; the feting of Bedini, likewise, was imagined to indicate that the city authorities had abandoned the egalitarian principles of the Republic. On Christmas Day, the anti-Bedini protestors marched to the Saint Peter in Chains Catholic cathedral, where the bishop was preaching. They burned his image in effigy (a piece of street theater the anti-Macready movement had performed many times in various cities) and chanted slogans. The Catholic bishop of Cincinnati, John Purcell, who had invited Bedini to come, was appalled by the "execrable charivari and music" of the marchers. He also claimed that they carried clubs, pitchforks, and pistols. The police charged to disperse the crowd, killing one protestor. There were sixty arrests. The next day, an "indignation meeting" was held and the violence of the authorities condemned for bringing the Republic down to the level of "Austrian despotism." Indignation was the characteristic formalized emotion of antebellum politics, a stylized form of moral outrage expressed through the ordered, restrained mechanism of resolutions proposed and adopted at public meetings.[46]

Unlike New York Mayor Caleb S. Woodhull, who gave the order to call up the militia in the Astor Place Riot, the mayor of Cincinnati, David T. Snelbaker, went home to spend Christmas with his family and later disassociated himself from the repression of the protest. He dismissed the chief of police, Thomas Lukens, and two weeks later Lukens, along with six lieutenants and 104 policemen, were called before a grand jury for inciting to riot. After hearings that lasted for six months, the grand jury refused to indict the policemen collectively, but some were cited for assault and battery.

The riots sparked by the actor and the bishop thus had much in common—a hate-figure burned in effigy and a locus of action (the Opera House and the cathedral) that was associated with a subversive enemy. Each also prompted violent repression. But the political choices made afterward were different. Unlike Macready, Bedini did not have friends and champions in high places. Whereas Macready's restrained model of theater modeled, for some, how to shepherd a democratic society through the storms of modernity, Bedini represented only the unreconstructed old order. The choices people made about the legitimacy of using lethal violence to restore order reflected, quite naturally, what they thought was at stake, and in the Macready affair the stakes seemed simply higher.

In various ways, violence had always been present in American public life, but in the middle decades of the nineteenth century heightened fears for the stability of the republic made violent outbreaks and their meaning one of the central questions of politics. Whether it was on the streets of American cities, on the plains of Kansas, in the California gold fields, in the treatment of en-slaved people or Native Americans, in the halls of Congress, or in mass mili-tary mobilization, violence dramatized political choices—forcing people to choose sides. Violence appeared to come with no warning, erupting as one observer put it in a much-used metaphor, like "the fires of a volcano."[47] And, like a volcano, the collapse of decorum was presumed to have deep causes. It was frightening because it was unrestrained and unpredictable. Violence that to earlier generations, occurring in smaller and more stable communities, could have been resolved more easily seemed to have far higher stakes in a rapidly expanding society. With the telegraph and railroads spanning out across the continent, moving people, goods, and news at previously unimagi-nable speeds, Americans both exulted at the revolutionary pace of change and feared its centrifugal force, asking themselves how, in such circumstances, a republic based on the principle of self-rule could provide political stability.

The Meanings of Revolution

The contrasting reactions to the Astor Place Riot illustrate that by mid-century the idea of revolution in American culture had achieved a kind of duality. On the one hand, the word "revolution" conjured images of the spirit of 1776 and the creation of America's "model republic"; on the other hand, "revolution" evoked the terrors of Maximilien Robespierre and Toussaint Louverture. The concept of revolution had always had a double meaning in American political culture—after all, if revolutions could make nations, they could also destroy them—but the Forty-Eighters who had fled to America after the failure of the revolutions in Europe found the conservatism of their new home surprising. Had Americans already "forgotten that this great land began with a revolution, that Washington, the father of the fatherland, was also a revolutionary?" asked the Indianapolis *Freie Presse*.[48] The answer was no, they hadn't—but Washington had been turned into a very different kind of revolutionary from those who manned the Paris barricades. To his fans—and there were some—the apparently uninspiring Millard Fillmore, who assumed office on the death of Zachary Taylor in 1850, exhibited the same "eminently conservative" principles as the nation's first leader.[49] Dorothea Dix was relieved that he had navigated "the ship of our destiny past shoals and sunken rocks, [into] deep secure waters."[50] That Fillmore was captaining the national destiny at that time was itself evidence of the superiority of American institutions.[51]

For Whiggish types, but also for many who retained an allegiance to the Democratic Party (or "the Democracy" as it was known), the turmoil of Europe, and especially in France, helped to clarify what they most valued about their Union. Catharine Maria Sedgwick was especially expressive about this. In a domestic analogy that came to her mind and pen naturally, the Union, she wrote, was like her "true idea of a home." By this, she meant "a place guaranteed against all foreign intervention; a sanctuary of domestic rights and freedom; a temple with open doors, but never to be entered by the profane." What secured the welcome "permanence of our institutions," and defended Americans against "centralization," were "religion and morality." Lacking these values, she wrote in 1852, the year in which Louis-Napoleon declared himself emperor, the French had suffered "the horror of being drilled for freedom through centuries of alternate revolution and despotism." It was, she speculated, "the utter moral unsoundness" of the French that was their downfall.[52] The Boston lawyer George Ticknor Curtis, an admirer of Daniel Webster, wrote a series of books and pamphlets explaining that the American Revolution was an entirely different sort of revolution from any other. It had preserved property and so had preserved liberty; and it had been fundamentally an expression of historical continuities, not a rupture. Americans, argued Curtis, owed the success of their free institutions to their origins in "the bosom of that mixed Saxon and Norman race, which had enthroned itself in the British Isles." And it followed that "the history, the glory of England—the great body of its law which centuries had built up with the fabric of its institutions, and which its emigrant children bore with them to the farthest bounds of their pilgrimage and planted on the remotest soil—are all ours." The American Constitution had its origins in the "days of Alfred."[53]

This spirit of patient faith in the gradual perfection of society through stable, free institutions was founded in a conviction that one could not speak of a legacy of freedom without understanding its Protestant basis. At the Princeton Theological Seminary, Charles Hodge argued that "as every tree or plant, every race of animals, so every nation has its own organic life." And so, for Hodge, the Puritan early settlers and the use of English Common Law (which was based on Christianity) made the United States a Protestant nation, "by the same general law that an acorn becomes an oak." The supremely Whiggish Hodge gave greater weight than most to this vision of history as a moral bond between past and present, but in a milder form these ideas were common fare. Since the Revolution, ministers had told their congregations that the nation was a moral being and its prosperity depended on a healthy religion and Christian rulers to inculcate a moral, virtuous citizenry, notwithstanding (in the case of the American republic) the constitutional bar on a church establishment.[54]

According to this Whiggish strand of antebellum political thinking, free institutions in America created social stability only insofar as republican citizens in a Protestant nation exercised discipline and self-restraint; that was why when they failed to do so, as at Astor Place, the response had to be so severe. Anarchy, warned Ohio Governor William Bebb in 1849, "is a despotism more to be dreaded than the arbitrary rule of a single despot. Just as the state was bound by law in America, so too must be citizens. "Laws, while they remain in force, should be implicitly obeyed," wrote Bebb, "and he who knowingly violates them, disregards his first duty as a good citizen and a patriot."[55] The heritage of free institutions and free thought, deeply rooted in the republican tradition in English history, created a polity in which there was never, under any circumstances, a justification for popular violence. Unfortunately for the defendant, this was also the view of Charles P. Daly, the judge who presided over the trial of Ned Buntline, the nativist writer who had the bad luck of being the one man the authorities could blame for the riot (he ended up doing a year's hard labor as a result). "If there is a government, gentlemen, upon earth, in which an unauthorized resort to violence is entirely without excuse, it is that under which we live," Daly told the jury in his summing up. Rioters who used violence to achieve their ends were daring to set themselves up against the people's law, to assert that they, through their possession of rocks and brickbats, were above it. "It was deemed a great point gained in the progress of English liberty, when it was conceded that no man was above the law," Daly said; "and the rioter now who stirs up a commotion, claims to exercise a privilege which was supposed to have expired with the barons of the feudal ages."[56] When Daly said that respect for the majesty of the law was the "vital principle of our political organization," he came to this view not as a hide-bound Whig but as an Irish-born Democrat. It was precisely his faith in the people's practical political sovereignty, he explained, that made him intolerant of mobs—since the people had made the laws, they must obey them.[57]

In the shadow of the 1848 revolutions, it became a commonplace in Northern politics to express the idea that American freedoms were the perfection of a common-sense English tradition of resistance to tyranny—and therefore that they owed nothing to the abstract theorizing of continental European radicals. Utopian projects with a vision of collective property ownership and social harmony, many inspired by the writings of the utopian French socialist Charles Fourier, had attracted modish attention in the 1840s (even Nathaniel Hawthorne had spent some time at Brook Farm, a commune championed by Transcendentalists like Margaret Fuller and Ralph Waldo Emerson, and later wrote a very funny book—*The Blithedale Romance* [1852]—about how absurd it all was). But in the light of the Jacobinism on display in Paris in June 1848, such experiments no longer seemed merely harmless eccentricity. Radical projects were quickly associated with the worst aspects of destructive revolution. For example, the Seneca Falls Women's Rights Convention of 1848 was denounced as a symptom of the "red plague of revolutions on these shores."[58] Little wonder, then, that there was less tolerance of organized crowd disturbances at Astor Place than might have been the case a few years earlier.

The post-1848 conservative turn even influenced Horace Greeley, the editor of the *New York Tribune* and famous champion of Fourierite ideas. Greeley was a celebrity politician-editor, as often lampooned as he was grudgingly admired. But "undisciplined" violence and "terror" had dampened Greeley's enthusiasm for the socialist dimension of the February revolution that toppled the French monarchy.[59] After a year or more of tumult in Europe, which had been lavishly covered in the columns of Greeley's *Tribune*, by the spring of 1849 the restless editor was now more aware of the ways in which popular action could lead to results that he considered regressive. The working classes of New York may have erected barricades, observed Horace Greeley, but unlike those who risked their lives against European despotism they had no justifiable revolutionary goals. "A revolutionary outbreak," the *Tribune* editor explained, could be a noble thing because it "evinces courage." But "a mob is essentially the impulse of cowards."[60] Greeley argued that anyone who tolerated mob action should be "execrated as a traitor" since in doing so he would be collaborating with the undoing of the basis of American nationality.[61]

Greeley had spent the evening of May 7, 1849—the night of the first riot, in which Macready had been driven from the stage—at the Anniversary Meeting of the New York State Society for the Abolition of Capital Punishment, a perfect example of a cause that Jacksonians regarded as faddish, effeminate, and meddling. Few issues could so exemplify the political gulf between Greeley and the anti-Macready protestors as did his quixotic campaign against capital punishment. And so, while remaining one of the touchstones of one-ideaism against which various types of conservatives railed, Greeley became, like so many other Americans, increasingly concerned about what was being lost and what needed to be protected in the years of midcentury crisis.

Partisanship and the Problem of Political Authority

As was obvious to observers at the time, the feud between Macready and Forrest replicated partisan warfare in caricatured form. At the most basic level,

Democrats took the lead in the anti-Macready movement because the actor and his supporters were presumed to be Whigs, while Forrest's Jacksonian sympathies were a core element of his appeal. One of Rynders's associates recalled how he had mobilized young men who had not paid much attention to the row between the actors. "Of course we said [Macready] slurred the Democratic party . . . and for an impudent English actor to lecture and abuse us from the stage about politics, &c, &c, was not to be endured! This ruse had a most wonderful effect, and brought out hundreds on that score who not care a pinch of snuff for *either* actor."[62] (The claim was misleading, but not entirely fabricated. In a speech to a sympathetic audience, Macready had indeed dismissed his detractors as merely a "*party* faction."[63]) It was no coincidence that on Tuesday, May 8, 1849—just two days before the fatal riot at Astor Place—Caleb S. Woodhull, a Whig, was inaugurated as New York's new mayor. A schism among Democrats had cost the party control of the country's biggest city.[64] What the *New York Tribune* hailed as a "release from the dreary reign of Jacksonian despotism" was a threat to Tammany Hall, whose power depended on being able to dispense patronage.[65] Together, the supposed Whiggish sympathies of Macready, combined with the unexpected loss of Democratic control of the city's government, created a combustible mix. Democrats had always warned that Whigs were bent on subverting the republic and what clearer evidence could be required than such a bloody, direct attack on the people? In the riot's aftermath Democrats laid blame at the feet of "Caleb S. Woodhull, the Whig mayor of the city . . . [Militia commander] General Hall, formerly a Whig State Senator [and] in fact the whole Whig authorities of the city [on] whom the people will pass in sentence upon the 5th of November next."[66] In cities and towns around the country, newspapers frequently divided on party lines in response to the news.[67] Democratic organs described the "murders" or the "massacre" by "insolent" city authorities while Whig papers railed that their opponents, in truth, cared "nothing for the blood of the innocent" except "to use it is as a libation to the god of Party."[68]

Without this party political element, the riot, its timing, origins, and aftermath cannot be properly understood. The broad political persuasions that Forrest and Macready embodied offered different ways of seeing the nature of political authority. The two tragedians' contrasting understanding of the appropriate relationship between actors and audience played out, in microcosm, the question of whether the will (and the taste, judgments, and values) of the majority should always prevail unfettered.

At Forrest's performances, true to the Jacksonian ideal, the audience was, as Walt Whitman recalled, "as much a part of the show" as anything that happened on stage; indeed the self-consciously dramaturgical approach of antebellum audiences was exemplified by a group of young men called the Forrest Life Guards who would appear in the pit at Forrest's performances wearing fancy French-style military uniforms; dressing up was not just for those on stage.[69] In his days as a drama critic for the *Brooklyn Eagle*, Whitman reported that at Forrest's entrance on to the stage of the Bowery Theater, "the whole crowded auditorium and what seeth'd in it and flash'd from its faces and eyes . . . burst forth . . . in one of those long-kept-up tempests of hand clapping." This was "no dainty kid-glove business" but "electric force and muscle from perhaps two thousand full-sinew'd men."[70] Whitman's breathless reports perfectly captured how Forrest himself saw his audience: as an idealized vision of the masculine, white American nation—freemen, unfettered by tradition, hierarchy, or a coercive state—given voice by their on-stage tribune.

In Forrest's vision of theater, the people came to participate, to feel, and to admire. In contrast, Macready's audience came to be improved. This genuine difference goes some way toward explaining one of the apparently petty causes of the two actors' feud. A few years earlier, while on a tour of Britain, Forrest loudly hissed his rival from the audience during a particularly foppish piece of stage business during a performance of Hamlet—bad manners to Macready's friends, but to Forrest's a manly expression of dissent.[71] Similarly, what to the "friends of order" was the mindless violence of the mob was to Rynders's the people's the deliberate exercise of their sovereign power. The same argument was used to justify the violent disruption of abolitionist meetings. (Some of the same crowd who drove Macready from the stage on Monday night may well have been among those who attacked delegates of the Anti-Slavery Society meeting later that same night and the following day.)[72]

If the anti-Macready movement embodied Jacksonian white, majoritarian nationalism, the "friends of order" drew on Whiggish anxieties. Taking the lead in his loud defense of the mayor's decision to send in the troops was the forty-eight-year-old founding editor of the *New York Courier and Enquirer*, James Watson Webb, a former army officer and suavely dressed, self-proclaimed "lady-killer" who had gained youthful notoriety by serving as a second to Henry Clay in a duel. To Webb, naturally hierarchical in instinct, the riot merely confirmed his suspicion of democracy. In this he was not alone. Former Whig mayor of New York Philip Hone, born in 1780, referred in his diary and, we may confidently presume, in private conversation, to the "dunghill of democracy." Appalled, naturally, by riots and entirely supportive of Woodhull's actions, Hone had nevertheless, by the time of his death in 1851 aged seventy-one, taken to making a distinction between the "*fierce* democracy" he disapproved of and the "good *honest* democracy" he did not.[73] The only way for popular sovereignty to work, from this perspective, was if the masses were subject to the discipline of what Webb called the "sternness" of authority, although, as in Macready's theater, sternness could be combined with a culture that instilled the right values of patriotism, discipline, and restraint.

Far from simply being a remnant of Federalist-era snobbery, Whiggish anxieties about universal white male suffrage franchise had a particularly modern focus: the city.[74] Cities, warned the *North American*, incubated "bad citizens, reckless of the restraints of law."[75] An analysis of the prevalence of demagoguery, rioting, and corruption by the Philadelphia *North American* sought to explain why such problems were "less manifest in the rural than in the urban population" and concluded that the answer was a greater sense of "deference" in the former. In the country, men were "usually fixed to the soil, trained to habits of reverence and obedience to law, less violently agitated by the spirit of partisanship, and suffering less from the alloy of unworthy and turbulent elements."[76]

The epitome of the propertied Whig conservative perspective, the Philadelphian Sidney George Fisher was an introspective man of independent means who spent his days visiting neighbors, making generally unsuccessful investments, reading the newspapers, and penning learned, anxious tracts about the state of the world. Bearded and fastidious, he gazes rather anxiously at the camera in a surviving photograph. Aware of his privilege, Fisher was determined to defend it, and at his lowest moments he thought urban violence the apocalyptic manifestation of literally all the multitudinous threats to civilization. "Rome was destroyed & with her the civilization of antiquity by the barbarians of the North," Fisher wrote, but the barbarians of the modern age came not from without but from within. There was a "dark mass of ignorance and brutality" beneath the "present civilization of the world," he wrote in 1844, after destructive riots in his city. Fisher saw popular government as continually threatened by demagogues, who whipped up popular passions without the leavening influence of pragmatic calculation or reasoned thought. "I always vote against the popular side on principle," he once wrote, a line that could well have served as his epitaph.[77] In this, Fisher merely reflected in starker form than was usual a mainstream anxiety within the Whig tradition (in 1838, the twenty-eight-year-old Abraham Lincoln had warned in a now-famous speech that free government was particularly vulnerable to the rise, one day, of a "towering genius . . . an Alexander, a Caesar, or a Napoleon" who would seek fame, whether at the "expense of emancipating slaves, or enslaving freemen."[78]) The popular hero-worship of Edwin Forrest—the on-stage avatar for Jacksonian manhood—was exactly the mass behavior that stoked Bonapartism.

The Democratic Party was the touchstone for everything that men like Fisher feared. And so, having conceded that municipal corruption and petty demagoguery existed under other party regimes, the *North American*—a newspaper to which Fisher contributed occasional editorial pieces—concluded that "one party, that which claims the name of democratic, has done more to bring our elections into thorough disgrace than it will ever be able to atone for."[79] As a man of property in a country with manhood suffrage, Fisher saw riots as the arrogant assertion of majority rule, which was, in fact, exactly how the defenders of extra-legal mass action also saw it. If popular sovereignty was real, a man like Rynders thought, then it was manifest in the crowd. For Fisher, this was precisely the problem. One of the many problems with "the tyranny of the many [and] the supremacy of numbers over mind," he argued, was that the "management of a great confederacy demands the ability to exercise self-denial, to sacrifice local interest & passions to great & general ends, & the masses are capable of neither comprehending the purpose nor of making the sacrifice." To Fisher the lack of restraint and discipline lay at the root of all the challenges confronting his world—whether it was the incidence of divorce, the headlong rush to pursue quick wealth in California, the on-stage ravings and off-stage histrionics of Forrest—or emotionally charged sectional antagonism. Temperamentally a deeply pessimistic man—though, like all pessimists, grimly pleased when he was proven right—Fisher thought the "mobcratic" spirit that prevailed meant the dissolution of the Union was a certainty: "It may last 20 years, or ten or 6 months, but go it must beyond doubt within half a century. I hope, however, it will last my day, for dissolution is synonymous with civil war, anarchy & misery & disaster of every kind."[80]

It is not, perhaps, surprising that traditional, propertied conservatives like Fisher, Hone, or Webb saw the Astor Place rioters as a threat that needed countering with lethal violence. But the "friends of order" coalition also included others of a very different temperament and background. The leading abolitionist William Lloyd Garrison, for example, who had, after all, been on the receiving end of mob violence numerous times in his life of radical political agitation, defended the authorities' actions against the Astor Place mob in his newspaper, *The Liberator*, arguing that "everyone who countenanced [riot] was the enemy of republican liberty."[81] When a citizen joined a mob, argued Garrison, he ceased to be a citizen. This was an important claim. The influential *Democratic Review* had charged that the militia action undermined popular sovereignty. Rebutting this assertion, Garrison countered that the militia were, after all, citizens, so it was *they*—acting as militias had in the American Revolution—who truly embodied popular sovereignty and not the mob. As the Washington-based antislavery paper, the *National Era*, put it, "Who were the soldiers? Not hirelings, not mercenaries, not the miscreant tools of a selfish Despotism, but the *People themselves*, assuming, for the time, the awful character of Conservators of the Peace, and putting forth energies, whose terrible nature they understood too well to resort to, except in an exigency when Law must be maintained, or the State overthrown."[82]

The crisis of political order was not therefore just about the propertied classes' concern to protect their interests, or even just about defending the disciplined, legitimate authority of government. It was also, as Horace Greeley explained, a necessary, justified reaction to the bullying, arrogant attempt by the anti-Macready mob to claim that, as the supposed majority, they had the right to impose their will. On similar grounds, he had condemned the action of Thomas Dorr, the leader of a rather shambolic attempt to overturn the colonial-era constitution of Rhode Island, which, in the early 1840s, still held out in refusing suffrage to propertyless working-class men. While strongly supporting the principle of a wide franchise, Greeley was indignant at Dorr's willingness to countenance force. If he was allowed to get away with it, "all Courts, all laws, all Constitutions, become the merest frostwork, which the next breath may dissipate, or which a bushel of voters, collected by a peddler on his rounds, may utterly set aside."[83] The popular will, thought Greeley, could not be "unfettered." On the contrary, democracy needed "fetters"—legal processes and formal institutions that might embody, channel, or interpret the popular will. The essence of the "Rhode Island question" was whether popular sovereignty was embedded in, and constrained by, duly constituted authority or whether the people, as Dorr claimed, retained an inalienable right to alter or abolish their governments at will. Dorr's cause was taken up by Democrats nationwide. The *Democratic Review* argued that Dorr's opponents, the Rhode Island "Law and Order Party," could not stomach power residing in "actual, real, living, flesh-and-blood People."[84] Democratic editors proclaimed Dorr a martyr of popular sovereignty while the Whig leader Henry Clay warned that Dorr represented a "dangerous spirit of disorganization, and disregard of law" that the "Democratic Party, as it calls itself" typified.[85] The Supreme Court did not rule on the Dorr case until January 1849, keeping in the public arena this fundamental question of the relationship between the sovereign people and a republican government in the months preceding the Astor Place Riot.[86]

And so, not for the last time, at Astor Place, antislavery activists, reformers, and those tagged as "radicals" aligned themselves with uniformed, disciplined citizens-in-arms against an undisciplined, violent mob. Popular sovereignty, they argued, should be embodied in duly constituted authority—in government and laws—and not the mindless partisanship or unrestrained emotionalism of the crowd. Antislavery activists here joined forces with traditional conservative Whigs in pathologizing partisanship (by which they meant, of course, Democratic partisanship) as a "madness."[87] It was one thing for old Whig conservatives like Philip Hone to be anxious about social order and the protection of property and quite another when men like Garrison and Greeley used similar language. These were men whom Hone would have regarded as precisely the kind of dangerous one-idea fanatics who, alongside demagogic class agitators like Mike Walsh, were likely to be a threat. Jacobinism and the fear of it had been part of American political discourse since the 1790s and the specter of senseless violence it conjured up was as important to the abolitionist imagination as to the old Federalist law-and-order tradition.[88] What had changed by midcentury was that democracy was no longer a dirty word. Whereas once the mob had been synonymous with popular rule, now mob rule was a threat to democratic government, properly constituted under law. The anti-Macready movement was representative, from this perspective, of a particular style of politics that was demagogic, unsophisticated, and undisciplined— and which stood in the way of progress and modernity.

The Astor Place Riot was a wake-up call for another Whiggish reformer with a prejudice against partisanship and demagoguery: the young Unitarian minister Henry W. Bellows. May 1849 was not the first time Bellows had been present when troops opened fire on a riotous mob in a city square; he had been in France and Italy in the spring and summer of 1848, and, like other Americans, he was awestruck by the historical importance of what seemed an unstoppable tidal wave crashing over the ancien régimes of Europe in that fateful year. "The people have learned their own strength," Bellows wrote, "and it is impossible that the populace will long be opposed."[89] At first, he was blasé about the disorder, breezily assuring friends in Boston that he had no concerns for his personal safety in Paris. But that was before the bloody June Days, in which Paris workers were killed in violent confrontations with government troops. Now, having seen the springtime of the peoples first hand, Bellows was home in New York—and the talk was that the revolutions had come home. Disgusted by the violence of the anti-Macready movement, Bellows thought the United States was reaping "the fruits of our political panderings to the ignorance and vanity of the people." The question the riot posed was existential: could "a federal Republic, the most artificial and consummate of all forms of government" be sustained in the "present imperfect stage of human development"?[90]

But unlike the pessimistic Fisher, Bellows's instinctive answer to this profound question was yes. He had a plan. On the Sunday after the killings, he told his well-to-do congregation that the salutary use of force was a necessary but insufficient response to the challenges of modern society. The core problem, Bellows argued, was the sudden explosion of a market economy, revolutionary new communication technology, and the dislocation and atomization that came with crowded urban living. These revolutions, emancipating as they were, presented challenges unique in human history. "All strangers who come among us remark the excessive anxiety written in the American countenance," Bellows had written in 1845.[91] The rise of worry was a consequence not of "poverty, nor tyranny" but "the restless desire to be better off." Just as unfettered democracy posed the danger of anarchy, so an unfettered free market created social and cultural strain.

And so, while his worldview was shaped by worries about the state of the world, Bellows had an optimistic faith that the solutions were in men's hands, should they be able to grasp them. Action, by government and by leading men such as himself, could redeem and reinvigorate a fractured society. New parks, theaters, and schools would elevate the masses, bind them into the national culture, and cement their patriotic loyalty. Such spaces, argued Bellows, would exercise "a good influence on the character of the people."[92] Among those who may well have heard Bellows's postriot sermon were not only Mayor Woodhull, who was to be a major supporter of new educational and recreational institutions for the city's poor, but also Frederick Law Olmsted, the creator of Central Park.[93]

Critically, in terms of the future alignment of Northern politics, this broad coalition of old conservatives, reformist Whigs, and abolitionists was joined—in spite of the anti-Democratic rhetoric of many of the "friends of order"—by a prominent group of Democrats, including Herman Melville, Washington Irving, Cornelius Matthews, and Evert Duyckinck. Walt Whitman's political trajectory also seems to have been affected by the events at Astor Place, which seemed to him to be a direct assault by the mob on culture and thus jeopardized his own idealized conception of democratic mores. Whitman detested violent excess.[94] And so, to a remarkable degree, the defenders of the militia's actions were those who either joined the Republican Party during the 1850s or who supported the full use of state power, including conscription and emancipation, in order to suppress the Confederacy. The

Astor Place Riot was a crisis moment when the imagined enemies, the political language, and the alliances that frame political choices were formed. In
the following years, anxieties about disorder, social fragmentation, and the
dissolving of the fabric of nationhood encompassed the threat from the "Slave
Power" as well as the threat from the "mob." The term "Slave Power" described
a conspiracy of immensely powerful slave-holding southerners to use their
sway over the Federal government to subvert American freedom in pursuit of
their own interests. Just like the mob at Astor Place, the Slave Power endangered the delicate balance between order and liberty in a democracy. Both
represented antimodern forces that ran counter to the civilizing, improving,
nation-building project.

The United States in 1849 appeared to be at a pivotal point. Would its
unique political institutions be able to withstand the class tensions and social
disorder that the anti-Macready riot seemed to represent? Did popular sovereignty invest in the city, state, and federal governments of the United States
the capacity to maintain order, by force if need be, without descent into European "despotism"? In one sense, these were questions—about whether the
principal threat to liberty came from excessive democracy or from abuses of
governmental power—as old as the republic. But in the context of the spread
of what James Watson Webb called "communionist" ideas from Europe and
with the scale of immigration and industrial and urban development challenging old notions of what the ideal Republic might be, the old questions were
given new urgency.

Macready's supporters sought, in effect, to reengineer the language of democracy to make it compatible with order. They wanted to invest the state, as
represented by the militia and the mayor, with the authority that came uniquely
from a democratic form of government, arguing that precisely *because* the
people were sovereign, the people—in the form of the militia—had the right
to suppress those who had abrogated their citizenship by joining a mob. But
their position was not merely reactive; their aim was to preserve American
institutions by constructing (or, perhaps, reconstructing) a republican culture that was respectful of the value of the necessary restraints that enabled
liberty to survive in a modern world characterized by giddying progress and
instability.

The Macreadyite syllogism was that in a republic, people must obey the
law because laws were made by the people and were therefore in the overall
public interest; that respect for the law ensured order; and that order enabled
liberty and prevented a French-style descent into despotism or anarchy. But
what if the law did not work in that way? What then?

CHAPTER TWO

Order and the Problem of Law
Fugitive Slaves and the Constitution

On the evening of May 26, 1854, thousands of people armed with axes, clubs, and pistols tried to storm the courthouse in Boston. Like the crowd in Astor Place and outside the Cincinnati Catholic cathedral, their object was a man inside the building—but on this occasion the crowd wanted to liberate not attack him. The man was Anthony Burns, who had escaped slavery in Richmond, Virginia and had been working for a clothing company on Brattle Street. Arrested by slave catchers, he was being held under the terms of the 1850 Fugitive Slave Act, which was, up until that point, by far the greatest assertion of federal government power into the legal processes of the individual states. Burns, like thousands of others accused of being fugitives, could not be bailed nor claim the right to a jury trial. Nor was he even permitted to testify in his own defense. Cases were heard by a federally appointed commissioner who was paid ten dollars for remanding the prisoner into the hands of those who claimed him as property but only five if he declared him free (not a bribe, claimed defenders of the bill, just a reflection of the amount of paperwork involved). Although one of Massachusetts's leading lawyers, Richard Henry Dana, spoke at his hearing, there were no grounds, under the law, on which Burns could be freed (Dana, an abolitionist, protested that the Fugitive Slave Act had turned "our temple of justice" into "a slave pen").[1] The Fugitive Slave Act not only suspended habeas corpus for the accused, it criminalized any Northerner who refused to cooperate with the federal authorities in the recapture of an alleged fugitive.

For Northerners, believing as they did that American institutions guaranteed their liberty, slavery posed a profound dilemma. One of the most common descriptors attached to slavery was "delicate"—an issue, some said, that was "too delicate" to even mention in the halls of Congress.[2] Key national decisions between 1846 and 1853 illustrated just how delicate the problem of slavery was and how multidimensional. Slavery, as a political and moral problem, sat at the intersection of the political anxieties that beset Americans at midcentury about how to maintain both stability and freedom in the face of remorseless change. But was the core problem the antislavery agitators or slavery itself? Did the emotional intensity of the conflict arise from a fundamental incompatibility of slavery with a free labor society or was it simply the consequence of slaveholders becoming aggressive in their demands? The Fugitive Slave Act was at the epicenter of that storm.

When Daniel Webster spoke in the U.S. Senate on March 7, 1850, to announce his support for the Fugitive Slave bill ("I wish to speak today, not as a Massachusetts man, nor as a Northern man, but as an American," he had begun in typically portentous manner), many of his Northern supporters had been shocked to the core. "The word *liberty*, in the mouth of Mr. Webster," observed the writer Ralph Waldo Emerson tartly, "sounds like the word *love* in the mouth of a courtesan."[3] There had been a federal Fugitive Slave Act before 1850, passed in 1793, a much weaker piece of legislation that provided ample opportunities for state courts to block an alleged fugitive's rendition. The 1850 act in effect required Northerners to acknowledge the legitimacy of human property—precisely the point that very few were prepared to concede. As a result, the act pushed many people in the free states to see for the first time the ways in which the need to preserve the claim to ownership of human beings corrupted free institutions. Challenging the axiomatic assumption that reverence for the law was the best means of preserving both order and the Union, the Fugitive Slave Act raised troubling questions for the mainstream majority of Northerners who, unlike Dana, had never been antislavery radicals.

The language of conservatism, deployed in force to defend the Fugitive Slave Act, became a powerful means of attacking it as well. Understandably, because underlying all Northern political discussion of slavery in the 1850s was the nagging feeling among increasing numbers of people from different political traditions that the arguments now being deployed by the South to protect slavery contained an ominous logic that threatened the freedom of white Northerners—figuratively, but perhaps literally too. The abolitionist Lydia Maria Child noted pointedly that when a hearing was held in Boston to determine whether to render an alleged fugitive back to slavery, citizens—who would normally be allowed to sit in the public gallery—needed to obtain a pass "as is the custom with slaves."[4] Slavery had a broad meaning in nineteenth-century republican political culture, so it is not surprising that that white Northerners who were imprisoned for obstructing the operation of the act felt that they had been literally enslaved. And so the act stoked Northerners' anxieties that slavery might not be confined only to black people. After all, did not slaveholders "look with sovereign contempt upon *all laboring men*," asked an old Jacksonian.[5] "Chaps thet make black slaves o' niggers / Want to make wite slaves o' you," the antislavery poet James Russell Lowell had his eponymous hero proclaim in the *Biglow Papers*.[6] In the light of what was happening in Boston in May 1854 that no longer seemed the paranoia of an abolitionist but a justifiable anxiety.

The act's passage was the cue for a series of violent confrontations over its enforcement. One of the best known took place in 1851 in a small Quaker settlement in Pennsylvania called Christiana, between armed abolitionists protecting a runaway and a posse of slave-catchers. The slaveholder, a man called Gorsuch from over the border in Maryland, was killed and his son seriously wounded in the shootout.[7] In Boston, also in 1851, Shadrach Minkins was rescued by an antislavery mob and spirited across the border into Canada. After attending a protest meeting at which people had "cheered for 'Shadrack and liberty' and groaned for 'Webster and Slavery,'" the nineteen-year-old Louisa May Alcott fervently declared herself willing "to do anything—fight or work, hoot or cry" to obstruct the working of this "wicked" law.[8] Senator Webster, incredulous at such disregard for the law in his hometown, wrote to President Millard Fillmore about the importance of convicting at least "some" of those who had rescued Minkins in order to demonstrate Massachusetts's allegiance to the Fugitive Slave Law.[9] A few months later in the same city the seventeen-year-old Thomas Sims was returned to slavery amid violent protests.[10] By 1854, when the crowd gathered outside the Boston courthouse, Webster was dead, his dream of becoming president on the back of a cross-sectional conservative alliance a failure and his reputation as a champion of liberty fatally wounded by his new guise as a "slave-catcher."[11] (On hearing of Webster's death, Richard Henry Dana, conveying the feelings of his many one-time admirers, wrote, "This great sun has gone down in a cloud.")[12]

The news that Anthony Burns had been "kidnapped within sight of Faneuil Hall," recalled the grandson of former president John Quincy Adams, "came like a lurid flash of lightning from amid [the] gathering clouds of a lowering political sky."[13] The mob outside the courthouse used long planks as a battering ram against the doors of the building. According to some reports, cries of "Rescue him!" were mixed with "Storm the Bastille!" The courthouse, wrote a newspaperman, resembled a "beleaguered fortress." As the west door burst open, someone fired a pistol almost at pointblank range into the abdomen of James Batchelder, a member of the fire department who was serving as a deputy U.S. marshal. He was killed instantly. The mayor called up two militia companies, who arrived with artillery pieces, as had the Seventh Regiment in New York five years earlier. The crowd eventually dispersed with no further fatalities. But over the weekend of May 27 and 28, Boston, in the words of one observer, was in a "state of siege," as U.S. troops defended the courthouse, angry crowds gathered, and ministers sermonized about the destruction of liberty in the very cradle of the Revolution. Handbills using terminology evocative of the revolutionary era were posted in surrounding towns urging "the yeomen of New England" to make use of railroads, the technology of the modern age, to come to Court House Square in Boston to "lend the moral weight of your presence" to the "friends of justice" in the city.

References to the "independent yeomanry" as "the chief conservative element of the republic" were increasingly common in the early 1850s and used by Whigs and Democrats alike.[14] But that such a quintessentially "conservative" and "sturdy" body of citizenry as the yeomanry should be appealed to as "friends of justice" in opposition to armed authority illustrates how far the Fugitive Slave Act threatened to rend asunder the relationship between law, on the one hand, and order, on the other. If the law undermined order, what were self-described "conservative" men to do? One answer was provided by numerous prominent Whigs who had supported the passage of the Fugitive Slave Act four years earlier and who now signed a petition in a Boston newspaper calling for its repeal. To the amazement of Richard Henry Dana, men who would not speak to him four years earlier, such was their anger with him for opposing the Fugitive Slave Act, now stopped him in the street and "talked treason." Even Amos A. Lawrence, one of the richest men in the city, who had offered warm support for the act when it was passed, now offered Dana as much money as he needed to defend Burns. Lawrence told Dana that he and "a number of active 1850 men" (supporters of the compromise measures) were determined to make a public demonstration that "conservative, compromise men" like them were as much "in favor of the liberation of the slaves" as the opponents of the passage of the act had been.[15] It was not that they were no longer conservatives, Lawrence emphasized, but that conservatism now demanded a different stance. Sallie Holley, a young woman who had been converted to abolitionism after hearing Frederick Douglass lecture, eagerly reported stories of previously unlikely people—Democrats as well as Whigs—suddenly showing sympathy for fugitives. Even "one of the most forward and staunchest supporters of General Pierce's election in the city of Boston," Holley reported, had aided a fugitive whose skin was "as white as any lady"—a factor that was presumably relevant.[16]

Drawing on the precedent of Boston's resistance to royal authority in the 1770s, residents formed vigilance committees to "preserve law and liberty" in the Commonwealth by resisting the implementation of the Fugitive Slave Act.[17] Abolitionists were the principal organizers of the vigilance committees but the language they used was steeped in respectability and order and their membership included some of the city's wealthiest citizens. Vigilance committees using a similar language of order emerged in other places to resist the law. The language justifying this self-regulation was the same as that used by the vigilance committees that seized municipal power in San Francisco on two occasions in the 1850s in the name of preventing anarchy.[18] Challenges to order, whether caused by immigrants in frontier California or the overturning of Massachusetts's judicial processes by federal fiat, prompted similar responses that were legitimized in similar ways.

President Pierce sent federal forces, including artillery pieces and a detachment of cavalry, to Boston (just as George III had done, Bostonians said) to help in the rendition of Burns back to slavery. After the inevitable court order, delivered by the federal commissioner, Judge Edward G. Loring, who claimed to detest the law he felt duty-bound to enforce, federal troops marched the manacled Burns to the wharfs where he was put on board a waiting U.S. naval vessel.[19] Fifty thousand Bostonians watched the scene in impotent horror as church bells tolled "the death of liberty in the birthplace of American liberty," as one heartbroken observer put it.[20]

Even one of the other federal commissioners for the state, the lawyer and editor George Hillard, was left distraught. "When it was all over, and I was left alone in my office," he wrote, "I put my face in my hands and wept. I could do nothing less."[21] Few men, in fact, can have found the Fugitive Slave Act as politically and personally disorientating as Hillard. A member of the faction of Massachusetts Democrats who allied with the Whig leader Daniel Webster, Hillard had supported the Fugitive Slave Act in the hope of preserving sectional harmony. Like Loring, he had accepted a post that required him to implement the act. Yet Hillard was also a law partner of the antislavery leader Charles Sumner, now a U.S. senator, and he had struck up a friendship with his fellow Unitarian, the passionately antislavery George Ripley, sometime advocate of the Utopian socialism of Charles Fourier. Perhaps most devastatingly for his attempts to tread a moderate middle path, upholding legal due process even if it was controversial, his own wife was active in the Underground Railroad helping runaway slaves escape to Canada. On several occasions, Mrs. Hillard hid fugitive slaves in their Boston townhouse in one of the servants' rooms on the top floor even, perhaps, as her husband was sitting in a Boston courtroom a few streets away ordering others back into enslavement.[22]

The drama surrounding the Anthony Burns case was so emotionally intense for many self-described conservatives because it dramatized the shocking underlying reality of the act—the massive use of federal force to capture and subdue a man who had committed no crime recognized under Massachusetts law. At the same time, it alarmed them because it brought into focus the ultimate "delicate" dilemma of the slavery issue: it seemed to force a choice between risking disunion by angering the South or disrupting the stability and order of their own free society. What could *compromise* mean in such circumstances, with the South demanding that Northerners limit their own freedoms in order to perpetuate the enslavement of African Americans in the South? In the face of what seemed to be such an egregious insult to the due process of law in a free state, the antislavery case now seemed entirely defensive and eminently conservative. Upholding the law—at least this one pernicious federal law—seemed to some, as in this dramatic incident in Boston, incompatible with maintaining social order. "The excitement of the Northern people is not the offspring of an exclusive sympathy with the black man," observed the antislavery *National Era*.

> True, their humanity is pained by a law which strips the ignorant, proscribed colored man of all defense against the kidnapper; but the law has other aspects equally revolting to their feelings. It tramples upon certain, great time-honored guarantees of right, held sacred ever since the Magna Charta was wrung from the reluctant hands of royal authority. It encroaches upon State Sovereignty—it establishes summary processes of trial and conviction unknown to the Common Law—it places the liberties of freemen at the mercy of ignorance, fraud, violence—it insults the people of the free States by commanding them, whenever it may be required of them, to become catchpoles to the slave-hunter.[23]

This recognition that slaveholder power demeaned Northern freedoms and honor was the fundamental shift that pushed people who had previously defended, even celebrated, the use of force against a mob to reevaluate their assumptions. Before 1850 it was antiabolitionists who were prone to use violence in Northern cities to break up antislavery meetings; afterward the militancy was on the side of those, as in the Burns case, who opposed slave catchers in the name of defending freedom—for whites at least as much as for blacks. The same language of maintaining political order and free institutions that was deployed to defend Mayor Woodhull at Astor Place was now used to delegitimize the Fugitive Slave Act.

Slavery, the Constitution, and Historical Precedent

The battle over the relationship between the federal government and slavery was framed by questions of historical precedent. That Congress's resolution of the question of the status of slavery in the new Mexican cession—measures that included the Fugitive Slave Act—were described at the time as the "Great Compromise" testified to the continuing appeal of the practice and principle of compromise in American public life.[24] The paradigm was the Missouri Compromise of 1820. That famous act of statecraft, credited to Henry Clay, had prohibited slavery above the line of latitude 36°30′ north within the borders of the United States as it was in 1820, thus, it was hoped, resolving in advance and for all time the status of slavery in future territories.[25] The implications of the Missouri Compromise were, first, that Congress had the indisputable right to determine the status of slavery everywhere outside the domain of an existing state and, second, that the fairest resolution of the slavery question was to divide the national domain between slavery and freedom. In this way, neither side could claim that their conception of property rights was the only one to be implemented by the federal government, which thereby protected slavery in some places and prohibited it in others. A house thus divided was the exemplification of those quintessentially conservative terms "restraint" and "balance," in public life.

One option in the wake of the Mexican War was to extend the Missouri Compromise line to the Pacific. For a while, that seemed the likeliest outcome. But the famous, incendiary proviso introduced by David Wilmot transformed the debate. Although the Pennsylvania Democrat's proposal to ban slavery in the new territories was condemned as fanatical by opponents, he claimed to be drawing on an even more venerable tradition than the compromise paradigm—that the default position of the Union was the preservation of freedom. Drawing on the precedent of the 1772 *Somerset* case heard by the King's Bench, which had established that slavery was contrary to common law, Wilmot's antislavery constitutionalism stressed that the natural condition of all men (including black people) was freedom.[26] Wilmot and his supporters believed that the federal government could and should not be a neutral umpire in the tension between free and slave states. Slavery could legally and constitutionally exist in a state, given the federal nature of the republic, but since Congress *could* prohibit slavery in the territories, it *should*. This was essentially the doctrine that the historian James Oakes, drawing on the terminology of the day, describes as "freedom national"—or, as one Indiana politician put it, "the ancient idea that slavery is sectional and freedom national."[27] But if this was a radical aim—and in the context of the prevailing compromise tradition it seemed radical—it was cloaked by two levels of conservative defense. Its proponents claimed, first, common law and constitutional precedent (the 1787 Northwest Ordinance banning slavery was often cited). Second, they argued that it was no more than a response to the inherent aggression of the Slave Power—the slaveholders who allegedly controlled the fate of the country in their own aristocratic interests.

The ideal of "free soil," as articulated by Wilmot, had roots deep in the egalitarianism of the Jacksonian tradition.[28] It was not simply the "free" but the "soil" part of the slogan that mattered: the emotive appeal to land and its availability for ordinary white men as the cornerstone of republican equality.[29] Slavery, free-soil Democrats argued, would undercut wages and push up land values, creating unfair competition for hardy republican homesteaders. What separated free-soil Democrats from fellow Democrats in the South was less their view of black people than their view of slaveholders. To Free-Soilers, the owners of slaves were not ordinary folks but a breed apart: in Jacksonian language, they were "aristocrats" amassing illegitimate concentrations of power and capital. Slavery and free labor could not healthily mix any more than monarchy could coexist with republicanism. "Shall we, in view of these struggles of all of Europe, with our model before them, renounce the doctrine of our fathers, and the sentiments of the civilized world, that slavery was an evil?" asked Oliver Cromwell Gardiner, a free-soil Democrat.[30] Since slaveholders were aristocrats in their antidemocratic values, they would, in the end, apply the same hierarchical logic to lower classes of whites.[31]

Wilmot's determination to prevent the extension of slavery led him, as it did a large faction of the Northern Democracy, to break with the official party organization in 1848 and support the new Free-Soil Party and its candidate, former Democratic President Martin Van Buren.[32] The platform of the Free-Soil Party, summarized one supporter, "pledges the party against the addition of any more Slave States, and to employ the federal government not to limit, localize, and discourage, but to abolish slavery wherever it has the Constitutional power to do so."[33] The principles of the Wilmot Proviso were thereby extended into a general rule. Channeling the Jacksonian tradition and appealing to people who disdained organized abolitionism, the Free-Soil Party brought to the surface the underlying Northern antislavery consensus. Captivated by the potential of this new movement, the New York *Evening Post*, edited by the old Jacksonian William Cullen Bryant, argued that it was not the "philanthropists, real or pretended" who would resist the "Slave Power," but "the laboring men of the North—the hardy sons of toil, who know that it is to labor that they must look for every thing of value . . . who cannot fail to see that slavery tends to degrade their calling."[34] To most of its supporters, the Free-Soil Party was profoundly defensive; it was simply the articulation of timeless verities. The principles of the Free-Soilers' platform in 1848 were, in the words of Marcus Morton, a Massachusetts Democrat, no more than "the doctrines of the declaration of independence, of our Constitution, of Democracy and of the Christian Religion." Morton's "political Bible," he said, was unambiguous: slavery was "*Anti-Democratic.*"[35] As an admirer of Edmund Burke, Morton's politics were—in his own mind—pragmatic and nondoctrinaire; so the free-soil politics he advocated were very different from the approach of abolitionists. "I am," he wrote, "in principle, decidedly opposed to slavery, but I am also equally opposed to all the measures and the whole organization of the Abolition party." This was not a soggy compromise or a slippery evasion but a genuinely held position. As Morton later explained, he was determined never to vote for "a Whig, a Socialist, an Abolitionist, a Slavery Extensionist, or a transcendentalist." To him, they were all "species of fanatics."[36] Morton's support for Van Buren in 1848 was no deviation from Democratic purity. On the contrary, as he explained it, the Free-Soil Party was simply the "real" Democracy.[37] In this analysis, the only reason why a Northern Democrat would not support free soil was the pursuit of patronage that had led Northern "doughfaces" to cooperate with the Slave Power.[38] This way of delegitimizing opposition was to become the standard line of attack against the entire Democratic Party by Republicans in the late 1850s but it had its origins in the intraparty factional battle of 1848. As it turned out, Morton's basic allegiance to the Democracy was hard to shake. To John Van Buren (Martin's son), he exclaimed, "I love old fashioned Democracy. I love practical Democrats. I love the Democratic party notwithstanding its degeneracy."[39] Countless other Northerners thought likewise, even many who ended up, for a time, in the Republican Party.

Although the Free-Soil Party failed to garner a single electoral vote, the response of the two established parties to the third-party challenge was an indicator of the breadth of Northern support for the principles of the Wilmot Proviso.[40] "During the last presidential canvass," wrote Free-Soiler Salmon P. Chase in 1850, "it was hard to find in the free States an opponent of slavery prohibition."[41] Northern Democrats vigorously denied that their candidate, Lewis Cass of Michigan, a jowly, sixty-six-year-old veteran of the War of 1812, was a slavery supporting "doughface." The *Boston Post* claimed "there was not a word, written, or uttered by Gen. Cass, in favor of extending slavery into territories now free."[42] During the campaign, William Cullen Bryant's *Evening Post* claimed that if you "ask a hundred men whether they are in favor of the extension of slavery to free soil," ninety-nine will say they are not. Why then were so many voting for Taylor or Cass? The answer, if you asked them, was "Oh they [Taylor or Cass] are opposed to the extension of slavery" too.[43] The

New York Tribune, edited by the antislavery Whig Horace Greeley, was confident that as a result of the election (and notwithstanding the victory of the Whig candidate, the Louisiana slaveholder Zachary Taylor), "the danger of an Extension of Slavery under our National flag is well nigh averted. The struggle is by no means ended, but the nature of the end is made certain." It had not just been an election in which Northerners had heard the cry of "Van Buren and Free Soil" but also "Cass and Free Soil" and "Taylor and Free Soil."[44]

Antislavery constitutionalism—the case that slavery could exist in law only as an exception to the general rule of freedom—was the justification for the passage by numerous Northern states of personal liberty laws. These measures, passed with widespread support in most places, tried to make the enforcement of the Fugitive Slave Act as difficult as possible. In Pennsylvania, for example, a personal liberty law outlawed the use of state facilities to hold captive fugitives.[45] By attacking the enforcement of the Fugitive Slave Act as a "ridiculous mockery" of justice and a "sham," opponents undermined an automatic correlation between the appearance of authority and its legitimacy.[46] "We make a great ado (and not unreasonably) about Italian despotism," protested a Harrisburg Free-Soiler, "but wherein is it more atrocious than [here] in Pennsylvania?"[47] As the legal historian Paul Finkelman argues, state laws attempting to undermine the operation of the Fugitive Slave Act were not conceived as establishing a radical new doctrine. On the contrary, they were simply efforts to reaffirm common law principles. It was one thing to suspend such principles in order to maintain national harmony by, for example, respecting the rights of sojourning slaveholders in the North to maintain their human property; it was quite another to accept the wholesale establishment in perpetuity of the underlying claim that human beings could be property, which was precisely and overtly what Southerners saw the Fugitive Slave Act as doing.[48]

The Missouri Compromise paradigm of drawing a dividing line between freedom and slavery on the one hand, and the "freedom national" doctrine on the other, both shared the assumption that Congress had the power to determine slavery's status in the territories even while offering very different views of the moral imperative that placed on the national government. In the end, however, it was a third constitutionalism that supplied the rationale—such as it was—for those elements of the 1850 Compromise that dealt with the status of slavery in the new territories. This was the concept of popular sovereignty: the position that the settlers in a territory, not Congress in Washington, had the right to determine the status of slavery for themselves. The supporters of popular sovereignty, like the supporters of the compromise and the freedom national doctrines, claimed legitimacy from a long historical tradition: it had been raised as an issue in every Congressional debate on territorial expansion since the Early Republic.[49]

The man who came to be more associated than any other with popular sovereignty, Stephen A. Douglas, did not oppose the Wilmot Proviso because he wanted slavery to expand, but because he thought it a huge distraction. "Why," he asked of Wilmot, "should such an exciting question be pressed now?"[50] Accurately anticipating a Southern backlash, Douglas was convinced that the apparently absolutist position of Wilmot would be counterproductive, an approach to the problem of slavery that, in essence, he maintained until the Civil War. For Douglas and many other Northern Democrats, popular sovereignty was a pragmatic, democratic solution.[51] Historians have sometimes dismissed popular sovereignty as a device to secure Democratic Party unity that fudged the critical issue of when and how the settlers in a territory could exercise their right to determine the status of slavery.[52] As we shall see, this underestimates the doctrine's political potency in the North over the coming decade. But it is certainly true that there was a fundamental ambiguity about whether settlers could prohibit slavery through their territorial legislature or whether they could only do so at a constitutional convention prior to admission as a state, and that this ambiguity had its uses for a fractious and divided party. The first of these options was the presumption of almost all Northerners; the latter of popular sovereignty's Southern supporters who, true to their basic conception of the Union as a compact between sovereign states, saw states (rather than territories) as the legitimate embodiment of popular sovereignty.

The Southern version of popular sovereignty in fact drew heavily on yet another constitutionalism: the claim most associated with John C. Calhoun of South Carolina that the federal government had a responsibility to protect all property, including slaves, in the common territory.[53] Calhoun's common property doctrine was quite deliberately an inversion of the Wilmot Proviso's freedom national doctrine: whereas the latter claimed that slavery could exist only in a state that specifically overturned the common law of freedom, the former asserted that slavery "followed the flag" (as Calhoun put it) and could be excluded only within the confines of a state.[54] Within a few years, the South united behind this common property constitutionalism, challenging both the Northern version of popular sovereignty and the freedom national concept.

In practice, to secure a deal, the critical question of when the settlers could exclude slavery was fudged in the legislation dealing with the territorial organization of the New Mexico territories.[55] But for its Northern supporters, the principle of congressional "noninterference" (the term was used inter-changeably with "popular sovereignty") gave the practical power of exclusion to the settlers whatever the abstract constitutional position might be. Ste-phen Douglas was adamant that his conception of popular sovereignty gave the power to exclude slavery to territorial legislatures and he successfully fought off parliamentary maneuvers by Southerners in Congress who wanted to prevent the New Mexico territorial legislature acting against slavery before admission to statehood.[56]

As the historian Christopher Childers has made clear, popular sovereignty therefore had distinctive Southern and Northern variants, and the Southern variant, by preventing prohibition of slavery before admission to statehood in effect asserted Congressional protection for slaveholders in U.S. territory. In contrast, the Northern version of popular sovereignty offered the prospect—indeed, many thought, the likelihood—that the new lands would remain free. But it did so without imposing that outcome from Washington. Instead, the principle embodied in the bill creating the New Mexico territory was that the settlers would decide on all local legislation, including whether to create the judicial apparatus needed to assure potential migrants that their human property would be secure. The freedom national constitutional theory em-bodied in the Wilmot Proviso demanded that Congress bolster the "natural" law of freedom; the popular sovereignty doctrine instead called upon politi-cians in Washington to resist the temptation to determine such matters for other people.

Leading Northern Democrats like the party's 1848 standard-bearer Lewis Cass as well as the young Douglas rallied behind popular sovereignty as a practical as well as principled resolution. Cass, his biographer has written, was "an opponent of slavery in the abstract, yet blithely accepted its existence as a condition of federal union" and in the hope of a final resolution of the sectional crisis he "sweated like a butcher" (in the rather unkind phrase of a colleague) through the sweltering summer of 1850 to gather the votes to push the measures through.[57] "We may well regret the existence of slavery in the southern States, and wish they had been saved from its introduction," wrote Cass in December 1847 in a published letter to a Tennessean slaveholder called Nicholson, "but there it is." The question of slavery, he argued, was "a great *practical* question," that could be resolved only by accepting that it could only be dealt with by local institutions.[58] Although Cass has been chided by historians for his possibly deliberate obfuscation on the crucial question of whether settlers could ban slavery before admission to statehood, Demo-cratic newspapers in the North at the time thought it was clear enough: he stood firmly for the sovereignty of a territory.[59] The question, Cass argued, was not how popular sovereignty could be defended, but how could it be denied? To prevent a territorial government from making a decision about slavery was "to call into exercise a doubtful and invidious authority [of Congress], which questions the intelligence of a respectable portion of our citizens." Such a power would give to Congress "despotic power, uncontrolled by the Constitution, over most important sections of our common country."[60] By this logic, Cass supported the right of territories to ban slavery just as fiercely as he opposed Congress's right to ban it.

As Cass's references to despotism and his appeal to the practical intelligence of the settlers showed, popular sovereignty struck a deep ideological chord with Jacksonians.[61] Some of the Democrats who had supported the Free-Soil movement in 1848 reconciled themselves very easily to popular sovereignty as an alternative expression of the same political impulses. Opposition to centralization was a recurring theme of the politics of the nineteenth century. Progress advanced, Jacksonians typically argued, through limiting government not expanding it, through entrusting political wisdom, in the words of an 1852 pro-Franklin Pierce campaign pamphlet, to the "unfettered" and "unbowed" people, whose natural instincts combined preservation with the "advancing, popular spirit" that "lives in the workshops and counting houses." The "conservative" people always opposed "high taxes, and all that obstructs the progress and prosperity of the masses."[62] Democrats, characteristically, were on full alert for any sign, especially at the federal level, of schemes that tended, as an ally of Stephen A. Douglas put it in 1852, "directly and fatally to consolidation."[63]

But in this instance, popular sovereignty also appealed to the Whiggish supporters of the compromise tradition. In a speech to the Senate on May 21, 1850, Henry Clay, newly converted to the popular sovereignty idea on purely pragmatic grounds, pointed out to his colleagues, "The bill is silent; it is nonactive upon the . . . delicate subject of slavery. . . . the bill is neither southern nor northern; it is equal; it is fair; it is a compromise which any man, whether at the North or the South, who is desirous of healing the wounds of his country, may accept, without dishonor or disgrace."[64] But it was not a compromise within the paradigm Clay had helped establish in 1820. Popular sovereignty stored up problems for the future, but in 1850 the potentially dangerous precedent of signaling Congress's lack of jurisdiction over slavery was less important than achieving a sectional truce. The young Illinois Whig Abraham Lincoln, for one, was willing to endorse the compromise, Fugitive Slave Act included. The administration's organ, the *Washington Union* argued that the settlement must be "religiously sustained: otherwise there is no safety for us. The ship cannot stand another tempest now that her masts are splintered, and her sails torn by the recent hurricane, which threatened to engulf her."[65] The challenge for Northern defenders of the compromise was to convince others that the Fugitive Slave Act steadied the tempest-ravaged ship. For many it made it list dangerously.

The Disconnection of Law and Order

The Burns case was a body blow to the four-year-long effort to define the new law as a conservative, necessary measure to which Northerners should "acquiesce" (no one ever claimed they should be more enthusiastic than that) in order to maintain the Union. After 1850, many political observers hoped or expected to see the emergence of a new, cross-sectional conservative party in defense of the compromise measures, including the Fugitive Slave Act. Its proponents hoped to create an alliance of pro-compromise supporters from the Whig and Democratic parties. Their strategy was to unite conservatives against opponents who could be labeled as extremists and fanatics, the peddlers of one-ideaism. One Whig leader looked forward to the emergence of a "great Conservative National party which will overwhelm the old divisions of Whig and democrat and make a new order of politics" based on the "finality" of the compromise as a comprehensive and permanent resolution of the delicate problem of slavery.[66] In the South, Whigs created Union parties in Mississippi, Alabama, and Georgia, hoping that their electoral prospects would be improved if they shed any link to the vocal Northern antislavery wing of the Whig Party. But in the North, the Union party movement struggled to develop any popular momentum, despite the enthusiastic leadership of Daniel Webster, who hoped that a new Union party might be a vehicle for his own presidential nomination in 1852 if the Whig party was unable or unwilling to perform that role for him. In New York and Massachusetts, Webster encouraged alliances between factions of Whigs and Democrats which supported the 1850 Compromise. In a public letter to a meeting at Castle Gardens in New York City in October 1850, which promoted a bipartisan slate of candidates for the state elections, Webster praised the organizers as "abject slaves to no party." Only by thus transcending petty partisanship, Webster suggested, were these men able to "uphold the Constitution and to perpetuate our glorious Union."[67]

A year later, Henry Clay also hailed bipartisan cooperation as a means of ensuring that the compromise was a final settlement of the slavery issue. In

November 1851, in a speech to a special joint session of the Kentucky legislature, Clay predicted that agitation against the Fugitive Slave Act constituted an anti-Union party that would be countered by a Union Party of which he would be proud to be a leader. If Northern Whigs grafted abolitionism onto Whiggery, Clay warned, "from that moment I renounce the party and cease to be a Whig."

So the key dividing line in American politics as Webster and Clay saw it was between those who endorsed the finality of the compromise, including the Fugitive Slave Act, and those who did not. The issue, argued "finalists" was simple: "Union or disunion"—the same binary choice that would be offered to Northern voters again and again until 1865. For many—including the Massachusetts lawyer George Hillard who was so shattered by the Burns case—the conviction that disunion and war was the only alternative led them to support the Fugitive Slave Act when it was first passed. A common defense of the act was expressed by a public meeting in a small town in Indiana that resolved, "We regard all sectional agitation as prejudicial to our interest and dangerous to the perpetuation of our free institutions."[68]

In the months after the passage of the compromise, numerous local meetings were held to endorse finality "without regard to party," though Whigs usually organized them.[69] In New Haven such a meeting was addressed by Ralph Isaacs Ingersoll, who was born in 1789, the year the French Revolution broke out. Coming of age around the time of the War of 1812, Ingersoll was a young lawyer and Connecticut state representative in the second post-Revolution political generation and, as the self-conscious heir of the Federalist tradition, was a firm foe of the Jacksonian party. Saddened by the indiscipline of the growing nation, Ingersoll's greatest anxiety was the epidemic, as he saw it, of extremism. Fanaticism bred violence, and violence was antithetical to the ordered genius of the free institutions created and sustained by the Revolution. Agitators against the Fugitive Slave Act, Ingersoll told the Union meeting in New Haven in 1851, however moderate and respectable they might seem, were, in effect agreeing with Garrison that the Constitution was a covenant with sin. In the face of the argument that the Fugitive Slave Act was offensive because it made slave-catchers of free citizens, Ingersoll stuck to the line that it did no more than put into effect the fugitive slave clause of the Constitution—and he was "not one to believe that we had grown wiser in reference to our moral or constitutional duties than the Founders."[70]

Ingersoll was in a minority. The reaction of most Northerners, including Whigs, to the Fugitive Slave Act, made finality a nullity. They may have tolerated the popular sovereignty resolution of the status of slavery in the Mexican cession with varying degrees of willingness, but the Fugitive Slave Act left most Whigs, including traditional elitists, deeply uncomfortable. For years, historians tended to argue that opposition to the Fugitive Slave Act died down after the first year of protests. This is true only in comparison with the first few months and the period leading up the Burns case. It does not indicate anything more than a grudging acquiescence, conditional on the lack of provocative, high-profile cases. The small free-black community was galvanized as never before, aided by sympathetic white allies, not just in aiding fugitives but in actively, vocally opposing the act. And, more generally, in most free states a majority of voters continued to try to nullify the effects of the act.

Correspondents to local newspapers in Harrisburg, Pennsylvania complained that the city's constables were seemingly more interested in capturing fugitive slaves than in dealing with "burglars, incendiaries and other villains."[71] When the high constable and three regular constables, who had all been elected as Democrats, ran for reelection in 1853, three who had been involved in fugitive slave cases lost, while the fourth, who had stayed clear of any controversy, was reelected with 79 percent of the vote. As one local newspaper concluded, "Our citizens have redeemed themselves from the mortification and disgrace of having a police that were engaged as the marshals of the slave commissioner in hunting up fugitive slaves."[72] By such means, opposition to the Fugitive Slave Act was naturalized, using language that Jacksonians had earlier adopted to describe the people's opposition to banks, or aristocrats, as the "manly" and "sturdy" position of the great body of the people. The only effect of politicians' support for the Fugitive Slave Act, argued the antislavery *National Era* was to "silence the office seekers and holders, while the mass of the people remain uncorrupt, unterrified and unbought"—the classic Jacksonian trifecta of adjectives describing what a republican people should be.[73] This was an optimistic assessment, but the culture of toleration for those who aided fugitives in many parts of the free states suggests the strength of continuing opposition; as Eric Foner points out, very few Northerners were ever, in fact, prosecuted for aiding fugitives, even though their activities were often an open secret.[74]

But if the Fugitive Slave Act was regarded as inherently at odds with stability, free institutions, and political order, the use of violence even in defense of a captured fugitive remained a delicate issue.[75] Even Harriet Beecher Stowe's brother Henry Ward Beecher regretted that "the mob spirit," which had once been antiabolitionist, was now, because of the Fugitive Slave Act, becoming pro-abolitionist as well. Mobs must be "put down promptly and effectually" from "whatever party the mob is raised" as it was at Astor Place.[76] Abolitionism could lead—as in the case of Garrison—to a dramatic, radical repudiation of the existing order, but antislavery principles also often fitted into a self-consciously conservative social vision, invoking ideas about natural order, social hierarchy, and, in some cases, notions of the divinely sanctioned nature of nationality and state authority. One Democratic newspaper in Michigan, accepting that "the Fugitive Law is one of the most iniquitous acts that ever darkened our statute book" nevertheless criticized violent opposition on the grounds that mob action had always been criticized in America: "We have a Government unequalled under the sun. . . . . Why, then, should we rush to pluck the weapons of anarchy, when the instruments of law and order are in our hands?"[77] Such opposition ran deep, which was why the Revolutionary-era language ("sturdy yeomen") to define those trying to free Burns in Boston was so striking.

The Whiggish Horace Greeley accurately described the Fugitive Slave Act, in an uncharacteristic understatement, as a "very bad investment for slaveholders" because it "produced a wide and powerful feeling among all classes averse to the institution itself."[78] Greeley thought the opposition to the enforcement of the "offensive" act, with its demands that Northern law and institutions bend to the recognition of human property, led people who may never have thought about the matter before to understand the inherent violence of the slave system itself. This analysis probably explains why James Watson Webb, once a vehement antiabolitionist, came to believe by the early 1850s that the Slave Power was the greatest danger to republican freedom. In contrast to Greeley—or Jacksonian Free-Soilers like Morton—Webb was un-moved by universalist arguments about natural rights; he continued to spec-ulate that slavery might be, in a practical sense, a blessing for black people even while becoming increasingly certain that it was a greater "curse to the country where it exists." Quarantining slavery by preventing its further ex-pansion came to seem to Webb to be the wisest, most conservative policy.[79]

By 1854, the Fugitive Slave Act had ensured that more Northerners than ever had been forced to think about the challenges slavery posed. Webb was representative of a growing number of Northerners who, notwithstanding their hatred of fanaticism and fear of anything that might lead to disunion, took a self-consciously conservative path toward opposition to the status and growth of slavery in the United States. Even so, Northerners' antislavery pre-sumptions, and even their dislike of the Slave Power did not lead to unanim-ity about what political action might be taken. Dorothea Dix told a friend she would not participate in the return of fugitives, and on a trip to North Carolina in 1850 mildly observed that "the Negroes are gay, obliging and anything but miserable." Yet at the same time, in an indication of the ambivalence that must have been shared by many others, she repeated her general condemnation of slavery, worried about the increasing disregard of the law that the fugitive slave issue was creating, and predicted that "whatever be the form or however remote the time, sure am I that a retribution will fall on the Slave-Merchant, the Slave-Holder and their children to the fourth generation."[80]

Sidney George Fisher was also torn between his instinctive desire to uphold the law and a growing sense that the nation was moving into unchartered and perilous waters in which the law was becoming part of the problem rather than the solution. Like Henry Ward Beecher, Fisher never under any circumstances condoned mob violence. Yet he also hated the revolutionary presumption, as he saw it, of the Fugitive Slave Act. This posed a dilemma that was brought home to him when a Pennsylvania abolitionist, Passmore Williamson, was jailed for ninety days without bail for failing to reveal the whereabouts of three escaped slaves. Williamson did not deny that he had been involved in the rescue of Jane Johnson and her two children, the slaves of John H. Wheeler, the U.S. minister to Nicaragua who was passing through Philadelphia on route to New York to board a ship back to his post, but he denied that the fugitives had ever been in his "custody, power or possession." This case kindled Fisher's considerable capacity for indignation. "A respectable man has been imprisoned because he is an abolitionist, on the pretext that he was guilty of contempt of court," Fisher complained. The heart of the problem, in Fisher's view, was that slavery could perhaps be justified as a "domestic relation" but should never be justified under the right of property in a free state. Convinced that the judgment in the case, by the Democrat John C. Kane, was "in error . . . badly written and argued," he nevertheless refused to be present at a public meeting to protest the decision since, as he put it, "I disapprove of public meetings to influence the judiciary." His sense of being torn between contempt for the underlying legal authority of the decision and the need to respect due process was exacerbated when he was asked to act as an intermediary between the defendant, Williamson, and the judge. Fisher drafted what he thought was a fair compromise in which Williamson would accept the authority of the court and in return Kane would release him from prison, but Williamson refused to sign it and Fisher was, once again, indignant. Williamson, Fisher wrote, "makes the mistake of thinking Judge Kane should concede to him & his position now, after Judge Kane's offer, is one of contumacious resistance to law." Feeling their slave property to be more vulnerable than ever, the South, Fisher realized, was demanding ever more control over the federal government. Judge Kane, meanwhile, had "fallen into the

[Southern] trap" of arguing that Northern laws denying property rights in human beings were essentially unconstitutional, a claim that would never be tolerated.[81]

In a deliciously perceptive inversion of the postwar Southern myth that localism and states' rights had driven them to secede, Fisher later pointed out that the Fugitive Slave Act was a manifestation of the fatal and counterproductive Southern desire to exercise centralized power. In prerevolutionary France, "centralized power had destroyed liberty [and] centralized consumption and expenditure had produced poverty." In contrast, the political stability of England, Fisher claimed, was because of its lack of centralization. After all, "even the Queen and the aristocracy" did not live permanently in London but on the land, in their estates.[82] So Fisher's Whiggish emphasis on the English roots of American freedom led to an argument about the importance of localism. (In this case, Fisher used the argument to attack the despotic, centralizing ambitions of the South, but the same Burkean line of argument could—and later was—used to support popular sovereignty.)

For a small number of Northerners, the Whiggish opposition to continental European-style faddishness, one-ideaism or radicalism crystalized into an ever more intense dislike of the rising tide of antislavery politics. In 1853, reflecting on the evidence of indiscipline in the opposition to the Fugitive Slave Act, the Whig *Boston Atlas* pronounced of a meeting at Faneuil Hall that "its most striking precedent is found in the action of Jacobin Clubs in the worst days of the French Revolution."[83] Seeing slavery as but one manifestation of the sinful state of fallen man, the Whig tradition could appear utterly hostile to all antislavery politics even if was not overtly supportive of slavery. A good example of this brand of Whig conservatism was the Rev. Nehemiah Adams of Massachusetts, whose book, *A South-Side View of Slavery, or, Three Months in the South* (1854), argued that the sins of slavery (and he conceded that it was an evil) had to be balanced against the sins that slavery prevented, including drunkenness, divorce, and riotous behavior. Adams was thankful that the "dispersal of the colored population to individual control" meant an "absence of mobs." They could not become involved in "labor agitation" nor in street brawls. "That fearful element in our society, an irresponsible and low class, is diminished at the south."[84] In an otherwise unfavorable review, the Whiggish *Boston Daily Advertiser* made the observation that there was "no danger that people at the North will fall in love with the peculiar institution; but if they learn to look with more charity and forbearance on their Southern brethren, no harm will be done."[85] This was an appealing idea to many: perhaps if slavery was not as cruel as they had been led to believe by radical agitators, playing on people's sensibilities (not least *Uncle Tom's Cabin*, then enjoying massive popularity), it would be easier to soothe the passions of the hour?

The Northerner who took this line of reasoning furthest—and attracted huge notoriety in the generally antislavery North as a result—was the Dartmouth College president, Dr. Nathan Lord, who peered humorlessly out at the world from behind thick round spectacles, looking startlingly like William Lloyd Garrison's wicked twin. Once, Lord had been an antislavery man ("America will not be governed righteously," he mourned in 1846 when contemplating the stubborn survival of slavery, "it has renounced the Puritan's God"). But he reversed his position in the wake of the 1848 revolutions.[86] Much mocked for his inconsistency, in fact Lord was faithfully wedded to the view that a virtuous community was one that hewed closely to the tenets of the Puritan Bible and did not presume to reorganize society on the whim of a theory. He became certain from his study of the Biblical evidence that slavery was part of God's plan. This did not make it beautiful or pleasant (hell was part of God's plan too, he pointed out), and it certainly did not mean it should expand, but it placed it beyond human capacity to abolish it.[87] In 1854, Lord appealed to his fellow ministers to focus on the "*divinities*" and not the "*humanities*" and to consider the question of slavery from its origin and foundations, as a question of divine right, rather than of prudence, policy, or economy, "a question of the moral sense and judgments, rather than of the sensibilities and sympathies."[88] In sermons, Lord warned of the dangerous Jacobinism first unleashed in France in the 1790s and now resurgent, he claimed, even in America.[89]

Reactions to the Fugitive Slave Act therefore cut across the two broad political persuasions of Jacksonianism and Whiggery, and consequently had ambiguous implications for party politics. In the 1852 presidential election, a divided Whig party nominated General Winfield Scott as their candidate (the only two Whigs to have been elected president had been military heroes, so to his supporters Scott was the only electable or, in the terminology of the day, the only "available" man.) Despite his Virginian roots, Scott was seen as in the pocket of the New York senator William Seward, who was firmly on the anti-Webster, anti-finality wing of the party. Consequently, there were some who deserted Scott because of what they perceived as his lack of support for the compromise.[90] To them, Franklin Pierce of New Hampshire, the dark horse candidate who had been propelled to the Democratic nomination ahead of far more charismatic but divisive figures like Douglas, seemed a more reassuring choice. He was so genuinely a dark horse that during the election almost any claim could be made about Pierce's specific political beliefs, which was of course precisely the intention of his backers. Consequently, bereft of a charismatic alternative like Martin Van Buren, many former Free-Soilers with varying degrees of reluctance, supported Pierce over Scott; Marcus Morton was among them. While the ideal of free soil was of massive importance to these people, as was resisting Southern domination of the party and the country, they were prepared to find ways of compromising on practical matters. The division over slavery extension, however, was an enduring one. In New York State, where the Democrats had long been divided, the Free-Soil defection of 1848 remained rancorous. "Hards" (who had supported the Fugitive Slave Act) opposed the readmission of the Free-Soilers. Many came back anyway, just as Morton reentered ranks of the Democratic Party in Massachusetts, and they continued to play a role in shaping the party, in a few prominent cases into the Civil War and beyond.

Meanwhile, Pierce's friend Nathaniel Hawthorne grimly concluded that slavery could not be subverted "except by tearing to pieces the constitution, breaking the pledges which it sanctions, and severing into distracted fragments that common country which Providence brought into one nation, though a continued miracle of almost two hundred years, from the first settlement of the American wilderness until the revolution." Abolitionists, Hawthorne feared, were "hell-bent on chaos." It was in this context that he said of Pierce (and, in effect of himself) in true Burkean style that he "loved his country not as he wished it to be but *as it is*."[91] Hawthorne presented Pierce as a pragmatic conservative opposed to dogmatism of any kind. Yet even Hawthorne, reflecting the ambiguities of maintaining a conservative posture, signed a petition opposing the Fugitive Slave Act. It was, he wrote, the only issue that "could have blown me into any respectable warmth on the great subject of the day—if it really be the great subject."[92]

Many in the Democratic Party were making strenuous efforts to focus attention on matters other than slavery in the hope that the manifest discomfort of most voters with the fugitive slave issue could be overcome. On a personal level, the affable Pierce was an unusually popular president in Washington and he seemed to be the right man to bring calm to troubled national waters. As it had been since the 1840s, the project of national expansion was intended to transcend sectional differences. Stephen Douglas was in the vanguard of this movement, confident that with an Empire of Liberty to be won, petty battles over slavery would soon be forgotten. The *Democratic Review* campaigned hard for Douglas to get the presidential nomination in 1852. They presented him as the man whose vision of perpetual growth would bind the nation together, transcending the "temporary" distractions of the slavery issue. Douglas had the energy, charisma and political world-view to be seen by his supporters as playing the same role on the national stage as Edwin Forrest did in the theater. Indeed, in one rather striking cartoon Douglas was shown posed as "the Gladiator"—Forrest's most famous role—with the sculpted calves for which Forrest was famous. The comparison was flattering to both men.

Plenty of Whigs also held fast to the notion that the Fugitive Slave Act was a price worth paying. A Whig newspaper in Illinois acknowledged that the "law in question may be defective—it may in some particulars be unnecessarily severe—its operation may, in a few cases, prove oppressive, perhaps unjust." But reverence for the law and the perpetuation of the Union meant "so long as it shall remain on the statute book . . . it will be the bounden duty of every good citizen to interpose no resistance to its execution."[93] A year after the Burns case, Abraham Lincoln expressed similar sentiments in a letter to Joshua Speed, his one-time roommate and closest friend. The two men's paths had diverged after each got married, and while Lincoln had risen in Illinois legal and political circles, Speed had married into Kentucky wealth and was now a slaveholder. "I confess," Lincoln told Speed, "that I hate to see the poor creatures [escaped slaves] hunted down, and caught, and carried back to their stripes and unrewarded toils; but I bite my lip and keep quiet."[94] Lincoln's respect for the rule of law, evident since his youthful speech to the Young Men's Lyceum in 1838, was at play here, but so too was an even bigger consideration—the belief that turning a blind eye in the face of wrong was a price that was being paid for Union. As Lincoln's words suggest, however, the strain was hard to bear. Very little was required to tip the balance against his willingness to bite his lip.

Even in Boston after the Burns case there were some holdouts who remained staunch in their defense of the Fugitive Slave Act. One was Rufus Choate, an acolyte of Webster's who haunted Boston's streets in his long black cape, reveling in his reputation as America's greatest courtroom advocate. Richard Henry Dana claimed that he visited Choate when preparing his defense of Burns asking him "to make one effort in favor of freedom" and support Burns in court. The "1850 delusion was dispelled," Dana recalled having told Choate. Conservative men now recognized that the demands of the act violated the social harmony and civil order that they so prized: did not Choate agree? Choate, in Dana's recollection, replied that he would "be glad to make an effort on our side" but that he had previously written in support of the act and could not change his mind now. "You corrupted your mind in 1850," Dana charged, to which Choate simply replied, "Yes, [I] filed my mind."[95] Choate, while apparently tacitly acknowledging the wrongness of the act in private, was still quick to condemn the crowd violence. "They counseled *no violence*," he told a courtroom a year later in a case about damage to property done by the protestors against Burns's arrest. "Oh no—no violence! . . . *three hours* afterwards, *Batchelder was killed!* Oh no—no violence! No violence!" As he reached this crescendo, recorded one witness in the press gallery, "all was stir and sensation in this court drama; in the midst of all which Mr. Choate stood erect, rampant, defiant, and with dilated nostril, as if snuffing up the air, in disdainful and daring arrogance."[96] In the 1856 presidential election, Choate threw his support to the Democrats.[97]

Slavery in the Free States

The revisionist historians of the early twentieth century, looking back to the political crisis of the 1840s and 1850s, thought their greatest challenge was to explain why white Northerners, the vast majority of whom were evidently not out-and-out abolitionists, became so agitated about the possibility that slavery might be allowed to expand to places where in practice, those revisionists claimed, it was never likely to go. One of Eric Foner's great contributions has been to explain how Northern culture and society was fundamentally incompatible with the economic interests and values of the slave South. Other historians have stressed the importance of the Slave Power conspiracy theory in mobilizing Northern anxieties about what otherwise may have seemed the abstract issue of slavery's expansion. Yet another, very helpful, insight has been provided by those historians who have emphasized that Northerners were as aware as Southerners that at stake in the 1850s was not just the status of slavery in the existing U.S. territories but, crucially, the prospect of the acquisition of a vast new slave empire in the Caribbean, an imperial project that, should it succeed, would dramatically alter the character and balance of the Republic.[98] All of these factors made Northerners anxious, but so too did the very real fear of a different kind of slave expansion—into the free states.

In 1848, the Ohio Whig Thomas Corwin tried to explain to Southerners the basic truth about Northern politics. What the South must understand, said Corwin, was the "deeply rooted" feeling of "men of all parties" in the free states that, while they "do not seek to disturb you in that institution as it exists in our States" they cannot "consent that you shall carry it where it does not already exist" and that "you or I cannot change this opinion if we would." So "enjoy [slavery] if you will, as you will," Corwin told his Southern colleagues, but never imagine that Northerners would accept its expansion as a good thing.[99] In the same year, and in strikingly similar language, Stephen Douglas warned Southerners that Northerners could "never take the position that slavery is a positive good—a positive blessing." After all, "if we *did* assume such a position," he pointed out, "it would be a very pertinent inquiry, Why do *you* not adopt this institution?" The answer was that "we have molded our institutions at the North as we have thought proper; and now we say to you of the South, if slavery be a blessing, it is *your* blessing; if it be a curse, it is *your* curse."[100] The Fugitive Slave Act, though, seemed, in effect, to be demanding of Northerners that they make exactly that kind of admission of slavery's basic legitimacy. Toleration of slavery, it seemed to be suggesting, was not enough: what was needed was active support. By making such demands in the face of Northern sensibilities, Southern political leaders, as Sidney George Fisher understood, had fatally overreached. The act was construed as a challenge to Northern honor and manliness. In such circumstances, even the staid Boston *Daily Atlas* began to refer to slaveholders as "these self-constituted dictators."[101] The Fugitive Slave Act helped to naturalize this kind of language, and, as language always does, it then framed the political choices Northerners made in the coming years.

More and more people in the midcentury North became convinced that proslavery politics must now be added to mobs and murderers as a threat to stability and order. Antislavery journals such as the *National Era* had long made this connection, arguing that in the South, as in old Europe, "Order is not Well-Being."[102] Greeley's *New York Tribune* hyperbolically castigated Judge Kane, the judge in the Passmore Williamson case, for having "done more at a single blow to shake the social fabric . . . than the vices of private criminals in half a century."[103] This notion that slavery was inherently disruptive of social order—and analogous in its effects to the use of arbitrary power by despotic regimes—spread during the 1850s. The law-and-order discourse so visible in the aftermath of the Astor Place Riot was applied to the survival of the nation against the inherently violent threat from slavery. The Fugitive Slave Act made slavery a cause of instability in the North; it forged the link between the imperatives of maintaining slavery and the exercise of tyrannical power over freemen; and it made men of property, and those who were disdainful of the "philanthropy" of the antislavery cause, see slavery as an active threat to them at home. Like the undisciplined violence of urban mobs, slavery had shown itself to be selfish and power-hungry, heedless of the need to respect local sensibilities, conventions, and orderly processes, an assault on all that men and women could fairly claim to be conservative values. The mob in Astor Place and Burns's uniformed kidnappers seemed to spring from similar, tyrannical impulses; both were insurgent threats to order and progress.

CHAPTER THREE

Storm over Kansas

Slavery Expansion and the Problem of Violence

Congressman Mordecai Oliver was pleased with the bill before the House to organize governments in the land once known as the "Great American Desert." The establishment of the territories of Kansas and Nebraska would open the prairies west of Missouri, Iowa, and the Minnesota Territory to white settlement; farmers priced out of burgeoning states like Illinois would be able to buy land; the federal government could subsidize the building of a transcontinental railroad with land grants—no longer would it be quicker to travel from New York to London than to California. Furthermore, Oliver hoped that by redirecting the people's attention toward the nation's bright future in the West, the bill would finally slay the "many-headed hydra of fanaticism" that so frightened him.[1] But as he rose in the House of Representatives on May 17, 1854, to give voice to these thoughts, the heavens opened. In a matter of minutes, the sunny spring afternoon became so dark that attendants were called to light the gas lamps in the House chamber and the noise of rain pounding on the roof was so great that Oliver could not be heard. Proceedings had to be halted until the storm abated; the "violence of debate," as a newspaper reporter put it, "was hushed by the impressive eloquence of nature." Outside, rain gouged at the thin crust of dried mud that had formed over Washington's streets, turning them into quagmires. The crashing thunder, ringing of fire bells, and raging wind gave the city a "most fearful character," reported one observer. Bolts of lightning killed two people: a woman sheltering on the corner of K and 18th Streets with her grandchildren and a slave working on a farm in Rock Creek.[2]

The weather, as observers were quick to note, was mirroring the politics. Only an hour before the storm unleashed its fury, one congressman had warned the House that they were in danger of raising "a storm that we could neither rule nor ride."[3] It was a prophetic remark, because however much its supporters stressed the opportunities that might be opened up by the territorial organization bill, there was, of course, a catch—and a pretty momentous one: the prospect of human slavery being legalized in an area from which it had hitherto been banned.

The bleeding sore of the fugitive slave issue ensured, as we have seen, that there was no era of good feelings after the 1850 Compromise.[4] And because of constant speculation about the annexation of slaveholding Cuba it was commonly assumed (with good reason) that slaveholders wanted to push ever wider the bounds of the United States.[5] Yet antislavery Northerners at least knew—or thought they knew—that slavery would be forever banned from the land between the existing free states and the Pacific. In the 1830s and 1840s, neighboring segments of the Louisiana Purchase had been admitted as the new states of Arkansas and Iowa with minimal controversy, the status of slavery in each being predetermined by the Missouri Compromise line. It was one thing to have a fight over the status of slavery in the additional land annexed from Mexico, but in the case of Kansas and Nebraska Northerners from all parties assumed that a decision on that most explosive question had long ago been made, and should not now be unmade.

But Stephen A. Douglas, chairman of the Senate Committee on Territories, his waistcoats ever more tightly stretched as his expanding girth raced to keep up with his territorial ambition for the Union, had a different order of priorities. To him, territorial organization was worth almost any price. He had been trying to organize this last remaining unorganized parcel of the Louisiana Purchase since he first entered Congress in 1844. Yet his senate colleagues from slave states—men whose support Douglas needed to maintain if, as the party's rising star, he wanted to rise further—made clear that they would never support a bill that did not give their constituents the right to carry their slaves unimpeded into any newly organized territories.

Douglas was not hard to persuade of the case for overturning the Missouri Compromise. The notion that a measure enacted when he was only a child of seven should be sacrosanct did not sit well with his temperament; moreover he genuinely believed that a top-down, centralized prohibition of slavery was a violation of settlers' right to self-determination. Douglas's argument, from which he never retreated, was that by allowing the status of slavery in Utah and New Mexico to be determined by popular sovereignty, Congress had established a new general principle. In the words of the bill, the Missouri Compromise was "superseded" by the Compromise of 1850 and rendered "inoperative and void."[6] This may have been one of the arguments Douglas used to persuade President Pierce to lend his support to the bill. In addition, Pierce's most astute modern interpreter, Michael F. Holt, makes a convincing case that the Democrats' electoral success in 1852 led the president to become overconfident about the ability of his party to win in the North on a platform of popular sovereignty. If he had been convinced that Douglas's bill could be defended on the same terms as Northern Democrats defended the Compromise of 1850, especially against a weak Whig opposition, then he may well have felt that this was a political risk worth taking.[7] Pierce's support turned the Nebraska measure into a test of Democratic loyalty. Before the bill finally passed the House on May 22, tempers had grown so frayed that weapons had been drawn on the floor of Congress.[8]

In the face of powerful, conflicting pressure from constituents and party leaders, Northern Democratic congressmen were evenly divided—exactly half voted for the bill and half against. But that was a sufficient level of support for the measure to pass, together with the overwhelming support of slave-state representatives. Unsurprisingly, Democrats from states sharing a border with a slave state or with large Southern-born populations were most likely to support the measure. In only three Northern states—Illinois, Indiana, and Pennsylvania—did a majority of Democratic congressmen support the bill.[9]

Unlike the storm that broke over Washington on May 17, the ferocious political response to Douglas's bill did not come out of a clear blue sky. The gnawing issue of the demands made by the 1850 Fugitive Slave Act had primed millions of Northerners who would never have dreamed of attending an antislavery meeting to be suspicious of the centralizing tendencies of slaveholders. *Uncle Tom's Cabin* had brought the question of the reality of the lives of enslaved people into the mainstream of public discussion for the first time. To the abolitionist Lydia Maria Child, the bill had been passed "in open defiance of the people" (she meant the people of the free states, of course) by a Senate "completely servile to the slave interest."[10] The public reaction in the North from across the political spectrum was no less violent for having been anticipated. For some of the Democrats who had joined the Free-Soil crusade in 1848, the bill was evidence of all they had long feared: the abandonment by the Democracy of its soul. There were millions in the free states, claimed the Democratic New York *Evening Post*, who had "relied upon the promise made with such emphasis and solemnity in Mr. Pierce's inaugural speech, that the agitation of the Slavery question should never be revived during the continuance of his Administration, if any power which he could exert might prevent it." Yet, "they have seen him consent to be made an instrument for reviving this agitation, wantonly, without necessity, [and] with the most deliberate predetermination. Not only the enemies of the Compromise of 1850, therefore, but its very friends at the North, are deeply offended."[11]

The day after Douglas introduced his bill, a faction of old Free-Soilers in Congress calling themselves the "Independent Democrats" raised the banner of rebellion, castigating the bill as "part and parcel of an atrocious plot" to make free Nebraska "a dreary region of despotism, inhabited by masters and slaves."[12] For all that its authors posed as above politics, the "Appeal" was very effective politics, catapulting its authors into the center of what was to become an all-consuming and extraordinarily bitter political fight, not just in Washington but in the editorial pages and meeting halls of Northern towns and cities. The self-described Independent Democrats had no prior party organization or institutional existence, but they leveraged the attention they received for their explosive language into a leading position in the political maelstrom that ensued. They would not have been able to attract so much attention, however, had they not been articulating—albeit in stronger language than most would have used—the reaction of many Northern politicians and voters. "The crime is committed!" declared the newspaper edited by the close political ally of New York's antislavery Whig senator, William H. Seward, when the bill was passed. "The work of Monroe, and Madison and Jefferson is undone. The wall they erected to guard the domain of Liberty is flung down by the hand of an American Congress, and Slavery crawls, like a slimy reptile, over the ruins, to defile a second Eden."[13] Meanwhile, John Nigley, a Pennsylvania Democrat desperately fighting to defend a seat in the state senate, was one of many supporters of the bill who spent his time desperately trying to persuade his party's usually reliable voters that the bill was simply an alternative route to a free territory. Yet he despaired that the "general opinion" which had "taken a pretty deep hold" among his party's habitual voters was that the act "*extends slavery* into all that territory."[14]

As Nigley recognized, the bill's opponents, contrasting the new dispensation with the outright prohibition under the Missouri Compromise, saw opening up the west to slavery as, in practice, tantamount to Congress determining that it should go there. The bill's defenders, however, emphasized that, objectively, the bill did not determine the question of slavery in one way or the other: it merely delegated the decision to local settlers. Consequently, Northern supporters and defenders of the bill talked past each other. For Douglas and his Northern allies, the problem was finding a workable solution that would enable westward expansion; for others, as Harriet Beecher Stowe expressed it in a public letter to the "women of the free States," the question was whether "we are willing to receive slavery into the free States and Territories of this Union."[15] An increasing number of Northerners, observing the defeat of the Wilmot Proviso and the passage of the hated Fugitive Slave Act, saw a systematic effort by slaveholders to nationalize human slavery.

Confident as he was of the soundness of his own position, Douglas was shaken by the protests he faced as he traveled home after Congress adjourned in August 1854. "All along the Western Reserve of Ohio [a hotbed of abolitionist sentiment] I could find my effigy upon every tree we passed," he reported.[16]

When he arrived in Chicago, he was warned to expect mob violence if he tried to defend the act.[17] "As for thee Senator Douglas!" wrote one of his constituents who claimed to have been a Democrat all his life, "In an evil hour thou didst think to barter the peace, prosperity and blessed hope of thy country, the last and the noblest of thine, for a miserable mess of potage."[18] Douglas's project of a railroad to California with an eastern terminus in Chicago was presumably the metaphorical potage, and for this writer it was clearly not worth the betrayal of allowing such a blatant Southern power grab.[19] Anti-Nebraska Northerners saw the Missouri Compromise as a covenant. To break it asunder was, by implication—and often by explicit reference—a Godless act.[20] Douglas assured a Southern colleague that "the storm will soon spend its fury and the people of the north will sustain the measure when they come to understand it."[21] A year later, some optimistically claimed that the tempest had finally abated, that all that was left was a mere trace of its existence whistling gently in the popular ear "like the last of a storm through the leaves of the forest."[22] Others, however, thought it just a temporary lull.

Like Washington residents sheltering anxiously from the fearsome torrents as the unpredictable lightning ignited fires in wooden buildings and haystacks, Northerners sought shelter as best they could from the political tumult sparked by slavery expansion and antislavery opposition. The imagery of violence—as both a threat and a response to the threat—suffused political language. The manner of the bill's passage showed that "aggression is as distinctive a feature of the political Slave Power as it is of slavery itself."[23] The act itself was typically described as having been pushed through Congress by "force" and "brutality" in order to unleash pain on a peaceful country. Opponents protested that the bill was a "violent infringement" of the Missouri Compromise, likening it explicitly to rape.[24] The violence of slavery was manifested, Northerners increasingly thought, not just in the tyranny of the owners over the enslaved but also in the conflict unleashed in the Kansas Territory between the supporters and opponents of slavery's extension, and in the "subjugation" by the South of the "whole North to servitude."[25] The lessons seemed clear: violent actions were the result of violent language, and the result was lawlessness. The question was whether the assumptions that had guided political action in the past provided an adequate response to the crisis.

The Storm of Politics

"Faction and violence will rage around this measure until they tire themselves out," accurately predicted one observer.[26] The political storm unleashed by the Kansas-Nebraska Act "washed clean" public offices in fall 1854 elections, wrote another political observer.[27] Democrats in the free states suffered a "violent schism."[28] Some who broke with the Democratic organization were later to claim that there was a generational divide: older Jacksonians ("The bold and Spartan band who in 1828 were open and resolute supporters of Jackson" as one put it) were more likely to reject their old party, while younger men—perhaps those who shared the young Stephen Douglas's determination to prioritize expansion at almost any cost—were more likely to stay. Whether or not that was true, there was, unsurprisingly, a link between support for the Free-Soil Party of 1848 and defection from the Democratic organization in 1854.[29] In some places, such as in old Free-Soil Party–supporting counties of New York, anti-Nebraska Democrats called meetings under the banner of the Republican Party in a conscious evocation of their Jeffersonian tradition. Silas Wright, a charismatic rising star of the Jacksonian movement in New York State, who died prematurely in 1847 but whose legacy remained potent, had referred to himself as a Republican or a Democratic-Republican to the end of his life.[30] In the tradition of Silas Wright, old Jacksonians saw in the Nebraska bill the same threat to liberty that the "money power" and that "many-headed hydra" of the Bank of the United States had once posed. One pamphleteer urged his fellow Democrats to realize that their party was captured by a "terrible POWER . . . subtle, despotic, and tyrannical in its very nature and essence—for slavery and despotism are the same the world over." For this writer, "the spirit of slavery in our country is the same in essence with that despotic spirit which crushed the liberties of Greece, trampled out the life-blood of Poland, [and] overwhelmed freedom in Hungary, Italy, and France."[31] In a world in which the central battle between despotism and freedom was being fought out on the barricades, with brickbats and bullets, in the Old World and the New, anti-Nebraska Democrats metaphorically, and sometimes literally, armed themselves for battle.

Initially, most local Democratic editors opposed the bill, although many acquiesced in time. The most dramatic indication of the public reaction against the bill was that of the forty-four Northern Democratic congressmen who supported the Nebraska bill only seven were reelected in the fall (thirteen declined to seek reelection).[32] The forty-four Northern Democrats who had opposed the bill did a little better but still suffered: fifteen of their number were reelected. Overall that meant that out of a total of 144 congressional districts in the North, the number won by Democrats fell from 93 in the 33rd Congress to just 22 in the 34th. (There were 234 House seats altogether.) The Democratic Party suffered catastrophic losses at the state level too, where by the start of 1855 it retained control of only two Northern state legislatures.

The Whigs, however, were not in a position to benefit from the Democrats' collapse. In a complex and chaotic series of local and congressional elections in 1854 and 1855, in which there were virtually no two-party contests, the biggest beneficiaries of the Democrats' troubles were the American (or Know-Nothing) Party, a network of insurgent anti-immigrant groups that made much of their supposed status as outsiders, freed from the corruption and compromises of professional politicians and party machines.[33] The extraordinary growth of nativist lodges after May 1854 and their entry into electoral politics was one of the most sudden and dramatic electoral developments in U.S. history. In the fall of 1854, Know-Nothings won the state elections in Pennsylvania, where Democrats had held power for a generation; and in Massachusetts, the insurgents took votes from both old parties to win a clean sweep of the state's congressional delegation, to the shock of the state's Whigs. In various western states groups opposed to the Kansas-Nebraska Act created fusion movements combining Whigs with dissident Democrats, sometimes calling themselves "people's parties" (as in Indiana) or Republicans (as in Michigan and Wisconsin.)[34]

Political nativism channeled Whiggish anxieties about immigration and social disorder, and nativist lodges had grown in response to urban violence and especially the migration of Catholic Irish from the late 1840s onward. But the political breakthrough of the American Party in 1854 was not because of any new religious or cultural controversies. It was slavery that drove what observers called this "great political revolution" or this "violent political paroxysm."[35] "Never were the wheels of any government so completely and unexpectedly and suddenly changed than by these nightly gatherings of the conspiring 'Know Nothings'" wrote an appalled Massachusetts Whig in 1854.[36]

Know-Nothingism arose in the space created by a collapse of faith in both the two main parties. "Because the old parties have become so thoroughly rotten," as a New York City Know-Nothing journal put it, "there has been a general rush from both of them" into the Know-Nothing lodges.[37] Disillusionment with politics as usual had multiple causes and was rooted in a long-standing Whiggish mistrust of professional politicians, demagoguery, and the corruption that oiled legislative wheels. But the flourishing of antiparty language in 1854 was not just a familiar Whig lament but also reflected a sense among habitual Democratic voters that something profound had shifted in the political world—the Nebraska bill suggested that the party of Jackson had been corrupted by the Slave Power. Even in Democratic strongholds like

Pennsylvania many Democratic voters surged to what seemed like a new alternative. Appealing directly to Democratic voters in Pennsylvania and deftly combining anti-Nebraska sentiment with anger at corrupt established parties, Know-Nothing literature accused Democratic gubernatorial candidate William Bigler of being unable to resist the "aggressions of Slavery, today or in the future" because he "is hopelessly rotten—unsound to the core, and will sacrifice his countries' highest interests and glory for mere partizan [*sic*] considerations."[38] No wonder a depressed Pennsylvania Democratic party manager reported to Bigler that "the Nebraska bill is hurting us badly," while a worried correspondent told James Buchanan that "too many of our young men . . . sons of Democrats" had joined the nativist movement. "They don't care," he continued; "they have no idea of the wrong that they are doing to their country."[39]

The Democratic share of the popular vote did not fall as dramatically as the number of state and congressional seats would suggest—probably four out of five voters stuck with the party.[40] Yet in key contests the drop-off in the Democratic vote was sufficient to deprive the party of the majority position in the free states that it had held, more or less, since the party's emergence in the 1830s.

The Kansas-Nebraska Act was also a blow to Northern Whigs who had followed the lead of the late Daniel Webster and put all their faith in the finality of the Compromise of 1850. Douglas and his supporters argued that his bill was "essentially conservative" because it represented continuity with the principles the country had committed to in 1850.[41] This was not how Northern Whigs saw it. Few free-state Whigs had been happy about the concessions made to the slaveholding interests—especially the notorious and politically toxic Fugitive Slave Act—but they had defended the measures as the final resolution of the one issue that everyone agreed had the potential to destroy the Union. Now, it seemed, the issue had not been resolved at all. It was the utter gratuitousness of the Missouri Compromise repeal that was so astonishing; it seemed hard to interpret it as other than either a sinister Slave Power plot or Douglas's selfish ambition, or, more likely, both. Dorothea Dix irascibly expressed all these thoughts in letters to Millard Fillmore. She was incredulous that this issue was now being opened up when it had seemed settled. Douglas, she scoffed, "already sees himself in the *White House*, and demeans himself like the tom-tit, which fancied itself an Eagle."[42] To Whig conservatives like Dix, it was especially offensive that so disruptive a politician as Douglas should claim the mantle of conservatism.

Repealing the Missouri Compromise, Northern Whigs felt that—contrary to Douglas's reasoning—meant the Compromise of 1850 had been undermined.

Worse, the idea that compromise between the slave interest and the free states was struck a perhaps fatal blow. "Who, after this, will ever [again] trust in a national compromise?" asked the Illinois Whig, Abraham Lincoln. If this compromise could be undone, so could any: "The spirit of mutual concession—that spirit which first gave us the constitution, and which has thrice saved the Union—we shall have strangled and cast from us forever."[43]

For Lincoln, as for many others, the Nebraska bill was a tipping point not because of its substantive consequences (opening the West to the possibility of legalized human slavery) awful though they were, but because it was a total rejection of the only kind of politics that had hitherto held the Union together. The Missouri Compromise was regarded as sacred because it was the most important manifestation of the principle of compromise itself. It had always been evident to Lincoln that human slavery was a political issue unlike any other, and that literally the only way he could imagine the Union maintaining its precarious half-slave and half-free balance was if there were clear lines drawn between each and if each side tolerated a different moral and legal foundation in the other's domain. It was the collapse of that principle that led him to his famous formulation four years later that a "house divided against itself cannot stand." And that realization was also presumably why, in deep despair, a Whig from Maine who had supported the Compromise of 1850 concluded blackly in 1854 that "if the Missouri Compromise is repealed, then nothing remains but sectional war."[44]

The radical antislavery Senator Charles Sumner agreed entirely with this analysis, but unlike finalist Whigs, he relished the implication. It was progress, he argued, in a powerful, much-reprinted speech, that Congress could no longer make any future compromise with the evil of slavery: "Thus it puts Freedom and Slavery face to face, and bids them grapple."[45] This was precisely what most Whigs feared would be the consequence of the bill: it would feed antislavery "ultraism" jeopardizing the Union that was ultimately the only guarantor of liberty. Millard Fillmore was one of those who made this point most emphatically. Even five years later, he contrasted the supposed finality of the Compromise of 1850 with the "Pandora's box of slavery" that had been opened in "an evil hour" by the repeal of the Missouri Compromise. "The flood of evils now swelling and threatening to overthrow the constitution, and sweep away the foundations of the Government itself and deluge this land with fraternal blood," he proclaimed, "may all be traced to this unfortunate act."[46]

Whigs who had worked so hard over the previous few years to try to elevate love for the Union over antagonism to the Southern slave interest desperately tried to frame opposition to Douglas's bill in conservative language. Sumner's senate colleague from Massachusetts, Edward Everett, received numerous letters urging him to take the lead in the anti-Nebraska fight so that Sumner's radicalism would not dominate the political battle.[47] And in New York City, finalist Whigs organized a meeting at the Broadway Tabernacle to protest the Kansas-Nebraska Act. A young Democrat who attended out of curiosity was relieved to find that the keynote address by Daniel Lord, an old Whig, was "conservative in feeling, and far removed from any sympathy with the Abolitionists."[48] Lord, by all accounts, testified to his sense of "betrayal." The 1850 Compromise, he argued, had marginalized radicals of all stripes, whether abolitionists or Southern fire-eaters. But the slaveholding interest had now overreached itself. By demanding that Northerners acquiesce in the abandonment of the longstanding congressional ban on slavery in the territories, they were demanding no less than subservience.

James Watson Webb—a Whig of Daniel Lord's stripe—warmly welcomed the meeting as indicative of the feeling of the "conservative men of the North, who are beginning to speak in terms of warning."[49] For Webb this act of aggression by the slaveholders demanded resistance by the "conservative, honest men of the North" to defend their "honor" and "manhood."[50] He described "true conservatism" as "that which seeks to save the country by restraining the aggressive spirit of the South."[51] This did not mean, of course, that Webb had succumbed to the fanaticism, faddishness, or one-ideaism against which he had always railed. On the contrary, "when we are found advocating any wild theories, any impracticable measures, any harum-scarum projects; when we are found promoting the schemes of feather brained fanatics or addle headed philanthropists, it will be time enough to charge us with radicalism, and destructive opinions and tendencies."[52] This was a sentiment echoed by the leading Whig newspaper in Ohio, which argued that "true conservatism" lay in adherence to the Founders, who would all have opposed the Kansas-Nebraska Act: "George Washington, Thomas Jefferson, James Madison, Henry Clay . . . if they were now on earth, and should presume to say what they have repeatedly said against the institution [of slavery], would be branded as 'abolitionists'" for their principles.[53]

For many Whigs, the Nebraska bill forced them to reflect more deeply than before on the political implications of their loyalty to the Union. The Congregationalist minister and writer Horace Bushnell argued that Northerners, having "as part of our moral nurture, this high virtue of attachment to the country and its institutions," had a duty not to submit to measures that "have only a questionable agreement with the institutions we have it as a

charge on our virtue to protect and perpetuate." In the past, Bushnell reflected, Northerners had made difficult judgments about whether particular
"concessions and compromises" would weaken the integrity with which they
could stand up for "the principles of American liberty." The Nebraska bill,
however, could never be defended as a means of securing the Union since it
undermined its foundations. The "violence" that slavery was doing to the
Union now had to be confronted in order to maintain what "our fathers have
bequeathed to us."[54]

The essential conservatism of opposing the "godless" Nebraska bill was
explicitly linked in the religious press to the destabilization of society. The
New York Observer and Chronicle, described by a Whig newspaper as "one of
the most careful and conservative of the religious journals in the Union," made
this point repeatedly. The editors of this Presbyterian weekly had devoted
many column inches to denouncing state legislation to liberalize divorce law
and were driven to distraction by the Free Love movement that had flow-
ered in the late 1840s calling for marriage to be solemnized by "love" not
"law." For them, the willingness of Congress to annul the "solemn compact" of
the compromise was indicative of the same indiscipline, if not outright li-
centiousness.[55]

Free-Soiler George Julian was not far off the mark when he said scornfully
of Whiggish opponents that they "talked far more eloquently about the duty
of keeping covenants, and the wickedness of reviving sectional agitation
than ... the evils of slavery."[56] Yet what his scorn missed was the importance
of the underlying antislavery consensus on which Whiggish horror at the
broken contract was based. They were sincere in their conviction that broken
covenants augured political instability and perhaps the ultimate nightmare of
civil war and the destruction of the Republic: their commitment to the Union
necessitated, as they saw it, an accommodation with the slave interest, and
they felt betrayed precisely because they were now realizing that slave owners
were no longer people with whom they could do business. Yet at the same
time, slavery's basic wrongness was axiomatic. "Is slavery a blessing to a community?" asked an anonymous writer in a pamphlet addressed to "the conservative masses." Clearly not: "The proposition is absurd." That did not
mean that slavery could not or should not exist. It was a concession the conservative masses, it claimed, were more than willing to make "for Union's
sake." But that faith was now being tested as never before. In an article entitled "A Conservative View of the Nebraska Question," a New England minister bemoaned the betrayal of the North by the South and of future states and
generations by present ones. Southern "aggressionists" should remember

that Northerners were increasingly conscious of the horrors of slavery—not least since the publication of "Mrs. Stowe's book." All now knew of the "separation of families . . . the avowed prohibition of the knowledge and reading of the Bible . . . [and] the debasing effect . . . upon the white population." Respecting the constitutional protection for slavery as they did, Northerners, could hold their sentiments in check for only so long.[57]

The Nebraska bill therefore profoundly altered the terms of debate in the North—even more so than the crisis over fugitives from slavery. It pushed self-described Whiggish conservatives to use a language of confrontation they would previously have avoided, willingly embracing the term "Slave Power," for example, that was first introduced into American politics in the 1840s by Northern Democrats. One self-described "conservative Old Whig" pamphleteer used language that would have been cheered at a Free-Soil Party or even a Liberty Party meeting, defining the Slave Power as the "Aristocracy, which . . . has planted its foot upon our necks." But this, he insisted, was the "purest," "truest" "conservative ground." In resisting the Slave Power, the aim was no more than to "make this nation again in reality, as it is in form and name, a Republic."[58] The Boston *Daily Atlas*, having previously been a staunch defender of the compromise, warned its readers of the inherent violence of the political force they now confronted. "We find in the nation a power, which little by little has aggrandized itself until it has become a despotism," it argued. This sinister power "mobs and shoots, tars and feathers, hangs and rips open mail bags, imprisons travellers, bullies Congress and debauches Courts. [It is] a power which sweeps away the sweet serenity of law and order, and substitutes in its place brawling anarchy and sanguinary semi-civilization." Support for slavery extension—at least support for slavery extension into territory that all had agreed would be forever free—was a threat to the stability of political institutions. "Who is the true conservative?" asked the *Daily Atlas* rhetorically, "He who seeks to rebuild that shattered barrier [the Missouri Compromise] against the black and bloody sea of slavery, or he who hangs his head, and folds his hands, and waits with oriental submission for his own destruction?"[59] For finalist Whigs, opposing the Nebraska bill was a matter of basic constitutional preservation. Precisely because they *were* conservative, wrote a Philadelphia Whig, the "conservatives of the North" could never accept "slavery as a national institution." Nor, for that matter, would they tolerate being branded as fanatical abolitionists.[60] The opponents of the act, protested the Whiggish *Ohio State Journal*, were "not the rabble" but "the solid men, the men of character and property . . . the bone and sinew of the American body politic." Those attending anti-Nebraska meetings were, it claimed, "almost without exception American born citizens," whereas the "offal of civilization cast upon our shores from the corrupt nations of the old world" supported the act.[61]

Political nativism and opposition to the Slave Power, it turned out, were natural bedfellows. In many of the violent and bitter confrontations over the rendition of fugitives there were anti-Catholic or anti-immigrant undertones. Antislavery newspapers routinely asserted that the Irish were the principal Northern supporters of slavery. Irish militia units in Boston had been the only ones—allegedly—that had helped in the rendition of Burns.[62] Just as the "friends of order" who supported Macready had associated violence with in-discipline and a threat to republican order, Whiggish Northerners had always made a connection between Catholicism and slavery. In a July Fourth address in 1854, Anson Burlingame, a Massachusetts lawyer who was shortly to be elected to Congress, explained that the twin forces threatening the republic were "Slavery and Priestcraft." They were "in alliance by the necessity of their nature," he explained: "for one denies the right of a man to his body, and the other the right of a man to his soul. The one denies his right to think for him-self, the other the right to act for himself."[63] A leading Ohio nativist grimly con-cluded that the Kansas-Nebraska Act had been passed due to "un-American influences" in the body politic.[64]

Such language hints at how Northern Whiggish conservatives saw the emerg-ing threat from the Slave Power as one symptom of a deeper malaise in the Republic that was manifested in urban disorder and moral declension. And Know-Nothings stressed their conservative credentials even as their movement succeeded, for a time, in rocking the old political order. The Northern Know-Nothings' opposition to the Nebraska bill was, they proclaimed, no more than a reflection of the "honest and manly . . . free men of the North of all parties" who were "determined to resist, to the last extremity, all further encroach-ments of the Slave Power." As a Pennsylvania Know-Nothing leader told a public meeting, "This is not an 'abolition movement,' but a movement of the moderate conservative men . . . who up until this time have stood shoulder to shoulder in support of the Compromise of 1850, fugitive slave law and all."[65]

Resistance to Aggression

The summer and fall of 1854 therefore saw a blurring of some political bound-aries within Northern politics that had previously been strongly drawn. To describe this process as one of moderates being radicalized is to miss the more complicated process by which conservatives reshaped the meaning of the political struggle against the South and slavery, emphasizing themes of preservation, stability, continuity with an older constitutionalism, and, above all, of heartfelt commitment to the Union.

At least three hundred public meetings were held in the spring and summer of 1854 to express indignation at the Kansas-Nebraska bill. "Indignation meetings," steeped in the republican language of a united people's morally righteous resistance to oppression, had been a characteristic political practice since before the Revolution but the anti-Nebraska storm in 1854 brought them to their peak of political effectiveness.[66] Since their political legitimacy derived from the assertion of a unified public will, such meetings always declared themselves to be nonpartisan. Participants and sympathetic press reports hailed the coming together of citizens "without distinction of party" and the resolutions passed by acclamation invariably asserted that party issues were obsolete, or, in the words of a meeting at New London, Connecticut, "that the subject rises far above all party considerations." Meetings typically defined the questions before the people as whether "plighted faith shall be observed" and "whether freedom shall be supplanted by slavery."[67] When expressed in such terms, it was hard not to feel indignant in the spring and summer of 1854. Procompromise Whigs like James Watson Webb could feel indignant, and so could battle-hardened antislavery free-soil Democrats like Salmon P. Chase or Whig opponents of the 1850 Compromise like Horace Greeley or William Seward. Anti-Nebraska meetings forged a shared political experience among such people: with their familiar structure of an organizing committee, speeches, and resolutions, they were a ritualized means of coming together and expressing strong feeling about a "public abuse." As the historian Michael E. Woods has explained, such meetings had the goal of turning individual emotional reactions into a collective political project. In nineteenth-century American culture, indignation was imagined to be disciplined, purposeful, and moral—the appropriate emotional response to sin. It was therefore quite distinct from the indiscipline of anger, an unruly passion that nineteenth-century Northerners strove hard to tame and banish from private and public life.[68] Ritualized expressions of righteous emotion, therefore, helped to fuse a common commitment to defend the high moral ground of the Union as the "ark of our liberties," as one speaker put it.[69]

Cloaked in this guise of righteous, disciplined resistance, opponents from different political traditions united in castigating the bill as a revolutionary innovation and charged that the South's aggressiveness was a challenge to the political order. They argued that the bill was disruptive in its intent and would lead to instability and violence in its effects. These arguments were confronted head-on by Douglas, who defended it as a conservative measure. It had the sanction of history and divine law, claimed the Illinois senator. "The Almighty breathed the principle into the nostrils of the first man in the Garden of Eden, and empowered him and his descendants in all time to choose their own form of government."[70] In a speech from the balcony of the St. Nicholas Hotel in New York City to a noisily supportive crowd of around two thousand young men of the Democratic Union club—always Douglas's favorite kind of audience—the "Little Giant" got cheers when he proclaimed that the Kansas-Nebraska Act proved that the Democrats were "the law-abiding party . . . the constitutional party!"[71] The antislavery journal the *National Era* dryly commented in April 1855 that the "first effort of men engaged in a bad cause is to adopt a respectable nomenclature" and hence the Slave Power was "noisiest in its professions of . . . reverence for Law, claiming to be pre-eminently 'conservative.'" This captured an important truth: each side in the battle over the Nebraska bill worked ferociously to legitimize their position as being founded on "respect for the laws and order of Society."[72]

In staking out a conservative basis for opposition to the Slave Power, Northerners—especially Whiggish types—turned instinctively to seventeenth-century precedents. The staid *North American Review*, Sidney Fisher's favorite journal, illustrated the seriousness of the threat to liberty by publishing a review of a lecture by Robert C. Winthrop on the seventeenth-century English politician and republican theorist Algernon Sidney. The pairing of Winthrop and Sidney pushed all the right buttons for the *North Americans'* conservative Whig readers. No one had more impeccable Puritan heritage than Winthrop, a direct descendent of John Winthrop, the first governor of the Massachusetts Bay Colony. Now in his early forties, Winthrop had read law with Daniel Webster, attended the Boston Latin School and—naturally—Harvard, and had served as a Whig congressman, his career in public office petering to a premature end when his mentor Webster died and his mild antislavery views were deemed too tepid for Massachusetts. Now, in 1854, with "propagandists of a fearful system of oppression [having] set aside the faith of solemn compromises," was a good time, the *North American* told its readers, to revisit Winthrop's discussion of Sidney and of what suddenly seemed an all-too-similar period of crisis in mid-seventeenth century England. Just as Charles I had abused the trust of his subjects with his passion to extend his authority, so now in America, those who already held the reins of government in Washington were "rioting most insolently in the exercise and extension of their power." The term "riot" (like the term "slavery") had a metaphorical power derived from its literal meaning: riots in this sense were not simply the pre-

rogative of the mob, but of the powerful when they lose all restraint. In introducing Winthrop's piece, the *North American* editors wrote that the "violence"
and "recklessness" of the Slave Power was a sign "of the madness with which
the Gods first smite those whom they would destroy." Sidney, meanwhile,
was the ideal Whig martyr: a republican eventually beheaded for treason but
who had opposed the king's execution (though he later changed his mind). In
his lecture, Winthrop quoted Sidney's famous line from the scaffold: "We live
in an age that maketh truth pass for treason," a sentiment to which Winthrop
would return a decade later when he found himself accused of treason for opposing what he regarded as the tyranny of the Lincoln administration.[73]

"I was born a Conservative," Winthrop wrote, accurately. He went on to
say that although he had about him "something of the Hampden" (an allusion
to John Hampden, another Parliamentarian who had resisted royal authority), there was "not a particle of the Cromwell."[74] For Winthrop (as for Algernon Sidney and John Hampden), Cromwell was as destructive and despotic
as Charles I. Yet Cromwell's reputation in America was rising. From being a
figure remembered as a fanatical destroyer of order, Cromwell was now being
reinvented in the post-Nebraska North as a righteous conservative willing to
take strong action to defend order.[75] Admiration for Cromwell did not con-
form to old partisan affiliation: the Jacksonian George Bancroft praised him
in his popular *History of the United States* (1837), as did the young Whig
Charles Francis Adams.[76] (Though not Winthrop, who pointed out that his
hero Sidney had, in the end, come to regard Cromwell just as Winthrop was
later to regard Lincoln: as a tyrant.) Adams and Bancroft, differing in temperament and political background, were in agreement over the threat of a
violent, tyrannical Slave Power. Both had supported the Free-Soil Party in
1848 (Adams had been the vice presidential candidate) and both ended up,
by the 1860s, in the Republican Party (although Bancroft remained loyal to
Douglas until the latter's death). For both, Cromwell illustrated and legitimized the use of righteous, disciplined force in defense of liberty—and if the
Jacksonian Bancroft gave the Lord Protector a more democratic, populist
spin than the unashamedly elitist Adams, that was less important than their
conviction that he demonstrated, as Abraham Lincoln was later to put it, that
"right makes might" and that the use of violence was justified if in response to
those who would deny liberty.[77]

A particularly enthusiastic proponent of the Cromwellian lessons for
Northerners of the crisis was Joel T. Headley, a beak-faced scribbler of rather
superficial history books (one critic rightly called them "flatulent and swoshy").[78]
In 1855, at the age of forty-two, Headley ran for the office of New York Secretary

of State as a nativist and to many people's amazement, he won, no doubt aided by his friendly relations with New York *Tribune* editor Horace Greeley, not normally sympathetic to nativists. In the campaign, Headley drew heavily on one of his best-selling works, *The Life of Oliver Cromwell*, which had been published in 1848 and was the first biography of the Puritan leader by an American author. Cromwell's appeal to anti-Catholic midcentury American conservatives is not hard to fathom: the sacking of Drogheda and Wexford during Cromwell's destructive Irish campaign in 1649 were referred to often in enough in American newspapers to suggest a general public familiarity with Cromwell's view of Catholicism.[79] Headley's biography made much of his hero's godliness—he was "no longer the Hypocrite, but rather the sincere Covenanter, when called to his last summons" as one sympathetic review in an antislavery journal put it.[80] By 1855 Headley was more interested in running against the Slave Power than against the Catholic Church (which is no doubt partly why Greeley was willing to support him), but in this quest too Cromwell was called in aid. Like his Roundhead hero, Headley declared himself to be "a conservative friend of 'law and order' " who was roused to public life (from their respective quietude as a farmer in Ely or a man of many letters in New York) by the threat of tyranny—in one case to become Lord Protector of England, in the other secretary of state of New York. Order and liberty depended on a government that respected law, as the Slave Power, Headley proclaimed, did not. In a speech at Albany in October 1855, he developed a gruesome metaphor to describe the sectional crisis. "A union formed between two discordant interests is neither healthy nor reputable," he wrote. "It reminds me of a Roman mode of punishment where a dead person was chained to the body of a living criminal and the foetid, festering mass of corruption he was compelled to drag with him wherever he went." If the South with slavery was that bad, the alternatives appeared to be either disunion or war but Headley rather skirted the choice: "I pray God that the other party will keep at a distance from us." This was a line that elicited "hearty applause." But the implication was clear: if the slave-bound South posed so appalling a threat, honor and freedom would demand a resolute response from a respectable, disciplined, civilized people.[81]

Contrary to Douglas's hopes, the political drama over his bill never went away. Violence in Kansas between free-soil and proslavery settlers in the years following the passage of the act was reported in great detail in the Northern press, and interpreted as yet more evidence of the violence inherent in the slave system.[82] And then, on May 22, 1856, came the brutal near-murder of Charles Sumner on the floor of the Senate. The assailant, South Carolina

Representative Preston Brooks, was driven to violence by a speech of Sumner's in which the antislavery leader attacked Brooks's relation, Senator Andrew Butler of South Carolina, in highly personal terms and likened slavery to a harlot and the extension of slavery to the "rape of Virgin territory." Brooks's attack was relentless. He had come upon Sumner after the Senate went out of session, sitting quietly at his desk writing. Accompanied by two Southern colleagues who kept onlookers from intervening, Brooks thrashed the sitting Sumner with full force over the head and shoulders so hard that he snapped in two the gutta-percha, gold-topped cane he had selected specifically for its robustness. Blinded almost immediately, Sumner was unable to defend himself. He staggered to his feet, ripping his desk from its fixings, and stumbled up the aisle. By some accounts Brooks then grabbed Sumner by his lapel and flayed his bleeding head with his broken cane until Sumner "bellowed like a calf" and slumped unconscious at his feet, at which point Brooks was pulled away. The attack was reported in great detail in the press.[83]

The reaction of Northerners from across the political spectrum was even more intense and personal than had been the response to high-profile slave renditions like that of Anthony Burns. "The outrage upon Charles Sumner made me literally ill for several days," reported Lydia Maria Child. "It brought on nervous headache and painful suffocations about the heart. If I could only have done something, it would have loosened that tight ligature that seemed to stop the flowing of my blood."[84] These physical reactions reflected a deep and literal sense that Northerners were personally being assaulted by the Slave Power and rendered effectively slaves themselves. As William Cullen Bryant put it, "Are we too, slaves, slaves for life, a target for their brutal blows, when we do not comport ourselves to please them?"[85] This was "but one of many scenes in the drama—or, more properly, the tragedy—which is now being enacted on the great political stage of our country" declared the resolutions in one of the many indignation meetings that once again sprung up around the country to express the "righteous outrage" of Northerners at the attack.[86] Lydia Maria Child's sense that her physical symptoms were the consequence of her own outrage seems to be mirrored in this very typical theatrical metaphor. The question now pressing itself, painfully, on Northerners, was: if they were the audience witnessing a tragedy unfold on stage, what course of action could they take? A Boston woman prayed, she confided to her diary, that the dreadful assault would "be the means of rousing the North more certainly, to the true nature of Slavery, and the tyranny they are striving to fasten upon us. Oh! can it be, that we shall longer submit to these things?"[87]

If aggression must be resisted for the Union and liberty to survive, and if the North was to "rise up" in a "manly" and "steadfast" way (to use some of the language deployed by editors) what about their culture must change? In widely circulated drawings of the assault, Sumner was represented in the North as a Christlike figure, passively receiving painful blows while holding nothing tougher than a quill pen in his hand. But was turning the other cheek, literally or metaphorically, enough? The challenge was how Northerners could defend the presumed superiority of the values against ruffianism with the "sternness" and "discipline" of trained militiamen against rioters.[88] After all, what connected "bleeding Kansas" with "bleeding Sumner" was the resort to "barbaric" violence in defiance of order and law. Even Dorothea Dix, searching so hard to maintain her reassuring faith that the only thing troubling the harmony of the Union was excitable extremists, began to use the language of civilization and barbarism to describe the clash of values revealed by the assault; like Charles I as he overreached, the slaveholders were a power that must be dethroned. The response of "civilization" and "patriotism" must be more "free Christian sentiment."[89]

Like the anti-Nebraska indignation meetings, the gatherings to express Northern feelings about the assault on Sumner claimed to transcend partisanship, and Northern Democrats, keen to demonstrate that they were no mere lackeys of the South, joined the condemnation of the outrage. The leading Democratic newspaper in Ohio, for example, insisted that while Northern Democrats may not "ring bells, and drum on old tin pans" like "professional agitators," they nevertheless felt "indignation . . . deeply and sincerely."[90] They had made the choice to stay and fight within the party rather than to join forces with the "allied army of *isms,*" as Douglas called his political opponents in the North. This was a choice grounded both in deep partisan loyalty and a principled conviction that the Democratic Party remained the last, best bulwark of Union—slaveholders were best restrained within the national party, argued one Democratic editor, rather than assailed from without.[91]

Sidney George Fisher read the reports of Brooks's attack on Sumner in his country house outside Philadelphia (strictly speaking, it was his father-in-law's house; Fisher never earned much money—he had reached a "elevated" position in society, as he ruefully confessed to his diary, without working for it). A few weeks earlier he had met Sumner at a dinner party and found him "fluent and clever" but "superficial" and "somewhat pretentious." Spotting instantly the egotism that was to so infuriate his political friends and enemies alike, Fisher airily concluded that the tall, elegant Sumner was "just the sort of person . . . to push himself everywhere & be endured. . . . I should tire of him very soon." But naturally the news of the violence ("the attack on *the Senate*" itself, as Fisher emphasized) filled him with astonished outrage. He sat down immediately to write an article for the *North American,* something he regularly did since he was a good friend of editor Morton McMichael. "It is a relief to express one's indignation" on paper, he commented. Writing for publication served the psychological purpose for Fisher that attending indignation meetings did for most other people; Fisher was decidedly not the sort of person to go to a public meeting, even if he agreed wholeheartedly with its aims.[92] In his own fussy, scholarly way, Fisher was contributing to the gathering willingness of Northerners to respond to Southern violence with violence of their own if need be—a restrained, disciplined violence of the kind the friends of order thought was meted out by the troops at Astor Place—but violence nonetheless.

By 1856, the Kansas-Nebraska storm had not abated; it had fueled the consolidation of a coalition incorporating former Whigs, Free-Soilers, Know-Nothings, and disaffected Democrats, and now becoming widely known as the Republican Party.[93] There is a debate among historians about how many Know-Nothings ended up as Republicans—the pattern evidently varied from place to place—but the evidence is overwhelming that in terms of leadership, voting strength, language, and issues there was plenty of continuity.[94] In 1856, the Northern Know Nothing Party was still running separate slates of candidates in some races, but elsewhere had faded as a separate organization as quickly as they had, clandestinely, arisen. The Republicans were an unstable, heterogeneous coalition, divided over many issues (even their party's name) but held together by the feeling among supporters that there was no alternative political organization capable—at this time of crisis—of standing up for the Union and liberty. Having emerged from the anti-Nebraska protests, Republicans in 1856 stood firmly on the ground of opposition to any extension of the domain of slavery in the United States. On this question, the difference between Republicans and Northern Democrats—in 1856 and in the years following—was that the former emphasized ends, the latter means. Republicans were refreshingly able to state clearly and categorically that since slavery was manifestly at odds with free institutions it should be placed on the retreat. Most Northern Democratic voters broadly agreed with this, but their priorities were different; to them, the wise course was to navigate a political path toward a free West while respecting, as the Founders had done, the divergent interests of North and South.

While radical antislavery people rushed into the ranks of the Republicans, for many these were not easy choices to make. Compared to the Know Nothing

Party, however, the Republicans were a vastly more welcoming alternative for many Democratic voters. Even the party's name was resonant of the Jeffersonian antifederalist tradition. This was probably especially true in New York, where the Republican name had been used by followers of Silas Wright into the 1840s. Many of the New York Democrats who had been leaders of the Free-Soil movement—Preston King, John Bigelow, William Cullen Bryant, and Reuben Fenton for example—became state leaders of the Republican Party by 1856.[95] James G. Blaine, a twenty-five-year-old Whig newspaper editor in Maine, later observed that ex-Democrats "infused into the ranks of the new [Republican] organization a spirit and an energy which Whig tradition could never inspire."[96] One Jacksonian, Francis P. Blair, summed up very simply why he left the party of his fathers with such indignation: "The Slave Power had got control of the Democratic party."[97]

Gideon Welles entirely agreed. He was a Jacksonian Free-Soiler from Connecticut who abandoned the Democrats in 1854 (he later served in Lincoln's cabinet), but his political principles, he claimed, were entirely consistent. All Welles's political choices, he wrote, were aimed at "supporting the rights of man and the rights of the states, and opposing the centralization of power in the hands of the federal government."[98] From Welles's point of view, the Republican Party, notwithstanding its large membership of ex-Whigs, had become the vehicle for expressing Jacksonianism. The crisis had forced this change: a switch in party labels had become necessary because of the threat now posed to the Union and to social order by the slaveocrat takeover of the Democratic Party. For old Jacksonians like Welles, with a view of the world that was populist, liberal, antistatist, and classically republican, there were many reasons to view the aristocratic Slave Power with suspicion.

Buchanan and Stability

The presidential race in the free states in 1856 was a contest among candidates who each sought to present themselves as the antidote to instability. It was a three-way race pitting Democrat James Buchanan against two men nominated by parties—the Republicans and the American Party—that had had no organizational existence four years earlier. With the crisis in Kansas mirroring the threat to law and order from urban riots as the discordant backdrop, Northerners confronted the prospect that Southern power was blocking free white settlers' access to the West while conspiring to create a slave empire in the Caribbean that would profoundly alter the character of the Republic. Northerners grappled with the problem of how best to preserve their honor, their manhood, and their Union in the face of the prevalence and prospect of violence.

In the end, the third-placed candidate was former Whig president Millard Fillmore, nominated by a rump of the Whig party and the nativist American, or Know-Nothing Party. His supporters promoted him as a "tried and tested man" endorsed by the "conservative masses, and by the ancient friends of our Constitution, without respect to party."[99] Aspiring to be a national campaign in this their first and only national race, and with the majority of their most antislavery Northern supporters now in Republican ranks, the American Party was hamstrung over the pressing question of slavery extension. One of Fillmore's biggest fans, Dorothea Dix, was quite happy about that. "The slavery question I positively ignore," she proudly, or defiantly, wrote in 1856, hoping that the country would simply turn to other matters. Dix was also increasingly enthusiastic about immigration restriction and claimed to see nothing but "reckless opportunism" in the Republican's opposition to all slavery extension.[100] But to other old friends and allies, Fillmore's embrace of, or by, the Know-Nothing Party, made him a compromised figure, notwithstanding his personal opposition to the Kansas-Nebraska Act. In the free states, if the Fillmore campaign stood for anything in 1856 it was for a yearning to a return to the pre-1854 political order, a goal that elicited much sympathy but which was less convincing as a political platform without any clear plan to achieve it.[101] Fillmore polled 13.4 percent of the free-state vote, splitting the opposition to the Democrats.

In contrast, Republican nominee John C. Frémont, a dashing Western explorer and military adventurer, polled 45.2 percent of the popular vote in the free states and captured 114 Electoral College votes, 35 short of victory. This was by many orders of magnitude the best performance by any candidate only seeking support in the free states, and it demonstrated that a sectional candidate could win outright if he could win a clear majority of the Northern vote.[102] In New England and some parts of Yankee-settled upstate New York and Ohio, Frémont completely dominated. In the ranks of longtime abolitionists or more recent Free-Soilers, there was a level of unanimity and enthusiasm for the Republican nominee not seen before, even in the Van Buren campaign of 1848. Even so, the limits of the Republican appeal were evident, especially in the free states he failed to capture: Pennsylvania, Indiana, Illinois, New Jersey, and California. Frémont's flamboyance, apparent radicalism (and untrue rumors of his Catholicism) meant that he was not perhaps the figure best placed to overcome the whiff of Jacobinism that hung over the Republicans. Dorothea Dix claimed she had heard hundreds of people say that had the steady and reassuringly conservative Fillmore been nominated on the Republicans' platform of nonextension he would have been elected, which is a plausible counterfactual.[103]

Not that James Buchanan was a weak candidate in the North, however. Notwithstanding the Republican sweep of everywhere north of Pennsylvania, Buchanan polled 80,000 more votes in the free states than had Pierce four years earlier, though an expanded electorate and a higher turnout meant that in proportional terms this was still a fall in the Democratic vote from 49.8 percent in 1852 to 45.2 percent in 1856.[104] The key to Buchanan's appeal in 1856 was his claim to be the only candidate in the field who represented continuity, stability, and reassurance. No previous presidential candidate, save perhaps Henry Clay, had as much experience as the sixty-five-year-old James Buchanan. Entering politics as a Federalist, "Old Buck" had first held elective office more than forty years earlier. In the terminology of the day, he was a *fogey*—but one who was so steeped in the tradition of the Democracy that all factions could rally behind him. Indeed, he was the only potential contender who offended no one. As Nathaniel Hawthorne (when he was the American consul in Liverpool at the same time as Buchanan was minister to London) observed, "He is the only Democrat, at this moment, whom it would not be absurd to talk of for the office." Douglas had insufficient support in the South and Franklin Pierce, angling for renomination, faced the implacable opposition of too many Northerners.[105] To the public, Buchanan was represented as embodying the values of a silent majority of ordinary white Americans and the pamphlets and speeches that supported him were saturated in a language of conservatism.[106]

Accepting his nomination for the presidency, Buchanan wrote, "This glorious party now, more than ever, has demonstrated that it is the true conservative party of the Constitution and the Union."[107] Speakers at nominating conventions spoke to Democrats' duty as "a great conservative organization."[108] Editors addressed "the conservative masses" and appealed to their "sound and conservative principles."[109] Buchanan's grey and uncharismatic demeanor—so different from the Byronic appeal of Frémont—reinforced this conservative, reassuring message. Buchanan described himself in an attempt at mild self-deprecation as an "old public functionary"—and, as one young Democrat, William A. Butler, dryly put it, "This, in fact, he was." Old Buck's conservatism was deep-seated and temperamental. As Butler recalled, the candidate was a man of "routine, careful of precedents, wedded to the doctrines which he had professed during his whole political life, and cherishing a horror of men given to change."[110]

When John W. Forney, one of Buchanan's Pennsylvania protégés, founded a newspaper in Philadelphia he used his pages to argue that Buchanan's "calm, conservative and constitutional policy" should appeal to Whigs.[111] And indeed, there were some prominent Whigs who offered support for Buchanan. Forney may have been instrumental in encouraging the publication during the campaign of an anonymous pamphlet "by a Philadelphia Whig" that appealed to the old partisans of Henry Clay, "in the spirit of peace and humanity," to support Buchanan as the best hope for maintaining peace.[112] A victory for Frémont, warned another old Whig, would equal "a triumph of mob law." By passing personal liberty laws that attempted to undermine the Fugitive Slave Act, as several Northern states had done, this new sectional party had set an alarming precedent.[113] Daniel Webster's old Massachusetts colleague Rufus Choate urged his fellow Whigs to "defeat and dissolve the new geographical party calling itself Republican." And since Fillmore could not win, the only way to do this was to support Buchanan, the man who "more completely than any other" served as the representative of "the great spirit of . . . conservatism" and "that sentiment of nationality without which, and the increase of which, America is no longer America." Here was the question, asked Choate, warming to his theme: "by what vote can I do most to prevent the madness of the times from working its maddest act—the very ecstasy of its madness—the permanent formation and the actual present triumph of a party which knows one-half of America only to hate and dread it."[114] Some Democratic politicians hoped that losses to the "Frémont bandwagon" from their own ranks were being more than offset by, as Joseph Cracraft reported from Mahoning County, Ohio, the "number of old Whigs going for Old Buck."[115] The election results suggest this wasn't so—Frémont won Ohio thanks to his overwhelming strength in the Northern counties—but there were certainly former Whigs who made the judgment that Buchanan now formed the most convincing bulwark against destruction.

The case for the Democratic Party was that it alone could provide certainty and stability because of what its adherents claimed was its unique fidelity to the Constitution and its status as the only truely national party with support in both North and South. The Democrats' "strict construction" of the Constitution was the only sure foundation of liberty, wrote Pennsylvania Democrat Charles R. Buckalew. Unlike their zealous, meddling opponents, Democrats would not exercise "the public power . . . except where a clear warrant and manifest utility authorize and justify it." To Buckalew this question of meddling by a centralizing government was at the root of all the political troubles facing the nation.[116] And so Democrats attacked Republicans for "legislating too much and spending too much," and for racking up too much debt and raising taxes.[117] The "meddling" party of one-ideaism, protested a New Hampshire Democratic editor, did not allow the people to be the "judge of their own institutions and local affairs" but wanted to place them under a "congressional despotism—the very essence of old toryism." And slavery was just one aspect of this: "They even go to the extent of proscribing what the people shall eat and drink, and what manner of religion they shall profess."[118] The New York state Democratic Party passed resolutions in the spring of 1856 attacking the "unsound" and "revolutionary" claim of the "theorists" of the Republican Party that under no circumstances could Congress admit a slave state.

Such was the continuing faith in the purpose of the Democratic Party that some evidently convinced themselves that in the end his election was the best way of halting the aggression of the Slave Power. A woman traveler reported that on a stagecoach ride in upstate New York just before the election she found herself among people who were "all on one side, all Buchanan men, and yet all antislavery. It seemed reasonable, as they said, that the South should cease to push the slave question in regard to Kansas, now that it "has elected its President."[119] Democrats, then, were simply acting out their historic mission of defending the Constitution. In the face of factionalizers and incendiary ideas, they alone "invoke the spirit of peace, of mutual forbearance, conciliation and compromise." The Founding Fathers, explained the New York Democrats, had understood the need to balance "the countless practical and certain advantages of Union against the vain hope of theoretical perfection in government." That pragmatism and worldly, Burkean wisdom, was contrasted with their opponents' "reckless spirit" and their "anger."[120]

Frémont the Conservative

What Rufus Choate called "the madness of the times" scattered men different ways in search of order.[121] Unlike Choate, some sought shelter from the storm of sectional conflict under the Republican banner. The *North American*, for example, threw its venerable Whiggish authority behind the "conservative Republican ticket."[122] Former senator and Whig vice presidential candidate Theodore Frelinghuysen assured an audience in Newark, New Jersey: "If I did not believe in my heart that the administration of Col. Frémont, should it ever come into power, would be as conservative and truly national as any of its predecessors, I would have nothing to do with it."[123] The traditionally Whig Boston *Daily Atlas* hailed Republicans as "men who are laboring in these stormy times to bring back the National Government to its primitive position"[124] By primitive they meant they would extinguish license by restoring liberty, that the indiscipline and disregard for basic principles of justice, for tradition, and for authority would be defeated, that oligarchy would be overcome, just as the revolutionary generation had overcome British tyranny. Whig New York Senator Hamilton Fish (later secretary of state under President Grant) reminded voters in 1856 that he was proud to continue to say he was a Whig even though the formal party organization had, in effect, collapsed, since to say one was a Whig was simply to say that one believed in "law and order, of the rights of person and property, of personal liberty and of social restraint, without which our republican institutions must cease to exist." The Republican national convention's resistance to the expansion of slavery into the territories was "no new doctrine" Fish pointed out: "Some years since it was the universal received doctrine."[125] Republicans therefore represented continuity and a liberal and national outlook, quite in accordance with Whig values. In a similar vein, former Whig Henry Raymond's newly established *New York Times* was at pains to stress its conservative credentials, using identical language to that deployed by countless pro-Buchanan editors. "The Republican Party is the one for all . . . conservative men to attach themselves to," ran a typical article, signed "A Conservative Fremont Man."[126] Keen to distance themselves from any sign of ultraism, especially in states with a minimal tradition of antislavery activism, Republican activists emphasized their candidate's honesty and steadfastness, and as someone free from the taint of corruption.[127] Above all, Frémont was presented as the embodiment of a disciplined masculinity: willing and able to use violence, as he had allegedly shown against Mexicans in California, but only where necessary and with the grim, restrained purposefulness shown (in his supporters' imagination) by uniformed troops responding to unruly rioters.

This image was burnished by an unlikely source: the hitherto Democratic *New York Herald*, a newspaper with a readership in the hundreds of thousands across the free states. The *Herald* enthused about Frémont throughout the summer and fall of 1856, publishing articles with titles like "Fremont the only conservative, national, constitutional . . . candidate." Having supported Polk and Pierce, and routinely referring to abolitionists as "nigger-lovers," the *Herald*'s willingness to sign up for the Republican campaign in the fall of 1856 was something of a surprise. The paper was edited by James Gordon Bennett, a Scottish immigrant, who had become fabulously wealthy through his newspaper entrepreneurship and whose newspaper self-consciously spoke for the "solid men, the conservative men" for whom "peace, law, order and prosperity are paramount." His opponents attacked him as amoral and unscrupulous; he regarded himself as a Romantic figure nurtured on the novels of Sir Walter Scott, and when his enemies mocked him for being cross-eyed, he riposted that it was the result of trying to follow their political movements.[128] But Bennett's support, as he made clear, did not reflect a weakening of his antiabolitionism. He was putting his editorial influence at the service of a candidate whom he hoped would be what he had once expected Pierce would be: the bulwark against "the nigger factions—the drivers and the worshippers." A crisis was approaching when, unless the conservative masses rallied to the polls to wrench the government out of the hands of these pro- or antislavery zealots, the "vitals of the republic" would be torn out by the fighting that would ensue. Bennett's newspaper almost never used the term "Republican Party," referring instead to the "Frémont Movement." Frémont was presented as a transformative, vigorous Jacksonian figure whose conservatism was a source of masculine strength and "steadfastness" in contrast to the "vacillations" of Buchanan.[129] Bennett's newspaper was consistently and viciously racist; it was a fervent champion of the continued and inexorable territorial expansion of the United States, including, in the short-term, Cuba. Yet it was also implacably antislavery and its support for Frémont in 1856 seemed to mark a turning point in its recognition of the political threat of the South.

In New York in the summer of 1856, two old Free-Soilers, James S. Wadsworth and David Dudley Field, echoed the *Herald*'s line by organizing a Democratic-Republican convention, which celebrated the lineage of a party back to the "early days of the Republic—to the days of Jefferson." Frémont's "professions and antecedents are all democratic" Field pointed out, and he stressed that, like the Democratic party of Jackson's day he wanted to make "no attack" on his "brethren" in the South, and emphasized his continued adherence to the old principle of compromise, which the South was now denouncing. It was the purpose of the Frémont Democratic-Republican movement, argued Field, to restrain the "northern traitors" (his term for abolitionists) as much as the "southern traitors" who were undermining the liberties of the North with their proslavery aggressions.

Similar public demonstrations were held in Connecticut, Ohio, Pennsylvania, New Hampshire, and other states. And especially in traditional Democratic districts anti-Nebraska candidates, running under a variety of party labels, claimed the mantle of the true democracy. In Philadelphia, for example, a pro-Nebraska congressman, Thomas B. Florence, a radical land-reformer and temperance advocate who was so associated with fighting for the interests of the poor in his working-class central Philadelphia district that he was known as "the Widow's Friend," faced a serious electoral challenge from Thomas G. Allen, a former Democrat running on an anti-Nebraska platform as a "People's" candidate. Allen's speeches and public addresses went out of their way to explain that he was running against Florence "*as a Democrat.*" He quoted with approval from a speech of Florence's about the need to silence "sectional agitators" with their "anti-republican conduct" as "language becoming of a Democrat." And he expressed deep sadness at the recent "votes against Freedom" from a man "who has been heretofore conspicuous in the work of promoting Freedom, who [has] manfully stood up and advocated the interest of the free laboring man." Florence, declared Allen, was no more than a "*professed* Democrat" who had abandoned the faith of his fathers.[130]

The other side of the conservative case for Frémont was the accusation that his opponents were dangerous radicals. Republicans argued that *Democrats* were now the peddlers of dangerous, untested new ideas. They "do not rest their [policies] upon historical precedent or ancient and established practice, but upon a THEORY which they contend must be and shall be, though never has been, carried out." That theory which "originated with the great *doctrinaire,* John C. Calhoun" was that human property should be respected and protected by the government of the United States on exactly the same basis as any other kind of property. "It behooves every Northern conservative to understand it clearly; for as applied, it is pregnant with rankest *innovation* and *mischief.*"[131] Republicans protested "the most dexterous and successful device of the Democratic party for getting and keeping power has been its claim of exclusive *conservatism.*" But this was no more than a humbug. Like the confidence tricksters that haunted unwary new arrivals in the cities, Democrats sought only to mislead.[132] The newspaper in Springfield, Illinois, for which Lincoln sometimes wrote, expanded on this image of Democratic "false conservatism":

> In these latter-day times . . . when all good things are put to base uses, and all just principles perverted, confounded, or ignored, the word "conservatism," like that of "Democracy," is made use of as a specious disguise for political cupidity. A certain class of long-faced, wise-looking, slow-tongued individuals have wrapped themselves up in the black folds of demagoguism, and labeled the covering "conservatism;" and there, and thus wrapped up like a band of friars, they presume to speak words of admonition, of solemn warning to the country, for whose welfare they profess to have the most profound solicitude . . . [But] to encourage slavery

in this country by extending it, is *not* conservatism. It is anything but that. By taking the opposite ground, we contend that the party of Freedom is the truly and only conservative party of the country.[133]

Where "the Pathfinder"—Frémont—was disciplined, Democrats were unrestrained, reckless, and a danger to the stability of the Union. Republican speakers and editors warned of plots to stage a "bloody revolution" if Frémont were elected.[134] The third candidate in the race, Millard Fillmore, was a difficult man to cast in this way, but his apparent admission, in a speech in Albany during the campaign, that he would rather accept disunion than war, was pounced on by his opponents, who thought he had destroyed his "national" and "Union-saving" credentials.[135] The use of violence was being imagined, even if tentatively and implicitly, as an alternative to the path down which the Slave Power was marching the country.

Frémont supporters, meanwhile, had no difficulty in presenting Buchanan as the candidate of the "Border Ruffian Party," the defender of license, disorder, and mob rule. Horace Greeley's New York *Tribune*, itself often accused of fanaticism, castigated the alliance between "the merchant princes of Wall Street and the Maratists and Jacobins" of the Democratic Party.[136] Drawing on a long strain of antipartisanship in Whig political culture, the Boston *Daily Atlas* reminded readers that Buchanan embodied the "JACOBIN principles" of the Democracy, meaning the pursuit of spoils and the sheeplike "unthinking" commitment to whatever the party platform said.[137]

Where Buchanan proved most vulnerable to charges of radicalism—notwithstanding his long record as a public servant seemingly almost entirely absent of innovation or imagination—was over his apparent sympathy for Cuba filibusterers. In 1854, while he had been stationed in London as American ambassador to the Court of St. James and generally advancing his political career by avoiding becoming embroiled in the storm over the Kansas-Nebraska Act, Buchanan had become associated, seemingly almost in spite of himself, with something close to a filibusterer's charter. At a meeting in Ostend with two Louisianans, the excitable Pierre Soulé, American minister to Spain, and John Slidell, minister to France, Buchanan had added his name to a position statement that became grandly known as the "Ostend Manifesto."[138] It was in fact a declaration of what many Americans in both sections assumed to be the case—that sooner or later Cuba would probably fall into U.S. hands, just as Canada probably would. Cuban annexation became one of the central questions of the 1856 election campaign. It was impossible to separate from the issue of slavery since manifestly the accession of what was (currently at least) a slave colony would strengthen the slaveholding interest. One of the reasons why Southerners had been pushing hard for annexation since the European revolutions of 1848 was because they feared that political destabilization in Spain would lead to emancipation in Cuba, just as the French Revolution of 1848 had led to emancipation in the French Caribbean colonies. "Africanisation"—the specter of a Haitian-style race war and a black-run state just ninety miles south of Florida—was anxiously discussed in the South. For Northerners in the Young America tradition, the annexation of new territory was never, or almost never, a bad thing. The New York *Herald* loudly trumpeted its support for Cuban annexation, although, in line with its anti- slave power conservatism it promised that annexation would be accompanied by emancipation.[139] As the *Herald*'s stance indicated, Cuban annexation was a complicated and crosscutting issue and by no means a test of antislavery credentials. In 1853, it was the uber-Whiggish Bostonian Edward Everett who achieved national acclaim when he published a letter he had written as secretary of State in the final days of the Fillmore administration telling the British government that the United States would not enter into a treaty binding them not to annex Cuba, an "acquisition" which, Everett wrote, might take place "in the natural order of things" as part of "the law of progress."[140] Admittedly, Northerners were more sensitive to slavery expansion in 1856 than they had been three years earlier, but fundamentally what made the Ostend Manifesto so politically incendiary was its supposedly Jacobinical style as well as its overtly proslavery objective.

Southerners considered themselves the bulwarks of conservatism against the fanaticism of "Black Republicanism," but Frémont supporters used identical language to make the opposite point. The Ostend Manifesto was sewn into the narrative of a violent, radical, undisciplined South. Filibustering was all of these things: "piratical," "brazen-faced," "savage," "lawless," "essentially revolutionary," and "barbaric" in its spirit. Happily for alliteratively minded slogan writers, Buchanan's name fitted nicely with the allegation that he was a "Buccaneer." The *New York Courier and Enquirer* warned that Buchanan's victory would mean "permanent war for slavery" in Central America and beyond, a war *"in which all mankind would be against us."*[141] Civilization had never been more conspicuously arraigned against the barbaric impulse of violence and enslavement, argued an old Whig; it was "neither safe nor patriotic" to vote for the Democrats.[142] To another old Whig, Sidney George Fisher, the Democratic convention's sinister-sounding pledge to assert U.S. authority in the Caribbean, which he took to mean that they would fight for Cuba, was no more than "the highwayman's plea, that 'might makes right.'"

From this perspective, the disregard for order and process evident in the Kansas-Nebraska Act was all of a piece with a similar willingness to encourage piratical filibusterers to wage war on foreign nations. Just as the "peaceful settlers of Kansas" had been thrown "into the midst of the terrors of a Jacobin club" argued the *New York Herald*, so the Ostend Manifesto threatened an equally Jacobinical war against the "combined naval powers of England, France, and Spain." The "masses of the conservative people of the North" were, claimed the *Herald*, rallying for the antitheses of Jacobinism: for "peace, law, order and the decent usages of civilized society." The *Chicago Tribune* wondered whether, having conquered Kansas, "Slavery" now imagined it could "push Uncle Sam into quarrels with its neighbors to acquire territory and slave states out of it." And if it wasn't plausible to present Buchanan himself as a Jacobin, then the danger lay in his weakness. "Mr. Buchanan concurred in the idea of seizing Cuba and revolutionizing Europe," pontificated the *New York Herald*, "merely because he met men of stronger will and more gorgeous imagination than himself . . . he was used by the enthusiastic wild revolutionaries . . . to serve their purposes, and he might be again."[143]

The political imagination of Republicans in 1856 therefore contained a heady mix of violent visions. The same people who had come to see slavery as representing indiscipline, violence, and a threat to "liberty under law" were among those who had praised the use of deadly force against the Astor Place Rioters—ranging from abolitionists and one-idea reformers to hierarchically minded old Whigs. That increasing numbers of these people were, by 1856, supporting Frémont, was partly because of the way that violence tied together different issues in a connected set of anxieties about the unraveling of society. And so the "brutal violence" on the plains of Kansas was linked to the "contagion" of "fearful homicides" in America; the "barbarism" of Brooks invoked in the same sentence as the mobbism that plagued cities; and prospect of disunion routinely compared to the problem of divorce.[144] The 1850s saw an explosion of class-based and ethnic-fueled violence in cities, raising again and again the question of the appropriate use of force. In New York City, party alignments fed into violent conflict on the streets. In 1857, a peak year for riots in the antebellum period, there was chaos on the streets of Manhattan once again when two rival police forces fought pitched battles against each other after the Republican-controlled state government created a new metropolitan police to rival the force controlled by the Jacksonian, proslavery Mayor Fernando Wood. The new force was responsible not to the elected city government but to an appointed board of commissioners whose president was Simeon Draper, a Whig turned Republican and a signee of the 1849 friends of order letter.[145] Working-class crowds attacked the new police, taunting them as Black Republicans.[146]

Such events fed into a Republican Party narrative that, echoing the friends of order response to the Astor Place Riot, associated disorder and the urban poor with disloyalty to the nation and an abrogation of citizenship.[147] When around six people were killed in an election riot in Washington in 1857, Republican newspapers blamed "base partisanship" and "inflammatory harangues made from the hustings."[148] The alternative was the "tyranny of the mob" or Kansas-style "anarchy." Southerners, naturally, saw in the instability of Northern society a sharp contrast with "the peaceful homes and pure hearths, the personal security and public tranquility of Southern life." As the *Richmond Examiner* explained it, slavery was "the great conservative element of our society, which builds up and sustains . . . the noblest social system in the world."[149] But for many Republicans, the opposite was true: slavery rested on implicit and actual violence. But so too did partisanship and mobbism. The social crisis must be met and overcome by principled, manly, nonpartisan, and conservative men.[150]

In the political imagination of Northerners, violence was both terrifying and emancipatory. It sharpened their sense of the South and of slavery as a threat, increased their anxiety about the stability of their society and the security of their freedoms, and gave them, at the same time, an imagined resolution. If the problem was violence, then the response was to pacify society; but if—as seemed increasingly apparent—the problem was violent enemies, then the response was to destroy those enemies, using violence as the only alternative to national destruction. The inherent violence of slavery or the violence imagined to lie beneath the calm of Northern towns and cities seemed as undisciplined as lightning strikes and as ferocious as a summer tempest. Yet, the crucial shift in Northern sensibility in these years was a gradual recognition that stern, disciplined violence was the necessary means of securing the Union and preserving freedom. In contrast, the appeal of an older, gentler approach—perhaps one exemplified by the old compromise constitutionalism—was lessened by its association with submission and, therefore, figurative enslavement.[151]

CHAPTER FOUR

An Engine for Freedom
Popular Sovereignty and Political Convergence

The visions of violence that haunted Northern politics in the 1850s drove a political realignment. By 1860, a purely sectional party stood on the brink of a dramatic victory that directly precipitated disunion. But the story of the North's path to war is not just the story of the Republicans; it is also the story of the half of the Northern electorate who made different choices about how best to defend their liberty. Sharing some of the fears of Republican voters about the encroachment of the Slave Power, loyal Northern Democrats nevertheless believed that their party represented the only chance of maintaining the Union. Democrats felt deeply that their party carried a historic mission to maintain liberty; never more so than with sectional "fanaticism" threatening the "untold horrors" of disunion and war.[1] "I belong to the great Democratic Party of the Union, that party that has supported the true honor and interest of the Country," wrote Lewis G. Pearce, a Pennsylvania farmer and stalwart of his local Episcopal church, expressing the conventional view of his fellow partisans.[2]

These were precisely the ideas celebrated in New York City after nightfall on September 18, 1856 when around 30,000 people gathered for a torchlight procession led by brass bands, with ritualized cheering, the mass consumption of hundreds of barrels of beer and whiskey, and the singing of patriotic songs. Vast canvasses with images and slogans were illuminated from behind by calcium flares known as Drummond lights (the sort also being introduced into theaters and today better known as limelights). Every few hundred yards a marcher carried a pole with a shield bearing an image of an eagle and a motto that, just five years later, was to embody the war aims of the North: "Union and Victory."[3] This was not just empty symbolism; it reflected a deeply felt emotional bond with the Union and what it represented, and a faith—grounded in a sense of history—of the Democracy as the great bond of that Union. While their opponents lambasted "partisanship" as synonymous with corruption, Democrats defended partisanship and party organization—at least their own partisanship and organization—as the organized manifestation of the people. "We do not claim for [party organization] the merit of infallibility," modestly acknowledged a Democratic newspaper editor in 1855, "but up to this period of time it has proved to be the best that our politics have known." Democrats contrasted their "time honored" and "open" organization with the "clandestine midnight conspiracies" against the people of the Know-Nothing lodges.[4] And above all, the rise of the sectional, opportunist, upstart Republicans left the Democrats able to proclaim their status as the only national party—and the only one with the blessing of generations past.

The crises of the late 1850s created a political convergence often overlooked by historians. Beneath the sound and fury of electioneering, Democratic and Republican voters in the 1850s were not different tribes; the storm drove people with similar concerns in different directions, but many of the underlying assumptions of the mainstream of Northern Democrats and Republicans were the same. This convergence in itself helps to explain why the Democrats did not disappear: they too represented and embodied core Northern values like the superiority of a small-scale capitalist, free-labor economy blessed with an abundance of available land, in which every (white) man could hope to own productive property. The Republican Party was not merely the Whig Party under a new name: it drew on a Jacksonian style and, in some respects, on Jacksonian ideas. Democrats, meanwhile, increasingly challenged Republicans for the mantle of best defender of the free North, albeit using different arguments and with, for the most part, a different political style.

One of the factors explaining the political survival of the Northern Democrats in the late 1850s was the surprising durability, through many assaults and setbacks, of the political appeal of popular sovereignty. The doctrine was contradictory—sometimes deliberately so—and distinctly different policies were defended under the same slogan.[5] But as a broad approach, as a slogan to trumpet in newspaper columns and on the stump, it had a political purchase that did not fade until the guns sounded over Fort Sumter. Its key tenets could be distilled into two core claims. The first was that local self-government was the best means of preventing centralization with its threat of despotism. Taking their cue from the Jeffersonian maxim "that government is best which governs least," popular sovereignty advocates insisted that good government meant resisting the allure of the moralizers and meddlers, the preachers and the proselytizers who sought to impose their values on everyone else.[6] The second claim was that the practical application of popular sovereignty, given the common sense of the common man, was that slavery would not expand—and without the needless provocation of the moralizing Yankee Republicans.

It tells us something about the continued political power of the concept of popular sovereignty in the North that even the opponents of the Kansas-Nebraska Act did not reject the concept entirely, even while pushing the alternative organizing idea for the territories that they should remain free because "freedom was national" and slavery sectional.[7] Douglas's bill was attacked from two directions: on the one hand, for introducing popular sovereignty in place of the Missouri Compromise's ban on slavery; on the other hand, for pretending to introduce popular sovereignty while not really doing so, or rather for subverting the true meaning of popular sovereignty in the interests of the Slave Power. Clearly, in theory, these two approaches were inconsistent. In practice, they meshed perfectly well.

The first approach drew on the logic of the "freedom national" doctrine: delegating the question of slavery to local settlers was an abdication of Congress's responsibility to uphold the principle that freedom was the norm, slavery the exception. "Liberty is National and Democratic," insisted an anti-Nebraska Democratic newspaper, and "we will not . . . be deterred from urging the right" simply because others "accused us of Abolitionism."[8] But critics also challenged the bill as a fraud, a swindle, and a humbug, objecting because it was not "true popular sovereignty." How much real sovereignty would the people of Kansas have, asked opponents, if the administration chose the governor who had a veto over the legislature? And since the Fugitive Slave Act would, of course, be operative, did that not so tilt the balance in favor of slavery that it was a sham to pretend local settlers could prevent it? Midwestern Democratic editors were especially likely to take this line, charging Douglas with using "the honorable term popular sovereignty" as a "clap trap."[9] More broadly, it was those most associated with the Young America style of bombastic expansionism who seemed most determined to save the principle of local decision-making over slavery from being corrupted by the Slave Power. We must "vindicate an honest doctrine from the sophistry of its false friends," argued an anonymous writer in the New York *Evening Post* who claimed to have supported popular sovereignty as a resolution to the slavery issue since boyhood. This writer made the perceptive charge that the lack of clarity over the timing and the manner by which settlers could exercise their right to exclude slavery meant that the matter would end up being decided by the courts. "In every aspect of the case" it transforms the status of slavery into "a judicial question and not a popular question—and such is the *true* purpose of the Nebraska bill." A bill that claimed to secure popular sovereignty would in fact ensure, through its deliberate, fatal ambiguities, that the Southern-dominated Supreme Court would be the final arbiter.[10]

The historian David Potter argues that the Kansas-Nebraska Act destroyed the legitimacy of popular sovereignty "by employing it as a device for opening free territory to slavery."[11] It is certainly true that the act gave popular

sovereignty a potentially proslavery meaning, but the term "popular sovereignty" itself retained its political prestige and it remained a viable alternative
political solution to those Northerners who were resistant to the absolutist
claims that the federal government should always act against slavery. Popular
sovereignty had, in fact, the allure of pragmatism and a smack of Burkean
common sense. Let the people decide! What could be more American than
that? Even the supporters of the "freedom national" doctrine saw the political
value of attacking the Kansas-Nebraska Act for not enacting what it promised. An example was Thurlow Weed's *Evening Journal*, the organ of the
Seward faction in New York, which acknowledged that "popular sovereignty
is a just principle" and "the only kind of 'sovereignty' recognized by pure Republicanism" but there was "no more 'popular sovereignty' in [the Kansas-
Nebraska bill] than was conceded to this country in the days of its Colonial
dependence." Indeed, in a familiar reference to European liberal nationalist
struggles, the *Evening Journal* claimed Kansas and Nebraska would be "less
'sovereign' than the people of Greece" had been under the Ottoman Empire.
While Douglas argued fiercely that the bill sought to do no more than give
the people "the capacity to legislate for themselves," the *Evening Journal*
charged that, on the contrary, under the terms of the bill the territories were
"mere dependences, where the People are held in a state of pupilage, because
they are presumed to be incompetent to exercise the high prerogative enjoyed under the practical operation of the true 'popular sovereignty.'"[12] This
line of criticism argued that the problem with the Kansas-Nebraska bill was
that it had betrayed Northern popular sovereignty as articulated in 1850 by
Cass and Douglas and replaced it with the Southern variant, which was in fact
no popular sovereignty at all since it prevented people in a territory from excluding slavery until admission to statehood.

The fact that critics ranging from antislavery Whigs like Seward to Young
America Democrats chose to attack the Nebraska bill in this way was a back-
handed acknowledgement of its political potency notwithstanding the reen-
ergizing of "freedom national" constitutionalism. Anti-Nebraska meetings
typically passed resolutions seamlessly combining "freedom national" constitutionalism with theoretically inconsistent attacks on Douglas's bill for not
implementing popular sovereignty honestly. For example, a meeting in Columbus, Ohio, on March 21, 1854, resolved that "freedom is national, slavery
sectional, liberty the rule, oppression the exception" and they condemned
the "breach of faith" by the South in striking down a sacred compact.[13] So the
"freedom national" doctrine was there, but in the very next sentence the bill
was also condemned for the "subversion of popular sovereignty." By imposing

a governor and officials from Washington, the "tory bill" subjected the territories to "colonial vassalage."[14] It was "miscalled" popular sovereignty.[15] The staunchly pro-Douglas Cleveland *Plain Dealer* was impatient with all this "balderdash" about the Nebraska bill "going too far and then again not far enough with its principle of sovereignty of the people"—but that was indeed a fair characterization of the criticism.[16]

As we have seen, the doctrine of popular sovereignty could mean very different things depending on *when* the settlers were able to make a decision about slavery. The Kansas-Nebraska Act also left ambiguous another, equally important issue: *how* settlers could exercise their decision. Was it necessary for a territory to pass "positive legislation" establishing slavery in order for slaveholders to uphold their claim of property? If so, the practical consequence of nonaction would be free soil. This was the position Stephen A. Douglas took, and it was one of the reasons why Northern supporters of the bill claimed to be so confident that slavery would not, in practice, expand into the new territories. Opponents warned, however, that unless a territory passed laws explicitly outlawing slavery it would in practice be legal because—whatever the supporters of the "freedom national" idea might wish to have been the case—established practice gave a case in law to a slaveholder. A writer in the free-soil, Democratic New York *Evening Post* explained that "if a slave is brought into a court in Kansas, the question will not be, 'How became you a slave?' or, 'is there a statute in this territory to establish slavery?' It will be, 'You were born a slave, your father before you was a slave, there is no statute to strip you of the property qualification, no notice to your owner, that to cross this line is to cross it at his peril, the Missouri Compromise is repealed, no legislative action contravenes his long-recognized rights, and you remain a slave, therefore, because there is no Law to make you free.' "[17] In the face of such arguments, the challenge of the Democratic Party after 1854 was to exploit the underlying acceptance of the principle of popular sovereignty and to try to argue that in practice it worked, both in the sense of giving settlers real power, and also—as a presumed consequence—by prohibiting the expansion of slavery.

The Binding Power of Popular Sovereignty

The "old Democratic Party [is] the true exponent of the principles of the Constitution," wrote John A. Dix. The former Free-Soiler and friend (but no relation) of Dorothea Dix retained his partisan faith despite opposing slavery's expansion because on the "ascendency of those principles," he thought, resided "the safety of the American people and the hope of mankind in general."[18] Coming into politics in the 1840s as a supporter of the Jacksonian antislavery campaigner Silas Wright, Dix had viewed the Wilmot Proviso as a conservative measure, entirely in keeping with Thomas Jefferson's Northwest Ordinance of 1787, which had banned slavery from what was then the Northwest Territory.[19] He was the Free-Soil Party candidate for New York governor in 1848, but completely opposed to fusion with antislavery Whigs. For Dix, the opposition to slavery was "a genuine Democratic tradition." He thought the Kansas-Nebraska Act "bad policy and bad faith." The Compromise of 1850 was supposed to bring finality. There was no need for "any more slavery legislation" since "the Missouri Compromise disposed of the Louisiana Territory" and "the Compromise of 1850 disposed of the territory acquired from Mexico." If the Kansas-Nebraska Act had not reopened the wound, there would have been "nothing left to quarrel about."[20] Yet in spite of all this, Dix chose to remain in the Democratic Party. Many years later, Dix's son explained his father's antebellum politics by claiming that while he was "firm in his opposition to slavery; he was not less firm in asserting the constitutional rights of the Southern people."[21] Dix's own voluminous antebellum writings make clear how far he was invested in the hope that so long as the Democracy retained national power there was no necessary conflict between those two things.

Another New York former Free-Soiler, Samuel Tilden, held a very similar position, rationalizing the party's position as both national and in the interests of the free-soil North. Most ordinary Democratic voters, in Tilden's judgment "expect the Democratic Party to rise again, purified."[22] And Horatio Seymour—who had not been an 1848 Free-Soiler but who had been a sympathetic fellow traveler—argued that the storm over the Nebraska bill was simply because people had not yet had the time to reflect properly on its "practical effect" (by which he meant that slavery would not, in his opinion, spread into the territories).[23]

It was not only former members of the Free Soil Party who kept the Jacksonian antislavery tradition alive in the post-1854 Democracy. One Ohio Democrat, whose support for the Nebraska bill was, at first sight, unsurprising, was David Tod. Having become wealthy through investment in coal, iron, and, latterly, railroad development, Tod was a former state legislator who sympathized with Jacksonian antibank views (on the grounds that banks hoarded capital unproductively rather than using it to foster development) and who had consistently opposed antislavery politics within his state—in 1838, he had sponsored a bill strengthening the rights of slaveholders to reclaim enslaved people who had escaped across the Ohio River.[24] Yet, impatient as he had always been with abolitionism, like many other Northerners, Tod was increasingly certain that slavery was a profound wrong. A spell living in Rio de Janeiro as the U.S. minister to Brazil from 1848 to 1850 seems to have shaken any illusions that Tod may have had about slavery's benignity.[25] During his term in office, he proved an effective and tactful opponent of the slave trade, and strongly supported U.S. efforts to suppress it. In 1857, at a dinner party in Philadelphia, Tod held the guests spellbound with a story about the horrors of the Middle Passage. He recalled that, while minister to Brazil, he had heard that an American vessel had just landed a cargo of slaves from Africa. "He went down to a cove to see them," reported Sidney George Fisher, who was listening, clearly agog. "He found 800 children from 5 to 15 years old on the beach, many of them sick, some dying. Several died while he was there. The slaver told him he had thrown 300 overboard during the voyage. On his asking what they had cost in Africa, the man showed him a stout boy of 15 whom he had bought from his mother for a handful of glass beads and some brass ornaments, all worth about 50 cents. They sold at Rio for $100 each, such as were sound. Those that were too sick were left on the beach to die! What a picture of human nature." To Fisher, Tod was "rather western in his manner" (which Fisher did not intend as a compliment), but his general demeanor was "sensible," making the emotion evident in his story all the more powerful. Yet Tod still supported the Kansas-Nebraska Act and he remained loyal to the Democratic Party, serving as president of the convention that nominated Stephen A. Douglas for the presidency in 1860. Tod hoped the Nebraska bill was a final (and probably fair) resolution of the slavery controversy. His powerfully felt objection to the slave trade demonstrated that Tod was not immune to the moral and humanitarian case against slavery, yet he still, like the vast majority of Northerners, accepted it as a regrettable but probably inevitable institution given the presence of African people in America and slavery's protection under the Constitution.

There were hundreds of thousands of free-state Democrats who had never met a slave. But there were also those like William A. Butler, more sensitive than most no doubt, who had personal encounters with enslaved people and were changed by it. In Butler's case, spending time in Washington when his father had a federal job opened his eyes to the brutality of separating mothers and children, wives and husbands. In one horrific instance, Butler recalled a tale of a respectable black government employee—a door attendant in Congress—whose wife and children were sold while he was at work. He went to the slave auction house to "recover them" with money gathered from sympathetic white politicians, including Butler's Democratic father, only to find that his wife, in total despair, had murdered their children rather than see them sold south. However much such tales turned Butler into a secret abolitionist, however, he would never have acknowledged as much because, as he rightly observed, "the very word 'Abolitionist' . . . implied criminal aggression upon constituted human law, and the divine order of things."[26] Butler, like Dix and Tod, supported the Kansas-Nebraska Act and remained a loyal "national Democrat" as he put it, until the war began.

There were hardliners in the party who wanted to drive out anyone who had associated with the Free Soil Party. Daniel S. Dickinson of New York led the "hardshell" faction in that state, opposing giving any nominations or patronage to men who had so much as flirted with the revolt of 1848. Similar moves were made in other free states. But though the poison of intra-party factionalism was a powerful motivator in antebellum politics, none of these attempted purges succeeded; even though support for the Kansas-Nebraska Act was made a test of party loyalty there were still former Free-Soilers who received patronage from Pierce in his final two years in office and from Buchanan thereafter. Former Free-Soilers could, in effect, reenter the Democratic fold so long as they embraced the doctrine of popular sovereignty—but, as we have seen, this was a doctrine malleable enough to be accommodating to those whose basic premise was opposition to slavery extension. In January 1856, the moderate "softshell" faction of the New York State Democratic Party—weakened after the defection to the Republican column of leaders like Wadsworth and Field—reversed course and praised the Kansas-Nebraska Act as a final resolution of the problem of slavery. But, crucially, staying loyal to the Northern Democracy after the Kansas-Nebraska Act did not mean abandoning the notion that the Slave Power was a danger. Plenty of Democrats expressed indignation at the attack on Sumner, in private and in public, and saw the assault as a manifestation of Slave Power brutality, just as Republicans did. While they might not venerate Sumner as a martyr, explained the Cleveland *Plain Dealer* (a reliably Democratic paper), they were "quite as indignant as the case demands," emphasizing the unity of the "whole north" in response.[27]

Stephen Douglas himself did not make the argument that popular sovereignty was a "practical" antislavery solution because he was still preoccupied with maintaining his support base in the South. But many of his supporters made exactly that case. On the ground in Kansas, ordinary antislavery Democrats were trying to make a new life in what they hoped would become a free territory. In practical terms, Democrats hoped that events in Kansas vindicated their opposition to both abolitionism and the Slave Power. It was, for such Democrats, immensely frustrating when President Pierce denounced the free-soil Topeka convention as a revolutionary act, implying that it was a partisan gathering of abolitionists. "I assure you on the honor of a man and a brother democrat that the president's position has no foundation in fact," insisted one Kansas settler, William Y. Roberts, to his old political mentor, William Bigler, the former governor and now a U.S. senator from Pennsylvania.[28] Far from being an abolitionist plot, Roberts argued, "nothing would please that infamous party" more than for the Topeka constitution to be rejected by Congress since their true aim was to foment trouble. It would be disastrous if the Democratic Party were held responsible for such an outcome, whereas, "I assure you that should we be successful and thus vindicate the theory of popular sovereignty [the abolitionists] would of all men be the most disappointed." Roberts claimed that "9 out of every 10" of the antislavery free soil settlers in Kansas were sound Democrats. The move to support a free-state constitution was initiated, he claimed, by Democrats who had done all the work in drawing up the document. And furthermore, if the Topeka constitution was approved it would at a stroke remove the "great stumbling block of 'the Kansas difficulties'" and "clear the presidential track" for the Democrats in 1856. If, however, the wound of Kansas was allowed to fester, and the people of the North became convinced that popular sovereignty was—as its opponents always claimed—simply a fancy term for slavery expansion, then the "Democrats were doomed to defeat.... Our next president and congress would be abolitionized." And then the Union would dissolve: "a blow will be struck that may terminate in a bloody civil war all over the Union." Roberts's antislavery was of a conditional kind: if he thought a majority of the settlers wanted slavery, he claimed he would respect their wishes (and even mused that since he had the capital to invest, he would probably personally profit from slavery's introduction). However, he was certain that the vast majority of Kansas settlers wanted it to be free soil, and—irrespective of the morality of the claim to hold a human being as "property"—he was "strongly opposed to the establishment of slavery in this territory" on the grounds that the prosperity of the state would be "retarded."[29] In short, as the Cleveland *Plain Dealer* put it, "all this is fuss is about a simple abstraction—a thrashing of water—a beating of air": slavery would not take root in Kansas.[30]

Roberts was right to claim that Democrats took the lead in Kansas in making the case for a popular sovereignty-based, free-soil outcome. The proslavery forces in Kansas who had effectively seized control of the apparatus of state government pointedly refused to designate themselves the Democrats, arguing that "the Pro-Slavery Party [must] know but one issue, Slavery; and that any party making or attempting to make any other, is, and should be held, as an ally of Abolitionism and Disunionism."[31] So it was the Free-Soilers who, in May 1855, organized the Kansas Democratic Party, committing it to popular sovereignty, the Kansas-Nebraska Act, prohibiting black emigration to the territory—and banning slavery.[32]

Many of the act's advocates also skillfully tied it to the prevailing distrust of politicians, and the fear of corruption and concentrations of power. "It was not the extent of territory that enervated Greece and Rome, and produced their overthrow," warned a Philadelphia minister in a sermon that called for an end to agitation over slavery, "but its opposite, *centralization*."[33] Great effort was expended by Democrats, including Douglas himself, to provide a lineage for popular sovereignty that would justify the use of the word "conservative" to describe it. The historian George Bancroft—who, along with that other Massachusetts writer Nathaniel Hawthorne, was a beneficiary of Democratic Party patronage—was enlisted to prove that history sanctioned popular sovereignty by showing that "colonial legislatures had control over slavery."[34]

Everyone wanted to be able to claim the sanction of history and specifically of the Founders. At an Independence Day celebration in the small town of Poland, Ohio, one life-long Democrat, Joseph Cracraft, got into an argument with a Republican neighbor about whether Thomas Jefferson, Henry Clay, and Daniel Webster had thought that Congress had any right to interfere with the right of people to decide for themselves whether to make slavery legal in new states. His neighbor hotly denied Cracraft's claim that these men had advocated popular sovereignty, but the doughty Douglasite, outflanked in public discussion went away to do his research which consisted of writing a letter to his political hero asking for some "proofs." Would Senator Douglas please provide him with "speeches or pamphlets" demonstrating that these great men in the Republic's history also supported popular sovereignty? It is not clear whether Douglas responded to Cracraft's letter, but if so, he would no doubt have cited Clay and Webster's support for the Compromise of 1850, and Jefferson's 1784 Northwest Ordinance.[35]

Whatever the specific claims that could be made and refuted about Clay and Webster's attitude to Congressional interference with slavery in the territories, the core argument for popular sovereignty was, as the New York Democrat Greene C. Bronson put it, that it "fully accords with the *spirit* of our institutions." Bronson was an old man, born in the year Washington became president; he had been involved in politics before Andrew Jackson even ran for office. Having witnessed the political storms over slavery that had erupted every time the question arose of admitting new states from the time of the Missouri crisis in 1819 onward, Bronson was convinced that had Congress never "attempted to legislate concerning the domestic policy of the States and territories, we should have escaped the Slavery agitation" which now "threatened the stability of the Union." The guiding principle from now on should be to "allow other people to manage their own affairs." Especially, Bronson implied, since that meant that free-soil settlers, who were, after all, ordinary folks just wanting to better themselves in the West, would not in reality have had to compete with slaveholders.[36]

Caleb Cushing and John O'Sullivan, Democrats from totally different political backgrounds with profoundly different temperaments, agreed that the Kansas-Nebraska Act was in effect a way of preventing the spread of slavery into the West. Cushing, a Massachusetts Whig-turned-Democrat of no discernible antislavery proclivities whatsoever, described the Kansas controversy as a "humbug" because slavery would never be established there. It was a fight over process not outcome, he claimed, whipped up by fanatics for their own ends.[37] For O'Sullivan, as for Douglas, the organization of the territories was an imperative that could not be delayed simply to pander to people's sensitivities over slavery. There was a bigger picture here that had been obscured, O'Sullivan argued, in all this bickering over the Missouri Compromise. "The day is not distant," he predicted, "when history will take this question out of the passionate hands of the partisanship of the hour." Before long the American people would see that the "unseen hand" of providential destiny was safely guiding the nation to its glorious future. More important than tedious disputes over slavery were the "hundreds of millions of souls" who had to be provided for in the glorious and not too distant future.

By the time of the Nebraska bill, O'Sullivan's view of slavery had undergone what he called a "material change." In 1848, he had supported the Free-Soil ticket on the same Jacksonian lines as Marcus Morton. At that time, he later explained, he had assumed "without question the old doctrine of the unity of the Human Race; carrying with it the consequence that the Negro was merely a Black White man degraded by a long course of external influences to a present merely temporary and accidental inferiority. Hence Slavery involved an idea, to me, of wrongful oppression, in conflict with the essential American idea." In 1852, however (he was very specific about the date of his conversion), he had become convinced of the "the error of that view" having read works on the "original diversity of species" by the Harvard zoologist Louis Agassiz. Scientific evidence of African Americans' "inferiority" had changed O'Sullivan's mind, and he now thought "slavery to the inferior race . . . is a better as well as more natural relation . . . than freedom side by side [with white people], especially in a democratic country."[38] But revealingly O'Sullivan wanted to keep private his proslavery conversion, presumably because he knew what a controversy it would cause in the North, and although he now believed that slavery was the appropriate condition for black people, he did not think it should spread into areas where ordinary white folk—always the people he was really interested in—wanted to go. Therefore he supported popular sovereignty since he had no doubts that it would lead to the West being open to free labor: "There is no chance of either Kansas or Nebraska becoming a slave state," he wrote.[39] (Cuba, however, was a different matter. O'Sullivan, with his new-found belief that slavery was morally right, spent much of the early 1850s conspiring with filibusterers like John Quitman on schemes to annex Cuba as a slave state.)

O'Sullivan's conversion was symptomatic of the growing acceptance of the theory of polygenesis—the notion, associated with Agassiz, that "races" had distinct moments of origins and therefore constituted different species. In its essentials this was not a new idea, and some of its Biblically minded defenders claimed that, notwithstanding the mainstream Christian belief in a single moment of human origin, the Book of Genesis could be used to support it. The most influential popularizer of polygenesis in the 1850s North, at least among Jacksonians, was John Campbell, one of the many former Chartists from the British Isles who continued their political activism in America. Steeped in British radical antiabolitionism, Campbell immigrated to Philadelphia in the 1840s and wrote a number of books and pamphlets aiming to expose "that philanthropy which will encourage the negro to rob his master, but which will not lift a finger in behalf of the oppressed and degraded of their own race."[40] Like O'Sullivan, Campbell had once been active in the Jacksonian free-soil cause, and even his conversion to polygenesis did not turn him into an advocate for slavery; his main concern was to use his discovery of "scientific" evidence for black racial inferiority to castigate abolitionists for failing to address the issue of the exploitation of white workers.[41] Ultimately, "new" racial theories, though of great interest to later scholars, remained, on the whole, marginal to the debate about slavery until emancipation became a reality after the Civil War broke out.[42]

While Cushing had contempt for "fanatical" antislavery politics, and O'Sullivan now thought slavery was, after all, the "appropriate" condition for black people, Horatio Seymour was probably more representative of the Democratic rank and file than either man. Seymour was a strident defender of popular sovereignty and an advocate of the superiority of the free labor system.

"The people of the North are uniformly opposed to slavery, not from hostility to the South, but because it is repugnant to our sentiments," he told a July 4, 1856 public meeting in Springfield, Massachusetts. But, he continued, "that doesn't mean that we should dictate to others, or that we should allow our repugnance to overrule our commitment to self-government." The Kansas-Nebraska Act, he argued, "only contains those principles of American freedom which cannot be assailed without attacking our own rights." Oppose the right to self-rule in Kansas, and where would it end? Acknowledging the chaos and violence in the territory, he denied that those who upheld the principle of noninterference were responsible. On the contrary, the problem, as ever, lay with the "press and political agitators" who "urge the sectional hatred and interference with local affairs." If the problems besetting the country were, as Seymour thought, the "fruits of meddling," of government interference by agitators, then the solution, naturally, was to end the meddling and end the agitation. As Seymour saw it, the Democratic Party was the guardian of the "democratic and liberal" theory that took control "away from central points and distributes it" to the "localities that are most interested in its wise and honest exercise."[43]

Here was a big philosophical divide: Seymour saw the Republican Party, like the Whigs before them, as the advocates of the "meddling theory" of government. They claimed "exclusive championship of morals, religion and liberty" just as, at the same time, they sought "guardianship of the finances and industry of the country." In both the economic and the moral sphere, the assumption that a centralized power could "dictate" was anathema to the "spirit" of the Republic, Seymour argued. This was not sophistry on his part. He made the case without for a moment gainsaying the consensus among all Northerners, as he saw it, that slavery was repugnant. The basic question of politics for Seymour was simply whether the "morals, religion, or liberty" of society would develop more harmoniously with or without such government meddling. The attempt to impose from the center a solution to the slavery problem would, he said, be no more successful than temperance, "Sabbatarianism, or Knownothingism."[44]

Underlying almost all Northern defenses of the act, then, was the insistence that in practical terms, the popular sovereignty it implemented was real and would have an antislavery outcome. Opposition editors attacked pro-Nebraska newspapers for "impudently tell[ing] their readers that the . . . repeal of the Missouri Compromise is a great and important measure in favor of human freedom!" and resorted to quoting at length from Southern newspapers to prove that in the slave states the bill was interpreted quite differently.[45]

So important was it to the pro-Kansas-Nebraska case that the act be seen as, in effect, an antislavery measure, that Douglas felt compelled to reply at great length when a colleague of his, the New Hampshire Democratic Congressman Edmund Burke, urged Northern Democrats to publically acknowledge that the act would "unquestionably revive and reestablish slavery over that whole region."[46] The editor of the newspaper in which Burke's article appeared backed up the Congressman's reading of the true position: "by this bill, slavery is permitted, to say the least, to go into Nebraska and Kansas, where it is now prohibited by the Missouri Compromise, and where it must remain, *protected by the Fugitive Slave law,* until the people of those territories, by their own action, shall expel it therefrom." Naturally, this article was gleefully reprinted across the North by the anti-Nebraska press. The act's supporters reacted with fury, launching ad hominem attacks on its author as a disappointed office-seeker with a grudge. Douglas called Burke's claim that the act would extend slavery a "wicked and unpardonable slander against every friend and supporter of the bill." A rival New Hampshire Democratic newspaper predicted that, contrary to Burke's claims, a "great tide" of emigration of "New England origin and character" would ensure that the "whole territory [of Kansas] will be parceled off into the potato patches and cornfields which distinguish the fatherlands of the hardy and enterprising adventurers." In short, "not one man whose opinion is worthy . . . pretends that slavery is likely to become a permanent institution any where in the domain of the Missouri Compromise."[47]

That, at least, was the line taken by Douglas supporters in the second half of the Pierce administration. But following the 1856 election, political decisions taken or abetted by leaders of the Democratic Party made such claims increasingly difficult to sustain. Those decisions meant that Northerners wanting to make the case that popular sovereignty was, in practice, a route to a free West were left no choice but to sunder their political ties with the South and even with the leadership of the national Democratic Party.

The Dred Scott Decision and the Lecompton Crisis

One of President Buchanan's first decisions was to appoint Robert J. Walker as territorial governor of Kansas. The two men knew each other well after many years of service in Washington. Like Buchanan, Walker was born in Pennsylvania, but at the age of twenty-five he had gone west, establishing himself as a lawyer and speculator in cotton and slaves in Mississippi. Predictably, he came into politics as a supporter of Andrew Jackson, and as a U.S.

senator and then treasury secretary under Polk he was a vigorous champion of Texas annexation, the Mexican War, and the expansion of slavery. Walker, Buchanan hoped, was the man who would resolve the problem of bleeding Kansas once and for all.[48]

For the great majority of Northern voters in all parties, it was self-evidently the case that only Kansas's admission as a free state would achieve that aim. George Bancroft was not alone among the new president's supporters in making this point explicitly: "I trust it will fall to your lot to bring Kansas into the Union as a free state," he told Buchanan shortly before the inauguration. Such an outcome, Bancroft wrote, would be a "great healing measure" that would "restore the country permanently to tranquility."[49] If popular sovereignty led to the admission of Kansas as a free state then the storm over the repeal of the Missouri Compromise would become of merely antiquarian interest. Even without the formal congressional ban, the West would have been preserved as free soil since surely it was inconceivable that with a free Kansas slavery could spread to its north. The remaining area from which slavery had been prohibited—now organized as the Nebraska territory—would then be entirely surrounded by free states or territories. Kansas was key. So, for Bancroft as for many other free-state Democrats who remained loyal to the party, while the philosophical appeal of the doctrine of popular sovereignty was defensible in theory, the political test was whether it could achieve, through the expressed will of the settlers, the same outcome as the maintenance of the Missouri Compromise would have done. Robert J. Walker seemed poised to play a decisive role in answering that question in one way or another.

For nearly two years, Kansas had been a byword for violence and political failure with free-state forces refusing to recognize the legitimacy of the proslavery territorial government in Lecompton. On Walker's watch, the Lecompton government organized a vote for a constitutional convention, the first step toward an application for statehood. Proslavery Missourian day-trippers participated in huge numbers, and the resulting convention proposed that the new state should legalize enslavement. When this was denounced as a fraud, a second election was held, but again Missourians came over to vote, and free-state settlers, in protest, boycotted the election. The convention, heavily dominated by proslavery delegates, drew up a proslavery constitution. Voters could only approve the constitution with or without a provision barring new slaves from being imported, which, as one free-soil Kansan observed, meant he could choose to take his arsenic with bread and butter or without bread and butter.[50]

At this point, Governor Walker intervened. To cries of betrayal from Southern Democrats, he publicly denounced the vote that produced the convention and stated that therefore the Lecompton constitution was illegitimate. To President Buchanan, Walker explained that free-soil Democrats comprised the largest number of settlers, followed by Republicans and then a much smaller group of proslavery Democrats and Know-Nothings.[51] If popular sovereignty were applied properly, Lecompton could not stand. Walker was not against slavery expansion per se: he suggested that a new slave state could be carved out of the remaining enclave of Indian country in present-day Oklahoma, and if Cuba was acquired as a slave state that would also meet with his approval. But Kansas, Walker said, should be free. If only Buchanan would follow this course, Walker urged, "your administration, having in reality settled the slavery question, would be regarded in all time to come as a re-signing and resealing of the Constitution."[52] The 1850 Compromise had promised finality, but the Kansas-Nebraska Act had rendered that promise hollow. Now, like Bancroft, Walker saw an opportunity to use popular sovereignty to create a new finality with the acquiescence of both sides.

It was not to be. Ignoring Walker's advice, Buchanan recognized the Lecompton constitution as the legitimate will of the people and urged Congress to admit Kansas as a slave state. Walker saw no alternative but to resign. He had been in the post for barely more than six months.

The subsequent political struggle over whether to approve the admission of Kansas under the Lecompton constitution left the Northern Democracy once again divided. Judging by the letters to congressmen and the tenor of editorials in Democratic newspapers, most saw it as the essence of tyranny to use federal power to impose a slave constitution on a territory where—as seemed uncontrovertibly the case—the majority of the population opposed it. As one young Illinois Democrat, the Virginia-born Amos Goodrich, put it, "for the first time in the history of our national existence, has the spectacle been presented to the American people of the strong arm of executive power being used to encroach on the liberties of the people." And this, he feared, was "the stepping stone to greater encroachments."[53] Goodrich's reaction was typical: the proslavery legislature in Lecompton seemed, to Northerners, hellbent on demonstrating that protection of slavery meant curtailing white men's liberty. They made the printing or distribution of antislavery literature an offense punishable by hard labor and prevented anyone who wasn't a supporter of slavery from sitting on juries that tried anyone accused of such crimes. "Outrageous laws" like this, argued a Kansas-based free-soil journal, made "extreme but pure & conservative steps necessary." This was exactly the reasoning that increasing numbers of self-described conservatives had adopted ever since at least the Fugitive Slave Act; they were compelled to stand up to slavery because slavery destroyed free government. A Douglas-supporting Kansas resident wrote to his local newspaper arguing that just as Washington and Jefferson were "conservative men [who] were not carried away by every ism and doctrine," so, in Kansas, it was only a "conservative and prudent course" that would lead the free-state forces to victory. For this Democratic free-soiler, only if "conservative men" took the lead would "the freedom of this Territory . . . be attained."[54]

There were three key differences between the congressional battle over whether to admit Kansas as a slave state under the Lecompton constitution and the battle, four years earlier, over the Kansas-Nebraska bill. First, the issue was now, more clearly than before, about the fate of republican institutions; not just the overthrow of the compromise tradition but an even more vital question about whether to recognize a process based on fraud, intimidation, and restrictions on free speech. If, in the Nebraska bill fight, opponents had warned that slavery was corrupting free institutions, that case could now be made more tangibly, with dead bodies and harrowing testimony to prove it. The second difference was that Stephen Douglas was now leading the opposition forces, deploying all his parliamentary skill and using all his political influence from the Senate to ensure that enough House Democrats opposed the administration's bill to defeat it. And the third difference followed from the first two: the administration lost. The House instead supported an alternative proposal (dubbed the "Crittenden-Montgomery resolution") that would have resubmitted the Lecompton constitution to the people of Kansas in a carefully controlled vote, which everyone expected would result in the rejection of Lecompton. The House vote on this measure was therefore the gauge of support for the administration's plan to admit Kansas immediately as a slave state. Northern Democrats split twenty-seven against the administration and twenty-nine in favor. Unsurprisingly, given the powerful patronage machine the president could wield in his home state, the bulk of the Pennsylvania delegation (eleven of fifteen) supported the administration. Likewise, ten of twelve New York Democratic representatives opposed the motion to submit Lecompton to a popular vote, reflecting the strong control of the New York State party by the "hardshell" faction, led by men who came as close as any Northerners to taking an overtly proslavery position. Connecticut, too, remained a bulwark of pro-Buchanan, pro-Lecompton politics, with that state's two Democrats also voting with the administration. Almost all the remaining House Democrats, including all the representatives from Ohio and Illinois, were opposed.

Pro-Lecompton Democrats fared catastrophically at the ballot box in the elections that fall and the following spring. Only six of the twenty-nine were reelected, all by much reduced majorities.[55] Even in Pennsylvania, where the president's patronage networks and longstanding ties of loyalty went deep and wide, only two of the eleven pro-Lecompton Democrats were returned. Thomas B. Florence, representing Pennsylvania's first congressional district, which contained the most working-class wards of Philadelphia and who had seen off a challenge from an anti-Nebraska Democrat four years before, was one of only two of the eleven pro-Lecompton Democrats from Pennsylvania to be reelected. Even Florence nearly lost to a challenger calling himself a "true Democrat." Newspapers spoke of "a Waterloo defeat for the administration."[56] Perusing the Pennsylvania election returns in the *North American*, Sidney George Fisher was, for once, cautiously optimistic. Perhaps this repudiation of the "shameful conduct" of the Democracy indicated that there was a "healthful and sound moral sentiment left among the people" after all?[57]

A compromise measure sponsored by William H. English, an Indiana Democrat who had voted against the administration on the Crittenden-Montgomery resolution, eventually did pass the House, allowing Kansas settlers a vote on a revised version of the Lecompton constitution with a smaller federal land grant than they had asked for. The English bill was, in effect, a face-saving maneuver for the administration; the alteration of the size of the land grant gave them an ostensible reason to support another vote by the settlers without having to concede that the first vote had been illegitimate. With a handful of additional votes from Northern Democrats like English, the compromise measure passed, but Douglas and his allies remained opposed. When Kansans went to polls to vote again in August 1858, they rejected the Lecompton constitution (with its altered land grant) by a margin of 86 percent to 14 percent. Kansas remained a territory until Republicans admitted it as a free state in 1861.

The alienation of such a large number of Northern Democrats from the Buchanan administration over the Lecompton crisis was a crucial political turning point. The South's willingness to support a slave constitution for Kansas in the face of overwhelming evidence that the great majority of Kansas's settlers were opposed to it was a terrible shock to those who had suspended their judgment and backed the Kansas-Nebraska Act. The majority of Northern Democrats felt betrayed—and said so repeatedly. The consequence was that the underlying antislavery consensus in the free states was strengthened by an increasing recognition of the aggression of the Slave Power. The rise of the Republican Party was accompanied by a rise in the sectional consciousness of the rest of the Northern electorate as a shared indignation at the Slave Power, and a shared sense of being under attack permeated the language of people from different parties and antislavery factions. So, after 1858, there was a perceptible convergence in Northern politics; the lines between the Northern wing of the Democratic Party, led by Douglas, and the Republicans were more blurred than before. They sang similar tunes and competed over similar ground.[58]

By the time of the Lecompton crisis, Northern Democrats had already been faced with the problem of how to respond to the Dred Scott decision, issued by the U.S. Supreme Court.[59] Announced only two days after Buchanan had been inaugurated in March 1857 and with the new president having already been informed of the decision, the majority verdict was, as Democrats immediately realized, a potentially fatal blow to popular sovereignty. Dred Scott, an enslaved man owned by an army doctor, was suing for his freedom on the grounds that he had been taken into a free territory. Notoriously, the court dismissed the case on the grounds that Scott had no standing to sue in a federal court. Black people could not be—and had never been—citizens, claimed the owl-faced Chief Justice Roger B. Taney of Maryland. But having thus dismissed the claimant, Taney went on to argue that even had the substance of the issue been admissible, Scott would still have lost since it had been unconstitutional for Congress to ban slavery from a territory. His reasoning was impeccable—*if* you started from the assumption, as he did, that property rights in human beings were just as valid as property rights of any other kind. Since the due process clause of the Fifth Amendment to the Constitution forbade, in the tradition of English common law stretching back to the Magna Carta, government to deprive a citizen of their life, liberty, or property without due process of law, so it followed that if slaves were property, Congress could not, in effect, take them away simply because of slaveholders' residence in a particular territory. Taney came from a slave state (Maryland) and although he was not a slaveholder he frankly told his son-in-law that the greatest problem facing the country was that the North was consumed by "evil passions" and wanted to keep the South in a "state of inferiority."[60]

When the news of the court's 7-2 decision was made public, old Whigs and Democrats were as stunned as any radical Republican. George T. Curtis, the Boston lawyer who had written much about the Constitution as a stabilizing force now feared that the very institution that was supposed to mediate conflict and rein in passions was working to do the opposite. Curtis had followed other Webster Whigs like Rufus Choate and Robert C. Winthrop in supporting Buchanan in 1856, yet he had also been a counsel for Dred Scott, and his brother Benjamin R. Curtis was an associate justice on the court and wrote a powerful dissenting opinion. Curtis had willingly taken the Dred Scott case not because he was a strong antislavery man (he was not, though he shared the general view that slavery was a regrettable institution) but because he was a constitutional expert who never doubted the federal government's right to exercise broad power within a limited range of areas, one of which was the regulation of property relations in federal territories. That the court decided otherwise, and by such a large margin, was, to Curtis, nothing short of a revolutionary act.

The Missouri Compromise had already been slain and buried. But now it was dug up and killed again—or, more precisely, retrospectively declared never to have been alive in the first place. It was only the second time that the Supreme Court had struck down an act of Congress as unconstitutional. (The first time was the *Marbury v Madison* decision in 1803 written by the bête noir of the Jeffersonian movement, the Federalist Chief Justice John Marshall.) Jacksonians had traditionally opposed such judicial activism as running roughshod over the will of the people as expressed in the legislature. George Bancroft was in despair that a court packed with Democratic justices could sink so low as to use a dastardly old Federalist doctrine to overrule the enacted will of the people expressed through Congress. George Bancroft was outraged by the chief justice's poor grasp of history. In Bancroft's home state of Massachusetts, African Americans had the right to vote and sit on juries; Taney's claim that black people could never be U.S. citizens purely on the grounds of race was demonstrably, historically wrong. It was also bad politics from the point of view of the South. By relying on the due process clause, Taney inevitably raised—as he must have anticipated—the prospect that the same logic could be applied to the status of slaves within free states: if a U.S. citizen could not constitutionally be deprived of his property in the Wisconsin Territory (the place where Scott had been taken), then why could he constitutionally be deprived of that "right" in Ohio? Taney pulled back from this implication, and since he was also basing his case on the argument that Congress specifically had no right to make regulations for territories, his defenders had a plausible riposte to the claim that the logic of Dred Scott would undermine the ability of free states to legally exclude slavery from their borders. (In this era before the Fourteenth Amendment, state governments were not regarded as being subjected to the due process requirements of the Fifth Amendment of the Constitution.) Nevertheless, as Bancroft pointed out, there was an irony in a proslavery decision that could be interpreted as being "to limit the rights of the states over the status of the coloured [sic] man."[61]

As a Jacksonian, Bancroft's dislike for the Dred Scott decision was firmly based in his adherence, as he put it, to the "old States-Rights School." The founders had meant to leave the subject of slavery "exclusively, unreservedly with the laws of the States." And that meant, in this case, U.S. territories. To prevent territorial legislatures from exercising their own judgment on this matter struck Bancroft as the essence of the kind of centralization and meddling that as a Democrat he had spent his life opposing. How ironic that it should be another old Jacksonian—Taney—who should be the instigator of this doctrine of centralization.

And there, in fact, was the heart of the problem, because what the Dred Scott decision—and then the Southern support for the palpably illegitimate Lecompton constitution—seemed to show was that the South was now demanding ever-greater centralized control. Only through universal acceptance of their right to slave property, it seemed, could slaveholders feel secure in the Union. But by making those demands they offended the deepest political commitments of Northern Democrats like Bancroft. It was a new, radical doctrine that the federal government should protect slavery as if it were just another species of property, and the overwhelming majority of Northerners resisted it fervently. The South was now putting forward "extreme notions," complained Bancroft, and was, in the process, doing itself great damage since the only effect was that "we of the Northern democracy have been dreadfully routed in consequence, and are handed over to the most corrupt set of political opponents that I have ever encountered." The only winners, in other words, of this radical overreach in slaveholder power were the Republicans and any other "fanatics" and "extremists" whose mission was to destroy the Union. Regretfully, moderate Republicans agreed. By "completing the nationalization of slavery, [this decision] has laid the only solid foundation for an Abolition party" explained the *New York Times*, edited by former Whig and supporter of the Compromise of 1850, Henry Raymond.[62] And Raymond did not think this a good thing.

Republicans tried to push Democrats like Douglas to acknowledge that popular sovereignty was destroyed by the logic of Taney's decision. In his debates with Abraham Lincoln in 1858, and on many other occasions too, Douglas tried to finesse the issue by suggesting that, in practice, a territory would have to pass positive legislation—such as a slave code—in order for slavery to exist and so whatever the default situation theorized by the court, the practical question on the ground would remain, as he wanted it to be, in the hands of local white settlers. As ever, Douglas was drawn to a pragmatic rather than a theoretical or historical argument and he was right that slavery needed positive protection. In itself the Dred Scott decision did not provide the security that slaveholders needed to take their expensive "property" into federal territories. What they needed was a federal slave code, equivalent to the slave codes in the slave states and replete with the provision to impress white folks into slave patrols. This was what Southerners would now start to demand, and a plank calling for exactly that was included in John Breckinridge's platform in the 1860 presidential election. To most Northern Democrats, including Douglas, this was completely unacceptable: a federal slave code would mark the final surrender of the ideal of local control to tyrannical centralizers just as surely as if the Republicans came to power.

And so, while the Dred Scott decision provided a rich seam for Republicans to attack their Democratic opponents as vassals of the Slave Power, the reality was that only a minority of Northern Democrats—close allies of President Buchanan—wholeheartedly supported the decision with its stark implication that slavery was being nationalized. The majority of free-state Democrats shared with other Northerners an anxiety about what the decision indicated about the power of the slave South over the Republic. The difference between Democrats and their opponents was one of political tactics and temperament more than underlying values. Arguing that the court's decision was much less important and certainly less innovative than their opponents charged, Democrats attacked Republicans for their lawlessness in attacking the court. All sides, in other words, framed their case as defending the Union against instability.

Popular Sovereignty as the Basis for Political Realignment

When Stephen Douglas broke with the Buchanan administration over the Lecompton constitution, Northern Democrats like Bancroft finally were able to support again a political movement in what they saw as the real Jacksonian tradition—opposing centralization, meddling, and fanaticism, and supporting localism and states' rights.[63] Douglas was terribly torn by having to take the lead in opposing the administration, but for thousands of Northern Democrats the Lecompton fight was liberating. From across the country, scores of Democrats wrote to Douglas hailing his "manly and conservative course," and showing that popular sovereignty was not a charade to enable slavery to expand but if implemented properly with due respect for the real wishes of the settlers, would be a democratic block on slavery's advance.[64]

Typical was a Hoosier now resident in California who described himself as an "anti Slavery Douglas Democrat" and who pledged never again to support Buchanan.[65] George Bancroft, appalled by the obvious fraud of Lecompton, was relieved that the man who was by now the unchallenged leader of the Northern Democracy was leading the fight for a free-soil Kansas. And one Pennsylvania Democrat wrote that "conservative men of all parties" stood with Douglas in opposition to Lecompton.[66]

Longstanding allies of James Buchanan felt free not just to oppose him on this one issue but also to break altogether from the kind of proslavery politics the president now seemed to have embraced. A prominent example was the Philadelphia editor John W. Forney, the former clerk to the House of Representatives and so committed to Buchanan that he had regarded the 1856 election as the "great battle of his life."[67] Forney had long been open about his antislavery views—Southerners had opposed one of his patronage posts for this reason—but he had also remained loyal to the Democracy.[68] Even before the Lecompton crisis, Forney's relations with Buchanan were becoming strained after the newly elected president reneged on a promise to make Forney the editor of the administration's mouthpiece journal in Washington when Southerners objected to an antislavery man in such a role.[69] But the Lecompton crisis was the real rupture. He negotiated with Republicans about dividing up state offices with anti-Lecompton Democrats and took the lead in trying to unseat Thomas B. Florence in his Philadelphia district.[70] And having taken a stance openly opposed to the administration, Forney was pushed down a track that led him eventually to become a committed supporter of the Lincoln administration. He arrived at that position, though, only after the outbreak of war, and via an energetic and committed support for Douglas and the anti-Lecompton Democrats. In September 1858, Forney went to Tarrytown, in the Hudson Valley, to speak at a public meeting in support of the reelection of John B. Haskin, a Democrat who had, like Forney, supported the Kansas-Nebraska Act but had now broken with the president. Forney told the meeting that Buchanan's endorsement of the Lecompton constitution was cataclysmic and "treacherous." He could never "betray his manhood" by supporting such a "dark and damning" policy as that which the president was pursuing. In his newspaper, Forney had pledged himself forever committed to "conservative doctrines, as the true foundation of public prosperity and social order." Imposing slavery against the will of the people was totally contrary to such beliefs. So what was to be done?

Insisting that the Dred Scott decision did not invalidate popular sovereignty, Forney spent the next three years championing congressional noninterference as the only solution to the sectional crisis. By supporting Lecompton, his old friend Buchanan was effectively abandoning popular sovereignty, as Forney saw it, and by accepting the argument that the federal government should determine the status of slavery the president had become just as much of a centralizer as the Republicans. And yet Forney now saw the Republicans changing tack. With Douglas having staked his political career on opposition to the admission of Kansas under the Lecompton constitution, there was now no difference between anti-Lecompton Democrats and the Republicans in terms of their desired outcome—a free Kansas—even if their routes to that end had been different. At Haskin's election meeting, Forney was speaking to an audience of Democrats like himself, but also of Republicans— the meeting had been advertised "without regard to party." What he saw in front of him, Forney proclaimed, was a "great coming together" of Republicans and Northern Democrats. Addressing the Republicans in the crowd, he had a message for them on the one issue that still formally divided them, and which, in his debates with Douglas in Illinois earlier that summer, Lincoln had made much of: popular sovereignty (or "squatter sovereignty" as Lincoln called it) versus the Republicans' "freedom national" doctrine. Forney saw this a false dichotomy. "You Republicans are coming to [popular sovereignty]," he predicted confidently. "The train is moving and the cars are filling up. Come on; let us take this for a single principle. Everything else that is right will follow, and in 1860 there will not be a white man in the North willing to say that he ever heard the name Lecompton!" Loud cheers followed.[71]

Along similar lines, Charles Goepp, a Philadelphia Democrat, also predicted a "great coming together" in Northern politics on the basis of "true" popular sovereignty: "It is most evident that the Republican party must add to its old platform the declaration that no constitution can ever be imposed on a state without full consent and approbation of the people thereof, a principle of self-evident justice, and not in any manner antagonistic to the position of the Republican party heretofore. . . . Nothing will [then] remain . . . to make [the Republican] platform identical, for all practical purposes with that of the Anti- Lecompton Democrats. . . . This seems to remove all difficulty in the way of the formation of a unitary opposition party."[72]

Buchanan's allies fought hard to remove from office the "despicable factionalizers" who opposed the administration; even the stance on Lecompton of potential appointees for postmasterships was heavily scrutinized.[73] In the New York district where Forney had gone to lend his support to the congressman's reelection campaign, feelings were intense and personally felt. " 'Down with John B. Haskin!' is our war-cry!" wrote one outraged Buchanan loyalist.

"Let the traitors tremble! Their dire fate is rapidly approaching and they shall reap quickly the bitter fruits of their iniquity."[74] Given the decades-long strength of Buchanan's support base in his home state, the ground war between the Buchanan faction and the anti-Lecompton Democrats was especially nasty in Pennsylvania.[75] In Douglas's Illinois, a beleaguered pro-Lecompton Democrat wailed that he had suffered "the most bitter and vindictive abuse from my former associates and co-laborers simply because I have dared to remain true to my former principles and professions."[76] One pro-Lecompton Democrat in Illinois, William D. Furness, was so convinced he was fighting a losing battle that he pleaded with one of Buchanan's Pennsylvania allies to try to heal the rift as soon as possible. "Much as I deprecate Judge Douglas and anxious as I am to defeat him," he wrote, the only outcome of a divided Democracy would be that the party would lose control of the state for many years to come.[77] Where the local Democratic newspaper opposed Lecompton, efforts were made to set up new organs to support the administration.[78] And meanwhile, Douglas was bombarded with fan mail (from old Whigs and Republicans as well as lifelong Democrats) declaring themselves delighted by his resistance to the administration.[79] Correspondents assured him that he had support "without regard to party distinctions, prejudices or partialities."[80] One confessed, "It is true I felt indignant towards you for the part you took in the repeal of the Missouri Compromise," but now "like the great body of the people" he relished Douglas's defiance of the "the present corrupt administration" and its ally "the aristocracy of the South."[81]

When Democrats of both factions lost ground in congressional and state elections in 1858, the alienation of the majority of ordinary Democrats from an administration they thought captured by the Slave Power intensified.[82] Long-standing party activists sometimes feared the "destruction of the democratic party" after the "shameful turn coat" Buchanan had decided, as they saw it, to wage war on the majority of the party in the free states.[83] Others, like John Forney, hoped that Douglas's leadership could forge a new, moderate antislavery, anti–Slave Power coalition that would sweep to power with the support of moderate Southerners, marginalizing the abolitionists and the proslavery fanatics alike. "And thereby," as one Illinois Democrat put it, "save the country from the sad fate in which the triumph of Black Republicanism would involve it."[84] The people, explained an anti-Lecompton Democrat in Berks County, Pennsylvania, where a prominent pro-Lecompton congressman was defeated in October 1858, believed what they had always believed—they "hate negroes and have no affection for slavery"—but those raw impulses no longer allowed them to support the Buchanan administration and the national party.[85]

Expressing indignation with Buchananites as well as radical Republicans, Douglas Democrats vied with Republicans for the role of champions of an aggrieved Northern public. Lincoln and Douglas jousted through Illinois in a series of debates that captivated the politics-obsessed, newspaper-reading Northern public and have been a rich source for historians who have mined them to understand the philosophical tensions between the two men. But these famous set-piece debates were also, at heart, an argument between people who in terms of practical politics—if not in underlying philosophy— had much in common, for all the distinction of style and the personal rivalry that gave those debates their spice. As Charles Goepp, the Philadelphia Democrat, put it, "*theoretically* there [is] a difference" between Douglas Democrats and Republicans, since "Republicans claim . . . that the people of the United States are not bound to increase the number of states, unless the candidate for adoption is so constituted as to make the admission advantageous to those admitting it." In other words, they didn't want any new slave states. But this, Goepp argued, was a moot point: "As the Republicans would only invoke the principle in case of a state giving itself a slave constitution, and as it is now manifest that the free-state party have the majority in all incipient states, there is no practical necessity for either approving or denying the proposition on a principle."[86]

It was relatively easy for Lincoln to expose the tension between Douglas's continued adherence to popular sovereignty and his determination not to repudiate the Dred Scott decision (largely for fear of completely alienating any remaining Southern support, but also out of a sense that it was the appropriate thing to do). Lincoln, with no Southern supporters to placate, was far freer to attack the Taney court. He was able, too, to cleverly expose the reality that beneath the sincere dedication of Douglas and his supporters to the principle of local self-rule it was, even for them, not an absolute principle in all circumstances. Why, Lincoln asked pointedly, was it acceptable for the voters of a territory to choose to enslave some human beings, but not for them to vote to adopt polygamy?[87] Douglas had generally been relatively tolerant of Mormonism, but the Utah territory (organized, under the terms of the Compromise of 1850, on the basis of popular sovereignty) was fast becoming almost as notorious a source of violence as Kansas: the worst incident was the so-called Mountain Meadows Massacre on September 11, 1857, in which more than a hundred people, trekking across the plains, were killed by forces said to be a combination of Mormons and Paiute Indians. In that instance, Douglas supported the use of federal force against the Mormons and the replacement of the Mormon territorial government—even for the Little

Giant, then, popular sovereignty had its limits if a territory was run by "alien enemies and outlaws denying their allegiance and defying the authority of the United States."[88] What, asked Lincoln, was the difference in principle between Utah and Kansas? "Why deprive the Mormons of the sacred right of squatter sovereignty?" he asked, ironically. Wasn't the truth that popular sovereignty was simply a cover for slavery expansion? "This thing of squatter sovereignty was never anything but a humbug, generated in the marshes and pools of South Carolina, and used as a pretext to run and pour slaves out of the land as hot lava is belched out from the crater of the fire mountain. It stinks of fraud."[89] But for millions of Northern Democrats Lincoln's attacks on popular sovereignty missed the point. Douglas's break with Buchanan and the attacks Douglas was now receiving from his Southern colleagues suggested that his policy was not a humbug at all, and that the slaveholders of South Carolina were certainly not now poised to belch their slaves into Kansas, even had that once been their hope.

Forney and Goepp were right to anticipate that Republicans would lessen their opposition to popular sovereignty. In the months after the Lecompton crisis, and especially in the 1860 election campaign, some Republicans did begin to champion popular sovereignty. The Indiana Republican Party endorsed it as policy in a convention in 1858.[90] And Henry Raymond's *New York Times* put the matter this way, in July 1860: "Whether that doctrine [of popular sovereignty] finds any warrant in the Constitution, in legal precedents, in the opinion of the Fathers, or not, it has a very strong hold upon the popular instinct. The great mass of the people in all sections, whatever may be their opinions upon its legal validity recognize it as a fair just and safe way of solving a very difficult problem. . . . [It is] ground which satisfies the instinct of nine-tenths of the American people." The *Times* concluded that even if Lincoln won the presidency, the truth was that "the slavery question will be settled on this basis [of popular sovereignty], whichever party may come into power." It was "under any circumstances . . . the *practical* solution of the difficulty."[91] In this view, the attention-grabbing debates between Lincoln and Douglas only served, as debates do, to exaggerate differences and obscure the underlying commonality of their supporters' positions. One of Lincoln's closest political friends, Edward D. Baker, who had migrated west from Illinois and was elected a U.S. senator from Oregon in 1860, went so far as to declare himself a "Popular Sovereignty Republican." In a speech in San Francisco in October 1860, Baker reiterated his view that popular sovereignty was a "safe doctrine" for the "friends of free labor" and addressed himself to the Democrats in front of him, telling them that the best route to enact popular sovereignty in the western territories was to vote for his old friend Lincoln. The Republicans, he pledged, "will stand by your doctrine of Popular Sovereignty as an engine for Freedom."[92]

Local political circumstances dictated that in Baker's California the ranks of the Douglas Democrats and the Republicans were largely fused, but not until after 1861. In the short term, in most places Republicans and Douglasites continued to fight each other at elections because to those who stuck with the Democrats, the Republicans remained a toxic brand, far too compromised by Jacobinical abolitionism to be trusted to do anything other than make the national crisis worse. Cultural differences lay deep. The Republicans in many parts of the North were embedded in the political style of Whiggish evangelicals, ineffably associated with the moralistic, meddlesome Yankees that Democrats loathed. Yet even so the lines between partisans in the North were more blurred and easily crossed than before. And in this post-Lecompton period there was, notwithstanding continued electoral combat, a bipartisan consensus on the danger of the Slave Power to the Union.

Pro-Lecompton Democrats

A few Northern Democrats defended slavery expansion by urging free-state voters to accept the reality of slavery's centrality to American economic life. New York's charismatic, dandily dressed mayor, Fernando Wood, for example, reminded audiences that "the profits, luxuries, the necessities—nay, even the physical existence [of New York City] depend on the products only to be obtained by the continuance of slave labor and the prosperity of the slave market!"[93] More often, however, Northern Democrats who supported the president's line on Lecompton tried to repeat the argument they had made in favor of the Kansas-Nebraska Act: that, counter-intuitive as it might seem, it was a pragmatic route to a free Kansas.

Former 1848 Free-Soiler John A. Dix was one who attempted to make this case. Accepting that the free-state settlers were "an overwhelming majority," he blamed their tactic of abstention for allowing a proslavery constitution to be drawn up: "They could have shaped their form of government according to their own wishes if they had not permitted the minority to control." Dix then went on to suggest that the best course of action for those who wanted a free Kansas (and he appeared to include himself in this number) was for it to become a state as quickly as possible—under a proslavery constitution since that was what was now before Congress—and thereafter the people of the state could change it as they liked. It was, unfortunately, true that there was a clause in the Lecompton constitution preventing the abolition of slavery in the state until 1864, but this, Dix argued, was "entirely nugatory" since "no power on earth" could prevent Kansans from altering their constitution whenever they wished once they had statehood since such power "lies at the foundation of all popular sovereignty."[94]

Another old Free-Soiler, Martin Van Buren's son John (still sometimes referred to in the press as "Prince John" because he had once danced with Queen Victoria), made a similar case. Van Buren had been one of the most powerful advocates for the Jacksonian antislavery case, but he had called on Democrats to "acquiesce" in the Kansas-Nebraska Act and now he argued that supporting the Lecompton constitution was another concession that had to be made, not just in the interests of maintaining the Union but also in the long-term interests of those who wanted to live in a free-labor society. "If Congress would confine itself to its own business, and let the people of Kansas confine themselves to theirs," he argued, "you would find that this whole subject would pass away with the occasion that gave it rise, and Kansas be admitted into the Union and form itself into a free State."[95] Van Buren and Dix were both implying that once Congress had dealt with this Kansas business they would have no need to ever discuss slavery again, a case that could only be made if they chose to ignore the ever-louder calls from Southerners to put the Ostend Manifesto into effect and annex Cuba and perhaps elsewhere in Central America as new slave states.

To many of their former supporters, Dix and Van Buren were making, to put it mildly, an implausible case. But one strong card they and others like them still could play was the appeal to party loyalty. For several years, a tension had been developing between, on the one hand, a proud sense of identification with a partisan organization and, on the other, an antiparty style. Know-Nothings and now Republicans presented themselves as the antidote to the old politics while Democrats sneered at their opponents' fleeting organizations who "like a man walking along a beach left no footprints behind them," as one put it. At the heart of Democrats' self-perception was the notion that they represented a long line of continuity stretching back to Jefferson, and that without them there would be no one to protect liberty. Had not the Democratic Party "crushed the financial monster" of the Second Bank of the United States and won a war with Britain? As one pro-Lecompton Democrat put it, "if any candid mind will turn back and see what the Democracy then did for us as a nation, he will at least feel that he owes it a debt of gratitude—an indulgence for its imperfections that cannot be slightly cancelled."[96] If you believed the continued strength and unity of the Democratic Party was literally essential to the maintenance of the Union and liberty, it was not unreasonable to be prepared to make unpalatable concessions in order to maintain it.

Thomas B. Florence, the Philadelphia pro-Lecompton Democrat who had narrowly survived reelection, protested that the Democracy's "piebald opponents" made it seem as if his party was "composed of Jacobins" or even of "assassins and thieves." As Florence explained it, the "national" Democracy (the term coming into general use for the faction that had supported the Lecompton constitution and Buchanan) was "neither pro-slavery nor anti-slavery" and although he himself "agree[d] entirely" with the principle that "every human being [should be] free," the fact was that slavery was protected by laws. As Florence pointed out, even "the boldest of the Republicans dares not avow the right, though he does not conceal the desire, to meddle with [slavery] within a State." And now that the judiciary had determined that slavery should also exist in the territories "by virtue of the Constitution . . . until the Territory becomes a State," he accepted it as the law of the land, whatever his private "tastes and judgments." The matter, then, was simple: given where we were, to oppose slavery in a territory or to imply you wanted to get rid of it within a state was to become "a traitor to the Constitution and the Laws."[97]

Pro-Lecompton Democrats claimed to see in their opponents a sort of collective madness. Their obsession with slavery was threatening to "break down the bulwark of the Constitution" and they predicted "the conservative masses" would, before long, have a "sober second thought." In private correspondence, supporters of the administration willed themselves to believe that if they could just ride out this storm, the slavery issue would be got "out of the way."[98] By embracing the Lecompton constitution, wrote one Pennsylvania supporter, the president had surely slain "this black-headed monster of agitation which has divided our party and threatened the peace and unity of our beloved Country."[99]

Unlike some political insults ("copperhead" being a relevant example), "doughface" was never appropriated with pride by its targets, but if anyone had done so, it probably would have been Buchanan. He had a long record of supporting proslavery positions, even those that most clearly threatened Northern liberties such as the gag rule that banned discussion of slavery in Congress in the 1830s, or the prohibition of abolitionist literature from the U.S. mail. Personally friendly with many slaveholders and with his home in Lancaster, Pennsylvania, only twenty-five miles from the border of a slave state, Buchanan appeared completely tone deaf to antislavery politics, genuinely believing it to be based on a delusion. Yet even Buchanan occasionally used the argument that the best route to a free Kansas was if it were admitted immediately under the Lecompton constitution. Only then, he suggested, would "the people have a more speedy opportunity of changing what they deem amiss in it than by any other practicable mode & the peace & the permanence of the Union will be best secured."[100]

The Shifting Calculus of Northern Politics

Too often historians have written about Northern politics in the run-up to war as if the insurgent Republicans made all the political running; the Democrats come into the story only in order to disintegrate and thus make possible final Republican triumph. But though they declined from their former majority position, the Democrats did not fade away. This large minority of free-state voters who supported either the Douglas or the administration wing of the Democrats did not operate according to a different value system from their Republican-voting neighbors; they simply made a different judgment about political priorities and the best strategy for defending the Union and the freedoms it guaranteed.

In 1854 the key line of division in Northern politics had been over whether to abandon the Missouri Compromise. Some Democrats abandoned the party when this became a test of party loyalty, but, as we have seen, many others remained, accommodating themselves to the idea that popular sovereignty was de facto an antislavery policy that might, once and for all, resolve the sectional problem. The Lecompton crisis shifted the key line of division again. Now the question became whether to accept the admission of Kansas as a slave state, in contravention not only of the Missouri Compromise covenant but also in the face of overwhelming evidence that the settlers themselves would prefer it to be free.

By 1859, Northern Democrats were torn between, on the one hand, recognition that Southern proslavery demands were at least as threatening as antislavery politics, and on the other, remaining loyal to the national Democratic party as the last bastion of the Union and hoping that if antislavery Northerners would just calm down, all would be well. Within each of these choices there were further questions, such as about how and with whom to cooperate locally, which may be different from the political choices one made at the national level. Making a choice about how to reconcile one's longstanding commitment to the Democracy with a commitment to prevent slavery's expansion westward and the Slave Power's corrosion of national life was never easy. But the choice one made would be shaped by whether one lived in a state like Illinois or Massachusetts, where the anti-Lecomptonites were in complete control of the state party, or in Pennsylvania or Connecticut, where the administration supporters remained in control, or in New York, where—as ever in that most factious, febrile political bear pit—neither side dominated.

Meanwhile, the Republicans remained a highly unstable coalition. In New England and Yankee-settled counties of northern Ohio and upstate New York it had already, in just a few short years, put down deep cultural roots as the perfect expression of the long-dominant Whiggish, evangelical-influenced reformism in that swathe of the country. Yet it also remained a political organization compromised by association with radicalism. Politicians as different as former Whig, now Republican, James Watson Webb and anti-Lecompton Democrat John Forney fretted about the hot-headedness of Northern radicals and continued to yearn for a truly national party that could be free both of Northern and Southern extremes.

As the presidential election of 1860 loomed, political observers understood that the route to a majority in the free states lay in offering reassurance against the perception of extremism and instability. Northern Democrats had gradually lost support for over a decade due, essentially, to a single cause: the perception that their willingness to compromise with the South was a sign of weakness not strength. Their argument was that the maintenance of a bisectional party organization was an essential bond of Union and that a pragmatic compromise over slavery that leached the emotional conflict from politics was the only way of avoiding the ultimate nightmare of disunion. Splitting with the Buchanan administration over Lecompton offered the great majority of Northern Democrats a way of continuing to make those arguments while also being able to show that there was nevertheless a line that they would not cross: they, too, could and would defend Northern values and interests. Administration, or "national" Democrats as they tellingly styled themselves, riposted that by splitting Douglasites had shown themselves to be no less sectional than the Black Republicans.

The underlying reality with which all Northern politicians had to deal was the consensus that slavery was wrong. The question was what the implications of this were, especially in a society that was profoundly racist. Republicans were quick to see in their Southern opponents' support for slavery a slippery slope toward an ever-increasing erosion of white men's liberties. As the former Free-Soil Party supporter David Dudley Field of New York put it, "If slavery be no evil . . . why should we make it piracy to bring a slave into the country? Why not let each man buy, according to his own conscience, what he finds to be property, or, which is the same thing, what he finds anywhere to be saleable?"[101] And if that was acceptable, by what logic would slavery only apply to black people? "If you wish to see the black flag of slavery waving its murky folds all over our broad land, go and enlist under its banner, and fight its battles," Field proclaimed. "But if, on the contrary, you desire the triumph of those great principles of FREEDOM embodied in the Declaration of Independence then, I conjure you, by your admiration for the fathers,—by your attachment to the ancient Democratic faith, by your innate love of justice and liberty, to unite with the noble company of those who are laboring to deliver our country from its most terrible scourge and most withering curse." Freedom must be made national or the Union, and freedom with it, would wither and die. Or, in Lincoln's famous, "house divided" metaphor, the nation must become "all one thing or all the other."

This was, potentially, a startlingly revolutionary line of thought, as Stephen Douglas tried to expose in his debates with Lincoln. He criticized his Republican opponent for his apparent hypocrisy in saying in one breath "slavery is wrong" and in the next that he did not wish to eliminate slavery where it currently existed. In effect, Douglas was mocking Lincoln for being moralistic about slavery while denying that he was an abolitionist. But in this respect, of course, Lincoln was typical of most Northerners in being chary about following his initial presumption to its logical conclusion. In a different sense, Douglas was guilty of this too: he would not condemn slavery as wrong, but he did not support human beings being treated as just another species of property by the federal government, hence his opposition to a federal slave code and the reopening of the Atlantic slave trade, and his effort to triangulate his way out of having to endorse the Dred Scott decision.

John O'Sullivan was rare in being honest about this failure to follow through on the answer to the basic question of slavery's justice. In the days when he had accepted as truth the doctrine of the "unity of the races" (before he changed his mind and decided that African people were inherently inferior) he conceded that it was a fair question to ask why he had not been an abolitionist. The answer was that he was "protected by my extreme State Rights Democracy"—in other words, he had not thought it appropriate to try to influence from outside the decisions about slavery made by the sovereign people of a state.[102] Most Northerners, had they been put on the spot and made to reflect on this same question—why are you *not* an abolitionist?— would have answered that they valued the Union or the Constitution or that they feared the consequences of emancipation for social order too much to risk acting on their antislavery views. This was why Lincoln repeated again and again that his political aim was to place slavery where the public could rest secure in the knowledge that it was "on the course of ultimate extinction."

The direction of travel was what mattered, more than arriving at the final destination. Similarly, Northern Democrats found ways of reconciling the theoretically incompatible elements in their position. The vast majority accepted slavery's "natural" wrongness *and* the notion that the practical solution to the problem was "congressional non-interference." One old Free-Soiler still loyal to the Democrats in 1856 summed up his core assumption this way: "Slavery must in the end be a losing game."[103]

The survival of the Democratic Party in the free states after 1854 is only surprising if you accept the Republican Party's view of the world: that only they were the true embodiment of Northern values, that the rights of free labor could be defended only by a sectional party willing to trash the presumption that republican politics must rest on at least an effort to forge a cross-sectional alliance. Democrats—and those many former Whigs who remained unwilling to sign up to the new Republican organization—firmly resisted that analysis. Inertia played a role, of course, as did the binding power of patronage for a party that still controlled the White House even as it lost control of many states it had been accustomed to run. But to most of its adherents the Democracy remained, as it had always been, the only true guardian of the legacy of the Founders, and the best guarantor of the conservation of the Union. Unlike the upstart Republican Party, Democrats saw themselves as the nonagitators, the nonshouters, the pragmatists in tune with the underlying conservatism of the Northern people. They therefore stood the best chance of securing the rights of free white Northerners while not destroying the Union without which the U.S. mission to advance the global cause of freedom would perish.

CHAPTER FIVE

Fear on the Campaign Trail

The Election of 1860

Early in 1860, two congressmen got into an argument on the floor of the House of Representatives and as one pulled his hand from his jacket pocket a loaded pistol fell with a deafening clatter to the floor. The owner of the gun was John B. Haskin, the anti-Lecompton Democrat from New York, newly endowed with a fashionable beard. There was a stunned silence, and, as one censorious journalist put it, the sight and sound of Haskin's gun "drew from every man . . . who was animated by courageous and honorable feelings the loudest expression of contemptuous condemnation." The incident was a gift to Haskin's opponents since it seemed to confirm rumors that administration opponents were "continually armed with revolvers and other deadly weapons and that they carried them every day on the floor of the House."[1] There had been daily reports of bad tempers and threats of violence as the 36th Congress became mired in a two-month standoff over the election of a speaker.[2] Republicans had a plurality but not quite a majority, even if they were allied with Know-Nothings, upper South anti-Democrats, and Northern anti-Lecompton Democrats like Haskin. The Republican speakership candidate, John Sherman, a second-term representative from Ohio, had a background as an anti-slavery Whig but his greatest offence to those who opposed him was his apparent endorsement of *The Impending Crisis*, a sensational, racist, antislavery tract by a North Carolinian, Hinton Rowan Helper. Was Haskin's supposedly accidental revelation that he carried a loaded gun an attempt to "frighten [his] political opponents," speculated a Washington newspaper. If so, it would fail, since the "man who would flourish his pistols in the presence of ladies is never a man who would use them bravely on a proper occasion."[3] For a few months critics referred to Haskin's gun, ironically or seriously depending on the context, as evidence that Republicans and their anti-Lecompton allies were resorting to violence as readily as fanatical Southerners. "Let Haskin's pistol drop once or twice more on the floor of Congress during a heated debate," warned the *New York Herald* "and the whole conservative sentiment of the North will rise against the abolitionized republicans, and settle their fate forever as a party."[4]

Hyperbole notwithstanding, this was a perfectly plausible political prediction. The perception of rising violence played into the sense of a coming

apocalypse, that the nation was on the brink of a catastrophe, driven by a failure of reasoned, conservative politics. As the year 1860 opened, no one could
confidently forecast the result of the upcoming presidential election. The Republican nominee, whoever he was, would have to sweep the free states as no
previous candidate had done, while a Democratic nominee would somehow
have to overcome a seriously fragmented party, a seemingly impossible task.
The result, then, might be a new configuration, perhaps led by Republicans
but—by excluding the fieriest abolitionists—able to reassure anxious Northern and perhaps even border state and upper South voters that they offered
the surest, safest course to preserve the Union.

In the still-shifting sands of Northern politics, some Republican leaders
had been making concerted overtures to former Whigs, Know-Nothings, and
anti-Lecompton Democrats—with some success, judging by the results of
the 1858 round of elections. Under the banner of the People's Party, Pennsylvania opponents of the Buchanan administration were making headway
in building alliances among Know-Nothings, Whigs, and anti-Lecompton
Democrats like John Forney. In Ohio, the conservative credentials of the new
antislavery opposition movement were immensely boosted by the support of
the charismatic, sixty-four-year-old Thomas Corwin, a veteran former congressman, senator, governor, and secretary of the treasury and general emi-
nence grise of the Whig Party who was elected to Congress as a Republican
in 1858. (Corwin had boosted his celebrity credentials in 1857 by serving as
the successful defense attorney for former Whig Governor William Bebb,
who was tried for manslaughter after firing a rifle at some local youths party-
ing outside his home and accidentally killing one of them.)[5] "I have been
constantly on the stump fighting the heresies of Republicanism and the delusions of Democracy," Corwin wrote in September 1859. "The former, I trust
are thoroughly expunged from the creed of the party, and the latter, I hope,
are somewhat damaged."[6] Corwin was one of a number of leading Republicans
from different political traditions—including, for example, Horace Greeley
and William Seward—who assumed, like their political opponents, that if the
party's policy of peaceful but determined resistance to the Slave Power was to
be successful they would have to build alliances with Unionists in the border
states and even the upper South, if only to signal clearly to voters in the North
that they were not the sectional disunionists that their enemies claimed. Two
distinguished politicians born in Virginia in the 1790s who had built careers
in the border slave states offered reassurance to voters about the Republicans'
essential safety: Francis Preston Blair, a veteran of Andrew Jackson's administration, and Edward Bates, a lifelong Whig.[7]

The question of Haskin's gun was whether it was an act of covert and therefore cowardly aggression on his part (as his opponents charged) or a manful and necessary act of self-defense (as his defenders insisted). These questions had far wider resonance than simply the conduct of the representative from New York's Ninth Congressional district, because it replicated in miniature some of the questions raised by a far more dramatic episode three months earlier. In October 1859, the nation was stunned by a failed attempt to seize the federal arsenal at Harpers Ferry, Virginia by a motley gang led by John Brown—a prophet-bearded abolitionist convinced he had a Holy duty to wage war against slavery. Brown apparently intended to seize the arms held in the arsenal, distribute them to slaves in the surrounding countryside, and foment revolution. Brown's actions are quite possibly better interpreted as a kamikaze mission designed mainly to dramatize his cause, but in any case, Brown became, as Frederick Douglass famously put it, the "meteor" that seemed, especially in retrospect, to have triggered the Civil War.

Brown—a veteran of "bloody Kansas" where he had murdered proslavery settlers—had no qualms about constitutionalism or social order.[8] To Northern abolitionists his boldness was inspiring and clarifying; but this was exactly why many Northerners reacted with such anxiety to the news of the raid, even if they shared, up to a point, Brown's moral condemnation of slavery. It quickly became apparent that a group of prominent New England antislavery men had prior knowledge of Brown's raid and provided him with funds, while church bells tolled in some Northern towns after Brown was hanged for treason.

The Harpers Ferry raid risked tarnishing the Republican Party as an aider and abettor of insurrectionary violence, just as it was attempting to shed its radical image. The core attack from non-Republicans was that Brown was merely carrying to a logical conclusion the Republicans' disregard for both the restraints of decency and the constraints of the Constitution. The party's violent language had led to violent actions, as it always would. "The teaching of [the party's] leaders had been the cause of the revolutionary outbreak," claimed a typical Democratic editorial.[9] Brown had made a "practical application of the 'irrepressible conflict' doctrine," charged the *Democratic Review*; his actions were no more than the "Logical Results of Republicanism."[10] The young Ohio congressman Sullivan S. Cox was reminded, chillingly, of the 1857 uprising in British India "in which Lucknow was besieged for months, by those fiends in human shape, who did what Brown would have had the negroes of Virginia do."[11] The *New York Herald*, which had daringly supported Frémont but had always remained steadfastly wary of Republican extremism, was reminded of a more distant historical precedent: "the Roman republic in the time of the wars of the patricians and plebeians, when the people withdrew to the Aventine Mount to take measures for the protection of their rights, and the whole republic stood on the verge of ruin and anarchy." Given how "strongly the antislavery sentiment of the North" was now arrayed against it, predicted the *Herald* accurately, Northerners should expect Southerners to demand yet more protection for slavery in the next Congress.

Douglas supporters saw the Harpers Ferry raid as clinching evidence that a national majority must be built around a platform opposing the Slave Power and abolitionism equally—and that they, not the Republicans, should lead it. "It behooves all conservative men ... whatever their previous political ... differences" to unite in "putting down the threatening demons of destruction," wrote one.[12] Democratic hopes of being in the vanguard of this conservative realignment were boosted by the horror at Brown's violence felt by former Whigs, some of whom now felt more wary than ever of the Republican Party. Dorothea Dix, for example, was predictably contemptuous of Brown's Northern sympathizers. That anyone would feel anything other than contempt for Brown's "mad scheme" she wrote to former president Fillmore, "is the strangest illustration of mistaken feelings overruling judgment and practical common sense that I have ever heard or read of."[13]

While some Republicans were happy to be associated with the bell-tolling martyrdom of Brown, others—essentially most outside the party's New England redoubt—were acutely aware of the political danger of doing so.[14] Republican newspapers and politicians all across the North—including in New England—called for Brown to be punished as a "pirate and a rebel." At the time of Haskin's faux pas, Republicans were redoubling their efforts to present themselves, in Corwin's words, as the "law-abiding party." Their strategy was to condemn Brown's actions utterly while describing them as an inevitable spillover from the lawlessness and vigilantism unleashed by the repeal of the Missouri Compromise. In a barnstorming speech in Brooklyn in November 1859 that was much reported in the press, Corwin proclaimed that popular sovereignty in Kansas "resulted in four years of civil war out of which came that spectre [sic] of insanity and treason, John Brown."[15] In the Senate, Democrat-turned-Republican James R. Doolittle of Wisconsin took this line a stage further, arguing that Brown was a filibusterer, behaving exactly like the lawless and violent filibusterers who came into Kansas from Missouri and from the Southern states into Nicaragua, where the "grey-eyed man of destiny" William Walker had led a bunch of American mercenaries in overthrowing the government and declared himself president. Republicans, Doolittle pledged, "would use all legal and proper means within the Constitution" to "put down this filibustering" whether that of abolitionists like Brown or pro-slavery expansionists like Walker.[16]

Abolitionists had long attacked slavery for its Jacobinical replacement of law with violence. "A slave-holding community necessarily lives in the midst of gunpowder," wrote Lydia Maria Child in a public letter to the governor of Virginia after Brown's raid, "and, in this age, sparks of free thought are flying in every direction. . . . Slavery is, in fact, an infringement of all law, and adheres to no law, save for its own purposes of oppression."[17] The difference between the moderate and the radical Republican response to Brown's raid was in whether they were willing to recognize Brown as a freedom fighter (which of course suggested that they would endorse similar and presumably more successful violent raids in the future) or condemned his aims (a slave uprising) as well as his actions as outside the bounds of acceptable political responses to the Slave Power. The vast majority of party leaders took the second course. Many Republicans (and other non-Democrats) pushed this argument further, welcoming Brown's sensationally reported execution on the grounds that it was a warning to potential secessionists in the South of the consequences of treason.[18]

These efforts by Republicans to present themselves as the sound, Unionist option were the background to the opening of the presidential race. One morning in May, Sidney George Fisher met one of his neighbors just returned from town who told him the surprising news that "a Mr. Lincoln" had been nominated by the Republicans for president. "I never heard of him before," said Fisher. Later that day, a friend confided that the Republicans' nominee was, unfortunately, a "screamer" who represents "Western coarseness and violence."[19] That sounded worrying, but over the next few months Fisher and his eminently respectable, formerly Whig neighbors were somewhat reassured by newspapers they trusted—notably the ever-cautious Philadelphia *North American*—that Lincoln was all right. Far from being a demagogic "screamer," the dark horse Republican candidate "in no way departed from the old [Whig] faith but stands today where Mr. Clay stood." In his one term as a U.S. congressman, Lincoln, the *North American* noted approvingly, had even voted against a resolution to ban the slave trade in the District of Columbia such was his lack of antislavery zeal. The Lincoln-Douglas debates were selectively quoted to show Lincoln's "essential conservatism." In short, "Mr. Lincoln" was "as much of a conservative statesman as any who has ever been presented for the suffrages of the people of the United States." And in any case, abolitionists didn't like him, so he must be sound. "The most dangerous and successful device of the democratic party for getting and keeping power has been its claim of exclusive conservatism," argued the *North American*, but it was now clearer than ever that they had lost all claim to this title. They had "torn up the compact" of the Missouri Compromise and abandoned "timeless" truths with "recklessness." Consequently, Republicans were now "the only conservative party."[20]

The Republican newspaper in Lincoln's hometown of Springfield, Illinois also made conservatism its consistent theme. The election, it stressed, was a battle between "conservative Republicanism [and] fire-eating, slave-extending Democracy."[21] One of Lincoln's supporters in 1860, the young ex-Whig, Manton Marble who later became editor of the vocally anti-Lincoln *New York World*, was convinced that support for the Republicans was the only true conservative course.[22]

Used in this way, the language of conservatism was a way of distinguishing its users from radical abolitionism, with its revolutionary, fanatical connotations, while at the same time legitimizing their determined resistance to slavery. The South, noted Fisher during the election campaign, was convinced that the free states had been "abolitionized"—and he thought they were right. "The North as a whole has become hostile to slavery," he wrote. It is "united on this subject, and when the North is united it must govern the country."[23] Southern anxiety about the direction of Northern politics was not paranoid but entirely rational. As Fisher understood, there was a basic determination on the part of the great majority of Northerners, including those who supported Douglas, that the Southern proslavery interpretation of American freedom had to be resisted. There was, to be sure, a noisy minority of free-state Democrats, led by President Buchanan, who steadfastly defended Southern leaders' demands even, in the end, for a federal slave code, and professed to regard all opposition to it as dangerous and fanatical. But most Northern Democrats stubbornly and indignantly resisted the attempt to impose a proslavery hegemony on their party. By demanding, as Southerners now seemed to be doing, that Northerners not simply accept the existence of slavery but acknowledge it to be a positive good and exert themselves to defend property rights in human beings struck the majority of Northerners as a dangerous and radical departure. It was also, Democrats argued, an unnecessary provocation to the antislavery "fanatics" and consequently jeopardized political stability on which "order, security of life and prosperity" depended.

Historians have written much about the fear that gripped the South as they faced the prospect of Lincoln's election, but fear was felt in the North too. If Southerners were motivated, in David Potter's words, by "a deeply defensive feeling" and were "united by a sense of a terrible danger," so were Northern-ers.[24] Historians have long recognized the role of emotions in the political crisis that led to war. Back in the 1930s, Avery O. Craven, one of the so-called revisionists who saw the Civil War as a needless conflict brought on by a "blun-dering generation" of politicians, argued that the Civil War came not because of any intractable clash between slavery and freedom but because of "emotions, cultivated hostilities, and ultimately of hatred between sections." Bloodshed, wrote Craven, was "the work of politicians and pious cranks!"[25] The revisionists were wrong that public fears were baseless (and ludicrously dismissive of the centrality of slavery to the conflict), but they were correct that political choices were driven by anxiety. Northerners in 1860 had good reason to feel their identity, or their "honor," was under threat, and they were right to believe that in tangible, material ways—by, most obviously, forming a barrier to Western expansion for ordinary white families, and by threatening destabilizing pro-slavery wars—the South was inimical to their best interests.

For Northerners, the 1860 election therefore came down to one basic question: how to combat the threat of political instability, or the "rapid down-ward tendencies of our popular institutions to revolution and Mexican anar-chy," as the *New York Herald* put it.[26] What policies—and what political style—would be most likely to preserve the Union without submitting to the Slave Power?

The Union Party Movement

In April 1860, a "Conservative Union" party in tiny Rhode Island elected the twenty-nine-year-old "boy Governor" William Sprague, who, the *Herald* re-ported, "represented the conservative elements of every shade."[27] "Glorious Victory!" rejoiced the *Providence Post*, "Rhode Island Rolls Back the Tide of Abolitionism!"[28] Sprague, who had been nominated by a convention of the "conservative men of Rhode Island," was also endorsed by the state's Demo-crats and defeated a Republican opponent regarded as too "Ultra."[29] Sprague's supporters presented the contest as a battle between "Union and Disunion . . . Conservatism and Radicalism" or between "agitation, anarchy and disunion" and "peace, harmony and the Constitution forever." Democratic newspapers claimed the Rhode Island spring election as a triumph for Douglasite Democ-racy over "black Republicanism."[30] The composition and political language of Sprague's coalition certainly suggested that party identities and alignments were still in flux, and it encouraged those who believed that the sectional crisis necessitated a grand conservative coalition that would, as the Philadelphia

North American put it, stand up for the North against the South while marginalizing forever "radicalism and fanaticism."[31] Manton Marble saw the Rhode
Island conservative movement as a template other free states should follow: a
coalition of old Whigs and Democrats on a platform of "conservative national
principles."[32] The impetus in the free states for a new conservative movement was illustrated by Fisher, who reflected on his reservations about the
Republican Party as it was currently constituted. The rise of the Republicans, Fisher observed, was a natural response to the "madness & crime & folly
of the South" but there was a danger of its "animus" and "hostility" to the South
"going too far." Fisher was perfectly willing to concede, as he always had, that
"slavery is hateful in itself" that "liberty . . . is the animating principle of all
our institutions, the ruling passion of our race" and that it was impossible to
"love liberty and love slavery." Yet at the same time, he fretted that "the masses"
rallying to the antislavery Republican Party "stop short at their hatred of
slavery & act on that" imprudently, rashly, without considering the implications.[33] At least in theory, then, there was political space in the North for an
organization that would do a similar job to the Republicans but in a more restrained way.

That there was at least some public appetite for a new party movement was
suggested by the large "Union" meetings held in Northern cities in the wake of
the Harpers Ferry raid. One of the biggest was in Philadelphia. Its organizers—
mostly former Whigs but also some Democrats—described its purpose as being "to bring a conservative influence to bear directly upon the incendiary
spirit which the late outrage has developed."[34] Of a similar meeting in New
York, a religious newspaper commented approvingly that "conservatives . . .
have been silent too long, have endured noisy agitation with commendable
patience, but now it is time to speak and be heard." Some hoped that religious
revivals in the winter of 1859–60 would turn people toward more godly concerns than the "pseudo reforms" of radicalism. A contributor to the Presbyterian
weekly, the *New York Observer*, thought "radicalism, infidelity, irreligion, sectionalism, [and] division" were all part of the same threat and all could be
overcome "by the active energies of those who hold to those great principles
in religion and in government which brought our Puritan Fathers in laying the
foundations of the State." After all, did not Christianity require "regard for the
strong truths which the Bible reveals" a "sense of submission to divine authority"? And was not that the same "class of emotions" that was identified with
"the spirit which dictates submission to law [and] acquiescence in principles
well established"? The "conservative fathers" of the republic had bequeathed
"a trust of infinite value" which, the writer argued, Christians were uniquely

capable of understanding. If conservatism had made the republic, it was even more important that conservatism should now save it.[35]

When Fisher heard about the raid on Harpers Ferry he decided, as he often did when public events agitated him, to share his thoughts with the readers of the *North American*. Fisher's articles appeared under the byline "Cecil," possibly an allusion to Elizabeth I's canny advisor who may well have been something of a historical role model for Fisher, steering a cautious middle path through the stormy religious wars of his age, persecuting Puritans as well as Catholics (although increasingly more of the latter). On this occasion, Fisher also published a little book addressed to the "Northern and Southern conservative party" (the only people worth addressing since "the fanatics of Slavery, and the fanatics of Anti-slavery, are beyond the pale of argument") in which he argued that the one good thing that had come out of the Harpers Ferry "tragedy" was that the "real people, the conservative classes ... the lovers of order and peace" had shown that they wanted the South to be part of the Union and understood Southerners' anxieties about having even "a small number" of "Northern enemies."[36] The question for the election year was whether this public sentiment could find appropriate political expression.

In May 1860, a national convention met in Baltimore to nominate candidates for the presidency who would capitalize on this inchoate sense that the "conservative masses" needed to be represented by a new party organization. The men who gathered in the Eastside District Courthouse were almost all former Whigs, and the men they nominated, John Bell and Edward Everett, both in their mid-sixties, had long records of public service as Whigs. The Tennessean Bell was an aloof man who liked writing long, detailed speeches and had a knack for parliamentary maneuvers, but had no popular touch. He was a slaveholder but had the distinction of being the only Southerner to have voted against the Kansas-Nebraska Act in the Senate, arguing it would be counter-productive for the South. Everett had shared his mentor Daniel Webster's faith in the finality of the 1850 Compromise. In the Senate debate on the Kansas-Nebraska Act, Everett had given an equivocal, cautious speech in which he opposed the bill even while claiming "that there is no great interest at stake. ... In the long run everybody admits that [Kansas] is not to be a slaveholding region." Compared to the full-blooded case for "freedom national" made by Everett's Massachusetts colleague Charles Sumner a few days later, it was a ponderous and seemingly pointless intervention and it helped to undermine even further the diminished credibility of Webster-style Whiggism.[37] Yet Everett still had one valuable political asset in 1860: as a famous orator who had toured the country giving a wildly popular speech about

George Washington to raise money for the purchase of Mount Vernon, he was as close a symbol as the North had to a living representative of the Founding Fathers. The Constitutional Union Party relied on the galvanizing, emotional power of the idea of the Union. The name of Washington, Everett told an audience in Boston on July 4, is "stamped on your hearts, it glistens in your eyes, it is written on every page of your history," while the principles of the Union are "as broad as humanity, as eternal as truth."[38]

Its emotional appeal was to defend the Union, but it was restrained manhood that would save it from destruction. Maintaining the Republic—with its unique guarantees of freedom—required "forbearance, concession and conciliation," explained the National Executive Committee of the Bell-Everett organization. These virtues were no more than the "rules of self-control and self-government as regulate in social life, or in the relations of business, the intercourse of gentlemen who may chance to differ widely on the gravest questions." The failure of such self-control, Constitutional Unionists argued, was a direct result of the low quality of political leaders. "Wise and good men" had been "repelled" from the "sphere of politics" because they were unable to make themselves heard amid the agitation of the slavery question that "dwarfs understanding while it inflames the passions."[39]

The Constitutional Union Party hoped to gain the support of self-conceived conservative Know-Nothings and Whigs who had been on a difficult political journey over the previous decade. An address to "Conservative Voters" published by the National Executive Committee of the Constitutional Union Party also made a pitch to former Democrats who had lost confidence in the party because of its "peculiar championing of Southern rights" and who, as a consequence, had been "induced temporarily to array themselves in the republican organization."[40] These were men who had heartily opposed the repeal of the Missouri Compromise but had quickly felt uncomfortable with their new antislavery bedfellows in the anti-Nebraska opposition. Since their chief objection to the Kansas-Nebraska Act was that it would stir up sectional antagonism, their hope had always been to oppose Southern aggressiveness without prompting a Northern antislavery reaction: a feat that, evidently, was impossible. In 1856, the Fillmore campaign had tried this tactic but made too many concessions to the South for the taste of many of his former supporters who, consequently, deserted to the Republicans. Others, like Rufus Choate, recognizing the electoral imperative, had gravitated to Buchanan. Choate died in 1859 so never had to make a choice again, but some of his former Whig allies hoped that Bell and Everett would now manage what Fillmore had not and stake out what they always called "national" policy. What this boiled down to was the strategy of avoiding contentious issues while galvanizing the popular emotional power of Unionism.

Fisher smiled indulgently at the Bell-Everett campaign—they were the only, truly "sound & safe party" he thought—yet still he could not bring himself to place their ballot in the box. "It is common to hear men say they prefer Bell & Everett, but to vote for them would be useless," he concluded. He did not, in the end, vote for Lincoln, either. "I am glad to hear that [the Republican Party] is to triumph," he wrote in explaining his abstention, "but I do not wish it to triumph by too great a majority."[41] Some of Bell's more optimistic supporters dreamed of a national reaction against pro- and antislavery "extremism" which might sweep him to power. More realistically the Bell-Everett campaign hoped that the election would be thrown to the House, as it had been in 1824, and that Bell, in such circumstances, would emerge as the natural compromise candidate. Partly with this long game in mind, the Constitutional Union Party platform contained no statement about the slavery controversy at all. It was a tactic that had worked for Zachary Taylor in 1848, but it would not work again. Bell ran well in the upper South, winning Virginia, Kentucky, and his home state of Tennessee. Old Whig planters in lowland Georgia and North Carolina, and some in the Mississippi Valley, supported him. But without substantial support in the North, the Constitutional Union Party was doomed. And that support did not come.

The Democratic Schism

One of the reasons it did not was that the Constitutional Union Party was squeezed from two directions. It faced not one but two parties trying to cannibalize its conservative appeal: not just the Republicans, but the Douglasite wing of the Democratic Party as well. When the Democratic National Convention met in Charleston at the end of April, Douglas was by far the most popular candidate but could not muster the required two-thirds majority among the delegates (the two-thirds rule having been originally introduced precisely in order to give the slave states a veto over any nomination). Having so publically and spectacularly broken with the administration over the Lecompton constitution, Douglas had irreparably lost the support of the Deep South. Simultaneously there was a battle over the platform. When a majority of delegates (a majority was all that was needed for the platform) refused to accept a plank endorsing the Dred Scott decision, fifty Southern delegates bolted. Reconvening two months later in the sweltering Front Street Theatre in Baltimore, the convention was again deadlocked; again Southerners bolted (this time more quickly than before) and two separate conventions ended up nominating two separate candidates on very different platforms. The bolters nominated thirty-nine-year-old Vice President John Breckinridge, a strikingly handsome Kentucky slaveholder and Mexican War veteran. Douglas duly received the endorsement of the remaining delegates—most of whom were from the free states. It was an acrimonious split, as intraparty divisions always are. In private correspondence Democratic politicians referred to members of opposing factions as "the enemy."[42]

The failure of the Democrats to unite on a single presidential nominee was not a great surprise to many observers; within the North the division between the Douglasites and the minority who supported Breckinridge broadly reflected the already-existing schism that had opened up over Lecompton. Some Southern Democrats worked quite deliberately to ensure that there would be a formal split as part of a maneuver to push the South toward secession by precipitating the election of a Black Republican president. That motivation certainly did not explain Buchanan's Northern allies, however. For them, on the contrary, the Union could only be preserved if the North conceded the Southern demand that slavery be recognized and protected. On that score, the election of Douglas would be as bad as the election of a Republican. Breckinridge was nominated on a platform that wholeheartedly endorsed the latest Southern demand for a federal slave code that would totally destroy any chance of genuine popular sovereignty by establishing protection for slavery everywhere the writ of the federal government ran. It was a logical legislative extension of the Dred Scott decision, which had, after all, said that slaves were no different from any other form of property. The vast majority of Northerners, including the great majority of Democrats, would never accept that the federal government should formally and forever abdicate any neutrality on the issue of slavery and commit itself to supporting slaveholder rights in any circumstances. That the Breckinridge platform offered up a federal slave code "as if it were a longstanding maxim" (in Sidney George Fisher's words) was an affront to reality and a radically innovative doctrine. It was a fallacy that government could not interfere with property rights under any circumstances. As Sidney George Fisher pointed out, "anyone with a passing understanding of the Anglo-American legal tradition" knew that "Government may declare what is & what is not property & how & on what conditions it may be possessed and enjoyed. A government that cannot do this is no government at all, and it is absurd to say that Congress has the power to *protect* only" and not to *define* what property was.[43] Most Northern Democrats completely agreed, and in Douglas they had a champion who could make that case while still posing as the legitimately nominated candidate of the moderate and "national" Democracy.

The Northern electorate would therefore be presented with a choice among four candidates offering four different theories of the appropriate relationship between the federal government and slavery. Lincoln saw the federal government's role as being to uphold freedom, notwithstanding the Dred Scott decision. Breckinridge promised the exact opposite: using the federal government to uphold slavery. Douglas's proposition was that Washington should have no role at all, devolving the decision to local settlers. Bell formally had no position at all, but his supporters often expressed a yearning for the restoration of a Missouri Compromise-style division of federal land.

The 1860 contest was, in practice, two parallel elections: one between Lincoln and Douglas in the North, and one in the South between Breckinridge and Bell.[44] But there were exceptions: there were a few Douglas loyalists in the South (his running mate Herschel Johnson was from Georgia) and Douglas polled well in northern Alabama, coming top of the poll in four counties in the Tennessee valley. In the North, Bell and Everett pulled in some votes in Massachusetts and in the far West. More surprisingly, perhaps, Breckinridge also had pockets of support in the North. Other than on the Pacific coast (where slave-state settlers gave him a solid base of support) one of Breckinridge's better performances in the free states was Maine, where he got 6.3 percent of the vote (compared to 29.4 percent for Douglas in a state with a big Republican majority). In Indiana he got 4.5 percent and in Massachusetts he recorded 3.6 percent. In all these places patronage may well have played a role, since in each case at least one prominent state party leader chose to interpret loyalty to the Democracy as loyalty to the president and hence to his favored successor. In five states (Illinois, Iowa, Michigan, Vermont, and Wisconsin), where Breckinridge got less than one percent of the vote, there was no notable Democratic figure supporting him locally. In Minnesota Breckinridge polled 748 votes (2.2 percent of the tiny electorate in this newly admitted state), and the testimony of one Breckinridge supporter, Charles H. Boone, suggests that most if not all of it may have come from Pennsylvanian migrants, many of whom had been active in supporting Buchanan and his allies.[45] Even Breckinridge's most zealous free-state supporters must have known their cause was doomed. The best they could possibly hope for was some Electoral College votes from Pennsylvania and, after the People's Party gubernatorial candidate triumphed in the Keystone state in October, any hope of this must surely have faded. Even if Breckinridge won every slave state— never likely given Bell's strength in old Whig states like Kentucky, Tennessee, and Virginia—it would still not have been enough to win an Electoral College majority.

Even so, there were three places in the North (east of the Rockies) where there was a functioning Breckinridge campaign complete with at least one supportive newspaper. The first was Connecticut, where he got 19.2 percent of the popular vote, just a fraction behind Douglas's 20.6 percent. Then there was New York City, where prominent party activists like Mike Walsh and Isaiah Rynders, together with a few financiers and merchants, supported the Southern candidate. And finally there was Buchanan's home state of Pennsylvania. But even there, staunch party loyalists acknowledged they were in a small minority. Writing to Senator William Bigler, who remained loyal to Buchanan and thus to Breckinridge, one party activist warned "there is no doubt that Stephen A. Douglas is the *man of the people* and the masses beyond all are for him before any other."[46] Fusion tickets in New York and Pennsylvania meant that the extent of Breckinridge's support in those places was not measured precisely at the polls but it is reasonable to imagine that it may have been similar to Connecticut, which is to say no more than about a fifth of the electorate. In New York City, Connecticut, and Pennsylvania patronage networks were certainly important in mobilizing the Breckinridge vote, although since the outgoing administration had little leverage in terms of the promise of future posts, patronage had less purchase than in previous elections. Given the very public act of voting, however, personal ties and loyalties to local bigwigs still carried some weight.

William Dock's tortuous experience in 1860 is a case in point. Born in the 1790s, Dock had grown up with the Jacksonian movement. He was a lawyer and judge in Harrisburg, Pennsylvania and had been involved in every election campaign since 1824. He had been a frequent speaker at public meetings and had served on county and state Democratic committees. In 1849 he had run for Congress for the 14th District but lost. And in 1851 he had been the chairman of the state convention that had nominated William Bigler for governor. He and Bigler went back a long way and corresponded frequently about local politics and business matters.[47] By 1860, Dock was living with his son George, a prominent physician, and was still a well-known figure about the city. But he was now, at the age of 67, increasingly frail and had formally retired from public life. During the election campaign, word got out that the elder Dock was unhappy with the direction of his old party. Simon Cameron, the wily head of a Nativist political machine that was now supporting Lincoln, concocted a plan to lure Dock—who he had known for years—into a public declaration of support. The defection to the Republican cause of a longstanding and well-known Jacksonian Democrat would presumably be a great publicity coup. Cameron had called with a local committee of Republicans at the Dock residence and tried to persuade the old man to accompany them to a nearby hall and preside at a public meeting. They failed, although it seems as if this may have been due to the intervention of Dock's son George who, as he recounted, "fought them off and reasoned and argued with Father so decidedly that I beat them out and prevented his not only presiding, but going out of the house that entire evening." One can imagine the Docks, father and son, sitting in uncomfortable silence by the fire for a couple of hours after Cameron's visit. But the excitement wasn't over. At 10.30 P.M., just as the elder Dock was making his way to bed, a brass band struck up outside the house, playing patriotic tunes. This was a "serenade," a conventional political ritual in the mid-nineteenth century; in return for the music and singing, a public figure would be asked to respond with a few words. In this case, any speech Dock made would, naturally, be taken down and reported in the papers the next day as an endorsement of the Lincoln campaign. Before George knew what was happening, old William was opening the door to go out and thank his serenaders. "Scarcely was the door open," reported George, when "up stepped Simon Cameron and urged Father to make a little speech to the Band etc.!" Knowing exactly what the game was, George "stepped right up [and] took Father by the shoulders. 'No Sir!' said I, '*Not a word*. Return your thanks to the *band* for the compliment they have paid you and *nothing more. Not a word more.*'" Cameron, George reported, "was very angry at me and I stood by until Father had in few simple words merely thanked the Band, and I then took him right into the house, leaving Cameron to walk off, *decidedly beaten* and disappointed."

The next morning George lectured his father, explaining to him "the *motives* of their sycophantic flattery." A few days later, though, George left Harrisburg for a week-long visit to his brother Gilliard, believing that he left with "a perfect understanding between Father and Mother & Myself that Father was to remain away from them & vote for Breckenridge [sic]." Cameron saw his chance, and called on William again. Promising the old man that should Lincoln be elected his younger brother Jacob would get a patronage post in Philadelphia, Cameron finally managed to persuade Dock to allow his name to be used as the president of a Republican meeting. With horror, George read about his father's alleged conversion to Republicanism in a newspaper ("as soon as I learned of it I wrote him a *scorcher* and then came home, but it was *too late*"). And so George wrote, apologetically to his father's old party comrade Bigler, assuring him that the Dock family would still vote for Breck-inridge "like *men*" and pleaded with the senator to "make allowances for Father. He is failing very much in elasticity and strength of mind."[48]

For George Dock, voting for Breckinridge was clearly an emotional com-mitment based on his family's long Democratic association. In Pennsylvania, with a powerful (albeit outgoing) senator and a current (albeit soon to be lame duck) president from the state endorsing Breckinridge, it is not hard to see how a vote for Breckinridge would seem to a man like Dock to be the loyal course, whatever the platform on which he stood. Other than in New York City and Connecticut, Douglas had the overwhelming support of the Democratic hierarchy—after all, as they argued fiercely, if tediously, he was the "regular" nominee (it was not the Douglasites who had bolted).

The deference to patrons, the pressure exerted on government employees, and the inertia of partisan loyalty no doubt explains many of the scattered Breckinridge votes in the free states. Some also supported him for the same reasons they had gone along with Lecompton and the Kansas-Nebraska Act: the hope that one more concession to the South would resolve the sectional issue for all time. One Pennsylvanian Breckinridge supporter thought the South simply needed to be assured that Northerners could "break down this [abolitionist] fanaticism."[49] The veteran New York Democrat Daniel S. Dick-inson spoke at a packed meeting at the Cooper Union in New York on July 19, warning that Breckinridge was the only candidate who supported the Dred Scott decision and thus the only one who could claim to be the protector of the Constitution ("the sheet anchor of our hopes; when that is gone all is lost") and so the only one who could keep the South in the Union. Dickinson argued there was no practical difference between Douglas and Lincoln. Popu-lar sovereignty in Douglas's version was indistinguishable in practice from Republican opposition to new slave states and both positions were unconsti-tutional according to the Dred Scott decision. The triumph of either would split the Union. Macready's nemesis Isaiah Rynders also spoke, summoning up his most fiery rhetoric to stir up the working-class crowd almost with the panache of Edwin Forrest in his prime. Dickinson's great intraparty enemy John A. Dix also supported Breckinridge, though he played a low-key role in the campaign. His sympathies he said, were with the South, which felt bullied by the North. But above all, he thought a victory for Breckinridge the only way of averting the ultimate calamity of Southern secession. Dix's son Mor-gan remembered "leaving my bed while suffering from severe illness, and tak-ing the risk involved in standing in the cold air on an inclement day, waiting my turn to vote, because I felt it a sacred duty to do whatever my one ballot could accomplish to prevent the election of Mr. Lincoln."[50]

Some Breckinridge loyalists were "fogeys" like Buchanan or Dickinson, men in their sixties long derided within as well as outside the party as "dough faces." But there was a younger cohort too: men like the thirty-two-year-old Samuel J. Randall, born into a Whig family in Philadelphia, who joined the Democrats after the Kansas-Nebraska Act, appalled by the rise of sectional politics. Or the thirty-eight-year-old Charles R. Buckalew, who grew up in a small town on the Susquehanna River, who was so frustrated by the way in which dominant Republicans were crushing opposition and speaking as if they represented the whole North that he became an enthusiastic advocate both of proportional representation for elections to Congress and of reform of the Electoral College. (He later argued that had the United States adopted his scheme of "cumulative voting" in the 1850s, the war would have been avoided because Southern Unionists would have been better represented and Republicans would not have been so dominant.[51]) And then there was the Indiana Democrat Daniel Voorhees, "the tall sycamore of the Wabash" as his fans called him, whom Buchanan had appointed district attorney.[52] "What is the great danger facing the republic?" Voorhees asked rhetorically in a campaign speech in 1860. His answer was uncompromising: it was "the seditious citizen [who] glories in the billows of popular fanaticism which roar around him, and rejoices in the sight of the fatal lee-shore on which the Union is drifting. No cry of horror escapes his lips. He rather jeers at the warning voice of others. He seeks with insane fury to grasp with his own hand the helm of the vessel to hurl her more swiftly and surely on to destruction." Echoing the language that had been used to defend previous concessions to the South, Voorhees framed the election as a choice between the "national" men and the "sectionalists." Voorhees's favored candidate, Breckinridge, was reviled by most Northern Democrats as a sectionalist on a par with the worst kind of abolitionists, but Voorhees presented him as the only candidate who understood the importance of treating the South with "equality." By that he meant giving the same status to their slave property in the "common territories" as to any other "species of property"—a concession that, as Voorhees must have known, very few Northerners were willing to make.[53]

As Lincoln had predicted in his "house divided" speech in 1858, the Breckinridge wing of the Democratic Party was now arguing that slavery needed to be normalized. Just as Southerners were, entirely rationally, fearful that the moral case which told Northerners that they should ban slavery in the territories set the nation on a path to ultimate emancipation, so Northerners, also rationally, saw that if they were being asked to accept that slavery was right and not wrong their own determination to ban it at home would come increasingly under pressure.

Most Northern Breckinridge supporters tried to argue that their candidate was in the conservative Democratic tradition of merely trying to hold the line between the sectional extremes. Few Northern antebellum politicians had expended as much energy condemning anyone who even so much as hinted at any sympathy for the most modest antislavery position as former senator Daniel S. Dickinson. And yet, even while defending slavery as a natural institution for black people, Dickinson staunchly, if implausibly, denied that Breckinridge's platform called for a federal slave code, calling the accusation a partisan charge by their enemies. Even Dickinson, it seems, had his limits when it came to making concessions to the South.

But if Dickinson uncharacteristically held back at least in this one respect, there were other free-state campaigners for Breckinridge who made an explicit proslavery case. "We are not fanatics hereabouts," wrote one Pennsylvanian merchant who supported Breckinridge, "we have seen the blacks from childhood, free blacks, lazy blacks, good-humored and very serviceable, but hardly our equals." And while he did not propose to reintroduce slavery into Pennsylvania he could see no reason why it would not, in principle, be a good thing. One line of argument by proslavery Northerners in 1860 set the question of slavery in the global, imperial context of how to manage "inferior" peoples; they contrasted the harmony of races in the slave states ("Go to the South and see those sunny black faces!") with the chaos and violence of Britain's Indian Empire. The Sepoy Rebellion, as it was called at the time—the 1857 insurrection in British India that was heavily reported in the U.S. press—suggested Southerners had found a better resolution of the question of how to rule "inferior" people than had the British. Here in America, wrote Dickinson, "we are benevolent" to our slaves, whereas "Britain has abused Africans, Celts and Indians" and has suffered rebellion as a result. Slavery, it seemed, was a modern and efficient system of managing race relations. Abolition in the British Empire had been a "mistake."[54]

Charles O'Conor, a New York lawyer of Irish Catholic descent was even more forthright in his full embrace of slavery as a positive good. O'Conor told a Breckinridge meeting that "the most fertile regions of the globe cannot be so cultivated as fully to develop their natural resources for the benefit of mankind except by negro labor. Negro labor cannot be there employed except through the judicious compulsion of a superior race; and in no way can so great a measure of physical enjoyment and moral improvement be imparted to the negro as by his compulsory servitude in these very regions." A storm of "pseudo-reformers" and "infidels" had launched "a moral war . . . upon this institution" and the fact that they were winning was simply because, "hitherto at least in the North no one has defended it, and its Southern advocates have not been heard." Absurdly, in O'Conor's view, "the idea that it conflicts with natural justice and with divine law has [therefore] taken possession of the northern mind." This was the heart of the distinction between Breckinridge and Douglas supporters. "We must, as a party," said O'Conor, "insist unqualifiedly that in the institution of negro slavery there is nothing whatever which calls for unfavorable action by government; that the right of the white master to the services of his negro slave is, in every moral sense, precisely the same as his right to any other property." Such overt proslavery arguments were marginal. No Douglas Democrat would have said this, but O'Conor had a long track record. At a public meeting after John Brown was hanged, he had insisted "that Negro slavery is . . . not only not unjust, it is just, wise, and beneficent."[55]

O'Conor took his proslavery crusade into the courtroom, arguing against the precedent set in London in the 1772 Somerset case in which Lord Mansfield had famously ruled that slavery was so odious that it could never be supported by common law and so in the absence of positive law to sustain it, no one could be held a slave. In 1852, six enslaved people had been brought to New York by Jonathan Lemmon and his family from Virginia. The Lemmons planned to stay only a few days before taking a steamer for Texas. Thousands of slaveholders before them had brought their human "property" into a free state in transit without incident under the inter-state "comity" principle by which the laws of one jurisdiction are recognized in another. But a black abolitionist, Louis Napoleon, who discovered the African American family in a boarding house, petitioned the courts for a writ of habeas corpus, which, in effect would emancipate them. Amidst scenes of much rejoicing from black New Yorkers who had crowded into the courtroom, a judge agreed: New York City's air was too pure for a slave to breathe. But in the wake of the Dred Scott decision an appeal was launched testing the basis of the original decision. (The status of the enslaved people themselves was no longer at stake: they had been formally manumitted by the Lemmons, who in turn had been the beneficiaries of a fund-raising campaign by New York financiers embarrassed by the case and keen to compensate them for their loss). It was at this point that Charles O'Conor strode into the national spotlight to argue that the common law assumption of freedom was wrong, and that, on the contrary, "by the law of nations," as well as the "privileges and immunities" clause of the Constitution which prevented one state from discriminating against the citizens of another, a visitor from the South could not be arbitrarily deprived of his property. O'Conor lost the appeal and Southerners raged at the decision. A Richmond newspaper urged retaliation: "if [New York] says that our negroes shall be free, if they pass through her territory, our legislature must pass a law rendering every vessel from the state of New York, that touches one of our ports, a lawful prize! No taxing, no half way measures—they destroy Southern property at a blow, let us do the same with theirs."[56] To O'Conor this was perfectly logical. Property was property. No distinction should be made between property one approved of and property one didn't. The Northern refusal to accept this. O'Conor claimed, was the cause of the sectional conflict.[57]

O'Conor became a Republican bogeyman, his proslavery speeches reprinted by his opponents as evidence of the reach of the Slave Power. Associating the principle of slavery with Old World despotism, as had been commonplace since the 1848 revolutions, one Massachusetts newspaper observed of O'Conor that "in Europe, he would be a devotee of Austrianism, as in America he is a champion of slavery."[58] Republicans seized on other proslavery spokesmen—notably the Dartmouth president Nathan Lord—to whip up anxiety among the electorate about the encroaching reach of the Slave Power onto free soil. They had plenty of material to work with. Breckinridge supporters in the North, small in number as they were, were far more open about expressing proslavery views than any Northerners had been before. An anti-Douglas newspaper published in New York, *The National Crisis* ("an antidote to Abolition Fanaticism, Treason and Sham Philanthropy" as it styled itself on the masthead) frequently called out the hypocrisy of Republicans and Douglasite Democrats alike who were not prepared to support slavery even though, they alleged, the North had rid itself of slavery only when it had the means of "realizing the full value of every slave, and of getting them without trouble or expense beyond their borders."[59]

Joseph Lovejoy was another striking proslavery convert. Lovejoy had been not just mildly antislavery like Lord, or a Free-Soiler like O'Sullivan, but a full-fledged abolitionist. One of his brothers, Elijah, an abolitionist editor, had been killed by a mob in Alton, Illinois in 1837. Another, Owen, with whom Joseph had once authored a book mourning their murdered brother and inveighing against the sin of slavery, was now a fiery antislavery congressman. But Joseph had changed his mind. "Have we not at the North, stimulated our own self-righteousness in contrast with the sins of the South, quite up to or beyond the healthy point?" he asked his brother Owen, in a letter that was reprinted in the press.[60] Still the stern Presbyterian he had always been,

Joseph placed at the top of his list of Northern sins that were at least as bad as anything abolitionists charged against the South the increasing availability of divorce: we "sunder the marriage covenant with as little consideration as the most ruthless slaveholder ... and our cities are dripping with the waters of Sodom." In 1859 Joseph publicly declared that he now realized that he had been "in error" to have once thought slavery wrong. Abolition, he now thought, had been a youthful passion. After all Edmund Burke "once was en-raptured with the voice of Liberty, as she cried from across the channel," but he had grown wiser, "in the full strength of his manhood"—just like Joseph Lovejoy. And like Nathan Lord, Joseph claimed to have reread his Bible and discovered clear scriptural authority for enslavement. Joseph was especially irked when his brother Owen made a speech in Congress arguing that those who sought Biblical authority for slavery could only do so by justifying the enslavement of all "laboring men." This was the basis, Owen had said, on which Israelites were permitted to enslave the Canaanites. Not so, responded Joseph: the Canaanites were enslaved because they were heathens; "and therefore so degraded that a transfer to the Hebrew commonwealth, where the true God was worshipped was a privilege and a blessing."[61]

The very public rupture between the Lovejoy brothers was an irresistible story for newspaper editors. And this specific issue of the justification in the Old Testament for the enslavement of the Canaanites was no esoteric matter. As journalists writing up the Lovejoys' spat understood only too well, at stake was the idea that once the legitimacy of slavery was acknowledged, how would ordinary free white men ever be sure that they themselves would re-main free? Some Republicans pushed this idea hard in the 1860 campaign. The barbarians, they implied, truly were at the gates.

For a decade, beginning with the Fugitive Slave Act, continuing with the Kansas-Nebraska Act and the Dred Scott decision, and culminating in the demand for a federal slave code, Southerners had been trying to use the con-solidated power of the federal government to preserve and protect slave property in the face of the opposition of the majority of Northerners. Those few, but noisy, Northern Breckinridge supporters who really embraced their candidate's platform (as opposed to just supporting him out of a sense of par-tisan obligation) argued that giving Southerners the guarantees they wanted would preserve the Union. But the severe limits of this argument within the free states were all too apparent. Douglas Democrats, like Republicans—and, for that matter, Northern Constitutional Unionists—simply could not accept the radical moral, political, or constitutional implications of a federal slave code. The Breckinridge campaign's role in the North was essentially to be the foil against which the other campaigns would compete to offer the most plausible, safe, conservative alternative.

Douglasites and Lincolnites

The path to victory followed by Buchanan in 1856 was not available to Douglas in 1860. The party schism meant the Little Giant clearly was not going to win many Electoral College votes in the South (in the end he won some from Missouri, but that was it). The Republicans, in contrast, could be fairly confident of 114 Electoral College votes from the states that had supported Frémont in 1856, plus another 4 from Minnesota, which had been recently admitted. That left Lincoln needing to gather another 38 votes to win. Pennsylvania was the key, with 27 votes. If Lincoln could win there, plus at least one of Illinois (his home state, but also, of course, Douglas's) or Indiana (with 11 and 13 votes respectively), he would be over the line. The Pacific states of Oregon and California had only 7 votes between them and were, rightly, considered impossible to predict (both, in the end, went for Lincoln on a plurality). New Jersey would always be a tough battle for the Republicans with a strongly entrenched Democratic tradition, although in the end Lincoln won a share of the split electoral vote in that state. The only two plausible scenarios in 1860, then, were either that Lincoln won a majority or that no one did. Douglas, like Bell, saw his most likely path to victory lying through the House of Representatives. Given this electoral reality, Douglas campaign newspapers devoted lots of space to electoral analysis purporting to prove that Lincoln could not amass enough votes to win, rather than to show that the Little Giant would do so.[62]

In the places where they needed to make electoral advances, Republicans needed to win over as many of those who had supported Fillmore in 1856 as possible. Those voters were mostly Know-Nothings and former Whigs and were the same people being targeted by the Constitutional Unionists. They were men who had resisted what they saw as the Republicans' sectionalism and fanaticism hitherto, and they were 18 percent of the 1856 Pennsylvania electorate and 16 percent in Illinois. Democrats, if they were to stop Lincoln winning a majority, needed to win over these same people. This meant that the battle between the Douglasites and the Lincolnites was over who would be the better bulwark against the many threats the republic now faced; who would best stand up for the time-honored, Revolution-sanctified liberties of free white citizens?

Consequently, and reflecting the underlying areas of consensus in the free states that had been developing for several years, Republican and Democrats were not so far apart on important matters of policy, and even in terms of political style and language. Republican supporters were almost as willing as Democrats to use violently racist language and everywhere, outside of the New England heartlands, editors and campaigners strove hard to distance the Republican campaign from any taint of abolitionism. Black people, wrote a contributor to Sidney Fisher's favorite paper, the *North American*, are "unquestionably at present of a type far inferior to ours in the scale of humanity, and will require many ages of culture and development to raise them to our level."[63] Republicans warned that Cuban annexation would lead to racial amalgamation. According to Lincoln biographer Michael Burlingame, one such article, in the *Illinois State Journal*, may have been penned by the candidate himself; tellingly, Lincoln appears to have used "Conservative" as one of his pseudonyms when he wrote for the press.[64] As Henry Raymond's *New York Times* asked, rhetorically, "How is the doctrine of negro equality to be 'forced upon the South' by the Republicans, when they scorn it for the free negroes of the North?" Republicans do not "have any more love of the negro—any greater disposition to make sacrifices for his sake, or to waive their own rights and interests for the promotion of his welfare, than the rest of mankind, North and South."[65]

Democrats had presented themselves as the embodiment of the common man for thirty years or more, but in 1860 Republicans worked hard to coopt this Jacksonian language for themselves. Republican clubs held meetings to celebrate Jefferson's birthday, and Lincoln was hailed as a "Jeffersonian Republican" in campaign literature.[66] Republican campaigners argued that the "so-called Democratic party" was "false to its name" and was now the "aristocratic" party, their support for slavery extension being in effect support for land monopoly by slave owners, securing "power to the few." Jefferson and Jackson were retrospectively enlisted as Republican spokesmen, since they had wanted to "give and preserve power to the people to enable them to become proprietors and secure them in their homes."[67] Lincoln's carefully projected image as a "Rail Splitter" and as "Honest Abe", as an "obscure child of labor" who was "an apt illustration of our free institutions," was a core component in the project of presenting Republicanism as a natural evolution of the Jacksonian tradition.[68] Notwithstanding Lincoln's background as a Whig, the presence of so many prominent Democrats in the party's leadership lent credibility to this image.

To many, the Republicans' warnings about Southern aggression seemed, in the light of all that happened since 1856, more plausible. During the campaign, Lincoln newspapers reported lynchings of Northerners in the South, stories which fed their narrative about the barbarism of the Slave Power.[69] The crucial context for their rise and success as a party was the growing feeling that electoral politics now barely concealed an underlying struggle for supremacy that was being fought out though violence—in Kansas, in Congress, in random episodes of violence in the South. And as a prime illustration of this seeming reality, the Harpers Ferry episode, in the end, simply made it harder for Douglas Democrats to deny the severity of the sectional crisis. If the threat was so severe, the Republicans were best placed to act as the defense shield for the North. Claiming roots for their opposition to slavery extension deep in the political culture of the Republic, former Free-Soiler Salmon P. Chase of Ohio called the Republican Party "the Liberty Party of 1776 revived." Its cause was profoundly defensive. It championed the established rights of equality and liberty, won in the Revolution, against "the party of *false* conservatism and slavery."[70]

Republicans also enfolded the threat of the Slave Power in a larger problem of corrupt and failing governance. A report by Republican congressman John Covode on the use of bribery by the Buchanan administration was a widely circulated campaign document.[71] Corruption of the venal kind was bad enough, but in a republican political culture the pilfering by officeholders and the disreputable reputation of parties and "wire-pullers" threatened to undermine the republic by draining it of virtue and honesty. In the Republican imagination, corruption scandals were symptomatic of the existential threat posed by the Slave Power.[72] There were two irrepressible conflicts, explained *New York Tribune* editor Horace Greeley, one pitting freedom against "aggressive, all-grasping Slavery propagandism" and the other, "not less vital," between "frugal government and honest administration" on the one hand and "wholesale executive corruption, and speculative jobbery" on the other.[73] Thousands of "intelligent men support the candidates of the republican party" wrote Manton Marble who did not "care a broken tobacco-pipe for the negro question." What motivated them instead, he thought, was their "fear that the democratic party has been so long in power that it has become corrupt."[74] The New York banker and Douglas supporter August Belmont had a similar analysis. "The country at large had become disgusted with the misrule of Mr. Buchanan, and the corruption which disgraced his Administration," he wrote in the aftermath of Lincoln's victory. "The Democratic party was made answerable for [Buchanan's] misdeeds, and a change was ardently desired by thousands of conservative men out of politics. This feeling was particularly strong in the rural districts, and did us infinite harm there."[75]

Douglasites tried to capitalize on this frustration with political corruption, playing on their opposition to Buchanan to vie with Republicans as political outsiders—but it was never a wholly plausible strategy. Republicans had channeled the Know-Nothings' talent for projecting a new style of antiparty politics. Republicans insisted that they were not a political party in the old sense at all but were, in the words of an Ohio supporter, "formed for a mere temporary purpose; namely the re-enactment of the prohibition of slavery in the territories."[76]

Republicans were the new broom that would sweep away years, if not decades, of rule in Washington by a corrupted national Democratic Party that had turned against the interests of ordinary free white men. This was essentially a conservative pitch to restore ancient liberties. There was a relentless focus in campaign speeches on the unprecedented threat to the Republic. Republicans warned tirelessly of the terrifying new demands being made by the South such as the reopening of the slave trade (a prospect mentioned by Lincoln in most of his 1859 speeches), or a Congressional slave code for the territories.[77] Posing as the conservative defenders of the liberties of the North enabled Republicans to secure the support of people who remained as appalled as ever by one-ideaism and "pseudo-reformers." Old Whigs like Fisher saw in the advance of the Slave Power the same kinds of threats as those posed by the demagogues and fanatics they had always worried about. The Democracy had always, to Fisher, been essentially demagogic in spirit; now, with its pursuit of dangerous innovations like the claim that the government could not regulate property, it had succumbed to single-minded fanaticism too. This republic, wrote one of Fisher's Philadelphia friends in the *North American*, "was intended and hoped by our fathers and by their children to be the example, the promise, the strength, the renewal and the glory of the world" and it must not "be broken to pieces by the arts of demagogues, of by the prevalence of one idea."[78]

Meanwhile Douglas's campaign rhetoric was far closer to Lincoln's than Buchanan's had been to Fremont's four years earlier. Douglas did not just endorse a homestead act, a Pacific railroad, and federal support for internal improvements, all policies that were championed by the Republicans, he claimed, not entirely implausibly, to have invented them all.[79] In 1860, Douglas Democrats, freed of their Southern wing, like Lincolnites, ran against the Slave Power (a phrase that had, after all, genuine Democratic origins). Northern Democrats indignantly warned that if the consequence of Southerners' bolting was Lincoln's election, they should no longer expect any support from Northern Democrats in returning "a 'fugitive' which they have not a dollars interest in." Douglas newspapers used the terms "slaveocracy" and "Slave Power," coinages associated with the Republicans, to describe Breckinridge, almost as much as they used the term "Black Republican" to smear Lincoln.[80]

Republicans certainly understood the danger of Douglasites stealing their best lines. "It is a notorious fact that the friends of Judge Douglas in the Northern States, solicit the vote of the people on the ground that he has done more for the freedom of the Territories, and that he is a truer champion of free labor, and besides a greater statesman, than any living individual," complained Carl Schurz, a veteran of the 1848 revolutions who had become a leader of the Republican Party in the West.[81] Yet their very similarity in some respects to the Republican alternative left Douglas Democrats with a problem of differentiation. The case for the Republicans in 1860 was that if, as a Northerner, one wanted to defend free institutions, why vote for Douglas who was compromised by his association with the national Democratic Party and who probably couldn't win anyway, when one could vote for Lincoln, whose anti–Slave Power credentials ran much deeper?

What Douglas supporters tried to do was to tell a story about their candidate as the only true nationalist, the one man who could save the Union against "fanaticism" in the North as well as the South. Douglas, simply because he was a Democrat, was (as Democrats, in their minds, had always been) a truer embodiment of the values of the ordinary white man than any candidate who represented, as Lincoln did, merely the latest manifestation of the Federalist-Whig "aristocratic" tradition. It was Douglas, not Lincoln, who could stand up to Southern disunionists, just as he could stand up—as Lincoln palpably could not—to Northern disunionists. Democrats too had the appeal of a popular candidate who had made his own way in the West. And they had the heritage of a Jacksonian tradition. They had always been the party of the ordinary white man, the enemy of "monopolists" and "aristocrats." The Douglas campaign was at least as enthusiastic as the Lincoln campaign in trying to profit from the anti-incumbent mood of the electorate through excoriating and often very personal attacks on Buchanan's administration. Douglas newspapers raked over the evidence of Republican support for John Brown's raid; they stressed the irresponsibility of talking about an "irrepressible conflict" (in Seward's phrase) as if no peaceful outcome were possible. If Douglas became president, they argued, compromise and peace could be secured. Douglas's success was "the only thing which can give peace and repose to this great Confederacy" wrote a Democrat from the predominantly Republican city of Pittsburgh.[82] The hope was that if the election was thrown to the House, Douglas could somehow attract enough upper South support to be selected as president on the basis of a popular sovereignty solution to slavery expansion. The national nightmare would be over.

Partly for this reason, Douglas never ceased trying to build support in the South, however hopeless his cause seemed. And the Douglas campaign trod a fine line between acknowledging the threat of the Slave Power while at the same time downplaying the "irrepressible conflict." They stressed the "common sense . . . conservatism" of the "masses" who did *not* see an inevitable show-down, who did *not* accept that a House divided, as the United States had always been, would fall unless it became all one thing or all another. As they had done for several years, Democrats wanted to separate the moral discussion of slavery's justice or injustice from statesmanship. Their popular sovereignty or doctrine of nonintervention—devolving decision-making about slavery to the lowest practical level—should remove the issue from national politics. Popular sovereignty was not some cobbled-together stitch-up, claimed Douglas supporters, but the embodiment of grand principles, of "the progressive principle of the age." Was nonintervention not what Kossuth had been fighting for in Hungary when "bloody Austria and Imperial Russia did intervene and the rising principle of Popular Sovereignty was there put down at the point of the bayonet"? The "interventionists of 1860"—the Republicans who wanted to "arbitrarily" declare all territory free, and the Breckinridge supporters who wanted to "arbitrarily" declare it slave—were the modern-day equivalent of the interventionists of the Revolution who wanted to interfere with the local right of self-government of American colonists. Tories "prated about the Divine rights of kings . . . and talked about 'rebel Americans' just as King James the First [Buchanan] and his tools now talk about the 'Rebel Douglas' and his Popular Sovereignty."[83]

Douglas saw himself as the only champion of moderation, the middle way between the extremes, the standard bearer of "the only political organization that is conservative and powerful enough to save the country from abolitionism and disunion." Trying to build links with Constitutional Unionists—with some success in Pennsylvania, Ohio, and New York—the campaign argued that Douglas's policy of nonintervention was the only practicable solution to the crisis: "The ultra men in each section demand congressional intervention upon the subject in the territories. They agree in respect to the power this duty of the Federal Government to control the question and differ only as to the mode of power. The one demands the intervention of Federal Government for slavery, and the other against it—Each appeals to the passions and prejudices of his section against the peace and harmony the whole country. . . . On the other hand the position of all conservative and Union loving men is, or ought to be that of non-intervention of Congress with slavery in the territories."[84]

DEMOCRATS PLEADED WITH VOTERS to see Republicans as hypocrites who were stirring up anxiety about the threat to white men's freedoms in the North, while running corrupt state governments where they were in charge. The slavery issue was one great smoke screen, charged one Douglas-supporting pamphleteer.[85] One correspondent of Stephen Douglas's claimed that only Democrats wanted a free Kansas because they really cared about the opportunities for white settlers; the "Abolition party" was "plotting to sell public land" for their own gain, he claimed.[86] "Popular sovereignty," to Douglas Democrats, was emphatically not, as their opponents (and some later historians) charged, a shallow fig leaf for a policy that benefitted the South. It was embraced as a doctrine that was in the spirit of the Jacksonian tradition, notwithstanding the practical, legal, and moral problems that had been exposed since 1854. Douglas, like Lincoln, was presented as the defender of Northern free-labor values, with "popular sovereignty," an idea rooted in the American tradition, as the guarantor of that promise. Douglas alone, the campaign asserted, would not only save the Union (in contrast to the "recklessness" of Lincoln and the "disunionist bolter" Breckinridge), but would also transform the opportunities available to white Northerners.

Douglas and Lincoln differed on an important point of historical interpretation, one with profound philosophical implications for the nature of the Republic. Did the Declaration of Independence have any relevance to the question of slavery? For Douglas, the Declaration was a practical document calling for self-government and thus provided a historical basis for popular sovereignty. For Lincoln, this was a pitifully limited vision. "When the white man governs himself, that is self-government," said Lincoln, "but when he governs himself and also governs another man, that is more than self-government—that is despotism." For Lincoln, banning slavery in the territories was not a violation of Southern whites' rights, but an acknowledgement of the universality of man's natural rights, at the very least the right to the fruits of one's own labor. For Douglas, this was the wrong language to use: since black people had no inherent right to inclusion in the polity of those who were entitled to self-government there was no philosophical problem with a vote among white people to enslave them (so long as that vote was free and fair). Since black people were usually excluded from citizenship as it was normally understood, Douglas struggled to acknowledge that they had any natural rights that could be separated from political rights.

Douglas was far from alone in seeing the Declaration in this limited way. The historian Don Fehrenbacher has shown that after 1820 the vast majority of Americans in the North as well as the South subscribed to the interpretation that the Declaration of Independence did not proclaim universal human rights "but rather applied to whites alone."[87] However, while this important point of principle separated the candidates in the Lincoln-Douglas debates, it does not follow that it was a meaningful philosophical cleavage among the broader electorate. In practice, the distinction between natural and political rights could be blurred, and the day-to-day campaigning of Republicans and Democrats very rarely addressed the implications of the Declaration. At the Republican Convention in Chicago there was even a battle over whether to include a plank endorsing the Declaration of Independence at all. The editor and Republican politico Horace Greeley, who was blamed by some for trying to scupper the pro-Declaration plank, was upfront that his motivation was blurring party lines. The path to victory for the Republicans, he thought, lay in embracing the lowest common denominator consensus in Northern society. Greeley explained that when he arrived at the Republican convention in Chicago he initially supported the Missourian Edward Bates for the nomination, on the grounds that he was "born in Virginia, a lifelong slaveholder, in politics a Whig, [and] was thoroughly conservative." He then recalled a conversation with a Seward backer, who thought the New York senator was the right choice because he represented the party's "most advanced convictions."

> "My friend," I inquired, "suppose each Republican voter in our State were to receive, to-morrow, a letter, advising him that he (the said voter) had just lost his brother, for some years settled in the South, who had left him a plantation and half a dozen slaves—how many of the two hundred and fifty thousand would, in response, declare and set those slaves free?"
>
> "I don't think I could stand that test myself!" was his prompt rejoinder.
>
> "Then," I resumed, "it is not yet time to nominate as you propose."[88]

People in the middle ground of Northern public opinion, some of whom ended up voting for Lincoln, as well as many who voted for Douglas and a few who voted for Bell, oscillated among a number of overlapping impulses: indignation at the behavior of the slaveholders; a genuine dislike of slavery on principle but also a deeply ingrained feeling that it was an intractable problem; a high moral disgust at the political corruption that seemed to flow both from slaveholders' selfishness and the demagoguery of abolitionist agitators; and deep fear about political destabilization, violence, and turmoil that would follow if disunion came.

In an article discussing the public spat between Owen and Joseph Lovejoy, a Wisconsin Democratic newspaper encapsulated some of the tensions that flowed from these conflicting emotions. On the one hand "the theory of the abolitionist is right": slavery was both immoral and unwise. It "has been a curse to every state which has adopted it among its institutions; it has depressed industry and enterprise and demoralized the public mind." But on the other hand, the premise of the abolitionist—that black people are equal to whites—was false. And so, while ideally slavery would disappear, the danger was that in practical terms emancipation would simply result "in making dependents and vagabonds of the millions of slaves now at least secure in the means of subsistence."[89] The editor of this paper went on to support Douglas. But a strikingly similar argument was made by Sidney George Fisher. On the one hand, he argued that slaves could not be considered as property in a legal sense ("it was a domestic relation only"), was indignant about the attempts to subvert the government by slaveholders, and thought *Uncle Tom's Cabin* a "true" (if badly written) book; yet on the other hand, he mused about how much better off were enslaved Africans in America ("far superior, intellectually & morally") than they were "in Africa in freedom."[90]

The categories of proslavery and antislavery barely allow for such ambiguities. In one sense, Douglasites and Lincolnites were all antislavery since they opposed slavery in their own society as an institution that would be harmful to them as well as distasteful and contrary to the spirit of republican institutions. But most in both parties were also unwilling to follow the idea that slavery was wrong to its logical end. The search for ideological or philosophical consistency in people who lived in the past is as Quixotic a quest as it is in ourselves.

The most striking differences between Lincoln and Douglas supporters were over their understanding of whether the conflict between the sections was truly "irrepressible." But even here the difference was more one of emphasis. The hope that somehow the old politics could still work pushed some old Whigs to support Douglas. Republicans were much more likely to see the election as a thinly veiled struggle for supremacy between North and South in which there could be only one victor. Republicans wanted to resolve the sectional crisis by peacefully asserting the control of the nonslaveholding majority over the direction of the Union. Consequently, and notwithstanding the creeping acceptance of popular sovereignty as a pragmatic solution by some Republicans, Lincoln supporters were far likelier than Douglasites to emphasize the importance of the free states—in other words, the large majority of the country—using their power in an unambiguous way to prevent the federalization (or nationalization) of slavery. Not, of course, to attack slavery where law, custom, and the Constitution made it seemingly impregnable, but to put it back where Republicans claimed the Founders had placed it. On this issue there could be no compromise, for Republicans. Committed to popular sovereignty, Douglasites wanted the federal government to keep out of the business of making rules on slavery one way or the other. Like Constitutional Unionists, Democrats were far more likely to acknowledge the legitimate concerns of Southern slaveholders about the protecting their property, up to a point. But Democrats also hoped congressional noninterference with its corollary of trusting settlers to make a decision about whether to protect human property would deliver much the same practical barriers to slavery's expansion without the confrontation of the Republicans' absolutist position. Democrats, in the main, did not like the confrontational language of an "irrepressible" conflict and they blamed Northern "fanatics" for needlessly provoking the South. Notwithstanding their own party's sectional fracture, they continued to believe that the Democracy was the only party of the Union and its success essential to avoiding disunion.

Although he could not, in the end, bring himself to vote for Lincoln, Fisher in effect made the conservative case for the Republicans—they were more likely to retain the character of the Union as bequeathed by the Founders, a stable, half-slave and half-free republic in which slavery remained a local exception, sanctioned as a domestic relation, to the general law and spirit of freedom. Fisher understood, as most Douglasites did not, that the insecurity of maintaining a slave system in the South forced slaveholders to make impossible demands of the free states, which by 1860 had led to a state of crisis. Slavery was first and foremost a claim about the nature of property; its security relied not just on legal protection but also on a consensus within the polity about the legitimacy of that property. Conscious of this, Southerners were forced by "fatal necessity" to demand from the North not just "toleration of slavery"—difficult enough in itself—but a "hearty approbation," which they would never get. Yet what could they do? Disunion might seem to solve their problems, but since "the North says that separation is treason and you shall not go, the result will be civil war and the first gun fired in such a war would sound the knell of slavery."[91]

The abolitionist Romantic poet James Russell Lowell, writing in the magazine he edited, made one of the most insightful of the many analyses of the sectional crisis published in the winter of 1860–61. There was literally nothing that could be done by the North to atone in the eyes of the South at this point, Lowell argued. The offense of the free states was that they were free with "the habits and possessions of freedom" and that in the preceding two decades they had been growing exponentially in number: "their crime is the census of 1860."[92] The census of 1860 showed that 63 percent of the population of the United States lived in the North, up from 55 percent ten years earlier. There were 20 million people in the free states in 1860, in comparison to 11.5 million in the slave states, of whom about 4 million were slaves. Since 1850 the total population of the country had increased by more than a third, but the North was growing much faster than the South. There was no reason to believe the trend would be reversed. The rapidly diminishing relative size of the South did not affect the prosperity of the cotton economy, which was booming—in seeming contrast to the recession-hit free states after the crash of 1857. Nor did it affect their ability to control their own affairs within the Republic's decentralized federal system. But it did mean that the character—legal, moral, and political—of the nation as a whole was harder to steer in the direction that slaveholders wanted. And that was the rub.

One Pennsylvania Democrat feared the Black Republicans would "entrap and carry the men who are national in sentiment but opposed to us."[93] Whether it was entrapment or not, the Republicans did successfully neutralize their perception of radicalism sufficiently to be able to win in the free states they needed to gain an Electoral College majority. In the free states, Douglas won nearly 1.4 million votes (a figure that includes the support for the fusion ticket in Pennsylvania, some of which would otherwise have gone to Breckinridge). It was not enough. Lincoln polled over 1.8 million, a majority in the free states, although less than 40 percent of the nationwide popular vote. Lincoln's victory in Indiana and Illinois was by the slimmest of margins, but his win in the crucial state of Pennsylvania was, in the end, comfortable. In a state where Frémont had polled 32 percent of the vote, Lincoln polled 56 percent.[94] It is not known whether one of those voters was the elderly William Dock, bravely defying his sons' orders.

Including an estimate of his share of the vote where there were fusion tickets, Douglas probably had the support of about 41 percent of the free state vote, which was a little more than Buchanan had won in the North four years earlier.[95] Douglasites mostly shared the opposition of their Republican neighbors to Southern aggression, and had shared their vision of a white republic expanding, prosperous, and free—even if they had disagreed over how to deal with the demands of the South. It remained to be seen how this sizable minority would respond to the raging storms that were about to hit the Union.

CHAPTER SIX

The Essence of Anarchy

Secession and the War against Slaveholders

Having virtually imprisoned his aging father to prevent him from endorsing the Black Republicans, George Dock, the Harrisburg doctor and committed lifelong Democrat, thought the nation was descending into madness. In the weeks following Lincoln's election, first South Carolina and then six other Deep South slave states seceded and formed a southern Confederacy while rumors swirled of slave uprisings and of arms being stockpiled in anticipation of civil war.[1] Dock anxiously watched the "political barometer of our nation, as its heavy mercurial columns had been heaving and vibrating under the wild perturbations and stormy convulsions that have been rocking our noble ship with their fearful surges."[2] The Union had never been lashed by storms so severe.

The conventional wisdom among Democrats, echoing the spirit of Jefferson, was that the larger the Republic, the safer liberty would be. A big country was harder to corrupt than a small one, went the logic. And those who had remained loyal to the Democracy still believed, as they had always done, that their party represented "the only hope for the Union."[3] The South should have stayed to fight abolitionist "heresies" from "*inside* of the Union," wrote an Indiana Democrat. That they had chosen to secede in response to an election— even one that had seen a "fanatical Black Republican" elected—meant they had "[forsaken] the maxims of Jefferson."[4]

Democrats' bewilderment that "our Southern friends" were in effect cooperating with Black Republicans to dismember the Union was accompanied by indignation.[5] Theo Williams, an old Illinois crony of Stephen Douglas, fumed that the Southern wing of the party had "proved themselves as much a sectional party as the Abolition Republican Party." The treason was first evident, Williams thought, when the Southern wing of the party reneged on the "common policy" of "non-intervention in the Territories" and demanded a federal slave code that they knew would "never, never" be acceptable to Northern Democrats: by giving up on the unity of the national party, they gave up on the Union.[6]

In those first weeks after Lincoln's election, Democrats often tended to pathologize the "fanaticism" on both sides.[7] As Victor Piollet of Pennsylvania put it, conservative men like him were surrounded, all of a sudden, by "insanity."[8] Anticipating the "blundering generation" thesis of the 1930s revisionist historians, the "insanity" analysis was often accompanied by resentment at the manipulation of these feelings by unscrupulous politicians. The Kentuckian Robert Anderson, a staunch Democrat and a major in the U.S. Army who was soon to find himself at the epicenter of the storm as the commander of Union forces at Fort Sumter, wrote sadly in early March 1861 that "dishonesty and bad faith" had "tainted the moral atmosphere of portions of our land. And alas how many have been prostrated by its blast."[9]

By reaching for the "insanity" explanation, these lifelong Jacksonians revealed their imaginative failure to understand how quickly politics had changed. Typical were the Bigler brothers—William and John—who had come of age in the 1830s when they set up a Jacksonian newspaper in Bellefonte, Pennsylvania. Their generation's unique destiny, it seemed to the young Bigler brothers, was to live through a golden era of national expansion, as autocrats and lesser races were cowed by the onward advance of American democracy. By the 1850s, both had risen to prominence in the Democratic Party of their hero Jackson. William became governor and then a U.S. senator from Pennsylvania, while John became governor of California in 1852 (the Biglers are the only brothers to have served simultaneously as state governors in U.S. history). In his inaugural address, John Bigler attacked abolitionists as "fanatical propagandists of mere moral tenets," a phrase that captures very well his inability to understand the forces driving politics.[10] For the Biglers, the rise of fanaticism was an incomprehensible disruption of the steady progress of national freedom they had anticipated. And an unforgivable one because it threatened all that the Founders had achieved and dismayed the "lovers of freedom throughout the world."[11]

The Biglers—and George Dock—were in a minority among Northerners in their complete tone-deafness to slavery as a political issue, but they were far from unusual in their anxieties about security and political stability. Secession exposed the tension in antebellum political culture between confidence that popular government was the wave of the future and the anxiety that it was inherently fragile. Private and public writing from the early months of 1861 reveals many Northerners shocked by the apparent discovery that their Republic was far from immune to the revolutionary instability they had seen all around them, especially since 1848. Their fears were expressed especially well by R. J. De Cordova, a West Indian businessman who had come to New York in 1849 and who, after losing most of his fortune in the 1857 crash, became an immensely successful lecturer and writer of humorous verse. After

Lincoln's election, De Cordova toured the country, packing large halls with paying audiences who listened to him say that the crisis they were facing was far from unique. "Trouble besets us on every side," De Cordova told them, asking his audience to cast their eyes toward the rest of the world. "In Italy a great war is concluding, only to make way apparently for a yet greater war afterward to take its place. Austria, crumbling to pieces, is brimming over with the waters of trouble. Turkey, even weaker and if possible more pitiable than Austria, seems bent on preparing for herself the deathbed on which civilization is preparing to lay her. In the vast empire of China, there is war. In Peru, war is threatening." And above all, De Cordova warned of the threat of "Mexicanization"—the prospect that the United States despite what he said was its greater racial "purity" and lack of "idolatrous" Catholic priests, may yet succumb, as had its neighbor, to "the worst of all wars, the maddest and most insane of all the sinful follies of which civilized men can be capable . . . Civil War." Still claiming to be optimistic about the possibility of a compromise solution to the sectional crisis, De Cordova urged his listeners not to assume that their Republic was so different from Mexico, a country which, he said, like the United States, had set out to demonstrate to the world "the capacity of a free people for self-government." In recent years, in both countries, different sections and communities had behaved in a "selfish and overbearing" way, "extreme opinions" had crowded out moderation, "violent orators" had stirred up "the already heated passions of excited men," there was widespread "disobedience of constituted authority" as men rioted in the streets. To avoid the fate of Mexico or Italy, and to fulfill their destiny to "bring together the nations of the earth," Americans must not "admit among us the family quarrel which will be the opening wedge for our destruction as a nation." In a fiery peroration that, according to observers, moved his audiences to tears, De Cordova concluded, "Let each man then speak and write to his neighbor: 'Peace, Peace!' "[12] De Cordova's lecture struck a chord with his audiences because it tapped into deep anxieties about the fragility of social order and republican freedom. What was less clear was what might be done about it.

The Dilemma of Disunion, the Dilemma of Coercion

In his inability to send out a clear message about how the federal government would, or could, respond to secession, President Buchanan was hardly alone. William Prentiss, one of the political lieutenants of the Douglas-supporting congressman Samuel S. Cox, described the Democratic Party of Ohio in early January as "paralyzed." Prentiss assured Cox that "the democracy of your district" is "without exception in favor of the preservation of the Union" but Democrats were "also almost as unanimous in their opinion that coercion is not only impolitic but suicidal." Suicidal, that is, to the nature of republican government since those rebellious states may be defeated in battle but they "will not stay whipped, and it will require an army of three or four hundred thousand men to keep them in subjugation."[13] A similar report came from the township of Wysox, Pennsylvania, a Douglas Democratic holdout in an otherwise Republican county in the anthracite coal-mining district of the upper Susquehanna River valley. "The masses of our people," wrote Victor Piollet, a local Democratic leader, "want all differences that now exist in all quarters of the Union compromised, settled and put out of the way."[14] To a man, wrote Piollet, Democrats in his district regarded secession as treason but also blamed Republicans for having provoked the South and were totally opposed to an "Abolition war" to suppress it.

In this ultimate crisis of national integrity, Democrats were outraged by the perception that Republicans were sticking to their "fanatical" commitment to oppose all slavery extension under any circumstances.[15] True, Lincoln had just won an election on this platform, but in circumstances Democrats saw as conveying a limited mandate. The election had seen the triumph of a "well compacted minority," as one Massachusetts newspaper put it, not inaccurately. In the Jacksonian tradition a majority was the arbiter of political legitimacy, and that the Republicans did not have.[16] In the light of the victorious party's refusal to compromise on their commitment to prevent slavery's westward expansion, responsibility for the crisis, wrote one Ohioan, clearly lay with the "traitorous Republican party."[17] The overwhelming lesson that must be drawn from the "present state of political affairs," thought Isaac Mayer Wise, the Douglas-backing editor of a Jewish newspaper in Ohio, was "that radicalism will not do in any province of human activity. There are no leaps in history. Like nature, history also follows its laws, and every thing develops itself slowly, regularly and certain."[18] The warring factions of the Democracy were united in their horror at Lincoln's election and the prospect of an aggressive war against the South that would surely destroy the Republic forever. "It will be useless to attempt any coercive measures," wrote the editor of a Hartford, Connecticut newspaper that had supported Breckinridge in the election. "We can never force sovereign States to remain in the Union when they desire to go out, without bringing upon our country the shocking evils of civil war."[19]

The fear that coercion would be, to put it mildly, counterproductive was by no means confined to Democrats. There were many old Whigs, with their long-entrenched horror of anything that smacked of radicalism, who regarded the breakup of the Union as a disaster but who thought war, with its attendant horrors and tendency to escalation, was even worse. Sidney George Fisher, for example, earnestly advocated recognition of secession rather than war. "Let us . . . open the door wide to our southern friends," he wrote in the *North American* on New Year's Eve 1860, "and say to them 'depart in peace, we will not detain you against your will.' "[20] Similar sentiments were expressed at a series of Union meetings called "without regard to party" and claiming to represent all "conservative citizens," which consciously echoed the similar gatherings held after the Harpers Ferry raid a year earlier.[21] In Philadelphia on January 16, the keynote speaker, Charles Macalester, a seventy-one-year-old Whig merchant, told the audience "the South should have remained loyal to the Union and fought the battle of the Union in the Union." However, since "they seem determined to go, let them go in peace, and let us say in a spirit of kindness and fraternal love, 'Let there be no strife between us, for we be brethren.' " Perhaps if the free states would for once simply "resolve to mind their own business . . . there will be no fighting to do."[22]

The problem was that in these early months of 1861 "coercion" was imagined as raising an army in the North that would be sent down to invade the rebel states and force them to submit literally at the point of a bayonet. Opponents of coercion expressed optimism in the power of reason to prevail in the end if forbearance was shown on all sides combined with the pessimistic calculation that the horrors of war were worse than the sadness of disunion. Perhaps if the North resisted coercion, the South—even now—would come to its senses and secession would be but a temporary breach.

It was not just Democrats who worried that a military reaction would be counterproductive. In the aftermath of Lincoln's election, Horace Greeley's *New York Tribune* published a leading article that made a reasoned case against disunion as a solution to any problem, urging the South to calm down and learn the discipline of electoral defeat (as, Greeley pointed out, he had been forced to do many times in the past). The *Tribune* conceded that "the right to secede may be a revolutionary one, but it exists nevertheless; and we do not see how one party can have a right to do what another party has a right to prevent." The difficulty, though, was that "the measures now being inaugurated in the Cotton States" with a view to secession were "destitute of the gravity and legitimate force" that such a momentous decision required. So while Greeley's paper hoped never to live in a republic "whereof one section is pinned to the residue by bayonets," it remained hopeful that the "passion" of the South could be "confronted with calmness, with dignity, and with unwavering trust in the inherent strength of the Union."[23]

But if coercion seemed impossible and secession was a cataclysm, what—beyond hope in calmness and common sense prevailing—could be done? Democrats, and many others too, could only pray that even at this late hour, the "conservative mind of the North" as one put it, could be brought to bear and resolve the differences with the "patriotic"—in other words, not fanatical—"men of the South."[24] This was certainly George Dock's view. Unable to see in the growing crisis over slavery and the Slave Power anything other than the raging of "fanaticism," the Pennsylvania Democrat invested his hope for a safe passage for the Union in the conservative masses. Indulging in his fondness for elaborate nautical metaphor, Dock thought that with "our vessel . . . tossing about, groaning and writhing . . . until she is foundering in distress" the only answer was to "call for the aid and opinions of the mighty and honest crew of *common sailors*, whose unselfish interestedness and innate love of their glorious vessel . . . *can* and *will* rescue her from being dashed upon the reefs which are now already, grating her very bow and threatening her with a fatal wreck!"[25]

Some Douglas Democrats, reflecting on the last few tumultuous years, began to regret their support for the Kansas-Nebraska Act. "The repeal of that [Missouri] Compromise ruined our party," wrote one, but perhaps even now "if we propose to reinstate it" the impending disaster of disunion could be averted. If the Republican Party opposed the restoration (on the grounds that it didn't go far enough toward their aim of ruling out all slavery extension), it might even provide the basis for a reverse of the Republican political tide, one ever-optimistic Democrat speculated. The Democrats may then "beat them [the Republicans] to death in the next elections!"[26] Democrats who had left the party after the repeal of the Missouri Compromise felt vindicated by events, and some now joined the chorus of their old partisans in calling for its reinstatement. Even most of those Northern Democrats who had supported not just the Nebraska bill but Lecompton as well now rushed to support the proposal to reinstate a federally enforced dividing line between slavery and freedom in the territories. A correspondent of Senator William Bigler insisted that "anyone with a claim to be considered conservative" should support such a move.[27]

Northern Democrats, drawing on the antimoralism of the Jacksonian tradition, retained a view of politics as a transactional business in which differences could be compromised if only excess emotion and piety were put aside. It was sheer hypocrisy of the "political parsons" and "crazed" abolitionists of the so-called Black Republican Party to suggest that they operated according to a higher morality than everyone else, Democrats told each other. As Isaac Mayer Wise put it, "politics in this country means money, material interests, and no more." The conflagration in Kansas that had caused so much trouble, for example, was, Wise argued, simply a clash of material interests. Striped of all "hypocrisy" and "exalted," "holy," or "lofty" rhetoric, the matter was deadly simple: "slaveholders favor the extension of slavery because it increases their wealth, and land speculators oppose it, because they find their present account by it."[28] If that were the case, common sense would suggest that compromise was possible.

Compromise was the quest of the old ex-Whig Kentuckian, Senator John Crittenden. In a series of resolutions and proposed constitutional amendments, Crittenden offered the restoration of the Missouri Compromise as the most tangible of a series of proposals, which—in the style of Henry Clay—he hoped would be the basis of another grand sectional compromise. Plenty of people wished Crittenden well. "I have not met a single Republican that did not endorse" the Crittenden proposals, reported one Democrat-turned-Republican from Pennsylvania, after a visit to Indiana and Illinois.[29] But the Dred Scott decision had changed the rules of the game. Following Roger Taney's legal reasoning, such as it was, the South now staked everything on a demand that property in human beings be treated as legitimately as property in real estate or livestock. Reviving the Missouri Compromise simply wouldn't cut it anymore.

Democrats, like all Americans, were defenders of the right of revolution, at least in theory. A few conceded that Southerners had the same right to leave the Union as the thirteen colonies had to exit the British Empire. But the consequences of revolution were also clear, explained Edmund Burke, the Democratic congressman from New Hampshire who tried hard to live up to the maxims of his famous namesake. Ten years earlier, in a long discussion of the history of popular uprisings, Burke had insisted that revolution could never be "a peaceable remedy." It was, he argued, "one of force, and in defiance of constitutions and governments." As "the last resort of an injured people" a revolution could never be something entered into lightly: it was "an act of war." And of course Democrats, like all Americans, had spent decades celebrating their own revolution as the forge out of which had come the liberties of an "unfettered," "unterrified," people, bound by the "covenant" of their Constitution the "sheet anchor" of their liberties.[30] It was one thing to stage a revolution against Austrian or British tyranny, but however much they disliked antislavery fanaticism, it was palpably not the case that Southerners met the high bar that Burke had set. The recent European revolutions, and the political instability in Mexico right on their doorstep, had, moreover, induced a deep anxiety about the uncontrollable consequences of the resort to arms.

The doctrine of the right of revolution, then, was not tantamount to having the right to break up a republic. And so, while nervous about whether coercion would work, there was also a parallel discourse that provided the basis for legitimizing the use of force by the United States in the right circumstances. "I am not one of those who believe that a collision or loss of life is an end of our government of liberty," wrote an Illinois Democrat to Douglas.[31] "A peaceable division of this Union is not admissible," fumed another. The precedent of peaceful secession would be fatal to the Republic, since "other states may do so too with out any fear of consequences" and in that event "our Government would be only a Government of form but destitute of power." The result would be a vulnerability to foreign invasion. Europeans would say the "republican bubble has burst at last."[32]

Trapped between utter horror at the prospect of coercion and even greater horror at the prospect of disunion, there were Northern Democrats who concluded that force would have to be used. "If the South expect aid or comfort from the Democracy of Ohio in disrupting the Union," insisted Douglas supporter John McCook from Steubenville, "they are mistaken, and the sooner they know the fact the better. Within the Union we will be found maintaining their Constitutional rights, but without the Union, we owe them no allegiance." A few Douglas Democrats immediately recognized that secession meant the end of the decades-long effort to conciliate slaveholders. "If the Union is ever despoiled," wrote McCook, in what was surely a conscious echo of Lincoln and a harbinger of the direction of Northern politics in the coming two years, "we become all free or all slave."[33]

Not many Democrats in the early weeks of the secession crisis talked about a clash between slavery and freedom in the stark terms that McCook did, but many others—including erstwhile Breckinridge supporters—urged a show of force from the lame-duck Buchanan, even if only because, they hoped, it would preempt the need for all-out coercion. One Pennsylvanian Breckinridge supporter named Hamilton, who had previously expressed proslavery sentiments, wrote to Senator Bigler urging him to tell the president to hold Fort Sumter and reinforce it with "every sloop or war vessel" available. A Democratic president must ensure that the American flag was respected or the values of the party would seem to be mere "humbug." Andrew Jackson had threatened to send troops to South Carolina during the nullification crisis in 1832, and now Buchanan must do the same to protect Fort Sumter. Otherwise, Hamilton prophesied, Lincoln would become the most popular president ever if he does it and Buchanan had not. "I hope and trust you will yield every thing to [the] South—vote for everything—even to making it treason to abolish slavery in the states which now have it if they so demand, but if a foot of our common property is molested fight for it, & let it be known far and wide that this is your opinion."[34]

So coercion—if that meant a full-scale armed invasion of the slave states—was one thing, but "manly" resistance to secession was, implicitly, something slightly different. Republican and Democratic newspapers alike argued that secession and then the firing on Fort Sumter were an assault on the legitimacy of democratic institutions, and that to "surrender" in the face of it would amount to "the suicide of government."[35] Through all the years that the expansion of slavery and the increasing influence of slaveholders had been the dominant question in Northern politics, politicians had competed to define their position as conservative. In the secession winter, increasing numbers of Northerners from different political backgrounds felt that conservatism now required resistance to the dismemberment of the nation; the question was what form that should take and how it would be justified. As the secession movement gathered momentum, and especially after a Confederate government was formed, some of those who had formerly opposed what they called "coercion" began to harden their attitude toward the seceded states. The widespread and not inaccurate perception that Southerners were not seriously engaging with Crittenden's compromise proposals only intensified this feeling.[36]

The spirit of President Jackson standing up to the South Carolina nullifiers was one frequently cited precedent; another was the decades-long Northern experience with confronting rioters.[37] The comparison of secession with a riot was not wholly convincing, as the *New York Herald* pointed out in February 1861. This was not the "Astor Place Riot all over again" in which the "firing of a few volleys" would dissolve the crowd. "If the movement in the South is a riot, it is the most important one in the history of the world."[38] Yet the Astor Place Riot was exactly what was cited by others as an example of how the allegedly "judicious" use of force could exercise a "salutary" influence. This was especially the case where secessionist sentiment was expressed in states that had not yet formally seceded. The New York *Commercial Advertiser*, in commenting on the efforts of the Unionist forces in Missouri to combat secessionism, thought the Astor Place Riot was an excellent model. Although "many of the killed [were] innocent spectators"—the unfortunate collateral damage to be expected—the use of force by the authorities in the name of freedom exercised "a most wholesome influence for years afterward in quelling the mobocratic spirit." Surely the same applied to the South? Would not a "baptism of fire and blood ... prove equally beneficial among the rabble who have wrought so much mischief" in the slave states?[39] The mayor who had called in the militia to deal with the Astor Place rioters, Caleb Woodhull, made this connection himself, arguing in March 1861 that time had vindicated his decision of twelve years before.[40] The Reverend Henry W. Bellows, one of Woodhull's staunchest defenders in May 1849, now told his friends and his congregation that "some *fighting* must be done, if necessary, for the preservation the National Integrity."[41] Even "if it strikes some thousands dead," Bellows wrote, the question of whether the Union should survive "must be decisively and affirmatively answered."[42]

The willingness to use violence was framed as a defense of values that otherwise would be destroyed. Cyrus Bartol, a Unitarian minister and friend of Henry Bellows, wrote: "War is bad, Civil War the worst war, but there are things worse than war. Treason is worse. Public plunder is worse. National disgrace is worse. The loss of national consciousness is worse."[43] The newly elected Republican governor of Connecticut, William Buckingham, described secession as "dangerous and revolutionary," while Walter Gresham, an old Whig from Indiana, had come reluctantly to the conclusion that "it is better to have war for one year than anarchy & revolution for fifty years—if the government should suffer rebels to go on with their work with impunity there would be no end to it & in a short time we would be without any law or order."[44] When secession was described as "Mexicanization"—in De Cordova's terms—or of "anarchy" it was not just because of fears about the integrity of the nation but of social order as well. Secession, Bellows feared, might precipitate "the whole chain of order into confusion and righteous chaos."[45]

This was precisely the case that Lincoln made in his inaugural speech on the front portico of the Capitol on Monday, March 4, 1861, a chilly spring day. The president-elect had entered, in traditional manner, arm in arm with his predecessor; Buchanan, wrote one observer, looked "pale, sad and nervous" while Lincoln was "slightly flushed, with compressed lips." Lincoln took a sheaf of papers from his jacket pocket and read a restrained, closely argued speech. Assuring the South that he had no intention of interfering with their property or rights, his key point was that the Constitution must and should be maintained, and that no right "plainly written in the Constitution" had ever been denied. But since "no organic law can ever be framed with a provision specifically applicable to every question which may occur in practical administration" a series of controversies had arisen over issues where the Constitution was ambiguous: "Shall fugitives from labor be surrendered by national or by State authority? The Constitution does not expressly say. May Congress prohibit slavery in the territories? The Constitution does not expressly say. Must

Congress protect slavery in the territories? The Constitution does not expressly say." In such circumstances, Lincoln said, there were two choices: either the minority or the majority must acquiesce. "There is no other alternative; for continuing the government, is acquiescence on one side or the other. If a minority, in such case, will secede rather than acquiesce, they make a precedent which, in turn, will divide and ruin them; for a minority of their own will secede from them, whenever a majority refuses to be controlled by such minority." Plainly, Lincoln said, "the central idea of secession, is the essence of anarchy." Since unanimity was impossible, and the rule of the minority on a permanent basis was intolerable, the basis of American republican government, Lincoln said, was that "a majority, held in restraint by constitutio-nal checks, and limitations, and always changing easily, with deliberate changes of popular opinions and sentiments, is the only true sovereign of a free people." Whoever would reject this notion of a restrained majority rule, conditioned by constant responsiveness to public sentiment, had no palatable alternatives: "anarchy, or despotism in some form, is all that is left."[46]

After Lincoln's speech, the hunched, crow-like figure of Chief Justice Taney administered the oath of office ("to protect, preserve, and defend" the Constitution of the United States). And among the first men to shake the new president's hand was his great Illinois rival, Senator Douglas, who had been overheard during the reading of the inaugural address muttering his approval ("Good!" "That's so" "No coercion" "Good again").[47]

By the time Lincoln was inaugurated the United States was in a twilight zone: seven slave states had declared their independence, congressmen from those states had left Washington, and Southern officers had resigned their commissions from the U.S. Army; but both the outgoing and the incoming federal administrations refused to acknowledge that the Union had dissolved. Many in the North continued to believe that secession was simply a bargaining position and that notwithstanding their new flag and provisional president, the Southern rebels could still be coaxed back into the Union fold. Hence, the path to preserving the Union remained unclear, as it had always been. It was one thing to speak of coercion in extremis, but how, and when, might such coercion be put into effect? Republican leaders had promised that by standing up to the South, the antislavery North could take control of the federal government without disunion resulting. That promise—always derided by their opponents, including Douglas Democrats—was now being tested to destruction.

Lincoln's core case that the minority must acquiesce if the system of free government were to survive suffered from a potentially important objection:

as a minority president, elected with only just over half of the Northern vote, and substantially less than half of the nationwide popular vote, his personal mandate gave him only a shaky claim to represent a clear majority. Hence Lincoln sought to describe the crisis in a way that Northern Democrats as well as Republicans would recognize. The only substantial dispute, Lincoln said, was that "one section of our country believes slavery is right, and ought to be extended, while the other believes it is wrong, and ought not to be extended." As a generalization this was fair. More importantly, though, Lincoln's careful framing of the conflict as a question of anarchy versus due process ensured that his address was, in the words of one fair observer, "generally regarded as high toned and conservative" even among Democrats in the North.[48]

Lincoln therefore did a good job of expressing a shared Northern position, but there was no masking the depth of the estrangement between the incoming administration and the South—not only the seven states that had already seceded, but the eight slave states which had not, including Virginia, the home of four of the Union's first five presidents. The atmosphere in Washington on March 4 was understandably tense, with an undertone of sublimated violence. The quasi-military "Wide Awakes"—companies of young men who had organized to demonstrate in favor of Lincoln in the election—were in evidence in the city's streets. The District of Columbia militia and thousands of badged policemen patrolled the area around the Capitol and the route of the procession to the White House. "While conservative people are in raptures over the Inaugural," observed the Washington correspondent of the *New York Times,* "it cannot be denied that many Southerners look upon it as a precursor of war." Earlier that morning, the new Secretary of State William Seward—the man who had wanted and expected to be the Republican presidential nominee—spoke to a crowd of well-wishers. He spoke of the wisdom of conciliation and taking the path of peace, but there was no mistaking the shadow of war that clearly lay on his mind when he urged the Northern people to "preserve the inestimable legacy of civil and religious liberty which they have received from their heroic fathers."[49]

In an almost unbelievable metaphor for the perilous state of the nation, the flag hoisted on top of the Capitol in the morning of the inauguration ripped in two when one of the supporting ropes gave way. "For a long while," reported an observer, "it could not be taken down, though finally an adventurous man climbed to the top of the staff, and tearing away the ill-omened standard, replaced it with an entire flag of the Union."[50]

Reflecting on the 1860 election campaign and its nerve-wracking aftermath from the other side of the precipice of war, it is striking how many

Democrats conceded, in retrospect, that they had been wrong. "Looking back to those days is like looking into a land of dreams," recalled John A. Dix many years later. "What broke the dream at once, and set me and others in my position face to face with facts never before understood, was the opening roar of the guns directed against Fort Sumter. With that portentous sound the old illusions passed forever and a new cycle came in."[51]

The Tensions of Unity

The Northern people wrought revolutionary change neither by accident nor prior intent but through what they saw as the logic of the situation in which they found themselves. And so it is difficult to overstate how important to Northern politics was the manner in which the first shot of the war was fired, in the darkness before dawn, on April 12, 1861, when a battery of more than four thousand guns and mortars opened fire on the federally held Fort Sumter in Charleston Harbor. The narrative developed in newspapers, sermons, and speeches in the following days was that the South had launched an unprovoked attack, and they had done so literally, as well as figuratively, on the American flag. The symbolism could not be starker.

The news from Charleston shocked Northerners who had become warily familiar with the nonmilitary political standoff between the self-declared independent Confederacy and the Union. In response, Lincoln called for troops to put down the armed rebellion against federal authority, and within days the geographical battle lines were drawn: four upper south states seceded, having been forced, as they saw it, to make a choice between cooperating with the armed coercion of their sister slave states or joining them in solidarity. Four more border slave states remained in the Union through a combination of force, heavy political persuasion, and a lack of strategic alternatives. Lincoln's call for troops to defend the flag was therefore the real moment when the war began. It was a clarifying moment. The question was no longer concession, or even the unprovoked resort to force when conciliation may still have worked; the question was starkly whether or not an armed assault on national authority should be resisted. And so this latest moment of choice was not one that many Northerners hesitated about, whatever feelings of foreboding many of them harbored.

Shock at the sudden violence was combined with a deep sense that there was something manly and ennobling about physical violence in pursuit of a moral goal—in this case liberty and Union. At last Americans had a taste of the thrilling nation-building romance that they imagined had driven Italians or Hungarians in their struggles for national liberation. As one New York woman put it, "The color is all taken out of the 'Italian Question.' Garibaldi indeed! 'Deliverer of Italy!' Every mother's son of us is a 'Deliverer.'"[52] Americans who had watched, rapt, as the peoples of Europe struggled to make nations that embodied the principles of liberty, now had the chance to make similar sacrifices for their nation. Elizabeth Cady Stanton told a friend, "This war is music in my ears. It is a simultaneous chorus for freedom; for every nation that has ever fought for liberty on her own soil is now represented in our army."[53]

Such language was a good deal too redolent of Jacobinism for most Northerners, but the circumstances of the first shot erased, at first, the tensions that otherwise would have been very visible behind any Northern military response to secession. Up until Sumter, the concept of coercion of the South had been imagined as an invasion of what were, after all, sovereign states. Now the mobilization of Northerners was imagined as a purely defensive reaction. It was no longer a military response to secession per se, but a military response to an assault on the flag: a subtle, but vital distinction. Even James Buchanan, now back in Wheatland, his pleasant federal-style mansion in Lancaster, Pennsylvania, was decisive in his support. "I hope that the Democratic party every where may adopt strong resolutions as you intend to do in Bucks County, in favor of a vigorous prosecution of the war to restore the Union," he wrote a party colleague. The man who had yearned for peace and compromise now declared, "To talk about peace and compromise, when we know that the Confederate States would accept of nothing less than a recognition of their independence is absurd. The Union must be restored and preserved if that be possible."[54] The sense of betrayal in Buchanan's words is palpable.

A sense of betrayal had been a theme of the politics of the preceding decade: at each political crisis from the imposition of the Fugitive Slave Act through the repeal of the Missouri Compromise to the Dred Scott decision and the Breckinridge Party's demands for a federal slave code, some Northerners felt themselves betrayed by the South. Now, even some of the staunchest defenders of the Southern position finally felt let down. Those who had worked hardest to be conciliatory in the past were among those who were now most indignant at the firing on the flag. Daniel S. Dickinson, for example, the leader of the New York "Hards" who had fought against antislavery politics for twenty years and supported Breckinridge in the presidential election gave fiery speeches denouncing the Southern traitors. Buchanan advised Bucks County Democrats that, as well as being the right thing to do, it was in their party's interest to pass resolutions supporting the war; and if even Buchanan felt betrayed by his erstwhile Southern colleagues, many Democrats felt far more strongly that they had no choice but to resort to arms in the face of a blatant attack on the flag. If the Democracy was the party of the Union and the Constitution, how could any other course be imaginable?

Beneath this consensus, however, there remained deep suspicion about the motives of the new administration, and the Democratic Party now faced a difficult struggle over how—or even whether—to maintain its identity in a war led by the Republicans. The impulse to maintain unity in the face of a common military enemy made partisan squabbles seem even more sordid and self-serving than had been the case in peacetime. In those first heady weeks after Sumter, politicians from all parties, expecting a short and decisive war, called for an abandonment of party politics. "Union meetings" were held on the model of the "indignation meetings" called in the wake of events like the assault on Charles Sumner, and like those earlier gatherings, they described themselves as being, in the words of one, as without any "taint of partisanship."[55] Stephen Douglas, his health broken after years of heavy drinking and overwork, died in June 1861 at the age of just forty-eight, but not before he exhorted his followers to abandon party fights for the duration of the conflict. As his biographer Robert W. Johannsen points out, for Douglas the question was not just Union or disunion but how to preserve order and stability. "Unite as a band of brothers," he told an audience at one of his final speeches, "and rescue your government . . . and your country from the enemy who have been the authors of your calamity." In the statehouse in Springfield, the venue at which Lincoln had warned of a house divided three years earlier, his voice weak and heavy with emotion, Douglas came close to acknowledging that he had been in error in making too many concessions to the Southerners who had now so spectacularly betrayed him, and their country. And to fellow Democrats he said this: "Do not allow the mortification growing out of defeat in a partisan struggle, and the elevation of a party to power that we firmly believed to be dangerous to the country—do not let that convert you from patriots to traitors to your native land. . . . Give me a country first, that my children may live in peace; then we will have a theatre for our party organizations to operate upon."[56] This was a clear answer to the many Democrats from across the North who had written to their leader for advice, such as Alfred Clapp, who confided that "many who profess to be Union men hesitate about boldly coming out against treason, fearing to be hereafter classed as Republicans" and who appealed to Douglas to "say to all of us who are your *friends, first, last & all the time*, to stand by our Government, and sink party for the present."[57]

A number of prominent Democratic leaders committed themselves to support the administration for the duration of the war. Douglas's old ally John McClernand argued that it was simply not possible to oppose the administration without also opposing the war "because there is no middle ground between loyalty and disloyalty" while former Breckinridge supporter Daniel Dickinson told a public meeting in 1862 that the war was "too great a question for party."[58] Elusive and shifting party labels make it hard to measure precisely how many ordinary Democratic voters similarly gave emphatic and enduring support to any candidate supporting the administration.[59] Yet, even as a tidal wave of antipartisan feeling swept across the free states in the spring and summer of 1861, there were plenty of Democrats who felt that, as the self-appointed defenders of popular government, they were needed now, more than ever, as the guardians of the people's liberty.[60] Democrats had always warned of the vulnerability of popular government, especially in time of war, and many were quick to see the threat coming from Washington as well as from secession. In June 1861 Joseph Ristine, a Democratic leader from Fountain County, Indiana, warned "an attempt will be made to place the whole country under military rule, that all the means of the government will be employed to arm the minions of the administration and to disarm all opponents." Tapping into deep-seated anxieties about Jacobins, Ristine feared "that an absolute reign of terror will be inaugurated, and when the means of resistance of the masses are removed a military despotism will rule until all state rights under the constitutional organization will be have been abolished and a monarchy absolute or limited established." There were many Northerners who harbored these anxieties, even among those who felt the nation had no choice but to respond to the firing on Sumter with military action. Perhaps a short conflict, they hoped, could avoid the assaults on liberty that a long war would bring. Anything else would, some Democrats feared, lead the United States into despotism. And as the carrier of the ideals of the Revolution (in its own self-conception), the Democracy would be on the firing line. "I look upon this war as much and more a war upon the democracy than anything else," Ristine told Congressman Daniel Voorhees.[61] To many, the battle against the Slave Power was the American version of the Italian struggle against Austrian autocracy. But the flip side of seeing the war in the light of European struggles was that so many Northerners were primed to see war as the handmaiden of despotism at home.

What made Democrats like Ristine feel especially paranoid were the calls to abandon Democratic Party organization. During 1861, Union parties were formed across the Northern states to fight local and state elections. The similarity of the name obscures the different makeup and leadership of these Union parties. Republicans led some and Democrats initiated others. In each state the balance of political forces to some extent shaped the nature of the Union organizations that emerged. Where the Republican Party was very strong, there was little incentive to change either the party's name or its organizational base; in places like Connecticut or Illinois where the parties were especially polarized and the Democrats especially prone to antiwar activism, there was less room for a genuine cross-party movement. But in other states, the outbreak of hostilities spurred a sincere effort to avoid partisanship for the duration of hostilities by uniting former political enemies on a general platform of support for the Union.[62] In Ohio and Pennsylvania, where Lincoln had won only narrowly, the ad hoc Union organizations were genuine coalitions of moderate Republicans with Douglas Democrats. Bell-Everett supporters were also prominent. In Ohio, the gubernatorial election in 1861 was won by David Tod, the Democrat who had regaled Sidney George Fisher with tales of the horrors of the slave trade even while supporting the Kansas-Nebraska Act. Tod ran as a Unionist and was supported by old Whigs like Thomas Corwin, who was pleased to endorse him as a "conservative."[63] In Pennsylvania, one of the leading champions of the new Union organization was John Forney, the old confrere of Buchanan who had broken with him over Lecompton and supported Douglas in 1860. All told, in only eight of the thirty-nine congressional races that took place in the fall of 1861 was there a straight contest between a Republican and a Democrat. While the idea of parties and party identities remained strong—including the pull of parties that no longer had any organized presence, like the Whig party—the reality was that voters in the free states were often not given clear-cut partisan choices, and this was never more true than in that first year of war.

While they were presented as a natural response to the exigencies of war, everyone understood that the idea of a Union party had a history rooted in the politics of conservatism and moderation. From Webster's efforts to form a finalist Union party to support the 1850 Compromise to the 1860 Constitutional Unionists, Union parties represented the hope that an antiparty party could transcend the corruption as well as the fanaticism of party hacks and "wire-pullers" and would bring together moderates and conservatives under one banner. That spirit fed into these new organizations. Whatever party their leaders came from, they invariably opposed radicalism as well as rebellion. The men who had described themselves as "national" and "Unionist" in their politics, who had hewed for as long as they could to the old politics of compromise through the crises of the 1850s, were, in a sense, now freed to pursue their Union party project as they had not been when they could be so easily dismissed as dupes of the Slave Power. An example is Robert C. Winthrop, the thoroughbred Bostonian who described himself as "born a conservative," and who spent the war attempting to resurrect, in essence, the old Whig party. Another is Marble's friend Samuel G. Arnold of Rhode Island, who wrote enthusiastically of the potential to bring together at last the "great mass" of Northerners who were "conservative men."[64] By 1864, Winthrop ended up supporting the Democratic presidential nominee, as did other Webster protégés like George T. Curtis. Arnold, in contrast, became more and more convinced that any Union party must be utterly loyal to the Lincoln administration, including its emancipation policy. But in 1861, both Arnold and Winthrop hoped that Union movements could transcend what they saw as the frustrating polarities of political choices hitherto.

Union parties were also, in part, a response to the genuine and widespread fear throughout the Civil War that popular government would not be able to stand the strain of conflict. In several towns and cities extralegal "Committees of Public Safety" were created at the outbreak of hostilities with the South, some appointing home guards to police neighborhoods and track down allegedly disloyal citizens. These organizations were deliberate echoes of the Committee of Safety that was established by Parliamentarians in England in 1642 as well as of the committees of public safety that coordinated resistance to royal rule in the colonies in the 1770s. They enacted a role long established in Anglo-American history: gathering citizens they considered stern, patriotic and resolute, to circumvent normal political processes. The vigilance committees in San Francisco had been justified on these grounds in the 1850s, as had the committees of public safety organizing resistance to the Fugitive Slave Law in Boston and elsewhere. In Philadelphia in 1861 a committee of public safety raised subscriptions to fund a complete artillery battery to defend the city.[65] And in August 1861 Henry Bellows floated the possibility that the entire national government should be replaced by a committee of public safety consisting of "fifty or a hundred men of character, weight, & boldness selected from every part of the country, men who could be trusted as having no personal ends to gratify, and under no political or party bonds." His friend Charles Eliot Norton cautioned that such a coup was not yet necessary, and might never be, but agreed that it would be prudent to identify such a group who would "pledge themselves to assemble instantly in New York or Washington, at any time of need, upon the call of any five or more of their number."[66]

In Rhode Island, where, as we have seen, the creation of a Union party predated Sumter, the spring 1861 elections to the state legislature saw a resounding triumph for the "grand conservative movement" (as one of its leaders called it) under the leadership of the charismatic young governor, William Sprague. Rhode Island lieutenant governor and later senator Samuel G. Arnold wrote enthusiastically of "a new party" that would "sweep the country" because it represented the sentiments of the majority: "Between the Chicago and the Breckenridge platforms stand the great mass of conservative men in the country and for them the constitutional Union party of R. I. offers a proper platform."[67] Delighted to have beaten the "straight" or "not-an-inch" Republicans, Arnold was nevertheless irritated to have been described in some newspapers as a Democrat "which I never was. . . . 'Conservative Republican' properly designates my position." Like Sprague, and indeed Rhode Island as a whole, Arnold had supported Lincoln in the 1860 election. That certainly did not mean that he considered himself a radical. The Rhode Island Constitutional Union Party was alternatively known (as its letterhead made clear) as "The Conservatives."[68] Barely a week after Sprague and Arnold's electoral triumph, Lincoln called for troops after the firing on Sumter, and Governor Sprague donned (a self-designed, gloriously elaborate) uniform and personally assumed command of the First Regiment of Rhode Island Volunteers, while Lieutenant Governor Arnold, slightly less gloriously clad, assumed command of a "battery of mounted artillery, with 6 rifled cannon, 142 men and 96 horses" and marched, as Arnold put it, "to the seat of war."[69]

The dangers of Union party movements to the Democrats were further illustrated in December 1861 when a Republican candidate (formerly a Democrat and a supporter of the 1848 Free-Soil Party), George Opdyke, was elected mayor of New York City. As with the surprise election of Caleb Woodhull to the same position twelve years earlier, Opdyke's election was made possible by Democratic division, but the *Herald* saw it as "the strongest evidence of the destruction of parties by the operation of the war" and argued, with some justification, that Opdyke's success was due to his appeal to "conservative votes."[70] As many Democrats accurately anticipated, however, the pressure to join Union movements would mean that anyone who stood outside them would be branded "disloyal" or "Tories."[71] While leading Ohio Democrats like David Tod not only joined the Union movement but took leading roles in it, many other grassroots Democrats understood all too well the power of language to frame political choices. "I can see no necessity for Democrats to change their names to Union," protested one. "We have always been Union men since the organization of our party so much so that the Black Republicans have styled us as *Union Lovers*."[72] Horatio Seymour argued that his party's dissolution "would seem like the last bond which holds our country together."[73]

Through the rest of the war, at least outside of New England and other centers of radical Republican strength, the best route to electoral success for candidates of whatever party configuration was to present themselves as the truest conservatives. When Republicans could be branded as dangerously radical, the existing Democratic organization could drape itself in a conservative mantle without formally joining nonparty Union movements. For example, in the fall of 1862, Horatio Seymour was elected governor by presenting himself as more in tune with the administration than his radical opponent, and his campaign freely adopted the designation "conservative" in place of "Democrat."[74] The *New York Herald* hailed Seymour as representing "the politics of moderation, conservatism . . . and common sense."[75]

Whether or not the vehicle for achieving it was through Union parties, the vast majority of Northerners who had supported Lincoln, Douglas, or Bell—and even many of those who had supported Breckinridge—could unite around the objective of restoring the Union as quickly as possible. The country backed a "conservative policy" remarked the New York *Independent* since "this war on the part of the Government and people of the United States is simply defensive. The war is waged in defense of . . . the Government . . . and the national Union." The conservatism of the war was essential to its success. If we "lose the advantage of our conservative position," we "become ourselves the revolutionary party." Conservatism did not mean any quarter for traitors, the writer stressed; "our conservative position" must not "hinder us from the most vigorous prosecution of the war." Yet only "*as conservatives,*" it stressed, could the revolutionary legacy of the Founding Fathers be preserved.[76] The *Independent* did not speak for everyone, of course. But it captured something important about the common ground of Northern politics. Notwithstanding the anxieties about war providing a fertile ground for radicalism, the vast majority of Northerners saw military action as a necessary, if regrettable, response to a threat to their polity, their values, and their future. Calls for the "vigorous prosecution" of the war are often assumed by historians to be code for the advocacy of emancipation or black military service—as was often the case. But the urgency with which many Northerners from across the political spectrum used this phrase in the first year or two of the war reflected a desire for more men and an apparently more concerted military effort—if only to ensure that the war was brought to a successful close before the really difficult questions about the future of slavery within the South would have to be faced.

For Whiggish reformers like Bellows fighting the war in a "conservative" way meant instilling a proper sense of "loyalty" in the people—one that could, he hoped, bind together the republic even after the rebellion had been defeated. "So debilitating, & demoralizing have been the influences of the last five and twenty years," Bellows wrote in 1861, that he was "afraid" of "our whole people," that they would be incapable of rising to the challenge of the conflict, that they were too selfish and factionalized to "endure hardship like good soldiers."[77] But Norton assured the uncharacteristically pessimistic Bellows that "this war is going to build up our national character on a firmer basis than that on which it has hitherto rested."[78] The process was not, however, to be left to chance. Just as in the aftermath of the Astor Place Riot Bellows had supported the creation of institutions designed to bind together a fissiparous society, so now he took a lead in creating the U.S. Sanitary Commission. It had the primary purpose of alleviating the suffering of Union troops by providing blankets and bandages and rudimentary health care. Yet in addition to this purely practical function, Bellows's Commission had a corollary purpose: re-creating deference and harmony between social classes in order to restore the old republican ideals of civic virtue and sacrifice for the common good. The commission, explained Bellows, "was not from its inception a merely humanitarian or beneficent association." It necessarily "took on that appearance," but the commission's leaders were "conservative men of strong political purpose" who sought to inculcate the "people of this country [with] a very much higher sense of the value of the Union."[79]

In a pamphlet published by the Loyal Publication Society, Bellows built on the case he had made after the killings at Astor Place that a government's authority came from God, even—in fact especially—in a democracy.[80] At stake in wartime, as in the face of the anti-Macready mob, was "Liberty under Law—whether of the Constitution or the Gospel." Bellows warned Democrats in 1863 that, by protesting about the unconstitutionality of seemingly everything the Lincoln administration did, they threatened to "loosen every link in that chain of law and order which binds society together," just as the triumph of the mob against Macready would have done. In either case, the result would be anarchy. Echoing these ideas, another New Yorker, the biographer James Parton, reflected in 1864 that "one evening about fifteen years ago, New York rowdyism fell, weltering in blood, in Astor Place, before the fire of the Seventh Regiment." The 1863 draft riots, Parton claimed, had been merely a "temporary resurrection" of this kind of backward-looking social disorder, "owing to a combination of causes never likely to be again combined." It was the defeat of the mob at Astor Place, Parton argued, that was the real turning point. The firm action of the authorities had "mitigated" the worst effects of democracy and assured the triumph of "liberty under law."[81] The military commander responsible for restoring order in the face of three days of horrific violence in New York in July 1863 was the old Democrat John A. Dix. His aim in restoring order in New York, he wrote, was identical with the aims of the Union in the war: to "vindicate the authority of the Government."[82]

By the time Dix wrote these words, however, the apparently uncontroversial aim of vindicating the government had become bogged down in the most serious internal conflict within the North since the Revolution. Coercion to restore national honor after the firing on the flag was relatively easy to support. In the early summer of 1861, there was a general assumption that this would be a short, sharp conflict in which the republic would demonstrate its capacity to subdue armed rebellion. Then there would be some sort of sectional compromise of the kind that had happened before, except this time the North would be in a far stronger bargaining position. The defeat at the first battle of Bull Run was the first shock to this assumption, but after the failure of the Peninsular Campaign in May 1862, Northerners had to confront the political ramifications of fighting a substantial and enduring war. That recognition placed the federal government's relationship to slavery back at the center of public debate and private anxiety.

Emancipation for Preservation

There is some evidence that some Northerners became less hostile to black racial equality during the war. The sacrifice of black soldiers after their eventual enlistment in the army was a powerful tool for reevaluating their capacity as potential citizens—at least for elite reformers and abolitionists. For the likes of Henry Bellows, preoccupied with moral order, freedmen fighting for the flag offered a better model of loyal citizenship than Irish workers rioting against the draft. The Union League Club in New York, of which Bellows was a leading member, famously raised a black regiment in early 1864, which, with deliberate symbolism, marched through the New York neighborhoods where only a few months earlier black people had been systematically targeted and killed by the antidraft rioters.[83] During the war, abolitionist speakers seem to have placed more emphasis on the humanity of black people than was the case before. Yet the moral symbolism of black soldiers, powerful as it was, did not substantially shift the racial assumptions of the vast majority of Northerners. White supremacist assumptions remained the norm.[84] Visual representations of black people continued to be largely pejorative—even the self-consciously positive depictions in *Harper's Weekly* painted African Americans as childlike in their loyalty. And when *Harper's* published an edition with a proud, straight-backed black man in uniform on the front cover, the editor's house was stoned by an antiabolitionist mob.[85] Certainly most Democrats would have agreed with the young Democratic firebrand Daniel Voorhees, who argued that "the theory of absolute human equality" threatened liberty for Anglo-Saxons. Having banished the Indian "into the shades of the forest as the white man enlarged the boundaries of civilization," asked Voorhees, why would Anglo-Saxons now give ground to the "negroes"?[86] There had always been a few in the North, as we have seen, who believed that slavery was Biblically ordained, or that it was practically beneficent, or both. And after emancipation became central to wartime politics, there were more outspoken proslavery polemics than ever before.

Entrenched racism remained a fact of life; yet it did not prevent the gradual acceptance of emancipation among a majority of Northerners, and nor was it by any means the only reason for the intense opposition to the administration's emancipation policy after 1862. Even at the very onset of the conflict it was certainly not necessary to be an abolitionist to assume that slavery would inevitably be at stake, whatever policy the government might adopt on the matter. Sidney George Fisher made what he thought a self-evident observation when he wrote that "the moral feeling of the North is setting strongly against slavery & the southern politicians [by their unreasonable demands and now their attempt to destroy the Union] are the cause of it." If even Buchanan's reaction to the firing on Sumter suggests his belated recognition that secession was post hoc evidence of slaveholders' malign intent it is not surprising that this was an assumption shared by most Northerners. Having long assumed that slavery was incompatible with Northern liberties, and wary (at the very least) of Southern attempts to demand ever-greater recognition for their property, it was a small step to conclude, as Fisher did, that secession—triggering a Northern effort to hold the Union together by force—might hasten the end of slavery. Slavery's death would come about not through any sense of revenge on the part of the North but simply through the instinct of self-preservation. The South's "material interest" in slavery, Fisher wrote, was so strong that within the Union, slavery would survive for a long time. But out of it, once the South made the survival of the Union an issue, slavery's "destruction must come at last." Despite his pragmatism and his deep temperamental opposition to radical change and social transformation, Fisher also believed that "moral truth is of a commanding nature; it will be obeyed" and since "Slavery is a wrong, an injustice" it would ultimately be destroyed by the "moral sentiment of the country."[87]

As with many other self-described conservatives, especially those in the Whig tradition, Fisher's view of slavery had gradually shifted as his perception of the greater cause of instability had moved from abolitionism to disunionism. In 1859, he noted, with some surprise, that abolitionism, once synonymous with mobs, was fast becoming "the cause of liberty [and] order." He had in mind the efforts of Southern politicians to undermine Northern liberties, and the ideals of due process, of respect for rational debate and free speech—all ideals that had been destroyed in the South by slavery. Garrison's strong support for the actions of Mayor Woodhull at Astor Place in 1849 had, in this sense, established an important template: abolitionists might be reckless and they might be hopelessly fanatical in their pursuit of a single goal, Fisher thought, but secession was the final proof that slavery was ultimately and irrepressibly at odds with liberal, free society. Such thinking aligned the old Whig Fisher with those whom the Jacksonian James Gordon Bennett sneeringly called the "Jacobin philosophers" of the *New York Tribune*.[88] Horace Greeley's paper framed the "Slaveholders' Rebellion" as a war of ideas: "the idea of slavery is fighting the idea of freedom."[89] In the spring of 1861 there was still reason to hope that the war may be brought to a swift end—presumably therefore with slavery still intact—yet that would not have altered Fisher and Greeley's view that the war pitted slavery against freedom, in the same way that slavery had eroded freedom in the preceding years of crisis.

A subtle but important difference separated Fisher's and Greeley's respective understandings of the place of emancipation in the war effort, however. Fisher accepted that the necessity of fighting the war would have consequences for slavery, whereas Greeley saw no dilemma in explicitly attacking slavery as a means of winning the war. One acknowledged that a natural process of prosecuting a war against a slave society would be likely, in the end, to lead to emancipation; the other wanted to actively use the army as an agent of abolition. It was Fisher's understanding of the legitimate path to emancipation that was more typical. Relatively few Northerners had objected to the first confiscation act, passed by Congress in July 1861, which empowered Union army officers to seize the property—including the slaves—of rebels.[90] That was, after all, simply a ratification of the generally accepted rules of war, that the property of the enemy could be impounded lest it be used to wage war. This was the reasoning employed by the commander of a federal-held fortress on Virginian soil, General Benjamin F. Butler, a red-faced, mustachioed Breckinridge Democrat from Massachusetts with not a particle of the abolitionist about him. Butler delighted radicals in the summer of 1861 by declaring that he would treat any enslaved people who reached his lines as "contraband of war" and thus, in effect, as free.

The New England man of letters Charles Eliot Norton, who heartily hoped that the war would end slavery, was savvy enough to recognize that the Northern public was driven not by a sudden desire to end slavery for the sake of the slave, but because the outbreak of war had "enormously strengthened" the "fear of the power of Slavery."[91] Writing in James Russell Lowell's *Atlantic Monthly* after the shocking defeat of the Union army at the first battle of Bull Run in July, 1861, Norton predicted that the unexpected loss would make Northerners realize that the war must be fought for a higher purpose. Inspiration, as always for a man with a deep consciousness of his own Puritan heritage, could come from the English Civil War. "When Cromwell's men went out to win the victory at Winceby Fight, their watchword was 'Religion.' Can we in our great struggle for liberty and right adopt any other watchword than this?"[92] In a letter to Henry Bellows, Norton explained at great length how, from his perspective, the question of the survival of the Union could never be divorced from the underlying problem of slavery or, more specifically, of the threat that slaveholders posed to freedom with their demands that Northerners acquiesce in its dominance. "The question at issue between the North and the South has become one of self-preservation on each side," Norton wrote, agreeing with Bellows's views, "but self-preservation at the North means the upholding and securing of the principles on which all the hope of future progress rests while self preservation at the South means present & future degeneration and decline. I have felt from the beginning that even if we were victorious over the Southern forces, we should fail in winning a true victory unless in some way or other Emancipation was secured as its result."[93]

Norton and Bellows wanted emancipation, but they wanted it done carefully. In a sermon delivered a month after he received Norton's extended explanation of how emancipation was implicated in the survival of the Union, Bellows warned that while slavery was a curse to the South as much as to the enslaved, and a threat to republican institutions, nevertheless, "abolition born of revolution was even worse than slavery itself." In the Burkean, incremental, terms that were characteristic of him, Bellows warned that a sudden rush to emancipate without proper planning for the fate of the freedmen would "risk our constitution, our union, our historic life and national identity." To abolish slavery "at a blow" was something that "only fanatics and reckless enthusiasts would dare to propose." The problem was a delicate one because like other revolutions it might become uncontrollable and contrary to the "conservative spirit" of the Union cause. As the Jacksonian *New York Herald* warned, emancipation might unleash a bloody "war against all kinds of property . . . according to the Fourierite . . . idea . . . that 'all property is robbery.' "[94] In short, while "riddance of slavery" was the wish of "every true American heart," Bellows wrote, "violent, unmethodized, rapid emancipation" risked disorder and was "the greatest wrong we could do the slave."[95]

Slavery was an unwise and an immoral institution, in Bellows's view, but there was no denying that it was deeply embedded by law and custom. The Harpers Ferry raid had been an early indication that it would take more than the spark of an antislavery man's musket to set the house of slavery on fire. In the early months of the war, there was a lot of publicity given to the numbers of refugees claiming a status as contrabands at General Butler's headquarters. *Harpers' Weekly* included a dramatic pictorial representation of slaves approaching Fortress Monroe in family groups, resembling the Jewish exodus from Egypt. Yet as many Northern newspapers also noted, the sudden and sweeping slave uprising that some abolitionists had predicted did not happen. This, to someone like Bellows, seemed evidence that one had to tread very carefully indeed when it came to ending slavery. However wrong it may be it had the sanction of time and the security of generations of familiarity. Abolitionists, still a minority within the antislavery mainstream, had no such restraints. But on occasion even they made their case using a self-consciously conservative language: "We are called 'agitators,' " the Rev William H. Furness, an antislavery Congregationalist minister from Philadelphia, told his congregation, "but we are in fact *true* conservatives."[96]

Notwithstanding the North's antislavery consensus, had the war ended quickly with the capitulation of the seceded states, emancipation may not have come. But the war did not end quickly. General George B. McClellan, the first commander of the Union's Army of the Potomac, charged with the central strategic objective of capturing Richmond from Confederate control, was one of the most influential and passionate Democratic advocates of the idea that the Jacobinism of the abolitionists should be kept at bay and the war conducted on limited terms, without disrupting slavery.[97] But when McClellan, having brought his army almost within artillery range of Richmond in May 1862, was defeated and forced to retreat by a resurgent Confederate force under the command of Robert E. Lee in the Seven Days Battles, the prospect of a short war died. And with it died the fragile unity in Northern politics. The battles over "true conservatism" between the advocates and the opponents of a targeted policy of freeing slaves, and between those who embraced the potential of war to instill patriotism and discipline in the citizenry and those who feared tyranny, were about to explode.

After Lincoln issued the Preliminary Emancipation Proclamation on September 22, 1862, abolitionists cheered a move that "inscribed freedom on our banner" while antiabolitionists denounced a "revolutionary" and "Jacobincal" act.[98] The administration had become disunionist, warned a Democratic newspaper in Ohio. Lincoln clearly intended to "annihilate the old Union our fathers made."[99] The proclamation, thought Horatio Seymour, had surely removed "the scales from the eyes of those stupid thick-headed persons who persisted in thinking that the President was a conservative man."[100] Between these two extremes, millions of Northerners reacted with caution. Many Democratic newspapers reacted dismissively, regarding the proclamation as a piece of ill-judged electioneering designed to shore up Lincoln's position with the radical wing of his party and unlikely ever to be put into effect. The *New York World*, for example, wondered what the president would gain by remaining wedded to an "impracticable policy." What was the advantage in nominally setting free millions of enslaved people outside of his jurisdiction? And if they were to be freed, what could they do but come North for fear of reenslavement, something which the North would never tolerate. If Lincoln went ahead with his promised second emancipation proclamation on January 1, the *World* predicted, the free states bordering the South—all of which, it correctly observed, now had Democratic-controlled legislatures—would "at once initiate measures to protect their laborers and tax-payers against the threatened evil. They will erect a dyke against the black inundation."[101] The *World* reported rumors that Lincoln's cabinet was largely against the emancipation proclamation policy and that it had only been issued to head off the prospect of intervention by Britain.[102]

Even the January 1 proclamation, however, did not strike many Northerners as tantamount to actually abolishing slavery. To declare slaves free when they were under the control of the Confederate government was not, in practice to free them.[103] In practice, what the Emancipation Proclamations did was to give further weight to the Second Confiscation Act, passed by Congress in July 1862, which mandated that Union troops should free slaves when they came into contact with them. Emancipating slaves individually or even in large groups as they came in contact under Union control—and even a presidential declaration of freedom applying to slaves in territory where the federal government's writ did not run—was not the same as the abolition of the institution of slavery, a process that still faced immense legal and constitutional obstacles.

Aside from abolitionists for whom January 1 was a day of jubilee, the mood in the North at the start of the new year of 1863 was somber not celebratory. Union forces under General Burnside had suffered a debilitating defeat at Fredericksburg. Twelve thousand men had been killed in an ultimately futile effort to push the Confederate defenders out of their entrenchments in the town on the south bank of the Rappahannock. "If there is a worse place than Hell, I am in it," Lincoln told a visitor when the news of the December 13 debacle came through. In such circumstances it was hard to discern what military advantages, if any, would flow from the January 1 proclamation. Even many Republicans offered only tempered approval, hoping that the measure would prove wise as well as just.[104] The *New York Herald*, with its long antiabolitionist tradition, was generally supportive of the Lincoln administration—and was to support his reelection in 1864—but it probably captured the feelings of many Northerners when it described a general sense of foreboding on January 1. "We shrink from the dreadful thought that this war is to ripen into the horrible scenes of St Domingo," read an editorial piece, invoking the deep-seated fear of a Haitian-style slave rebellion. Lincoln "against his own good judgment in this matter" seemed to be steering the ship of state "among the breakers of a perilous coast."[105]

Circumspect as ever, Sidney George Fisher allowed himself to be persuaded that the proclamation would, on balance, be helpful. Fisher's friend Morton McMichael, editor of the Philadelphia *North American*, assured his readers that the administration's policy was largely a ratification and reflection of what was happening on the ground anyway. "When the United States army landed at Port Royal [on the South Carolina coast] and every planter fled to the interior, leaving his slaves without even the means of subsistence, could we or should we have still held those poor negroes for their rebel masters?" Since the experience of the war was that the white population "is hostile" while "the slaves are our friends" surely it would be wrong to "continue their friends in bondage out of regard for these enemies." But—crucially—what was being done to slavery, and recognized in the president's proclamation, was the "consequence of no fanaticism, but of the inevitable and irresistible tendency of events."[106]

Charles Hodge, the principal of Princeton Theological Seminary, made the conservative case for the Emancipation Proclamation.[107] A deep and abiding "temperamental conservatism," in the historian Richard Carwardine's words, underpinned a "continuous spine of thought and ambition" as Hodge moved from his early Federalism into the Whig party and eventually, with some reluctance, into the Republicans.[108] (It was Hodge who proudly told his students at Princeton that "a new idea never originated in [this] Seminary.")[109] In an article that appeared in January 1863, Hodge did not oppose the Emancipation Proclamation but argued that it was justified only because it did not alter the goal of the war—reunion—but was simply a strategy for achieving it. "The difference between being a means and an end," he wrote, "is as great as the difference between blowing up a man's house as a means of arresting of a conflagration, and getting up a conflagration for blowing up his house." His support for the proclamation was therefore conditional on the way the policy was justified. He retained his suspicion of both abolitionists and of the power of slavery. As he explained, his concern that emancipation not become an avowed object of the war had nothing to do with whether slavery was good or bad. Hodge, for all his lifelong preoccupation with social, moral, and political order, was clearly of the view that slavery, at least as practiced in America, was a moral evil. Yet, as he pointed out, there were many other good objects for which one could go to war: "false religion," for example, or the "despotism" that was such "a grievous yoke on the neck" of European nations. Yet such issues did not, to him, justify conflict. "Nothing can be a legitimate object of a war but something which a nation has not only a right to attain, but which also it is bound to secure," he wrote. The preservation of its own existence fell into that category. Emancipation, however, was "one of those objects which may be benevolent, useful, desirable, but [is] to be attained in some other way. War is a tremendous evil. It is no slight matter for parents to give up their children to death. . . . There must be a moral obligation on a people to make war, or the war itself is a crime. Now it cannot be asserted that the abolition of slavery, however desirable in itself, is one of the ends for which our national government was instituted. We are not bound to abolish slavery by war, as we should be bound to resist invasion, or as we are bound to suppress rebellion by force of arms."[110]

This nuanced support for emancipation—as desirable, justifiable in context, but not in itself a legitimate war aim—was commonplace. And at the same time as they framed the policy as conservative, some supporters of emancipation attacked its opponents for "assuming the name Conservative." This was a "dexterous" (for which read: shifty and underhand) move by the "managers" of "what was once the Democratic party" observed the Philadelphia *North American*, but it hoped and predicted that it was destined to fail, since the people would soon realize that theirs was no more than a false conservatism.[111] "Our chief fighters are our chief conservatives," argued *Harper's Weekly* shortly after the preliminary emancipation proclamation had effectively transformed the means of the conflict. Since the war as directed by the president was now "the only way to preserve our liberties," only "demagogues and radicals" could oppose it.[112]

There was, however, a clear tension in the efforts to align the emancipation policy with conservatism. While the *North American* reassured its readers that Lincoln's course was "essentially conservative," other publications were more willing to acknowledge that desperate times might well require radical measures. At about the same time as Lincoln issued his preliminary emancipation proclamation, in September 1862, the New York illustrated weekly *Frank Leslie's* made the observation that "conservatism" was the "*juste-millieu* or mean" position between the extremes or "ultras." This was an expression of the conventional notion of conservatism as the middle path, the designation of the vast majority—the "conservative masses"—who wanted to avoid lurching into the arms of Jacobins, fanatics, one-ideaists or aristocratic counter-republicans. *Frank Leslie's* then went on to make the point, though, that the stubbornness of the rebellion made that middle ground look less solid and more risky. If "conservatism means the preservation of our Republican institutions, we of the North, are certainly Conservative" but what if it is now necessary to "become a Radical to save the nation"? As *Frank Leslie's* put it there were two "antagonistic elements," slavery and freedom, locked in deadly combat. The mainstream position in Northern politics since the mid-1850s had been that the South was vying for mastery, demanding that oligarchy replace democracy. If that was indeed the choice, and if the war, as was now evident, could not easily be won, then what room was there for a "*juste-millieu,*" asked *Frank Leslie's*. Praising the "conservatism of the present administration" up until then, the paper speculated that conservatism might henceforth demand its own sort of "ultraism." "If Ultraism consists in rescuing the Union at all hazards, we say Ultraism all hail!"[113] (Or, as another Republican was to say almost exactly a century later, "I would remind you that extremism in defense of liberty is no vice.")

Seen in this way, Northerners were confronted with a choice about whether to accept that they were being radicalized by the war. This too, was Lincoln's challenge in his Message to Congress in December 1862, in which he made the case that unprecedented circumstances required new thinking. But a remarkably large number of Northerners refused to see their situation in this light, even though, by1863, it was becoming harder and harder to sustain the idea that Northerners were fighting to restore the old Union of April 1861. To general approval, even from many Democrats, Congress abolished slavery in the

District of Columbia on April 16, 1862. And on June 19, slavery was abolished in the U.S. territories—thus ending at a stroke decades of struggle. The sign of how much had changed was that no one seemed to worry that the Supreme Court would try to strike down the measure—though Chief Justice Taney still presided, and if the Missouri Compromise had been unconstitutional then by the same reasoning so would this act.

Just as had been the case before the war, Jacksonian and Whiggish political traditions continued to frame what people believed to be the principal threats facing their society, but—as again had been the case before Sumter—the question of slavery cut across these divisions. Many Jacksonians thought the "fanaticism" of the administration was a frontal assault on popular liberty—the culmination of many years of warnings about one-ideaism and the monarchical tendencies of the opponents of the Democracy. Other Jacksonians, however, thought that, in the greatest crisis the Republic had ever faced, the people must rise up to use force to defend their freedoms against assault from aristocratic slaveholders.[114] Within the Whiggish tradition the desire for compromise and amelioration was in tension—as it had been since the 1840s—with the countervailing sense that only a stronger government could safeguard the institutions and social fabric of the nation. And, as it had been since at least 1848, the term "conservative" was much invoked by Northerners in their attempts to make sense of what was happening around them and to justify their political choices. Few in the North would have dissented from the judgment of Alexis de Tocqueville's self-appointed heir as an interpreter of Anglo-Saxon politics, Duvergier de Hauranne, who carefully explained to his European readers that, "the men of the North are the true conservatives."[115] They would, however, have disagreed—as always—about exactly what that meant, and would have done so even while embracing, with varying degrees of enthusiasm or reluctance, changes that were nothing short of revolutionary.

Democrats like John A. Dix who became fervent supporters of the war were especially determined to argue that what had been radical before the war was now the only responsible, conservative course.[116] Dix wholeheartedly supported the Lincoln administration without in any way feeling that he was betraying his lifelong commitment to the core ideals of the Jacksonian Democrats. His namesake Dorothea Dix, meanwhile, in her new position as Superintendent of Women Nurses, put all her efforts into crusading for national redemption, shocked by the savagery of the Confederates ("even the Sepoys fall harmless in comparison") but also by the rampant alcoholism and prostitution among the troops billeted at Washington, "this modern Gomorrah."[117] John and Dorothea Dix came from from different political traditions, but for both the war brought out their iron determination to go to any length to destroy the rebellion, even while it reaffirmed many of their prewar assumptions. For others, however, the war had assumed a far more sinister complexion—as a contest within the North between "freedom and arbitrary power."[118] The trouble with the Republicans, warned John A. Dix's former party comrade Horatio Seymour, was that while "one wing . . . is conservative and patriotic, the other is violent and revolutionary."[119] As "led by the Abolitionists," echoed a Philadelphia Democrat, the Republicans "have not about them an iota of conservatism; they are essentially a revolutionary party."[120] Whether that was so was the central question of wartime politics.

CHAPTER SEVEN

How a Conservative People
Conducted a Long War

By the early 1860s, Edwin Forrest was a wilder, heavier, and more polarizing figure than ever. His public image had never recovered from his alleged role in the riot at Astor Place and his sensational divorce, yet the American Tragedian could still drum up an enthusiastic crowd with his old strutting tricks.[1] In the first two years of the Civil War, Forrest found a topical vehicle for his on-stage persona in *Brutus*, an epic tragedy by John Howard Payne, who is now remembered, if at all, only as the author of the sentimental song "Home Sweet Home." The play was about the failed conspiracy to overthrow the new Roman republic and reestablish the monarchy. The title role, of Brutus the Roman Consul, defending the new-founded republic against counterrevolution suited the Jacksonian-inspired, vainglorious talents of Edwin Forrest excellently. When the antirepublican conspiracy is defeated, Brutus's rebellious son Titus pleads for mercy to his father ("What! I must perish like a common felon?") and Forrest's character replies, witheringly, devastatingly, "How else do traitors suffer?"

Never one to knowingly undersell a line with a contemporary payoff, Forrest played this one for all he was worth in a touring production up and down the east coast during 1862. To the theater critic of the *Washington Chronicle*, "the tone and manner" of Forrest's reply "was electrical, and the audience caught the suggestion and responded with hearty applause." At the end of the play, when his rebel sons had been executed, Forrest as Brutus spoke of the unique crime of launching a rebellion against the freedoms of a young nation.

> To strike their country in the mother-pangs
> Of struggling child-birth, and direct
> The danger to freedom's infant throat—
> Is a crime so black my foiled tongue
> Refuses it a name.

"No words," wrote the *Chronicle's* theater critic, "are requisite either to show the fearful application of these lines to our national troubles, nor the excitement they created when they were repeated." Forrest, the critic admitted, "has played better plays" but "he has never yet acted a part which was more entirely appropriate to the great tribulations of his country, or more creditable to himself or the American stage."[2]

Indignation at the breathtaking treachery of the rebels was one of the most powerful political emotions during the war—and indeed for many years afterward, as the "bloody shirt" election campaigns of the Republicans in the late nineteenth-century shows. It was an essential component in binding together people in support of the administration's war policy. But indignation only carried people so far. It might bring people to a public meeting to express their sense of outrage, but could indignation sustain people through the sacrifices required of a long and costly war? That was the question explored in a best-selling pamphlet by a Philadelphia lawyer Charles J. Stillé, *How a Free People Conduct a Long War*. Drawing inspiration from the ways in which the English coped with the long-drawn-out civil wars of the seventeenth century and the more recent wars against Napoleonic France, Stillé advised that people should cultivate a "stern endurance . . . rooted in a profound conviction of the justice of the cause."[3] The indignation of Forrest's Brutus, Stillé implied, needed to be transformed into a grim purposefulness; a sense of righteous outrage must be supplemented by discipline, resourcefulness, and patience. Stillé thought that English history provided examples of how a nation could maintain freedom while demanding loyalty in wartime, but in practice, as he also recognized, this was a difficult balancing act to pull off.

Finding this balance was made even harder by 1863. Just as the Kansas-Nebraska Act and then the Lecompton constitution fight had compelled people to make choices between unpalatable alternatives, so the response of the Lincoln administration to military failures in the summer of 1862 created new lines of division. To Northerners steeped in a political culture suspicious of centralization and national authority, the suspension of habeas corpus, military arrests, and the attempt to impose military conscription were exactly the sorts of organized assaults on freedom that had long been feared. Democratic congressmen S. S. Cox warned that "the conservative masses" were being pushed "beyond endurance" by the administration's susceptibility to one-idea radicalism.[4] It was, it turned out, perfectly possible to believe that, on the one hand slavery had in some sense fueled the disloyalty of the South, and yet, on the other, to be deeply anxious that it was counterproductive to make a bold declaration—as the Emancipation Proclamation of January 1, 1863 seemed to do—that abolition of slavery was now a goal of the war. The Philadelphia Democrat Charles J. Biddle was not "blind," he said, to the "evils of slavery" but the "intemperate and aggressive policy of the political antislavery party" was designed neither to benefit "the negro" nor to restore the Union. Was it not a "standing reproach of American history against George III," Biddle asked, "that he called in the Hessian against his British subjects"? Yet "we are to call in the negro!" This "plea of necessity" by the administration—the argument that it had no choice but to emancipate, to conscript, to suspend habeas corpus—was, Biddle charged, the thinking that led to the Reign of Terror.[5]

Anti-Jacobinism and the Opposition to the Lincoln Administration

The so-called Jacobinical reasoning of the administration made millions of Northerners nervous. In this respect the old Jacksonian Edwin Forrest serves as a window into the feelings of millions of others. Forrest had strong and conflicting emotional responses to what was happening around him. As Brutus, he channeled his ferocious opposition to secession as an assault on the Republic—a conspiracy against freedom the like of which all his great stage heroes had confronted and destroyed.[6] Yet at the same time, Forrest expressed fears that the Republican Party was corrupt and despotic and had conspired to provoke the war. And, at least at first, he could not entirely suppress his natural sympathy for the South. He had been acting in Richmond in the spring of 1861 and hyperbolically described the marshaling of Union troops on the Potomac as "the invasion of [Virginia's] sacred soil."[7] So while Forrest may have postured against rebellion in character as Brutus, he was, to say the least, deeply ambivalent about whether Lincoln was a Brutus-like figure, defending the republic, or whether he was a usurper using massive state power to destroy liberty. Forrest's letters suggest that he was sympathetic, at least at times, to the proposition that any war to keep the Union together by force was inherently subversive of liberty. When Lincoln was reelected in November 1864, Forrest concluded that it was yet more evidence that "those whom the Gods would surely destroy, they first make mad."[8] In this view, a free people could not conduct a long war without losing its freedoms.

Although hardly anyone in the North advocated the breakup of the Union as a good thing in itself, a few, at one time or another, came close to at least tacitly accepting the prospect—albeit, they hoped, temporarily—as preferable to war. "I am not opposed, but on the contrary, am in favor of an undying Union," wrote one Pennsylvanian Democrat in 1864, "so long as the states comprising it, are willing parties to the Compact. But I am opposed to any Confederation which must be formed by force, and sustained by military law, and fraud."[9] For Daniel Voorhees, the war against secession was as great a danger as secession itself—indeed, like others who were branded with (and sometimes accepted as a badge of honor) the label "copperhead," for Voorhees "armed resistance" on behalf of the "principles of free government" meant resisting Lincoln at least as much as it meant resisting secession.[10] Voorhees had become notorious for a speech he made at Greencastle, Indiana in April 1861—just days before the firing on Sumter—in which he had pledged to his constituents that "as your representative, I will never vote one dollar, one man, or one gun to the administration of Abraham Lincoln to make war on the South."[11] This was a piece of hyperbole that even Voorhees came to regret. The congressman remained a fierce critic of the administration, though, persistently framing his opposition in terms of the eternal republican polarities of liberty and power.

Voorhees's Ohio colleague Clement L. Vallandigham, an equally urbane and articulate Democrat, similarly cast his defense of ancient liberties in a long historical context. "Cowardice and servility before Executive power were the disgrace of the English Bar and Bench in the days of the Stuarts," Vallandigham told students at the University of Michigan in November 1863, just weeks after losing a high-profile contest for the Ohio governorship that had taken place while he was in exile in Canada. The question Vallandigham posed to the trainee lawyers in his audience was whether they buckle before tyranny or follow the "glorious example" of Hampden and Sidney and rise up to defend the liberties of the people.[12] Illinois Democrats meeting at a state convention in Lincoln's hometown of Springfield in June 1863 warned that the Lincoln administration was creating "misrule and anarchy" by imposing emancipation and conscription, and that the "further offensive prosecution of the war tends to subvert the Constitution and Government." For these Illinois Democrats, the Union should be restored (of course) but only by the tried and tested old measures of compromise and ameliorating Constitutional amendments—exactly the old politics of compromise that had failed in 1861.[13] At certain points in the war—for example in the summer of 1863, as conscription was being first imposed even while progress in the war seemed elusive—these kinds of arguments became mainstream at Democratic gatherings. This was especially true in the Midwest, but also in parts of Pennsylvania, Connecticut, and New York City where there had long been an organized anti-antislavery movement (and where the Breckinridge vote had been strongest in 1860).

While the Illinois resolutions rejected the use of force in seemingly absolute terms, more common was to distinguish between, on the one hand, the acceptable use of force (which, after all, Andrew Jackson had threatened against the South Carolina nullifiers, a precedent constantly cited) and, on the other, the manner in which the Republicans were going about it. "I never in my life saw [among the Democracy] that man who wanted this Union divided; no sympathy with the effort to break down this Government in the breast of any Democrat that I ever met," claimed Victor E. Piollet, the Pennsylvania Democrat. Summarizing the views of millions of Northern Democrats he then went on to say that, nevertheless, there were many "who, while devoting all their efforts to put down the rebellion and overthrow secession, wanted the liberties of the people preserved, and the Constitution and laws of the country held sacred and not violated under the plea of 'military necessity.'"[14]

For those inclined to see it, there was proof aplenty that the Republican Party had revolutionized the government and were bent on destroying the constitutional liberties of the people. "The great heart of the people is massing against the madness of this administration," wrote Democratic Congressman John Dodson Stiles, hopefully. The "rapid increase of a national Debt" and "onerous taxation" was so at odds, Stiles thought, with the "conservative temper" of the American people, and so contrary to the spirit of the Republic, that it "*must* cause the people to repudiate this cursed crusade."[15] John Brewster, an Ohio Democrat, was similarly optimistic, telling Congressman Samuel S. Cox that he knew "many persons" who had voted for Lincoln but who now felt "deceived by the Abolitionists" and so "will vote with the conservatives and repudiate the fanatics of the North."[16] The wealthy Philadelphia Democrat Charles J. Biddle thought that while a war against secession was justified, it ought then to have been conducted with a view, as he put it, "to the attainment of an early and desirable peace." Writing in the spring of 1863 to his friend Charles Stillé, Biddle argued that many Republicans seemed to want to prolong the war for reasons of their own. By way of evidence, Biddle told the author of *How a Free People Conduct a Long War* that "I have on my table a pamphlet by a clergyman—Rev H. Barking—sent to me for my conversion by an esteemed friend. The pamphlet lauds and expands this sentiment: 'how can any northern man, hoping and praying for the destruction of slavery, desire that the war should be a short one?'"[17]

That Stillé published his advice to his fellow countrymen to be stoical and steadfast within a few weeks of receiving this letter from Biddle is not a surprise; the spring of 1863 was the time when the twin pressures of conscription and emancipation and their highly contested relationship to the restoration of the Union assumed central importance in Northern politics. Contrary to the assertions of many newspapermen and Republican politicians at the time, there was no large-scale, organized antiwar movement within the Union.[18] But ad hoc, localized resistance was widespread—especially in the rural, economically more marginal, and often traditionally Democratic regions of southern Indiana and Illinois and western Pennsylvania. As the historian Robert Sandow has written, opposition to Republican war measures "brought intimidation, destruction of property, and acts of individual and group violence." The targets of violence included "civilians, soldiers, and government officials, especially those of the Provost Marshal General's Bureau."[19] Draft resistance was rooted in a community's traditional desire for local autonomy grounded in republican political culture. Conscription directly threatened families economically as well as in other ways. The draft's opponents used the term "abolition slavery" to refer to the metaphorical slavery imposed by abolitionists on white men impressed against their will into the army. Federal officials trying to enforce the draft noted that women were in the forefront of the resistance. Draft resisters may rarely have declared overt support for the breakup of the Union but they could certainly understand the impulse to secede in the face of tyranny. A Democratic Club in Columbia County, Pennsylvania, denounced the conscription law as "unjust, in that it favors the rich . . . while it consigns the poor man to the hardships and dangers of the battlefield [and] tramples upon the rights of the States, disregards the civil laws and places whole courts under despotic military rule." "All we ask," wrote one opponent of the draft, "is to be let alone that we may peaceably pursue our various vocations."[20]

When Northerners saw uniformed soldiers patrolling polling places at election time or read about the suspension of habeas corpus, the images and comparisons that came to mind were drawn from the Reign of Terror in revolutionary France. The readiness with which Northern newspapers and pamphleteers compared political factions to the Gironde or the Jacobins, and Democrats inveighed against "freemen of the North crowded into Bastilles" suggests these were terms with which readers would be familiar.[21] Especially after 1848—when revolutionary violence returned to the streets of Paris—American popular culture exhibited a Gothic fascination with the Terror, the guillotine, and the horrific fate of imprisoned nobles. Much of the imagery was imported from Britain but found a ready audience in America, not least in theaters. In one popular melodrama, *The Destruction of the Bastille*, which opened in London in 1844 but later ran in New York for several years, Robespierre sacrifices his own life in order to save his daughter's, titillating audiences with graphic depictions of the great revolutionary's bloody demise.[22] Even more successful was Don Bouciclout's melodrama, *Geneviève*, about a woman who disguised herself as Marie Antoinette, willingly placing her own beautiful head under the guillotine so the queen could escape. Dickens's *A Tale of Two Cities* was much discussed in the American press during the Civil

War (and also adapted for the stage). In 1845, a Philadelphia writer, H. N. Moore, published not only a series of books about the English Civil War but also a long and salacious compendium of breathlessly dramatic stories of 1790s France under the title *The Reign of Terror*. It was reprinted at least a dozen times in the following decade and a half, with an appendix adding bloody tales from the 1830 and 1848 revolutions added by another prolific Pennsylvania scribbler, John Frost.[23]

With liberty so susceptible to violent subversion by fanatics drunk on power, Democrats portrayed themselves as the last bulwark of freedom. By 1864, Democrats were routinely warning that this "government of the law" had been "subverted" by a "prostitution of the powers of the Federal Government."[24] Conspiracy theories abounded that elections had been rigged.[25] Democrats saw their voters as those who could "neither be deluded, nor purchased, nor intimidated."[26] They were the "conservative power of the nation" who retained their "holy faith" in the Union, as Democrats always had.[27] The party "will still support, and finally vindicate the Union under the Constitution, the rights of the States and the liberty of the people. No principle is changed, no position will be abandoned. It will never surrender the Union to Davis, nor liberty to Lincoln."[28] The great majority of Democrats had sympathy with these views. Naturally, inherently, in favor of the Union—that, after all was the core purpose of the Democracy—they were equally naturally and inherently the defenders of liberty and they refused to accept that these two principles could ever be in conflict.

One especially potent fear was that not only had Republicans subverted the government in Washington through an "intoxication" with power, but had also worked to subvert the people through the insidious use of secret organizations.[29] Charles J. Biddle contrasted the Democracy's open and transparent partisanship with the underhand designs of "lodges and secret organizations," a sinister way of organizing practiced a few years earlier by the Know-Nothings and now taken to extremes by the Republicans.[30] Union leagues—lodges of "loyal men" that were created in 1863—were, Biddle wrote, "conspiracies against liberty" which the organizers tried to "scare" people into joining under the "false but plausible plea" of nonpartisanship.[31]

Some cautious ex-Whigs came to the same conclusions as some old Jacksonians about the corruption of freedom in a long war. An example is Manton Marble, a dapper aspiring poet from Massachusetts who had supported Lincoln in 1860. By 1863 he was the editor of the *New York World*, which he had transformed from a gentle repository of literary and religious musings into one of the most strident opponents of the administration—not coincidentally after a group of wealthy Democrats bought shares in the paper.[32] Marble explained his political migration as the natural move for a "conservative man."[33] But there was a personal price to pay in terms of longstanding friendships. One old friend, James McClintock—like Marble an ex-Whig from New England who had supported Lincoln in 1860—wrote in despair that the *World*'s opposition to emancipation was doing more harm than good. It was not as if emancipation, in these circumstances, meant the triumph of radicalism, McClintock argued. The "radicals cannot triumph, if Mr. Lincoln, Mr. Seward, Mr. Weed, who are in the saddle, will only lead the country in the way of righteousness." The North, McClintock suggested, would unite against slavery if only Lincoln took the lead and people like Marble got behind him. Apparently invoking an antebellum free state consensus about slavery's basic wrongness with which he still assumed Marble agreed, McClintock urged his old friend to adopt emancipation, "and you have with you the spirit of the Age, the destiny of civilization, the sympathy of European liberals, and above all, Almighty God."[34] Marble disagreed, his mild antislavery views of the 1850s now overwhelmed by horror at the Jacobinism of the manner, language, and "revolutionary" agenda of the "abolition party."[35]

In a series of flirtatious letters Marble's friend, the novelist Elizabeth Drew Stoddard, who, like Marble, came from a traditionally Whig Massachusetts family, teased him for the extremity of his reactions. ("I hope you are not so distracted by the behavior of those amiable gentlemen messers Lincoln and Stanton, that your artistic sense is strangled," she wrote, after sending him a painting as a wedding present). After a series of letters criticizing the "speciousness" of the *World* "in this emergency," Stoddard asked, "When you write such articles do you put your common sense as well as your conscience in your pocket?" And on another occasion, she exclaimed, "Upon my soul I pity you—I would rather have you working your way," as he once had been, "as a literary man, than to have you where you are now. Don't you wish so too sometimes dear?" Yet Stoddard, while remaining, generally speaking, a supporter of the Lincoln administration, also worried about the "freedoms" and "habits" being sacrificed in the interests of reunion.[36] In her anxiety and uncertainty, Stoddard probably spoke for many people caught between seemingly incompatible desires.

Another of Marble's friends, the self-described conservative Republican from Rhode Island Samuel Arnold, complained in September 1862 that if only the government would "show its vitality on the enemy as it does on the people of the North there would be some hope." As it was, repeated military failures combined with the "interference" in the freedoms of the North meant his "faith [was] running out."[37] Unlike Stoddard or McClintock, Arnold praised Marble for his newspaper's support for the victorious 1862 Democratic candidate for New York governor, Horatio Seymour. For Samuel Arnold, a Douglas Democrat like Seymour offered a "conservative" alternative to the "radicalism" of the Republican candidate in New York, James S. Wadsworth, a former Democrat and 1848 Free-Soiler who had never returned to the Democratic Party. For Arnold the Conservative Party of Rhode Island remained the model political project that the North should follow—supporting candidates who wished to maintain the Union through war while fending off the attempt (as he saw it) of radicals to use the crisis for their own transformative purposes. But Arnold sadly, and, as it turned out, accurately, warned his friend Marble that it was difficult to oppose a Republican nominee without ending up on the same side as out-and-out peace men like Vallandigham and Voorhees. While Marble (Arnold imagined) wanted to pursue an "independent course," he would be identified in public with the "Vallandigham Democracy" and "that is the worst of it."[38]

Worried, respectable Democrats and ex-Whigs saw a world going mad around them: old party lines destroyed and old assumptions buried; all they could cling on to was the hope that the "old ideas of civil liberty and constitutional government" would, in time, come to be appreciated by a "distracted" people. These were the views of the New York former Free-Soiler Samuel Tilden, whose longstanding antislavery presumption did not make him any less appalled by how "unwise" this "calamitous" administration had been in disregarding the Constitution and its protections. This was why, he later explained, he had participated in the formation in 1862 of the Society for the Diffusion of Political Knowledge, an organization dedicated to "the dissemination of documents" that "might be useful in a time when men's minds are unsettled."[39] When the Democrats won the governorship of New York, Tilden described this "triumph of the conservative sentiment" as in no way indicating "consent to disunion either now or hereafter" but reflecting a desire for the "restoration" in "the *North*" as well as in "the South, of that Constitution which had secured every right, and under whose shelter all had been happy and prosperous."[40] At stake, in the words of Manton Marble, was not just the Union, but the "the old form & spirit of Gov[ernment]." While the radicals may be pursuing the former, they were destroying the latter.[41]

What Democrats shared with some former Whigs like Marble was a conviction that the freedoms inherent in the Union were founded in a centuries-old tradition of liberty dating back to the struggles of Hampden and Sidney in seventeenth-century England, and ultimately to the Magna Carta. Was a monarchical power now, as earlier in the history of England, abusing the argument of military necessity to undermine those sacred liberties? An old Philadelphian from a once-Whig now-Democrat family, Edward Ingersoll spoke out and wrote repeatedly during the war, arguing, "Conservatism is our only chance of safety. Conservatism of our own American institutions; such as our forefathers gave, such as our people have lived under and understand. Liberty of speech, liberty of the press, liberty of the person." Such values were "the only guides that we know, the only lights that our people recognize, the only landmarks that they understand. They are as essential to the safe conduct of the government in this hour of peril, as they are to the happiness of the people; and it is as great an administrative madness in the emergency, to attempt to throw them aside, as it is indicative of popular madness, to be willing to relinquish them."[42] If, as one Democratic newspaper put it in 1863, "conservatism is the true Americanism," then radicalism could win only by two methods: by relying on a "temporary madness" in the people, or by hiding its true colors. Or, of course, as now seemed to be the case, both.[43]

Drawing on the Jacksonian tradition, plenty of Democrats focused on the centralization of the wartime administration. Conscription, the suspension of habeas corpus, and massive increases in taxation, all pointed, wrote a friend of Charles Biddle, to a "Jacobin plot" to create a "permanent central controlling power."[44] This was the same battle that Democrats had been fighting since Jefferson's day, argued the nephew of Pennsylvania Democrat George W. Woodward. In the Republican ascendency "the principles and maxims of the old Federal party" were now becoming "the avowed and proclaimed rules of our political system." Already, by 1863, there were signs that the republic had become "a despotism, with all its brood of enormities in the shape of a peerage, a pension list, a standing army, a muzzled press, and a political police." The "supine" response of the people to the "trampling" of their liberties was, Woodward feared, the "fruits" of thirty years of experimentation with a common schools system, state-funded agricultural colleges, and "a government based on the theory that all the private interests of the citizen, and all the fundamental rules in the constitution that guaranty his rights, are at the mercy of that administration which for the time being, may be in power."[45]

Sympathetic to this analysis was former president Franklin Pierce, who in a poorly timed speech on July 4, 1863 (just hours before news of Lee's defeat at Gettysburg reached New Hampshire) condemned the war as "parricidal," "cruel," "heartless," "aimless," and "unnecessary." Of course Pierce sternly reiterated his lifelong adherence to the Union, but he concluded that the administration was undermining the work of the framers of that Union. The framers, Pierce said, were conservative men: unlike the present administration, they were "no desperate reformers, madly bent upon schemes which, if consummated, could only result in general confusion, anarchy and chaos." On the contrary, like Edmund Burke, they "saw society as a living fact, not as a troubled vision," and they "knew that national power consists in the reconcilement of diversities of institutions and interests, not their conflict and obliteration." It was the demand that "the House" must cease to be divided, the intolerance of opposition and the requirement for uniformity that had led to the war, Pierce said, and those same illiberal, despotic, revolutionary impulses were now destroying any chance of reunion. Pierce's fear of the despotism of the Lincoln administration was reinforced by personal experience. Secretary of State William Seward had ordered that the former president be monitored, suspecting him of treasonable activity. Pierce insisted on a Senate investigation that cleared him. "Even here in the loyal states, the mailed hand of military usurpation strikes down the liberties of the people," Pierce protested, "who, I ask, has clothed the President with power to dictate to any one of us when we must, or when we may, speak or be silent upon any subject?" To Republicans, Pierce became notorious for his alleged "disloyalty" in making these arguments, but he only echoed many other Jacksonians in portraying wartime politics as a battle between the liberties of the people, historically preserved by republican government, and the reactionary impulse of monarchy exhibited by the apparently authoritarian tendencies of the administration. In 1863, Democratic newspapers amplified this theme by repeating a remark they alleged Secretary of State Seward had made to British ambassador Lord Lyons that "I can touch a bell on my right hand, and order the arrest of a citizen . . . and no power on earth, except that of the President, can release them. Can the Queen of England do so much?" Democratic newspapers saw this unlikely story as proof that "our Glorious old republic has become a perfect despotism."[46] His old friend Nathaniel Hawthorne shared Pierce's sense of alienation. Hawthorne had been in despair about the future of the country since the war broke out. In a wry article for the *Atlantic Monthly* in 1862, he reluctantly conceded that "since the matter has gone so far" only military victory would in the end bring peace, but this would be done only in "another generation, at the expense, probably, of greater trouble in the present one than any other people ever voluntarily suffered."[47]

As all these critiques of the Lincoln administration reveal, it was rarely possible to talk about the issue of slavery and emancipation in isolation from a broader set of concerns about the fate of liberty for white Americans. This had been true in the crisis years that led to war, and it remained true until Appomattox. Of course the opposition to emancipation in the North sprang from fears of race wars and deep-seated white supremacism. Yet these anxieties were shared by many of those who supported emancipation—albeit in some cases reluctantly and with caveats—so were not in themselves enough to explain opposition. Emancipation also provoked anger and anxiety because it was seen as one symptom of the threat to republican liberty posed by a tyrannical government. The New Jersey Democratic Party protested the week after the preliminary emancipation proclamation had been issued that it was "a clear subjection of the civil to the military power. It is a declaration that the Constitution is insufficient for the purposes for which it was made, and that it must yield to the claims of a supposed necessity." Of course the New Jersey Democrats were alarmed at the practical effects of emancipation as well, but their main argument (pitched, naturally, to "conservative men") was that an administration that subverted the Constitution undermined the core purpose for which the war was supposedly being fought.[48] Similar ideas were expressed by an old Whig who wrote to the Boston *Daily Courier* in July 1863 asking if the abolitionists who had turned the war into a crusade for their "one idea" had asked if "the 'idea' for which they are contending is really worth the *price* the country very unwillingly, I think, is paying for it?" How could it be, he ended plaintively, when "it destroys the ancient landmarks"?[49]

Just as proslavery advocates like Charles O'Conor had become more outspoken in the late 1850s, the emancipation issue prompted a few defiant attempts to convince Northerners once again that slavery was right. For example, the Whiggish anti-Catholic nativist turned Democrat S. F. B. Morse argued that slavery was a success story for the enslaved. "Christianity has been most successfully propagated among a barbarous race, when they have been enslaved to a Christian race," wrote the elderly inventor of the electric telegraph in a pamphlet published by the Society for the Diffusion of Political Knowledge.[50] For Morse, the ending of slavery—through "military fiat"—was terrifying not just because he supported slavery in an abstract sense but because it was a symptom of the collapse of political order as he understood it. It was the manner and method as much as the outcome that alarmed him.

As for Nathan Lord, in 1863 he was forced to resign. Lord's nemesis was Amos Tuck, a former Democrat, then an early convert to the Republicans, who was a Dartmouth trustee and who found the college president's continuing opposition to the policies of the administration embarrassing.[51] Tuck moved a resolution of the board of trustees expressing support for the war, nominating Abraham Lincoln for an honorary degree, and hoping that "American Slavery with all its sin and shame . . . may find its merited doom, in consequence of the war which it has invoked," a sentiment with which he knew Lord could not concur. Congregationalist weeklies and some New England Republican newspapers had for some time been mounting a sustained attack on "disloyalty at Dartmouth."[52] Protesting against the trustees' "right to impose any religious, ethical, or political test," Lord protested in his resignation letter that he was being arraigned "not for misconduct" but for his private opinions "on questions of Biblical ethics and interpretations."[53] "Fanaticism rules the hour," Morse wrote. "The fanatic is on the throne." Like many others, Morse pathologized the concept of fanaticism, calling it "a frenzy, a madness . . . a spirit of the pit, clothing itself in our day in the garb of an angel of light, the better to deceive the minds of the unthinking and the simple."[54]

Leaders of the Democratic Party represented a wide spectrum of views on the nature of the conflict, but most who were drawn to the party after the Emancipation Proclamation shared, at the very least, a discomfort about the prospect that the administration's approach to slavery was prolonging the war. For some the solution to the conflict was now, as it had always been, that the "conservative men" of both sections come together and "overthrow" abolitionism.[55] Plenty of people who had followed the general drift of the late 1850s toward support for the Republicans' stern opposition to the Slave Power began to worry that the country was losing its way due to the influence of "fanatics" in Washington. As a soldier who had voted for Lincoln in 1860 put it, "We have lost sight of the real object we all commenced the fight for, the Constitution and the Union."[56] Some Democratic leaders, however, put their case far more strongly. The blunt words of a resolution passed by the Connecticut Democratic state convention in February 1863 proclaimed that, having once been a war against slaveholders' attempts to break up the Union, the conflict was now being "waged for the destruction of the Union."[57] By the summer of 1864, a writer in the *Cincinnati Enquirer* was one of many to argue that "peace—lasting peace" could be obtained if only talking would replace fighting, but that such an approach could never succeed so long as "the freedom of the negro" was "the basis of negotiation" as it would be so long as Lincoln was president.[58]

The perception that emancipation was prolonging the war was fueled by Lincoln's apparent declaration in an ill-judged public letter in June 1864 that his terms for negotiation with the rebels included not only reunion but also emancipation.[59] William Bigler told a public meeting in the summer of 1864 that the president's letter had convinced him that he was the "worst" of his party, rather than, as he had previously hoped, the "best." In a more-in-sorrow-than-in-anger tone, Bigler said Lincoln "was now attempting to act the part of an usurper and a tyrant." His attempt "to prosecute the war to the overthrow of the local institutions of the revolted states was unlawful, revolutionary ... and a falsification of the oft-repeated promises of Mr. Lincoln and his friends that the war should be for the Union and for no other purpose." Having been let down by the South in seceding, Bigler now felt betrayed by the government of the Union; there was, it seemed, subversion on all sides. Only the Democracy, as he had always advocated, could hold together the old idea of the Union. "Mr. Lincoln," said Bigler, has "divided a united North and united a divided South." Had he had the "wisdom and patriotism" enough to have "conducted the war for the Union and not for the gratification of fanatics ... Peace and Union might have triumphed, long since." To make his point, Bigler asked a hypothetical question: "Suppose Jeff Davis were to make the ultimatum of peace, the establishment of slavery in the North?" In such an eventuality, there "would be no peace Democrats on such an issue." None would submit to that kind of dictation. Equally, he suggested, Southerners who otherwise would support a peace deal would fight so long as the North tried to dictate emancipation to them. Not even, necessarily, because they were desperate supporters of slavery, but because of their stubborn, and (Bigler could have added) distinctively *Jacksonian*, resistance to outside interference.[60]

The climactic 1864 presidential election exhibited the different understandings of the "true" conservative choice facing the country. Lincoln's supporters, under the banner of the National Union Party, emphasized their distance from the old Republican Party and presented the issue as one of "war with Union" or "peace with disunion." Even as they prepared the ground for definitive constitutional abolition by means of what was to become the Thirteenth Amendment, Lincoln's supporters emphasized the essential conservatism of emancipation. If they used the word "abolitionist" at all, Unionists drew a distinction between the political abolitionism of antebellum times and the practical abolitionism that justified the freedom of the slave in the interests of the nation.[61] The continuance of slavery had become incompatible with the maintenance of free institutions.[62] The "*patriotic* policy of the President," concluded William E. Chandler, chairman of the New Hampshire Union party, "is to unite men of varying shades of sentiment upon a policy radical enough *to destroy slavery*, conservative enough *to save the nation*."[63]

Some Democrats had long recognized the potential of creating a new conservative party under their leadership that would include former Whigs, Know-Nothings, and moderate Republicans.[64] During 1863 and early 1864, Democrats reported big accessions to their ranks from disillusioned voters who had supported Lincoln in 1860 but who were now convinced that he had succumbed to radicalism.[65] There was widespread expectation among political observers that the perceived radicalism of the administration was a potentially fatal electoral liability. One Democratic leader told Manton Marble in August 1863 that "scores of the rank and file of the republican party" were "declaring that they have got enough of old Abe, and will vote for any person nominated . . . [by the Democrats] if he is not an ultra peace man."[66] At about the time Marble received this letter, the self-described conservative former Whig Henry Raymond, chair of the Union Party that had renominated Lincoln, was gloomily informing the president that he faced defeat.[67] In such circumstances, there was a concerted push by a group of moderate Democrats and former Constitutional Union Party supporters to ensure that Lincoln's opponent would stand, as the old Whig Robert C. Winthrop put it, on "conservative, national" ground—supporting the war, but renouncing any taint of one-idea fanatical rhetoric. For such men, the military emancipation policy was a symptom of the administration's dangerous radicalism but not in itself the rationale for opposition. Winthrop always insisted that he hoped one day slavery would end, but not believing in the Republicans' conservative bona fides, he trusted neither their motives nor their means. The key to allying anti-Jacksonian Whigs like Winthrop to the Democratic Party, wrote one party leader, was that it "must show no lukewarmness or hesitancy in sustaining or prosecuting" the war. Only then would "all the reflective, substantial conservatism of the nation" support a Democratic nominee for president.[68]

For a brief period in the summer of 1864, it seemed plausible to imagine that the circumstances might be right for Winthrop's Websterian dream of a grand conservative Union party that would marginalize both radicals and copperheads.[69] A conservative Union party, made up in the main of former supporters of the 1860 Bell-Everett ticket, initially hoped to nominate Millard Fillmore, who declined.[70] They then attempted to nominate the Democrat John A. Dix, who was by 1864 serving as military commander of the military district that included New York City, but Dix was dismissive of the idea.[71] In the end this group nominated George B. McClellan but did so on a prowar platform that was very different from the Vallandigham and Voorhees-inspired virulently antiwar platform on which McClellan was also nominated by the Democrats meeting in convention at Chicago at the end of August 1864. Almost by default, then, a group of Whig conservatives ended up in the same presidential camp as the Democrats, supporting the same man on a different platform. McClellan's "artful" letter of acceptance to the Democratic National Committee, as one Republican Party operative put it, unnerved Lincoln supporters by its potential to "conciliate many conservatives."[72] Distancing himself from the convention's peace plank, he promised to prosecute the war but abandon emancipation. One formerly Whig newspaper argued that McClellan in 1864 now occupied the "conservative ground" on which Lincoln had once stood before he "gradually abandoned it."[73]

It was never McClellan who inspired much enthusiasm among ex-Whigs, though, but the underlying issue of maintaining the Union through war while not sacrificing freedoms—exactly the dilemma that had been identified by Stillé. In a well-reported speech, which McClellan praised as the most "calm dignified & able & exhaustive exposition of the questions at issue" during the entire campaign, Winthrop set out the conservative case—not in favor of McClellan so much as against Lincoln.[74] Winthrop represented the Republicans as dangerous radicals who had no vested interest in restoring the Union because it would deprive them of national political power.

Having declined a nomination by the conservative Unionists, Fillmore ended up, with some reluctance, supporting McClellan—the first Democrat he had ever voted for. Fillmore, like Winthrop, always passionately asserted his loyalty. But unlike his friend Dorothea Dix, who called McClellan a traitor for running against Lincoln and whose letters showed bitter contempt for the rebels, Fillmore always advocated "Christian forgiveness" as the "best policy and the only one which can restore the Union." He urged an all-out struggle to win the war, but in a speech in Buffalo, New York, in February 1864, he spent more time mourning the devastation of a war that had "loaded the country with an enormous debt that the sweat of millions yet unborn must be taxed to pay; arrayed brother against brother, and father against son in mortal combat; deluged our country with fraternal blood; whitened our battlefields with the bones of the slain, and darkened the sky with the pall of mourning." Overwhelmed by the tragedy of the conflict, it seems that it was as much the tone of McClellan's approach—fighting the war to a victory that would be generous and forgiving—as it was Lincoln's unwelcome closeness to radicals that pushed Fillmore to cast his vote against the administration in November 1864.[75]

In the end, Winthrop and Fillmore carried too few of their conservative friends with them.[76] Their efforts were frustrated by a combination of the administration's ability to distance itself from radicalism and their own hardline antiwar members—"longhaired fanatics," as the *New York Herald* called them.[77] Henry Raymond used the columns of the *New York Times* to observe that "the student of history hereafter will hear with profound surprise that the purest of the New England Puritans, in the great crisis of his country's history, placed himself on the side of oppression against the party of liberty, excusing slavery."[78] Sidney George Fisher was confident that "the great majority of the northern people of both parties are determined to restore the Union," the

difference among them being that the "larger portion of the Democrats believing that it can be restored . . . by making concessions to the southern
people" and by "refusing to destroy" slavery. This was simply misguided, he
thought: "Two things are necessary for a permanent & satisfactory peace—the
utter destruction of the military power of the rebels & the actual emancipation of all the slaves."[79] This conviction that, as the taproot of the rebellion,
slavery must go had grown logically out of Fisher's analysis of the sectional
crisis, but convinced as he was of the necessity for conservative men to support Lincoln's reelection Fisher continued to worry as much as ever about
the "fanaticism of the abolitionists [and] advocates of Negro equality." As
soon as he heard news of the election result, Fisher told a friend that he
now felt "at liberty to criticize [administration] measures" and that as soon
as the rebellion was destroyed, the greatest danger to the Republic would
be from "excessive and extreme ideas" and the "abuse of power" by the party
in power.

There were, of course, many other paths by which self-consciously conservative men made a political choice in 1864. One was by John McNeil, born in
Nova Scotia in 1813, the son of loyalists who had fled to the British province
after the Revolution: few in the United States therefore had a more genuinely
Tory background than he. Apprenticed in New York City as a hatter, always
voting the Democratic ticket, McNeil plied his trade in slaveholding Missouri
for twenty years before the war. "I was a Conservative in times of peace," he
recalled in 1864. "I felt Conservative; I felt like sustaining everything that kept
peace and quietness between our neighbors." But when slaveholders broke
up the Union, he said, "that contract was broken. . . . We will have a new deal
entirely and before this war is done we will do away with the cause of it." As a
soldier in the Union army, he rose quickly through the ranks, ending the war as
a brigadier general. War, he thought, changed the political calculation about
slavery entirely. "Bayonets," he said, "are radical." Much as he may have liked to
keep the issue of slavery at bay, he soon found, as did many soldiers, that it was
not possible: "It was a ghost that would not be laid" and gradually, McNeil recalled, "the conviction forced itself" upon his mind "that behind the rebel army
of soldiers the black army of laborers was feeding and sustaining the rebellion,
and there could be no victory till its main support be taken away."[80]

In the years from Astor Place to Appomattox, the frames of references and
the language deployed in the free states remained largely constant even while,
as McNeil's testimony illustrates, circumstances changed. Old assumptions
led to conclusions that in an earlier time would have been unimaginable, but
the old assumptions remained. The sense of crisis that developed in the 1840s

gathered in intensity after Sumter, but its fundamental characteristic—a well-founded anxiety about the fragility of their government and society—was unchanged. Jacksonianism, with its fear of centralization, and Whiggery, with its fear of the mob, shared a similar, albeit differently accented, faith in a pragmatic politics that eschewed ideology in favor of preserving a unique inheritance of liberty. Slavery cut across these political traditions and generated a series of moments of choice in which Northerners had to make relative judgments about the greatest threat they faced. Even in 1864, there were plenty of Jacksonian arguments for emancipation and the unconditional surrender war policy of the administration, just as there were some Whiggish arguments in favor of one last attempt at conciliation and compromise. Opponents of Lincoln sincerely believed that the greater threat to the Union and to liberty came from the president's reelection, while his supporters had convinced themselves that if McClellan won, it would be tantamount to surrendering the Union to the rebels. Lincolnites enfolded the electoral struggle in the North into a Manichean conflict that would determine, as Lincoln put it at Gettysburg, whether popular government would survive or "perish from the earth." To them, their electoral choice was quite simply a referendum on that question. Lincoln's opponents rejected that formula entirely: almost all of them also wanted the Union restored and very few mounted a direct defense of slavery, but in addition to the danger of disunion, they saw another, even more venerable, set of threats to liberty from a "despotic" government.

Lincoln was reelected with a slightly increased share of the popular vote compared to 1860 in the free states, which now included the barely settled Nevada, Maryland (which had abolished slavery by the slimmest of margins in a referendum held a few days before the presidential election), and West Virginia (the Unionist mountainous counties of Virginia where there were few slaves and which had seceded from Virginia and been fast-tracked into the Union as a free state in 1863). The Democratic vote was proportionally higher than in 1860 too, with, however, only one Democrat and no Constitutional Unionist on the ballot. In defeat, McClellan supporters warned of a coming "absolute monarchy"; their anxiety about the perilous state of American liberty was genuine, their effort to capture the language of conservatism a deeply felt response to revolutionary times.[81] On the other side of the electoral divide, Democratic Lincoln-supporter John A. Dix insisted the result was "not a triumph for radicalism." Lincoln had been supported by the people, Dix wrote, not as a Republican or an abolitionist but merely because his resolve ensured "the prosecution of hostilities to a successful termination, and the preservation of the Union."[82]

Vindication

When the news that Richmond had fallen reached Philadelphia there were spontaneous celebrations. Sidney George Fisher saw "firemen parading & sounding steam whistles, guns firing & bells ringing." Such scenes were repeated all over the North. "The people," pronounced Fisher, "feel that the ... country and the government have been saved. Truly it is a glorious event."[83] Four years to the day after the firing of the first shot, a ceremony was held in the ruins of Fort Sumter to raise the Stars and Stripes. The famous Presbyterian minister Henry Ward Beecher, brother of Harriet Beecher Stowe, was the principal speaker. "Are we come to exult that Northern hands are stronger than Southern?" he cried. "No! but to rejoice that the hands of those who defend a just and beneficent government are mightier than the hands that assaulted it." They had gathered not to "exult over fallen cities" but that "a nation has not fallen." Even Beecher's powerful voice struggled to carry to the edges of the crowd such was the blustery wind that day, but his speech read well. Newspapers praised its eloquence. He was "speaking for the nation," said the *New York Times*, when he declaimed, "We *believed* in our institutions and principles before, but now we *know* their power."[84]

It is, understandably, a commonplace to describe the Civil War as a transformative experience. Echoing generations of previous scholarship, David Goldfield sees the war as "both the completion of the American Revolution and the beginning of a modern nation." In a thought-provoking study written from a libertarian perspective, Jeffrey Rogers Hummel describes the conflict as "America's real turning point," in which the balance between liberty and power was tipped decisively in favor of power. And the most influential Civil War historian of the last half-century, James M. McPherson, has placed the transformative nature of the war at the center of his work. "The North went to war to preserve the Union," McPherson writes, "It ended by creating a nation."[85] The abolition of slavery—an institution more embedded in the economy and culture of the United States than anywhere else in the nineteenth century—was an event that easily merits categorization as a revolutionary change. It is also true that many features of modern America can be traced to the wartime experience—or, at least, to the changes that occurred in its wake, and which, to some extent, were dependent on it. For example, the ending of slavery made easier both industrial expansion and the development of the West in the postwar years, as Progressive-era historians recognized more than a century ago.[86] The Fourteenth Amendment to the Constitution, ratified in 1868, established a template and a precedent for the black freedom struggle of the twentieth century by defining equal citizenship of the United States in a way that included black people—at least in theory.

In less formalized ways too, the war reshaped the relationship between the people and the federal government. Historians who see a new nationalism forged in wartime can draw on writers as diverse as Henry Bellows and Walt Whitman, each of whom described battle losses as baptismal or coming-of-age moments for the nation as a whole.[87] At the same time, Northerners had more personal contact with the federal government in wartime, not least through tax collection and the circulation of greenbacks. A "decentralized antebellum republic," McPherson explains, "in which the post office was the only agency of national government that touched the average citizen, was transformed by the crucible of war into a centralized polity that taxed people directly . . . created a national currency and a federally chartered banking system, drafted men into the army, and created the Freedmen's bureau, the first national agency for social welfare."[88] More than a million men served in the Union army, tens of thousands more were employed by the expanded Treasury Department, and countless others benefitted directly or indirectly from the more activist state brought into being by the Republican-dominated Congress. The Land Grant Act, for example, established what would become public universities.[89] Unlike in the devastated South, the war brought prosperity to the North. It was not equally distributed prosperity of course—sudden and disruptive changes to the basis of a market economy always create winners and losers. But overall, despite price inflation and a depression in real wages in some sectors, the free-state economy boomed, driven by the demand for agricultural products and raw material from the army and abroad, and by the increasing efficiency of railroad networks.

It is possible to exaggerate the significance of the growth of central government power in wartime. Many of the innovations of wartime were pioneered at the state level before Washington adopted them. The war effort was characterized not by an all-powerful government but by ad hoc cooperation between Washington and a plethora of semipublic voluntary bodies, and local and state governments. Many of the changes that did take place were temporary. Contrary to the fears of many Democrats, the vast Union armies were rapidly demobilized and did not turn into a permanent standing army. During the period of Reconstruction and after, the federal government shrank in size and ambition, and Americans' cultural antipathy to visible government authority remained undimmed.[90] Even so, there is no gainsaying some long-lasting changes. Veterans and their widows would benefit from a federal pension for decades to come. And the new paper currency and the mass selling of government bonds meant that, as the historian Heather Cox Richardson has put it, by the end of the war "the government belonged, literally, to the people."[91]

Above all, for millions, the war was a personal and emotional watershed. As the guns fell silent in 1865 and Northerners celebrated the extraordinary accomplishments of their citizen armies, there were few who had not been touched by the death or maiming of a loved one. For those who had served and had risked everything in disease-ridden camps and brutal battles, the war would remain forever the touchstone of their lives. Dorothea Dix emerged from the war painfully conscious that those who had thrown themselves into the war would "*never* be the same persons again."[92]

Yet at the same time, for the vast majority of white Northerners the storm through which they had passed reaffirmed their underlying values. For Dix it had enabled men and women to display "noble traits of character . . . that ordinary circumstances would never have quickened [to] visible expression."[93] The emotional toll of the conflict compelled Lincoln to reflect ever more deeply on God's will, leading him to deliver, in his second inaugural address, a speech of extraordinary humility in which he asserted very strongly that the war had been sent as a punishment to both North and South for the sin of slavery: "If we shall suppose that American Slavery is one of those offences which, in the providence of God, must needs come, but which, having continued through His appointed time, He now wills to remove, and that He gives to both North and South, this terrible war, as the woe due to those by whom the offence came, shall we discern therein any departure from those divine attributes which the believers in a Living God always ascribe to Him?"[94]

Such language from Lincoln would have been unimaginable four years earlier. Yet he had always been antislavery, and his view of the Providential purpose of the Union was affirmed, not undermined, by the war. It was not that Lincoln had changed his mind about slavery so much as that the circumstances had determined that emancipation must come to pass on his watch and under his political guidance, rather than at some distant time.[95] There was continuity, too, in the values that Northerners associated with military conflict; despite the shattering experience of increasingly industrialized warfare, a heroic ideal of gallant sacrifice remained remarkably persistent right through to war's end.

One of the words most often invoked by Northerners to express how they felt at the defeat of the rebellion was "vindication." Henry Bellows, for example, wrote with relief of the "overthrow of rebellion and the vindication of the Union." Beecher spoke of the flag unfurled at Sumter symbolizing a "vindicated government." The struggle that culminated (in Northerners' minds) with Lee's surrender was not about changing the country but preserving it. Revolutionary transformation was not the result of revolutionary intent. Appomattox was widely seen as a providential affirmation of Northerners' long-held values.

Those values—translated into war aims—did not come into being with the firing at Sumter, of course: they were forged through the preceding decade in which Northerners *of all parties* sought to come to terms with what, in the end, proved to be an existential threat to their nation. For the majority, the great task before them was to save the Union—and therefore the cause of freedom around the world—from those domestic foes who wanted to subvert it. The real point at issue was never whether or not slavery existed in Kansas, or any other particular place, so much as the larger agenda of the slaveholding interest to reverse the proposition that slavery should be the exception to the general rule of freedom. At stake was the fundamental character of the Republic: a beacon of liberty in which there were, for a time at least, pockets of enslavement; or a slaveholding republic in which there might be, for a time at least, some pockets of freedom. Lincoln said he wanted to "turn slavery from its claims of 'moral right,' back upon its existing legal rights, and its arguments of 'necessity.'" He wanted to return it to where he thought the Founding Fathers had placed it: tolerated but disapproved.

Historians have debated whether Lincoln's historical claims about the fundamentally antislavery character of the post-Revolutionary United States were accurate. But what matters to our understanding of how Northerners navigated their political choices in the mid-nineteenth century was that most shared Lincoln's assumption that it was so. An influential book by Gary Wills claims that in the Gettysburg Address, Lincoln reconfigured the basis of American nationality, transforming a contractual Union of sovereign states based on a principle-free Constitution into a purposeful nation with a Providential mission, conceived in liberty and dedicated to equality.[96] But at the time no one seemed to think there was anything new in what the president said. Supportive newspapers praised it as "appropriate" and even "eloquent" but Lincoln's central claim—that the Union cause was that of freedom and popular government around the world—was unremarkable.[97] The assumption that there was anything radical about claiming those resonant opening sentences of the Declaration of Independence as the basis of the Union is impossible to square with its sacred status in July Fourth addresses in the antebellum years. What the defenders of slavery were doing, especially from 1854 onward, was therefore, in the eyes of increasing numbers of Northerners, tantamount to staging a coup. Attacking the proposition that all men are created equal as a "self-evident lie," as Senator John Pettit of Indiana notoriously did in a debate on the Kansas-Nebraska Act, was alarmingly subversive to most Northerners, even when they shared Pettit's presumption that black people could never truly be the equal of whites.[98] Once that ringing claim to equality and liberty was jettisoned, what guarantees would there be that the Union would continue to be the "last, best hope of earth"? As Dorothy Ross has argued, Lincoln's use of the Declaration was simultaneously more expansive and more restrictive than that which had become mainstream in the North in the 1830s and 1840s. On the one hand, Lincoln was willing, as all Republicans were, to include black people among those who possessed the natural right to the fruit of their own labor. On the other, by defining the rights enumerated by the Declaration as applying universally, he was implicitly separating natural from political rights.[99]

This was a genuine crisis; the outcome was in the balance, and the perceived stakes—liberty or destruction—could not have been higher. In such circumstances, preservation, or restoration, could not be achieved passively or quietly. In the end, the Union was saved, and made forever worthy of the saving, only through a revolutionary, fiery trial and by adopting policies that in normal times would have been unthinkable. But we mistake the driving force of free-state politics and the impetus behind the Northern war effort if we imagine a people determined from the outset to change their world.

In an age in which politics was shaped by men who described themselves as conservative, most Northerners thought the war a triumphant vindication of their society and their values. That even many Democrats, following Lincoln's reelection, accepted emancipation as a fait accompli was a reflection of how far changed circumstances could push men and women to accept radical changes without it necessarily shifting their underlying values.[100] Lincoln, once again, can serve as a guide here. He could not have been clearer that his aim was to put slavery back where "the public mind" could rest in the knowledge that it was "on the course of ultimate extinction," a process that might take decades.[101] The direction, not the speed of travel, was what mattered. James Oakes argues that Republicans saw nonextension as a quasi-abolitionist device. Like a "scorpion girt by fire," slavery would destroy itself, they believed, if cordoned by freedom. But most Northerners did not see the process as lucidly as Oakes does.[102] Hoping, in a general sense, to be reassured that they would continue to live in a free (white) republic and not one in which slavery was positively celebrated and sanctioned by the central government, most Northerners stumbled into a situation where abolition took place. Many—probably most—Northerners were quite sincere in opposing slavery extension, strongly wanting not to live in a slave-based society themselves, yet

being content for slavery to continue to exist in the South for fear of the consequences of emancipation. That view persisted for a long time into the war,
driving opposition to emancipation as reckless. Where Oakes sees Republicans' preservationist language as a thinly veiled distraction from their radical
agenda, I believe we need to take it far more seriously as an expression of what,
ultimately, mattered most. Furthermore, slavery was impossible to think about
other than in relation to a host of other concerns—about social order, the
Constitution, the character of the republic, race, and social mobility, for example. So abolition could never be the singular polestar for most Northerners. In short, the relationship between politics and the ending of slavery was
messier and more contradictory than Oakes's clean lines allow.

Gary W. Gallagher makes a very different case from Oakes: that emancipation, insofar as Northerners embraced it, was always subsidiary to the over-
arching cause of Union. "The loyal citizenry," Gallagher writes, "initially gave
little thought to emancipation in their quest to save the Union." Emancipation
was supported as a tool to defeat the rebellion and little else, he suggests: "A
minority of the white populace invoked moral grounds to attack slavery,
though their arguments carried less weight than those presenting emancipation
as a military measure necessary to defeat the Rebels and restore the Union."[103]
As Gallagher rightly points out, administration supporters invariably cast the
defense of military emancipation in terms of its contingent effect on the war.
My own analysis of the language of politics largely supports Gallagher's case.
Even antislavery men rarely described the crisis without foregrounding the
preservation of the nation. When Charles Eliot Norton, safe in his library in
Cambridge, wrote, "It is not often that men can have the privilege to offer their
lives for a principle," the principle he had in mind was the defense of free government not freeing the enslaved.[104] And as Gallagher points out, sacrifice for
the preservation of the nation was the unifying theme of the memorial biographies of the slain that proliferated in the postwar years. The classic of the
genre was a two-volume work by the abolitionist Thomas Wentworth Higginson commemorating Harvard College alumni who had died in the service
of the Union. "Many a true and brave and noble soldier died on that bloody
field," wrote Higginson of one of his subjects, "but none truer or nobler or
braver than he. Many a patriot consummated there the long record of his sacrifices, but none left a brighter and purer record of sacrifices than his." The
biographies were peppered with references to the martyrs' "devotion to duty"
and "chivalrous self-sacrifice."[105]

Making abolition an objective of the war remained hugely controversial; it
was one thing for slavery to be undermined as a consequence of the war and

another for its destruction to be an explicit goal. Yet large numbers of Northerners—probably, in the end, a majority—were pleased to see the destruction of slavery by the time the rebellion was defeated. Slavery had to end because it was incompatible with the Union as they saw it—as the treason of slaveholders had amply proved. Most inhabitants of the free states presumed that slavery was, in an abstract sense, wrong. This did not mean that most Northerners were concerned about the humanitarian plight of the enslaved; they were not. Still less did they have any desire to share the benefits of their free society with free black men and women. What it did mean, though, was that most Northerners accepted that slavery made claims about the possession of human property that were inherently antagonistic to the ideals they believed in, which was why no one—or virtually no one—ever proposed the re-adoption of slavery in the free states. In the minds of many of those Northerners who lived through it, the national crisis of the mid-nineteenth century was one of moral and social order in which slavery came to be seen as an emblem of all that was wrong. It was as much the presence of slaveholders as the presence of the enslaved that was troubling in a republic: the ownership of people created an aristocratic class who disdained the mass of the people. Even though Northerners assumed the racial inferiority of black people, they were increasingly conscious that the claims slavery made could never be inherently bounded by race, as the visible presence of "light skinned" enslaved people showed.

There is a danger, therefore, in making the distinction between Union and emancipation too schematic because in the everyday thinking of ordinary Northerners, the association of the Union with liberty made it easy to elide the two. The Union that most Northerners went to war to preserve was, after all, one in which slavery was a tolerated but alien presence; it was a Union dedicated to freedom but which for noble reasons accommodated local differences, including slavery. Abolitionists like Higginson typically spoke of the sacrifice "on the altar of the nation" in a way that implied that destroying slavery was always—as Lincoln had suggested in his second inaugural—the moral purpose of the nation. Most nonabolitionist Northerners—the "conservative masses" with whom this book has been concerned—would never have foregrounded abolition even in the implicit way that Higginson did, yet all knew that the war for the Union was also a war against slaveholders. That was very different from a war against slavery, to be sure: they wanted to maintain a Union that had hitherto protected slavery and freedom alike.

Confident in the Providential destiny of their free-labor society, in which any man had the right to rise, free from the aristocratic constraints of the Old

World or the stifling presence of a system of forced bondage, Northerners took it for granted that the political economy they had developed was both morally and economically superior to any other—including the slave South. Northerners from different political traditions were anxious about many things—from the influence of Catholics and the undereducated poor to the aristocratic pretensions of a newly moneyed elite or the one-idea fanatics whose politics defied Burkean common sense. But on the superiority of their free labor society, Northerners, in the main, were in agreement: they did not want slavery for themselves, even if some understood and, to some extent, sympathized with Southerners who had it in their midst. The Union that Northerners went to war to defend in 1861 had been given meaning in the preceding years not just by what it stood for, but by who its enemies were. Those enemies existed in many guises, but for the overwhelming majority of Northerners by 1861, top of the list were slaveholders. It is true that most Northerners—including Republicans—also blamed agitators in their own section for making matters worse through needless provocation. John Brown's raid was the prime example, many Northerners thought, of how fanatics could inflame, counterproductively, a delicate situation. But while they condemned agitation in their own midst, few Northerners were unaware of where the real threat lay. They might condemn abolitionists and secessionist fire-eaters in the same breath, and many saw moral failings in both, but that did not mean that they placed them on an equal footing in terms of their power to destroy. This recognition that the greatest danger to Union, peace, and prosperity came from the slaveholding elite was one of the most consequential shifts in Northern politics between the riot at Astor Place and the Sumter crisis.

The political implications of the Northern antislavery consensus were far from straightforward. There was a small radical minority who remained pure, and purely consistent, in their recognition of the impossibility of being true to antislavery beliefs without trying to destroy a Union that, as everyone acknowledged, contained constitutional protections for slaveholders. Such people—William Lloyd Garrison being the prime example—ultimately placed allegiance to a universal conception of human rights over and above the moral claims of the nation. The vast majority of Northerners never did this. The system of bondage had to be tolerated in the interests of maintaining the Union, antebellum Northerners thought, and because they simply could not conceive that a social institution which, however undesirable, was so well embedded could easily or safely be dismembered. The revered Founders had, after all, placed slavery under the protection of the Constitution, where it remained until the passage of the Thirteenth Amendment, and while there were huge disagreements about where and how slavery was entitled to protection, only a tiny number even among the abolitionist movement argued that Northerners could destroy slavery in the South other than through secession and war and ultimately—as happened—profound constitutional change.

Many Northerners had come to think of the Union in millennial terms as a redeemer nation.[106] If the Union was the "last, best hope of earth" how, logically, could *any* cause—*any* goal—be deemed more morally justifiable? The answer was that it could not. The core goal of most political actors in the free states in the antebellum years and during the war can be simply expressed: Northerners fought to prevent national disintegration. But the moral cause of maintaining free government was given purpose by who its enemies were. And those enemies were undoubtedly fighting for slavery. The treason of the slaveholders in the South, as Northerners saw it, altered the balance of their political calculus about slavery and Union but it did not upend it completely. As Dorothy Ross puts it, the "moral weight of national allegiance . . . began to count *against* slavery, although not necessarily *for* emancipation."[107] This distinction between antislavery and pro-emancipation sentiment seems paradoxical but it captures an important truth: Northerners were against slavery and its influence even while remaining deeply skeptical that slavery could ever be safely abolished without doing incalculable damage to the Union.[108]

In the end, emancipation came because in the interests of upholding the nation—always the highest moral good—slavery had become an obstacle. Always predisposed to see slavery as wrong, it was natural that most Northerners would accept its ending, so long as they could be assured that in this extraordinary context of war, it was reinforcing and not undermining the larger purpose of the struggle. In the Gettysburg Address Lincoln made the case that Northern victory would bring about a "new birth of freedom" by proving to the world that self-rule could survive. To modern readers, it may seem as if Lincoln's purpose in saying these words was to laud the moral case for emancipation, but this would be a profound misreading. In that brief speech, Lincoln did not, of course, mention emancipation directly, but even insofar as the ending of slavery was implied by his words, people at the time understood him to be talking about emancipation as the vindication of what always remained in their minds a predominantly white man's government. Emancipation was, as Gallagher writes, a "tool" to destroy the rebellion, but it was also more than that—the ultimate validation of the idea of free government, embodied in the Union, to which Northerners had long subscribed.

Had Richmond fallen in the spring of 1862, the Union would have been secured without emancipation—and a majority of Northerners would have been entirely satisfied with that outcome, including Lincoln and most Republicans. At every stage in the war the suspicion that emancipation was being prioritized over Union was politically toxic. Yet at the same time, the war expanded Northerners' horizons—and, at least in retrospect, when there was no longer any doubt that it did not undermine military victory, the abolition of slavery was reimagined as natural and inevitable. The Union, shorn of slavery, triumphant over the reactionary attempt to break it up, was not so much transformed as vindicated.

Even some of those Democrats who had been labeled "doughfaces," who had bent over backward to defend slaveholders' interests so long as the Union was intact, were prepared to accept emancipation. Among those who did not support the administration's emancipation policy, their objection was to the practical consequences: the chaos and violence of a biracial polity, the prospect of a longer and even more brutal war, and the ascendency of fanatics to power in Washington. In this light, the relative shallowness of Northern support for black rights after the war is unsurprising; what is more astonishing is how a coalition of radicals, aided by a political crisis in Washington, managed to get as far as they did in laying the basis for a future multiracial democracy. An article in the April, 1865, edition of *Atlantic Monthly* reminded readers that "our war . . . [was fought] for the preservation of our national power and greatness" rather than "distinctly and avowedly for the extinction of slavery." Nevertheless, looking back at the close of the war, the author saw clearly the inseparability of emancipation and national preservation. "A higher reason," he felt, had been moving the public will "in a game where the stake was the life not merely of their country, but of a principle whose rescue was to make America in very deed a New World, the cradle of a fairer manhood."[109]

Conclusion
After the Storm

"It is a fact," claimed *Frank Leslie's Illustrated Newspaper* in 1873, in one of those trenchant aphorisms that litter the pages of nineteenth-century periodicals, "that the American people dislike change."[1] As an unqualified generalization this was manifest nonsense: Americans embraced progress with the zeal of a people convinced of their own providential purpose; but the political culture of the Civil War era contains more than enough evidence that the dreamers of a different world were heavily outnumbered by those who thought the central challenge of public life was to preserve and maintain a sacred heritage. In 1875, an anonymous article in the Philadelphia *North American* offered a revealing summary of the course of politics since the mid-1840s. Before 1854, it claimed, "Northern men did not approve of [slavery], but they knew that it was beyond the reach of their lawful power, and therefore they let it alone. That was justifiable conservatism." What changed in the wake of the Kansas-Nebraska Act, according to this narrative, was the attempt of Southern slaveholders to purloin the term "conservatism" for themselves and to accuse of radicalism Northerners who remained true to their longstanding principles and opposed the extension of slavery. "*Conservatism*," lamented the *North American*, "has been the convenient disguise of all who have sought to overthrow free institutions, to protect and extend slavery and caste, and to prevent the liberalism under which the north has become so mighty, from being extended over the whole land." For the South to claim that their revolutionary course was conservative was but a "cheat and a snare." "True conservatism," lay in perpetuating and protecting the "incessant advancement, development, [and] achievement" of the Republic. This statement captured something important about the Whiggish conservatism that had proven so enduring despite the demise of the party of that name. The "spirit of American democratic institutions was intended to be free, liberal, progressive, [and] enlightened," concluded the *North American*, and those who defended such values were therefore "best entitled to the designation of conservative." Such conservatism, in fact, was "the conservatism of Christianity, of humanity."[2]

As Louis Hartz and Alexis de Tocqueville both recognized, the United States, for obvious historical reasons, has largely been without the ancien régime conservatism of Europe. Yet, paradoxical as it may seem at first glance, the defense of liberty—of the supposedly unique form of government created in a specific revolutionary moment in the 1770s—generated its own peculiar conservatism. By casting their politics as the defense of a revolutionary settlement and by elevating the founding moment and the founding fathers into moral guides, Americans developed a distinctive combination of celebrating expansion and progress in a political construct defined by the past. The antebellum years saw the establishment of state historical societies dedicated to collecting and preserving the material records of the past. Public rhetoric celebrated the greatest generation of Americans who had gifted the new nation its freedoms. But the consciousness of the past was curiously ahistorical: the Revolutionary moment was always vitally relevant, to be remembered as a living thing not as an antiquarian artifact.[3] As the mid-twentieth century conservative intellectual William F. Buckley observed, "One of the most revealing American traits is moving forward while facing backward—a conservative posture."[4]

The circumstances of its founding allowed American political culture in the mid-nineteenth century to be freer in its embrace of the language of conservatism than many European countries. Unlike in Britain, a society and polity that the United States still resembled in many ways, conservatism in America was less tied to party identity. As ex-Chartists from the British Isles or ex-Revolutionaries from Germany often found, in America they could shed their radicalism. Largely freed of negative connotations, conservatism became a language of legitimation—used to defend, explain, and advocate policy positions precisely because it spoke to such a deep-seated understanding of what was at stake. It was not an ideology (indeed it was anti-ideological in its embrace of the doctrine of "common sense"), and nor did it connote opposition to change: it was most often simply an expression of faith in what Henry Ward Beecher described in a speech in Liverpool, England, in 1864, as "the conservatism of self-governing men."[5] Conservatism was therefore the language used to defend, justify, celebrate, and preserve the Union, with all the moral authority and world-historical significance that implied. The Whig and Jacksonian political traditions that continued to shape political attitudes through this period emphasized different aspects of the conservative defense of popular government. Determining where the balance lay between liberty and power remained the age-old republican conundrum. Yet, in contrast to the politics of other nations in the mid-nineteenth century, U.S. politics was about how to retain and shape American institutions, not whether to overthrow them.

From the Whig tradition, men like Bellows drew on arguments about the divinity of duly constituted authority and sought to bolster the physical as

well as the moral power of the state. Yet antistatism remained deeply entrenched on all sides, and even Bellows's defense of central authority was
weak compared with the defense of authority mounted by some European
conservatives. Most Americans in the free states agreed that their society and
economy worked best when it was—to use the term they invoked often—
unfettered. Some saw the fetters coming from the intimidation of the mob and
others from an overconcentration of power. The Slave Power, of course, was
imagined to be fettering the freedom of the republic. Beecher's "conservatism
of self-governing men" was the idea that, freed from the shackles of hierarchy,
established in a field of political equality, and given the opportunity to succeed
in what Lincoln called the "race of life," men would recognize that their own
interests lay in defense of the established order that gave them those privileges.
Carl Schurz, a German émigré, contrasted the free states of the Union in which
the mass of men had a stake in society to defend, and the hierarchical world of
his homeland in which only a privileged elite had a motive to resist change.
Schurz confessed that his political views had "undergone a revolution" since
coming to America. "All the great educational establishments, the churches,
the great means of transportation etc., that are being organized here," he
claimed, "owe their existence not to official authority but to the spontaneous
co-operation of private individuals." Looking back on his own past, he was
now highly critical of the "lust for government" he saw as characteristic of the
"hot-headed professional revolutionists" in Europe. In such circumstances,
for Schurz, conservatism meant the encouragement and the defense of this
"social anarchy."[16]

A sentimental attachment to an idealized past was a byproduct of the revolutionary changes mid-nineteenth-century Americans experienced around
them as well as of their veneration of their own formative, revolutionary moment. The coming of railroads was truly revolutionary, cutting journey times
from Chicago to New York from several weeks to a couple of days and, while
people marveled, they were also conscious of all that might be lost. As the
cultural historian Lewis Perry has observed, the antebellum period was an
age of "widespread and ritualized nostalgia."[7] Popular culture was suffused
with a sense that the astounding onrush of technological modernity was
sweeping away old communities and ways of life. Old dialects were said to be
disappearing along with the old rural ways and they were captured for people
to smile at by humorists like Charles Farrar Browne, in the form of his en-
dearing half-literate character Artemus Ward. The play that Lincoln was
watching when he was assassinated, *Our American Cousin*, was written by a
prolific British scribbler of satirical prose, but its success in America during

the war was due to the way Laura Keene's production changed the role of Asa, the eponymous cousin, from a pitiable rube into the voice of home-grown American good sense. The America Asa represented was one firmly rooted in a Yankee, bucolic past, his wisdom gleaned from real life rather than a classical education. Asa dressed in backwoodsman's jeans and a felt hat, just like Lincoln had back in his youth when he split logs and worked at odd jobs as he made his way in the world, but he could outsmart the English (and win the girl, naturally).

Nathaniel Hawthorne expressed this nostalgia for a vanishing past in all his work. Even the popularity of blackface minstrelsy might be seen in this light: as a romantic evocation of a stable plantation society. Politicians claiming to be born in log cabins (Lincoln really was; Daniel Webster was not, but he liked to talk about his elder brothers who had been) were not just laying claim to a powerful narrative about social mobility, they were also hinting at a connection to what was imagined to be a simpler, purer past. But it would be a mistake to conclude that the appeal of conservatism in American politics lay in a widespread resistance to modernity. Of course there were some—the Dartmouth president Nathan Lord, for example—who comfortably fitted the model of conscious resistance to what he saw as the immorality and craven materialism of the modern age. Yet, the appeal of conservatism went far beyond such people and such concerns. The nineteenth-century United States saw itself as simultaneously the embodiment of modernity—the "great nation of futurity" as John O'Sullivan put it—and the guardian of a historical moment that gave it a universal mission.[8] The language of conservatism—more than ever appealing in stormy times—legitimated progress just as it also served to conserve the past. Even the coming of emancipation, as we have seen, was explained in conservative language.

As it had since the late 1840s, conservatism continued, in the immediate postwar years, to be a lodestone guiding political language. To some self-described conservatives the survival of the Union—welcome as that was in principle—had come at an unacceptable cost: a new despotic federal government had risen up. As one Pennsylvania Democrat put it in 1865, "The Yoke [of despotic rule] is upon our necks and it only remains to be determined what efforts we shall make to shake it off."[9] To such people, "true conservatism" lay in restoring the antebellum balance between liberty and power. The challenge now, wrote Manton Marble of the *New York World* in 1867, was to restore that core conservative principle: "freedom of all local communities to manage the local affairs without central interference."[10] Marble's conservatism fused his original Whiggish liking for order and self-improvement with a new-found Jacksonian conviction that overmighty Jacobinical Republicans were bent on driving a social revolution—one that may even upend white racial supremacy. The New Hampshire Democrat Edmund Burke placed postwar political struggles for a free white republic in a universal frame, as a battle for "Liberty" that was "eternal" and which had been fought "in every age and nation." The Democracy, said Burke, was now, as it ever had been, the "leader and champion of the People," and its enemies were "the monarchists, the aristocrats, the artful demagogue, the corrupt plunderer of the People's subsistence, the saboteur of the public virtue, and their dupes and abettors." Once, in President Jackson's day, Burke's Democratic Party had cast itself as the radical champion of ordinary white men in their struggle against monopolists and aristocrats. In the years after 1848, the party became increasingly identified as conservative as they faced new challenges from the rising antislavery movement. Popular sovereignty in the territories seemed to be a perfect encapsulation of Jacksonian masculine democracy, even if opponents—from within Jacksonian ranks as well as from the Whiggish tradition—assailed it for in practice abetting the advance of the Slave Power to the ultimate detriment of the ordinary white men who were supposed to benefit from it. Democrats like Burke hewed to the traditional old Jacksonian language of universal liberty but did so in increasingly conservative ways—*defending* an idealized white man's polity from radical revolution. The "monarchists, ... Consolidationists [and] enemies of freedom," wrote Burke, now operated "in the guise of radical republicanism." And thanks to a war that "should have been avoided," they had regained power.[11]

In the midst of the 1864 election, a pro-Lincoln Massachusetts newspaper had mused that once slavery was overthrown, the Democratic Party would became once again "politically speaking essential truth," since it was "the party of the country."[12] And by 1867 some of the Jacksonians who had supported the Lincoln administration in the war were calling for a rebalancing of power. A number returned to the Democracy—senators James Doolittle and Lyman Trumbull being prominent examples. Even Salmon Chase—always labeled a radical Republican by historians and contemporaries alike—sought the Democratic nomination for president, returning to his instinctive political roots. John A. Dix did not return to his old party after Appomattox, but he too became increasingly concerned about the denial of political rights to some Confederate leaders and the continued exclusion from Congress of former rebel states.[13]

In other respects, however, the larger lesson of the war was that American institutions emerged in a new light as truly resilient, a bulwark of "true conservatism," as the *North American* put it.[14] This was also the perspective of European onlookers who were struck by the resilience of American institutions in the wake of Union victory. In Britain, Tories who had disdained the lack of restraint in American society were, in spite of themselves, impressed by how effectively the Union had waged a long and difficult war. Increasingly, the United States served as a model for how democratic tendencies could be constrained within fundamentally conservative constitutional and social structures.[15] To the *The Times* of London, for example, increasing inequality in the paradigmatic democratic nation merely served to make democracy seem far less threatening. And in his sprawling discussion of the United States, *The American Commonwealth* (1889), the Liberal politician James Bryce observed that those "English writers and politicians of the very school which thirty or twenty years ago pointed to America as a terrible example, now discover that her Republic possesses elements of stability wanting in the monarchy of the mother country." Similarly, in France, the conservative features of the U.S. polity attracted renewed attention. In the debates on the constitution of the Second Republic in 1848, and again in the making of the constitution of the Third Republic in 1875, liberals and conservatives alike argued for American-style bicameralism and a strong executive, thereby distancing themselves from the more radical legacy of the French Revolution.[16]

Even so, fears of national instability understandably continued for at least a decade after Appomattox.[17] To Sidney George Fisher, the war had resolved one source of instability, slavery, only for another—the problem of mobs, ignorance and recklessness—to assume an even greater significance.[18] The fight of conservatism against fanaticism continued. Nor could Union victory resolve some of the underlying issues with which the problem of slavery had always been linked: violence in the booming cities, the strains of mass society, the loosening of moral order, all of which were intensified by the increasingly violent struggle over the future status of African Americans in the republic. To some conservatives, the war offered a model for how to combat such ills through patriotic discipline and a restored social and cultural hierarchy. As the war drew to a close, the annual report of the elite Union League Club that Henry Bellows had founded addressed this issue squarely: "to the military and naval power, which protects us from the violence of armed enemies" it called for the addition of "a moral power" that would protect us from the enervation of politics by corrupt, self-interested "factions."[19] The war had demonstrated that a conservative people could sustain self-government, but only through constant effort and moral exhortation. For Whigs like Bellows, the problems that the Union had confronted in the 1850s were not intrinsic to the republic, they were corruptions of it, and the war had demonstrated ways of overcoming them. Bellows's friend Charles Eliot Norton wrote of the "self materialism, the mass of ignorance, the corruption of politics [and] the atrocities of slavery" as mere "excrescences" on a basically sound and healthy body politic that could be removed, although constant vigilance would be needed to ensure they did not regrow.[20]

On the fourth of July, 1871, in the bright sunshine of Providence, Rhode Island the local Episcopalian bishop Thomas March Clark recalled that back in 1861, there had been those—especially in Europe—who advised that "the ship having struck the rock and gone to pieces, we had better abandon at once the old Federal hulk, which was never fit to navigate a stormy sea and find our way to the shore as best we might on the broken State planks of which the ship was originally built." But the fortitude, perseverance, and patriotism of the American people had proved otherwise. Though "we did thump hard when we struck, so that the timbers bent under the shock, still the keel was so firm and the planks so well bolted that no vital harm came to the sound old craft, and to-day she rides the waves stronger and prouder than ever, and the flag at her masthead is saluted by men of every clime with a profounder reverence than ever given in days gone by."[21]

And so the war did not break the mold of American politics. From Astor Place to Appomattox, politics was shaped by preoccupation with the various sources of opposition to liberty, with a narrative of history in which freedom did battle with despotism and generally won, and by an enduring faith in the conservatism of ordinary self-governing, liberty-loving people. Everything had changed, and yet nothing was different.

Acknowledgments

I owe a debt of gratitude to John Thompson, Jack Furniss, Kathy Burk, David Sim, and Mark Power Smith, all of whom kindly read the whole manuscript and gave me invaluable feedback. Thank you also to those who read selected chapters: Daniel Peart, Richard Carwardine, Julia Mitchell, and Andrew Heath. I am grateful to Mark Simpson-Vos at the University of North Carolina Press for his advice and support, and to the Press's readers, Aaron Sheehan-Dean, Matt Mason, and Liz Varon, for their careful and thoughtful input. Many other friends and colleagues—whom I hesitate to try to list for fear of accidently forgetting someone—have generously helped me to formulate arguments, critiqued my ideas in conversation, or given me encouragement. I have presented material included in this book at the Nau Center for Civil War History at the University of Virginia, the History Department at Dartmouth College, the American History research seminar at the University of Cambridge, the U.S. History research seminar at the Institute of Historical Research in London, and the annual conference of the association of British American Nineteenth Century Historians (BrANCH). On each occasion I have benefitted from comments and criticism from participants. I hope it goes without saying that my understanding of this period of American history has been formed by years of reading some brilliant history by wonderful scholars. I have tried to keep the text mostly free of historiographical discussion, although the notes, I hope, convey some sense of my debt. It would be remiss of me, though, not to mention in particular the work of Eric Foner and Michael Holt, two very different historians whose work I have read and re-read many times since I first encountered it as an undergraduate, and which I never fail to find stimulating. I am privileged that both scholars have been very kind to me in person.

My research was made possible by financial support from the Hale Bellot Fund, the UCL History Department, the Arts and Humanities Research Council, the British Academy, the Gilder Lehrman Institute of American History, and the University of Chicago, which awarded me a Robert L. Platzman Memorial Fellowship. I began the project as a visiting professor at the University of Pennsylvania and I am grateful to the History Department at Penn, and especially then-chair Kathy Piess, for making me feel very welcome during a happy stay in Philadelphia. Visits to archives in New York, Chicago, Boston, and Washington have been made infinitely more enjoyable because of the company and hospitality of friends, including Larisa Mendez-Penāte, Graham Peck, Sarah Snyder and Danny Fine, Mike Ebeid and Kira Gould, Sanjay Ruparelia, and Tanni Mukhophadyay.

Much as I love research and writing, probably the best part of my job is teaching. If you were a student in my final-year course on the American Civil War at UCL between 2011 and 2016 you will probably recognize ideas, phrases, and modes of argument in this book that were formed in those tutorials. Without doubt, my ability to write this book has, more than anything else, been shaped by years of discussing these historical problems with very clever and engaged students. Thank you to them—and, I hope, to the many more to come. In recent years I've also had the pleasure of supervising some very talented PhD students working in nineteenth-century U.S. history. Conversations with them about their own work have also helped shape this book. Thank you to Billy Coleman, Alys Beverton, Gareth Hallett Davis, David Tiedemann, Matt Griffin, and Andrew Short—as well as to Mark Power Smith, whom I've already mentioned: I hope they will recognize ways in which their influence has shaped this work.

But my deepest thanks are due to my wonderful wife, Caroline, who I feel so lucky to have married, and to my daughters Rosie, Eleanor, and Lucy. I wrote this book in what I call my "shed"—a beautiful sedum-topped, book-filled wooden office at the bottom of our little garden—and so my memories of tapping out prose about Civil War politics are happily mingled with memories of a spell of months in which I could pick up the older girls from school almost every day and chat with our youngest during my writing breaks. The children never understood why Daddy's book was taking so long and occasionally asked me pointedly if I'd even got round to drawing the front cover yet. Sadly I hadn't, and still haven't. Having written books in the past while not surrounded by small people, I can say definitively that in my experience it's more enjoyable to do it with them there. It was very refreshing when sitting trying to get myself into the heads of long-dead people to be interrupted by someone with an entirely different set of priorities, such as a toddler wanting to show me a snail she'd just found. Writing history books is good fun, but it needs to be put in its place.

AIPS
St. Albans
England
September 15, 2016

Notes

Abbreviations in Notes

CWAL Roy P. Basler, ed. *The Collected Works of Abraham Lincoln*. 9 vols.
     (New Brunswick, NJ: Rutgers University Press, 1953).

MHS   Massachusetts Historical Society, Boston, MA

Fisher, *Diary* Citations from the diaries of Sidney George Fisher refer to the edition
     published in installments in *The Pennsylvania Magazine of History and
     Biography*, beginning with Vol. 76, no. 4 (October 1952) and continuing
     through Vol. 89, no. 2 (April 1965); reprinted as Nicholas B. Wainwright,
     ed. *A Philadelphia Perspective: The Diary of Sidney George Fisher,
     1834–1871* (Philadelphia: Historical Society of Pennsylvania, 1967).

LC   Library of Congress, Washington, DC

NYPL   Manuscripts and Archives Division, New York Public Library

NYHS   New York Historical Society, New York City

HSP   Historical Society of Pennsylvania, Philadelphia

SADP   Stephen A. Douglas Papers, University of Chicago

LCP   Holdings of the Library Company of Philadelphia

Introduction

1. CWAL, 5: 537. The plan, laid out in detail in his annual message to Congress, proposed to use federal funds to "compensate" slaveholders for the loss of what they regarded as property.

2. The combination of anxiety and confidence is a common theme in studies of mid-nineteenth-century culture in the Anglo-American world. See, for example, Welter, *Mind of America*; Nye, *Society and Culture in America*; Daniel Walker Howe, "Victorian Culture in America"; Howe, *Political Culture of the American Whigs*, 31; Parish, "Confidence and Anxiety in Victorian America"; McLoughlin, *The Meaning of Henry Ward Beecher*; Yokota, *Unbecoming British*.

3. Bacon, *Recollections of Fifty Years Since*, 24–25.

4. On divorce rates in the antebellum period, see Riley, *Divorce*, 35–38. On anxiety about the rebelliousness of young people, see Hersinger, *Seduced, Abandoned, and Reborn*. For an analysis of the fear of Jacobinism in the American imagination in the early republic, see Cleves, *The Reign of Terror in America*.

5. On sensational murder cases, see Haltunnen, *Murder Most Foul*; Cohen, *The Murder of Helen Jewett*; Srebnick, *The Mysterious Death of Mary Rogers*; Stampp, *America in*

1857, 40. On homicide in general, including data showing that murder rates rose during the 1850s, see Roth, *American Homicide*, 150.

6. On the discourse of disunion in the antebellum era, see Varon, *Disunion!*

7. A preoccupation with stability has recently been identified as a defining feature of the postwar years; I think it applies with equal force to the antebellum decades too. See Downs, "The Mexicanization of American Politics"; Downs, *After Appomattox*; Summers, *The Ordeal of the Reunion*.

8. CWAL, 7:282.

9. This twin commitment to, on the one hand, reform and rational solutions to deep problems, and on the other, to hierarchy, order, and the universal acceptance of God's grace was characteristic of Whigs according to Howe, *Unitarian Conscience*. See also Howe, *The Political Culture of the American Whigs*.

10. For the sake of clarity and to avoid repeating convoluted formulations, I use the terms "North" and "Northerner" to mean those states where slavery was banned and the inhabitants thereof. This means that at times I describe places like Illinois or Iowa as "the North" even though contemporaries also knew them as the West. I touch upon the new Pacific coast states of California and Oregon only very lightly in this book, but they too, as free states, come under the umbrella term "the North." It is in the nature of being border states with relatively small slave populations but also many ties to the North that some of what I say here also applied to Missouri, Kentucky, Maryland, and—especially—Delaware. But I do not have those states in mind when I make generalizations, even though they did not secede. My usage is entirely in line with most contemporaries who thought of the North as the domain of freedom, juxtaposed against the slaveholding South.

11. The pervasiveness of the language of conservatism in nineteenth-century politics has received scant attention from other historians, but there are important exceptions. See especially, Mason, *Apostle of Union*; Varon, *Disunion!*; Knupfer, *The Union As It Is*; Frederickson, *The Inner Civil War*. A very useful essay that supports the general line of my argument is Higham, *From Boundlessness to Consolidation*. Higham describes a tension in antebellum American culture between a sense of limitless possibility and a need to impose discipline, with the latter tendency coming increasingly to the fore as the Civil War approached. Of course most people in most societies at a given moment desire social order, even if they mean different things by it. Higham's use of the term "consolidation" is more specific than that, contrasting it with the lack of discipline that comes from excessive individualism. Urban historians have identified other sources of anxiety that led to a push for "consolidation" in the 1850s, including the failure of party politics. See, for example, Scobey, *Empire City*, and Bernstein, *New York City Draft Riots*. Both Scobey and Bernstein explore the sources of conservative impulses in the 1850s, even if they do not directly reflect on the use of that keyword.

12. A sample of recent work on abolitionists and other antislavery radicals includes Newman, *The Transformation of American Abolitionism*; Newman, *Freedom's Prophet*; Sinha, *The Slave's Cause*; Blue, *No Taint of Compromise*; Stewart, *Abolitionist Politics and*

the Coming of the Civil War; Rugemer, *The Problem of Emancipation*; Brooks, *Liberty Power*; Stauffer, *The Black Hearts of Men*.

13. This book builds on other scholars who have taken the role of moderates seriously in their analysis of the coming of the Civil War, including Ashworth, *Slavery, Capitalism, and Politics in the Antebellum Republic*, vol. 2: *The Coming of the American Civil War*; Quitt, *Stephen A. Douglas*; Huston, *Stephen A. Douglas*; Furstenberg, *In the Name of the Father*; Belohlavek, *Broken Glass*; McClintock, *Lincoln and the Decision for War*; Varon, *Disunion!*; Woods, *Emotional and Sectional Conflict*; Knupfer, *The Union As It Is*; Morrison, *Slavery and the American West*; Mason, *Apostle of Union*; Salafia, *Slavery's Borderland*. For a reading of the Northern public during the Civil War that beautifully conveys the dilemmas of the mass of ordinary folks who were neither abolitionists nor copperheads, see Gallman, *Defining Duty*.

14. *Campaign Plain Dealer and Popular Sovereignty Advocate*, June 30, October 13, 1860.

15. I use the term "political culture" to refer to the shifting, often unarticulated assumptions implicit in political discussion; it is an especially apt phrase to use in this context because in the mid-nineteenth-century United States, politics and culture were inseparable. On the uses of the concept of political culture in political science and in U.S. historiography, see Formisano, "The Concept of Political Culture"; Gendzel, "Political Culture: Genealogy of a Concept"; Jacobs and Zelizer, "The Democratic Experiment"; Freeman, "The Culture of Politics: The Politics of Culture."

16. Influential studies of the American conservative tradition by Russell Kirk and Clinton Rossiter both treat the antebellum and Civil War eras as a low point in which the only authentic conservatism existed in the slave South. See Kirk, *The Conservative Mind*; Rossiter, *Conservatism in America*. On Southern conservatism, see Genovese, *The Slaveholders' Dilemma*; Genovese, *The Southern Tradition*; Bruce, *The Rhetoric of Conservatism*; Nakamura, *Visions of Order*; O'Brien, *Conjectures of Order*, esp. vol. 2, 820–36; O'Brien, "Conservative Thought in the Old South"; Tate, *Conservatism and Southern Intellectuals*. Recent examples of scholarship that creates a genealogy of conservatism include Allitt, *The Conservatives*; Dunn and Woodward, *The Conservative Tradition in America*. When historians of the antebellum and Civil War North use the term "conservative," they almost exclusively refer to those who defended slavery. An exception is Howe, *Political Culture of the American Whigs*, especially chapter 9.

17. *Trumpet and Universalist Magazine*, February 19, 1848, 141.

18. *Ohio State Journal*, December 23, 1848.

19. *North American and United States Gazette*, August 7, 1849.

20. *American Whig Review*, March 1849, 221–34.

21. *Daily Illinois State Journal*, September 1, 1856.

22. There is a substantial body of scholarship that conceptualizes conservatism as the political manifestation of certain psychological traits such as uncertainty, anxiety, intolerance of ambiguity, or the need for structure and order. The classic statement of this view is Adorno et al., *The Authoritarian Personality*. Some neuropsychological research provides evidence for this view. See, for example, Jost and Hunyady, "Antecedents

and Consequences"; Haidt, *The Righteous Mind*. This approach is helpful to an understanding of the meanings attached to conservatism in the nineteenth century, but only up to a point. This book, unlike Haidt's for example, does not describe an ideologically bifurcated political world, but one in which emotions like anxiety and—insofar as they can be guessed from the sources—personality traits place people on a shifting political spectrum rather than on either side of a political battle line.

23. Quoted in Meyers, *The Jacksonian Persuasion*, 58. Cooper was famously ambivalent about democracy, as best expressed in his essay *The American Democrat*. See also Parrington, *Main Currents in American Thought*, 2:222–37.

24. Gross, Medvetz, and Russell, "The Contemporary American Conservative Movement"; Kendall, Willmoore, and Carey, "Towards a Definition of 'Conservatism.'"

25. For an incisive analysis of the multiple ways in which U.S. political culture in fact contained entrenched hierarchical, racial, gendered, and other forms of exclusion, see Smith, *Civic Ideals*.

26. Obviously some self-described conservatives did, and do, express reactionary ideas at times, a theme explored trenchantly by Robin, *The Reactionary Mind*. Robin's book is part of a long tradition of asserting that conservatism is no more than an effort to resist change, or, as William F. Buckley Jr. famously put it in the mission statement of the first issue of *The National Review* (1955), is a matter of people who "stand athwart history, yelling 'Stop.'" Without question, anxiety about change—its nature and pace—was at the heart of why the language of conservatism was so powerful in the mid-nineteenth century. But, as Buckley would have agreed, leaving the analysis at that is completely inadequate, not least because pretty much everyone is anxious about some change, to some degree, and virtually no one is against any change at all.

27. *Daily Atlas*, July 20, 1853.

28. *Pennsylvania Freeman*, December 9, 1852. For context on Beecher, see Applegate, *The Most Famous Man in America*.

29. *American Whig Review* January 1, 1845, 1.

30. *Daily Atlas*, July 20, 1863.

31. *Pennsylvanian*, February 21, 1858; *New York Herald*, March 5, 1857.

32. *Boston Daily Traveller*, September 3, 1857.

33. Carens, "Compromises in Politics." For valuable reflections on the importance of both agitation and compromise in antislavery politics, see Oakes, *The Radical and the Republican*, esp. 27–28, 136, 169–70. See also the reflection on the problem of compromise by the Victorian Liberal British politician John Morley, *On Compromise*.

34. *Trumpet and Universalist Magazine*, February 19, 1848, 141; *North American and United States Gazette*, June 30, 1858. Italics in original.

35. *New York Observer and Chronicle*, March 4, 1852.

36. On British political culture in this period and its preoccupation with historical precedent, see Hawkins, *Victorian Political Culture*; Craig and Thompson, eds., *Languages of Politics in Nineteenth-Century*. On the use of the term "Victorian" to describe the United States, see Howe, "Victorian Culture in America"; and Rose, *Victorian America and the Civil War*. The value of the term is that it highlights a common Anglo-

American culture in this period, framed by common concerns and a shared understanding of their respective nations' historical development.

37. Current, *Daniel Webster and the Rise of National Conservatism*.

38. Everett, *Works of Daniel Webster*, 6:221.

39. Everett, *Stability and Progress*; *Daily Cleveland Herald*, July 13, 1853. See Mason, *Apostle of Union*.

40. Quoted in Miller, *Salem Is My Dwelling Place*, 381.

41. Hawthorne, *The Life of Franklin Pierce*, 112. Hawthorne, Russell Kirk has written, "dwells almost wholly upon sin, its reality, nature and consequences, the contemplation of sin is his obsession, his vocation, almost his life." Kirk, *The Conservative Mind*, 254. Hawthorne, like most of the people I discuss in this book, had powerful conservative impulses. His sense of history was ironic and nuanced and he was an instinctive skeptic, especially toward radical or Utopian schemes of social transformation. Even so (and, again like most of the characters mentioned in this book), Hawthorne was far too interesting and thoughtful a figure for it to be possible to label him a conservative and be done with it. On the relationship between "progressive" and "conservative" impulses in Hawthorne's writings, see Arac, "The Politics of the Scarlett Letter." In a subtle study, Charles Swann argues that Hawthorne viewed history as morally complex and fraught with tensions. Swann, *Nathaniel Hawthorne: Tradition and Revolution*. An excellent recent biography of Hawthorne is Wineapple, *Hawthorne*.

42. Abraham Lincoln's now-famous address to the Young Men's Lyceum of Springfield in 1838 was a classic statement of the inherent conservatism of a postrevolutionary society. "Let every American," the twenty-nine-year-old Whig declaimed, "swear by the blood of the Revolution, never to violate in the least particular, the laws of the country . . . Let every man remember that to violate the law, is to trample on the blood of his father." CWAL 1:112. Reflecting on Lincoln's lifelong reverence for law in a shrewd study of his views on slavery and race, the historian George M. Frederickson has concluded, "If it is legitimate to call the abolitionists 'radicals', it is equally justifiable to call Lincoln a 'conservative' of a certain kind—conservative in his respect for constituted authority and his resistance to reformist militancy." This seems entirely fair: adherence to the faith that liberty only existed by virtue of the rule of law was foundational to Lincoln's politics and to that of the culture in which he lived. Frederickson, *Big Enough To Be Inconsistent*, 53. Lincoln, however, was not among those who deployed conservative language (see Seymour, " 'Conservative'—Another Lincoln Pseudonym" for a partial exception).

43. Baker (*Affairs of Party*, 53–54, 181–82) recognizes the attractions of Burke to Northern Democrats and emphasizes that their fundamental purpose was defense of the Constitution. Similarly, Howe (*The Political Culture of the American Whigs*, esp. 235–37) has written about the attraction of Burke to Whigs. See also Macaig, *Edmund Burke in America*; Handlin, *George Bancroft*, 151; Ralph Waldo Emerson, "Edmund Burke" (March 1835) in Whichter and Spillar, eds., *The Early Lectures of Ralph Waldo Emerson*, 184–201; Emerson, "The Conservative," in Porte, ed., *Ralph Waldo Emerson: Essays and Lectures*, 171–89; Clark, *Coherent Variety*, 119–20.

44. *Harpers' Weekly*, December 3, 1859.

45. What Angus Hawkins has written of mid-nineteenth-century Britain applies also to the United States: "In English mouths [ideology] carried the pejorative connotation of impractical and inflexible theorizing, the misguided application of rationalist and abstract ideas to practical and moral issues." *Victorian Political Culture*, 5.

46. Bacon, *Recollections of Fifty Years Since*, 27. Italics in original.

47. Quotes from Brown, *Dorothea Dix*, 269–70.

48. Lord, *The Improvement of the present state of things*, 32. Italics in original.

49. *Patriot* (Harrisburg, PA), February 3, 1855.

50. Whitman quoted in Reynolds, *European Revolutions*, 51. See also Brasher, *Whitman as Editor*, 138–39.

51. McCoy, "Jackson Men in the Party of Lincoln"; Mach, *"Gentleman George" Hunt Pendleton*, esp. 213–15. Mach argues that Pendleton remained committed to Jacksonianism throughout his political career; he even saw it as the basis of his postwar campaign for civil service reform. "As Pendleton faced new issues and challenges for the party during Reconstruction and beyond," Mach writes, "he considered them in the same framework and from the same philosophical foundation that he had laid prior to the firing on Fort Sumter" (217). On the continuities of popular partisanship over the mid-nineteenth century, see Silbey, *A Respectable Minority*; Silbey, *The Partisan Imperative*; Silbey, *The American Political Nation*. I share Silbey's view that a fairly stable and coherent set of Jacksonian ideas persisted over the middle decades of the nineteenth century, although I place far more emphasis than he does on the fluidity of party identities. For the debate about the extent of political fluidity in the electorate in this period, see Formisano, "The 'Party Period Revisited"; Holt, "An Elusive Synthesis."

52. A key concept in the Jacksonian tradition, "plain dealing" was the antidote to the imposture that plagued modern commercial societies and the deceit and game-playing of aristocratic elites; the term proliferated in the 1830s and 1840s and was adopted, most characteristically, as the title of newspapers.

53. Earle, *Jacksonian Antislavery*; Wilentz, "Slavery, Antislavery, and Jacksonian Democracy." The literature on reform movements overwhelmingly concentrates on evangelical reform, but for an important corrective that emphasizes how Jacksonians could enlist Romanticism in the service of radical reform, see Grow, *"Liberty to the Downtrodden."*

54. For major interpretations of Jacksonian democracy, see Meyers, *The Jacksonian Persuasion*; Kohl, *The Politics of Individualism*; Ashworth, *"Agrarians" and "Aristocrats"*; Baker, *Affairs of Party*; Wilentz, *The Rise of American Democracy*.

55. *North American Review* 101 (July 1865), 109. I am grateful to Mark Power Smith for drawing my attention to this article. A similar point is made in Ross, "Lincoln and the Ethics of Emancipation."

56. Elizabeth Cady Stanton to Susan Brownell Anthony, June 14, 1860, in Blatch and Stanton, eds., *Elizabeth Cady Stanton, As Revealed*, 82–83.

57. Day, *The Democratic party as it was and as it is!*, 2.

58. Hartz, *The Liberal Tradition in America*.

59. Elizabeth Cady Stanton to Lucretia Coffin Mott, September 30, 1848, in Blatch and Stanton, eds., *Elizabeth Cady Stanton, As Revealed*, 21.

60. Alexis de Tocqueville quoted in Meyers, *The Jacksonian Persuasion*, 43. Meyers coined the term "venturous conservative" to describe Tocqueville's depiction of Americans caught in the posture of conservatism while relishing progress.

61. On the role of emotion in contemporary U.S. politics, see Neuman, Spezio, and Belt, eds., *The Affect Effect*; Haidt, *The Righteous Mind*. In recent years, the "history of emotions" has had a broad influence on the writing of history. For an overview, see Reddy, *The Navigation of Feeling*. Some key works on the history of emotions in U.S. history include Stearns and Lewis, eds., *An Emotional History of the United States*; Burstein, "The Political Character of Sympathy"; Eustace, *Passion Is the Gale*; and Summers, *A Dangerous Stir*; Woods, *Emotional and Sectional Conflict*.

62. *Portland Advertiser*, July 29, 1856; *Washington Union*, March 27, 1856.

63. Hodge, "The War," 141.

64. Brown, *Dorothea Dix*, 270.

65. *Illinois State Register*, April 30, 1856; *New York Reformer*, December 4, 1856; *Ohio Statesman*, March 6, 1856.

66. Roitman, *Anti-Crisis*. See also Koselleck, *Critique and Crisis*.

67. *New York Ledger*, October 25, 1856.

68. Lydia Maria Child to Sarah Blake Sturgis Shaw, October 27, 1856, in Child, *Letters*, 85.

69. *Boston Recorder*, December 5, 1855; *Daily Union*, July 17, 1850.

70. Burke, *A Philosophical Enquiry*, 32, quoted in Robin, *Fear*, 4. Or as the *New York Ledger* rather cryptically put it on October 25, 1856, in a discussion of the "national crisis considered in the abstract": "Even if the crisis result disastrously many people would experience a pleasure as intense as the Californian who expressed his satisfaction with the exhibition at a circus, because it terminated with a feat of gymnastics in which the actor broke his neck."

71. Marcus, *The Sentimental Citizen*, 106. Marcus's work has been controversial. For a critique, see Ladd and Lenz, "Reassessing the Role of Anxiety in Vote Choice."

72. Rodgers, "Republicanism: The Career of a Concept"; Shalhope, "Toward a Republican Synthesis"; Shalhope, "Republicanism and Early American Historiography"; Smith, *The Enemy Within*; Holt, *The Political Crisis of the 1850s*, 4–5.

73. On the relationship between republicanism and melodrama, see McWilliam, "Melodrama and the Historians"; Hadley, *Melodramatic Tactics*; Joyce, *Democratic Subjects*, 192–204; McConachie, "The Theater of Edwin Forrest"; Mallett, "'The Game of Politics'"; Martin, "Interpreting 'Metamora'"; Lehning, *The Melodramatic Thread*.

74. There has been much scholarly debate about how far and in what circumstances "republicanism" gave way to "liberalism." The key text arguing that republicanism became a very diffuse idea in the face of the rise of market relationships and individualism is Appleby, *Capitalism and a New Social Order*. See also Appleby "Republicanism and Ideology"; Diggins, *The Lost Soul of American Politics*. A middle-ground position was staked out by McCoy, *The Elusive Republic* and Kloppenberg, "The Virtues of

Liberalism." My thinking about this issue has been influenced by Ethington (*The Public City*), who stresses that American political culture at mid-century was both liberal and republican, an amalgam he labels "republican liberalism." By the middle decades of the nineteenth century, republicanism was a diffuse ideology that is best understood as a repository of powerful images and associations rather than an all-encompassing worldview. The idea, core to republicanism, that politics was about identifying a singular public good retained a powerful imaginative hold, which was why politicians instinctively portrayed their enemies as illegitimate and unrepublican—a tendency that, as one might expect, intensified during the Civil War. But even this notion faced challenges from a variety of political actors who began to develop a more pluralist idea of politics as a site of competing interest groups. Similarly, the republican emphasis on community coexisted (as it still does in American political culture) with a "liberal" ideal of individualism.

75. During the 1960s and 1970s, nineteenth-century American historians began to coalesce around the idea that the North and the South were characterized by profound social, economic, and cultural differences. See, for example, Genovese, *The Political Economy of Slavery*, which argues that slaveholders were "the closest thing to feudal lords imaginable in a nineteenth-century bourgeois republic" (23) and that they rose up in rebellion in 1860–61 when they felt that the values of a modern, bourgeois, urbanizing society in the North were about to be imposed on them. For a similar interpretation of the South see Johnson, *Toward a Patriarchal Republic*. In some respects, Genovese's picture of the South was the mirror image of Eric Foner's description of a self-consciously distinct North in *Free Soil, Free Labor, Free Men*. Foner saw the free states as a society bound together by the conviction of the superiority of their supposedly distinctive small-scale capitalist economy. James M. McPherson embodied the contrast between a modernizing North and a backward South in his influential synthesis of the war, *Battle Cry of Freedom*. For an even clearer materialist analysis of the sectional differences, see Ashworth, *Slavery, Capitalism, and Politics in the Antebellum Republic*. For discussions of the "modernization thesis" and the contrast between the sections it implies, see Foner, *Politics and Ideology in the Age of the Civil War*, 19–24; Slap and Smith, eds., *This Distracted and Anarchical People*, 1–10; Towers, "Partisans, New History, and Modernization." An important corrective, setting out some of the essential similarities of the sections, is Pessen, "How Different from Each Other." More recently, historians have returned to the notion that the slave states and the free states were neither homogenous blocks nor in inherent conflict. Edward L. Ayers, for example, has described societies interconnected in multiple ways despite the difference of slavery. See Ayers, *What Caused the Civil War?*, 138; Ayers, *In the Presence of Mine Enemies*. Meanwhile, a huge amount of scholarship has dismantled the notion of the Antebellum South as a precapitalist society. See, Hahn, *The Political Worlds of Slavery and Freedom*; Barnes, Schoen, and Towers, eds., *The Old South's Modern Worlds*. William Freehling has argued that it was divisions *within* the slave states that created the dynamic that led to secession. See Freehling, *The Road to Disunion*; Freehling, *The South vs. The South*.

76. Fisher, *Diary*, June 11, 1848.

77. The quote, from the New York Whig Hamilton Fish, continues, "but it is only as a sentiment that it generally pervades; it has not and cannot be inspired with the activity that even a very slight interest excites." Hamilton Fish to John M. Bradford, December 16, 1854, Hamilton Fish Papers, LC.

78. The term "slavery" was used very broadly in the nineteenth century—as many historians have demonstrated—to describe varying conditions of "unfreedom," real or imagined, and was applied, for example, to white wage workers or people living under a despotic regime just as readily as to chattel slaves. But in practice, everyone knew that slavery had a very specific meaning as well: it referred to a claim that it was legitimate to own a human being as just other species of property. See Glickstein, *Concepts of Free Labor*; Cunliffe, *Chattel Slavery and Wage Slavery*.

79. By the word "consensus" I do not mean to imply unanimity, only that this basic disposition constituted what Lincoln would have called "the central idea" of "public sentiment" on the question: it constituted, for the great majority, the often unarticulated, operative assumption.

80. For studies arguing that Northern Democrats were, in the main, proslavery "doughfaces" see Landis, *Northern Men with Southern Principles*; Richards, *The Slave Power*; Ashworth, *Slavery, Capitalism, and Politics in the Antebellum Republic*, esp. 1:336, 340, 346, 364–65. Though they do not address the nature of the Democrats' position on slavery in any detail, a similar perspective on the Democrats is implied by two of the most influential interpretations of U.S. politics in the Civil War era over the last half century: Foner, *Free Soil, Free Labor, Free Men*; Oakes, *Freedom National*.

81. *Advertiser*, November 16, 1852.

82. See, for example, *Plain Dealer*, February 20, 1854.

83. In her study of the changing tone, focus, and audience for antislavery polemics, Carol Lasser has shown how opponents of slavery increasingly cast "free white men, rather than enslaved African American women . . . as the victims of the 'peculiar institution.'" Carol Lasser, "Voyeuristic Abolitionism,"113.

84. The importance of the anxiety that the argument in favor of slavery logically applied to whites as well as blacks is brilliantly examined in Tewell, *A Self-Evident Lie*.

85. Gallagher's *The Union War* provides statistics on the black population in the free states in 1860 on 42–43. African Americans comprised a total of 1.2 percent of the population. In Illinois, where Lincoln and Douglas famously debated, among other things, the question of racial equality (with both of them denying they favored it), the black population was less than a half a percent of the population. On "whiteness" and national identity, see Saxton, *The Rise and Fall of the White Republic*; Roediger, *The Wages of Whiteness*. The relationship between race and nationhood in the early republic and antebellum period is traced in Horsman, *Race and Manifest Destiny*; Melish, *Disowning Slavery*; and Stewart, "The Emergence of Racial Modernity." Recent works that frame the politics of this period in terms of race include Stauffer, *The Black Hearts of Men*; and Reynolds, *John Brown, Abolitionist*.

86. Sim, *A Union Forever*, 44. On Irish immigration, see also Miller, *Emigrants and Exiles*.

87. The historian David M. Potter made this point in his great study of the coming of the Civil War, *The Impending Crisis*, published in 1976. Potter criticized historians for being content to ask "a simple question: Did the people of the North *really* oppose slavery? rather than a complex one: What was the rank of antislavery in the hierarchy of northern values?" Potter, *The Impending Crisis*, 44. I am grateful to Matthew Mason for drawing my attention to this quote.

88. Grant, *North over South*, 61. I have added italics to the quotation from Webster's speech, as contemporaries often did.

89. As the historian W. R. Brock has put it, if antebellum Northerners talked all the time about "Union" it was because "it was the only way in which an American could summarize his romantic conception of national existence." Brock, *Conflict and Transformation*, 130, quoted in Gallagher, *The Union War*, 47. On American nationalism in the antebellum period, see also Stampp, "The Concept of Perpetual Union"; Grant, *North Over South*; Parish, "The Distinctiveness of American Nationalism"; Murrin, "A Roof without Walls"; Zelinsky, *Nation into State*; Yokota, *Unbecoming British*; Haynes, *Unfinished Revolution*.

90. On the Democrats in the 1850s, see Eyal, *The Young America Movement*. But the work that has most shaped the field has focused on the rise of the Republicans. Both the revisionists and the fundamentalists agree on the importance of the growth of the Republican Party. The revisionist perspective (see Holt, *Political Crisis of the 1850s*; and Gienapp, *The Origins of the Republican Party*) emphasizes contingent factors that explain the Republicans' rise, while fundamentalists (the classic example being Foner, *Free Soil, Free Labor, Free Men*) see the new party as a manifestation of irrepressible sectional differences. But all agree that Lincoln's presidential victory in 1860 was the tipping point that turned secession from a minority enthusiasm to a mainstream position in the South. Even moderate Southerners struggled to envisage a continued bright future in a Union where the president came from a party that did not hide its moral as well its political and economic objection to the claim that it was legitimate to own human beings (even human beings widely regarded as racially inferior). Unsurprisingly, increasing numbers succumbed to the lure of new empires for cotton and slaves, spectacular new stages on which Southern men could find honor and riches, freed of Yankee meddling and moralizing. Without doubt, therefore, the coming to power of the Republican Party was the trigger for the secession movement, which had swept seven states by the time Lincoln was inaugurated, and that is why so much scholarly attention has been devoted to explaining the phenomenal rise of this new sectional party. But accounting for the rise of the Republicans does not give us the whole story of the outbreak of the conflict.

91. Eisenschiml, ed., *Vermont General*, 47.

Chapter One

1. My description of the riots at the Astor Place Opera House on Monday, May 7 and Thursday, May 10, and the aftermath on May 11 is based on newspaper accounts in the *New York Herald*, *Evening Post*, *New York Courier and Enquirer*, and *New York Tri-*

bune together with the following sources: Clippings File, Astor Place Riot, Charles P. Daly Papers, New York Public Library (NYPL); Edward N. Tailer Diaries, New-York Historical Society (NYHS); Ranney, *Account of the terrific and fatal riot*; Caleb B. Woodull to Peter Erben Jr., March 22, 1861, Miscellaneous Manuscripts, Astor Place Riot, NYHS; Toynbee, ed., *The Diaries of William Charles Macready*, 2:425–27; Nevins, ed., *The Diary of Phillip Hone*, 876; Walling, *Recollections*; Andrew Stevens, "Secret History of the Astor Place Riot, with glimpses at the Forrest Divorce Case," Daly Papers; John W. Ripley, "Account of Astor Place Riot of 1849, written by John W. Ripley, a Participant (1897)," Seventh Regiment Archives, NYHS.

The principal scholarly works on the riot are Buckley, "To the Opera House"; Moody, *The Astor Place Riot*; Cliff, *The Shakespeare Riots*. Other useful material can be found in Burrows and Wallace, *Gotham*, 761–66; Kasson, *Rudeness & Civility*, 225–27; Berthold, "Class Acts"; Wilentz, *Chants Democratic*, 359; Evelev, *Tolerable Entertainment*, 79–111; Spann, *The New Metropolis*, 215; Adams, *The Bowery Boys*, 39–46; McConachie, "'The Theatre of the Mob'"; Haynes, *Unfinished Revolution*, 96–105. Most of the previously mentioned works analyze the riot in terms of class and nationalist tensions, but there is also an important strand of literature that sees Shakespeare and his place in American culture at stake in the conflict. For Lawrence Levine, Macready was the vanguard of an elitist movement that made Shakespeare worthy but inaccessible, while Forrest represented the authentically populist Shakespearean tradition. In this view, the Astor Place Riot was a pivotal moment in the bifurcation of American culture into high-brow and low-brow forms (Lawrence Levine, "William Shakespeare and the American People"). Other works that interpret the Astor Place Riot through the prism of the place of Shakespeare in nineteenth-century U.S. culture are Foulkes, *Performing Shakespeare in the Age of Empire*; Sturgess, *Shakespeare and the American Nation*; Cartelli, *Repositioning Shakespeare*; Bristol, *Shakespeare's America, America's Shakespeare*; Teague, *Shakespeare and the American Popular Stage*.

2. On the theater culture and its influence over ideas of democracy in the early republic, see Evelev, "*The Contrast.*"

3. As David Grimsted has shown, theater riots occurred regularly in Jacksonian America, involved larger crowds than any other type of riot, and were often characterized by antagonism to foreign artists, usually Englishmen. See Grimsted, *Melodrama Unveiled*, 65–75; Grimsted, *American Mobbing*. Edmund Kean, Fanny Kemble, and James Anderson, among others, had suffered this fate in the 1820s and 1830s for allegedly making disparaging remarks about the United States. See Haynes, *Unfinished Revolution*, 76–105. On Forrest, see Moody, *Edwin Forrest*. The American theater historian Charles Shattuck has aptly described Forrest as "a sort of theatrical frontiersman." Shattuck, *Shakespeare on the American Stage*, 63.

4. Evert Duyckinck, quoted in Baker, *Sentiment and Celebrity*, 130.

5. Toynbee, ed., *The Diaries of William Charles Macready*, 2:240.

6. On Macready, see Downer, *Eminent Tragedian*. Ironically, in the context of British politics, Macready was a radical and—at least before his experiences at Astor Place in 1849—a great admirer of the United States and its democracy.

7. Harlow, *Old Bowery Days*, 264.

8. On Rynders, see Anbinder, *Five Points*, 166; Spann, *The New Metropolis*, 236. Rynders's associates included other figures well known to newspaper reporters for instigating the communal violence for political ends, men like "Si" Shay and "Butt" Allen according to a police officer who was at the scene on May 7. See Walling, *Recollections*, 44. The best account of Rynders's role is John W. Ripley, "Account of Astor Place Riot of 1849, written by John W. Ripley, a Participant (1897)," Seventh Regiment Archives, NYHS.

9. On Forrest's possible direct role in funding the disruption of Macready's May 7 performance, see Cliff, *The Shakespeare Riots*; Andrew Stevens, "Secret History of the Astor Place Riot," in the Charles P. Daly Papers, NYPL. On the Opera House, see Kasson, *Rudeness & Civility*, 223–27; Dizikes, *Opera in America*, 160–62. On class politics and theater in the 1830s and 1840s, see Buckley, "To the Opera House"; Rodger, "Class Politics and Theater Law"; McConachie, "New York Operagoing."

10. Nevins, ed., *The Diary of Phillip Hone*, 876.

11. *New York Courier and Enquirer*, May 9, 1849. The letter was reprinted in most of the other New York dailies.

12. Some of the signatories of the letter to Macready had previously been very supportive of Forrest and his efforts to create a true American literature, Herman Melville being the most famous example. Others, including Parke Godwin and the judge at the trial of the alleged ringleaders of the riot, Charles P. Daly, brother of Austin Daly, later a theatrical impresario, were among the hosts of a public dinner to honor Forrest's return from Europe in September 1846. The signatories were overwhelmingly Whigs; forty-four of the forty-nine signatories were identified publicly with Whig causes or candidates, had served on party committees, had addressed Whig meetings, or had run for office. For more on Herman Melville's role in the petition, see Berthold, "Class Acts." For more on the petitioners, see Bernstein, *The New York City Draft Riots*, 148–51. Nevins and Thomas, eds., *The Diary of George Templeton Strong*, 1:351–53.

13. On one level, the two tragedians' culpability is undeniable. Forrest probably could have prevented the violence had he given a clear signal to his supporters to back off, and there would have been no performance at all had Macready just shrugged his shoulders and walked away. Some accounts of the riot explain it purely in terms of an actors' rivalry that got out of hand. See, for example, Headley, *Pen and Pencil Sketches*, 127.

14. According to some reports Rynders's men also printed a companion handbill purporting to be from Macready supporters urging Englishmen in New York to support him, in order to lend some credence to their claims. Walling, *Recollections*, 44.

15. Toynbee, ed., *The Diaries of William Charles Macready*, 2:426.

16. Walling, *Recollections*, 43–46. Although he gave the order to call up the militia on the advice of the police chief, Mayor Caleb S. Woodhull later denied responsibility for the deaths, emphasizing that he delegated decisions to the commander in charge of the Seventh Regiment, General Sanford, and that since he had only just assumed office, he had not had time to effectively prepare. Caleb S. Woodhull to Peter Erben Jr., March 22, 1861, Miscellaneous Manuscripts, Astor Place Riot, NYHS.

17. Reverend A. T. Scott to Levi Lattomas, May 14, 1849, Scott Manuscripts, Historical Society of Delaware, Wilmington, DE.

18. Ranney, *Account of the terrific and fatal riot*; *New York Herald*, May 11, 1849.

19. For casualty figures, see Cliff, *Shakespeare Riots*, 240–41. According to contemporary sources, the number of Americans killed at the Battle of New Orleans on January 8, 1815 was thirteen. See James, *A Full and Correct Account*, 563.

20. Edward N. Tailer Diaries, May 11, 1849, NYHS.

21. *New York Herald*, May 12, 1849. On Walsh, see Wilentz, *Chants Democratic*, 327–35.

22. *New York Herald*, May 12, 1849.

23. *Clarion*, October 6, 1849.

24. *Democratic Review*, June 1849.

25. *Irish-American*, undated clipping in Daly Papers.

26. *Evening Post*, June 4, 1856.

27. Brace, *The Dangerous Classes*, 29.

28. On the impact of the 1848 revolution on the United States, see Roberts, *Distant Revolutions*; Spencer, *Louis Kossuth and Young America*; Levine, *Spirit of 1848*; Honeck, *We Are the Revolutionists*; Fleche, *The Revolution of 1861*. Two other works illuminate how European events became embedded in nineteenth-century American political conflicts: Gemme, *Domesticating Foreign Struggles*; Katz, *From Appomattox to Montmartre*.

29. *New York Herald*, March 29, 1848.

30. Fisher, *Diary*, February 26, 1849.

31. Foster and English, *The French Revolution of 1848*, 10.

32. For a revisionist account of the supposed period of reaction following 1848, see Clark, "After 1848."

33. On American reactions to the movement for Italian unification, see Gemme, *Domesticating Foreign Struggles*.

34. *National Era*, April 20, 1848.

35. Foster and English, *The French Revolution of 1848*, 47.

36. Quoted in Reynolds, *European Revolutions*, 100.

37. Williams, *History of the San Francisco Committee*; Ryan, *Civic Wars*; Ethington, *Public City*.

38. *Philadelphia Inquirer*, August 17, 1854; Baughn, "Bullets and Ballots."

39. Reemelin, *Life of Charles Reemelin*, 86.

40. *Weekly Advertiser* (Portland, ME), June 28, 1853.

41. *Philadelphia Inquirer*, November 26, 1851.

42. Catharine Maria Sedgwick to Katharine Maria Sedgwick Minot, January 11, 1852, in Dewey, ed., *Life and Letters*, 335–36.

43. Whitney, *A defence of the American policy*, 171. Italics in original.

44. *North American Review*, September 1849.

45. Connelly, *The Visit of Archbishop Gaetano Bedini*, 98; Mach, " 'The Name of Freeman is Better Than Jesuit.' "

46. Quoted in Connelly, *The Visit of Archbishop Gaetano Bedini*, 102.

47. Fisher, *Diary*, May 26, 1844.

48. Quoted in Levine, *The Spirit of 1848*, 106–7.

49. *Boston Evening Transcript*, July 18, 1850.

50. Dorothea Dix to Millard Fillmore, March 26, 1852, in Snyder, ed., *The Lady and the President*, 126.

51. This is a paraphrase of the sentiments expressed in, for example, *Daily Chronicle* (New London, CT), March 19, 1852.

52. Catharine Maria Sedgwick to Katharine Maria Sedgwick Minot, January 11, 1852, in Dewey, ed., *Life and Letters*, 335–36. Emily VanDette has argued that Sedgwick's novels "sought to bring together the republican values of virtue, selflessness, and patriotism, and the democratic principles of equality, opportunity, and independence." VanDette, "'It Should Be a Family Thing.'"

53. Curtis, *The True Uses of American Revolutionary History*; Curtis, *History of the Constitution*.

54. Carwardine, "The Politics of Charles Hodge."

55. *Annual Message of the Governor to the State Assembly, January 5, 1849.* http://www.ohiomemory.org/cdm/ref/collection/addresses/id/2160; *Zanesville* [Ohio] *Courier*, January 23, 1849.

56. *The Home Journal*, September 3, 1849, clipping in Daly Papers, NYPL.

57. *New York Herald*, September 3, 1849.

58. *Nantucket Inquirer*, August 12, 1848.

59. Tuchinsky, "'The Bourgeoisie Will Fall,'" 482.

60. *New York Tribune*, May 14, 1849.

61. *New York Tribune*, May 15, 1849.

62. Stevens, "Secret History of the Astor Place Riot," Daly Papers. Italics in original.

63. *Philadelphia Public Ledger*, November 21, 1848. Italics in original.

64. On Woodhull, see Scoville, *The Old Merchants of New York*, 1:142–43. Whigs also won three-quarters of the seats on the Common Council. Democratic divisions broadly reflected the national division in the party in 1848 caused by Martin Van Buren's candidacy for the presidency under the banner of the Free Soil Party but—as occurs so often in New York—were complicated by other, local factors.

65. *New York Tribune*, April 12, 1849.

66. *Ned Buntline's Own*, undated clipping, Daly Papers, NYPL.

67. See, for example, in Brattleboro, Vermont, the exchange between the (Democratic) *Vermont Patriot*, May 17, 1849, and the (Whig) *Eagle*, May 28, 1849.

68. *National Era*, May 18, 1849.

69. *New York Herald*, May 9, 1849.

70. Quoted in Moses and Brown, eds., *The American Theatre*, 85.

71. On the hissing incident, see Toynbee, ed., *The Diaries of William Charles Macready*, 2:327; Moses, *The Fabulous Forrest*, 221–22. Both actors issued pamphlets setting out their version of what exactly happened on Forrest's British tour: Macready, *Replies from England*; Anon., *A Rejoinder*.

72. *New York Herald*, May 8, 1849.

73. Nevins, ed., *The Diary of Philip Hone*, 1:384 and 2:693, 905. Italics in original.

74. For example, the New York banker George Templeton Strong observed in 1858 that "people are fast coming to the conclusion that democracy and universal suffrage will not work in crowded cities." Nevins and Thomas, eds., *The Diary of George Templeton Strong*, 1:404. On postwar efforts to restrict the franchise, see Quigley, *Second Founding*.

75. *North American and United States Gazette*, June 30, 1858.

76. Ibid.

77. Fisher, *Diary*, May 26, 1844.

78. CWAL, 1:114. Some historians have read this passage as an eerie anticipation of Lincoln's own future role as an emancipator or as a veiled reference to his local, far more successful, political rival, Stephen A. Douglas. Maybe so, but the most straightforward reading is that it was simply an expression of conventional Whig anxieties.

79. *North American and United States Gazette*, June 8, 1858.

80. Fisher, *Diary*, March 4, 1850.

81. *Liberator*, June 1, 1849, 86.

82. *National Era*, May 24, 1849.

83. *New York Tribune*, May 24, 1842.

84. Quoted in Fritz, *American Sovereigns*, 266. On the Dorr rebellion, see Gettleman, *The Dorr Rebellion*; Dennison, *The Dorr War*; Conley, *Democracy in Decline*; Wiecek, "Popular Sovereignty in the Dorr War"; Wilentz, *The Rise of American Democracy*, 539–45.

85. Clay, *Speech of Henry Clay*, 16.

86. In the Jacksonian era, Daniel Walker Howe has argued, the Democratic Party "celebrated popular sovereignty and expressed relative indifference to the rule of law when this conflicted with the will of 'the people' as defined by the party." Howe, *What Hath God Wrought*, 599.

87. Bacon, *Recollections of Fifty Years Since*, 34

88. Cleves, *Reign of Terror in America*. An anti-Jacobin sensibility, Cleves suggests, led abolitionists to use imagery of the reign of terror both to condemn the violence of slavery and to condone the prospect of a violent end to slavery.

89. Bellows Journal, May 1848, Henry W. Bellows Papers, Massachusetts Historical Society (MHS).

90. Bellows, *A Sermon*, 14. Bellows's sermon was favorably reviewed in the *Literary Messenger* and the *New York Courier and Enquirer*, May 26, 1849. It was reprinted in full in the *Christian Inquirer* (Bellows's own paper) as well as being published as a pamphlet.

91. Bellows, "The Influence of the Trading Spirit Upon the Social and Moral Life of America," *American Review* 1 (January 1845): 94–98.

92. Henry W. Bellows, "Cities and Parks: With Special Reference to the New York Central Park," *Atlantic Monthly* 7 (April 1861), 420. On Olmsted and Central Park, see Rosenzweig and Blackmar, *The Park and the People*; Blodgett, "Landscape Architecture as Conservative Reform."

93. For an analysis of the development of this reform impulse between the Astor Place Riot and the Draft Riots of 1863, see Bernstein, *The New York City Draft Riots*;

Evelev, *Tolerable Entertainment*, esp. 79–90; Scobey, *Empire City*; Beckert, *The Monied Metropolis*.

94. See Reynolds, *Walt Whitman's America*, 163–66.

Chapter Two

1. Quoted in Gara, *The Liberty Line*, 131.

2. *New Hampshire Patriot and State Gazette*, December 17, 1851.

3. Emerson quoted in Collison, *Shadrach Minkins*, 53.

4. Lydia Maria Child to Francis George Shaw, January 22, 1854, in Whittier, ed., *Letters of Lydia Maria Child*, 71.

5. Anon., *A Plain Statement*, 4. Italics in original.

6. Lowell, *The Early Poems*, 43.

7. On the events at Christiana, see Katz, *Resistance at Christiana*; Slaughter, *Bloody Dawn*; Smith, *On the Edge of Freedom*, 115–40. On the impact and enforcement of the Fugitive Slave Act, see Gara, *The Liberty Line*; Campbell, *The Slave Catchers*; Lubert, *Fugitive Justice*; Pease and Pease, "Confrontation and Abolition"; Foner, *Gateway to Freedom*; Fehrenbacher, *The Slaveholding Republic*, 92–103; Litwack, *North of Slavery*, 146–58; Wilson, *Freedom at Risk*; Oakes, "The Political Significance of Slave Resistance." The most recent work on the Burns case is Maltz, *Fugitive Slave on Trial*.

8. Chaney, ed., *Louisa May Alcott*, 53. The Alcott family had been involved in the Underground Railroad for several years. At this point they lived in Concord, Massachusetts, and moved in the same social and intellectual circles as transcendentalists Emerson and Thoreau. See Reisen, *Louisa May Alcott*; Cheever, *American Bloomsbury*.

9. Webster quoted in Collison, *Shadrach Minkins*, 194.

10. Rantoul, Loring, and Curtis, *Trial of Thomas Sims*.

11. Dalzell, *Daniel Webster*, 259–304.

12. Lucid, ed., *The Journal of Richard Henry Dana*, 2:512.

13. Adams, *Richard Henry Dana*, 1:264.

14. *American Whig Review*, June 1852, 547.

15. Adams, *Richard Henry Dana*, 1:269–70.

16. Chadwick, ed., *A Life for Liberty*, 108–9.

17. On the inherently conservative aims of vigilance organizations, which have been common throughout U.S. history, see Kirkpatrick, *Uncivil Disobedience*.

18. On the Boston vigilance committees, see Bearse, *Reminiscences of Fugitive-Slave Law*; Collison, "The Boston Vigilance Committee"; Grodzins, "Constitution or No Constitution." Grodzins's article is especially good at showing how vigilance committees allowed their members to reconcile the tension between their respect for law and order and their dissent from federal law. On the use of vigilance committees to aid fugitive slaves more generally, see Quarles, *Black Abolitionists*, 200–203; Foner, *Gateway to Freedom*, 12–16.

19. Adams, *Richard Henry Dana*, 1:266. On Judge Loring and the subsequent, ultimately successful, effort to remove him from office as retribution for his role in the Burns case and other fugitive slave cases, see Cover, *Justice Accused*, 180–84. Cover makes the case that

Loring was typical among antebellum Northerners in feeling his antislavery views to be in conflict with his determination to uphold the law. An alternative reading is that antislavery judges were influenced not by their neutral conception of the role of the judiciary to uphold the law but, because the constitutionality of the Fugitive Slave Act was contested, more by their political conviction that upholding the act was the best means of preserving the Union. For this argument, see Schmitt, "The Antislavery Judge Reconsidered."

20. The description of the events surrounding Burns's arrest and rendition in this and previous paragraphs is drawn from press reports reprinted in Anon., *Boston Slave Riot*; and from the documents appended in Stevens, *Anthony Burns*.

21. George S. Hillard to Francis Lieber, June 1, 1854, Francis Lieber Papers, Henry E. Huntingdon Library, quoted in McPherson, *Battle Cry of Freedom*, 120.

22. Von Frank, *The Trials of Anthony Burns*, 350; Clarke, *Anti-Slavery Days*, 83.

23. *National Era*, October 24, 1850.

24. *Plain Dealer*, June 5, 1850. On the Compromise of 1850, see Russel, "What Was the Compromise of 1850?"; Hamilton, *Prologue to Conflict*; Morrison, *Democratic Politics and Sectionalism*; Waugh, *On the Brink of Civil War*; Remini, *At the Edge of the Precipice*; Potter, *The Impending Crisis*, 63–89; Holt, *The Rise and Fall of the Whig Party*, 414–583. To Henry Clay, who first attempted (and failed) to bring forward an omnibus bill to resolve all the outstanding questions about slavery's expansion, the genius of republican government lay in the ability to compromise. As Peter B. Knupfer has explained, there was a political tradition dating back to the origins of the Republic that celebrated compromise as a virtue, not an abrogation of principle. The followers of this "constitutional unionist" tradition believed that public life should be characterized by "rational discourse" and "attachment to procedure." Knupfer, *The Union As It Is*.

25. Wilentz, "Jeffersonian Democracy."

26. On the Somerset case (sometimes spelled Somersett), see Finkelman, *An Imperfect Union*, 16–17; Dyer, "After the Revolution."

27. Oakes, *The Scorpion's Sting*; Oakes, *Freedom National*. The quote is from Oliver P. Morton, later the wartime Union Party governor of Indiana, in *Scorpion's Sting*, 28. Oakes emphasizes that antislavery politicians in the 1850s did not see "freedom national" as a recipe for stability; instead, they anticipated that by restricting slavery they would exterminate it by suffocation, leaving it to die by suicide "like a scorpion girt by fire" (*Scorpion's Sting*, 19). Oakes has persuasively argued that for some radicals this constitutionalism was a quite deliberate abolition strategy. The antislavery "freedom national" constitutionalism that Free-Soilers drew on did not push the case that hard, however. Wilmot, for example, was far more interested in ensuring free access to the West for white men than he was in the long-term future of slavery where it remained. I suspect that, in this respect, Wilmot's position was more representative of the Northern public than was that of the antislavery radicals Oakes writes about. See also Wiecek, *Sources of Antislavery Constitutionalism*, 189–93.

28. A strong case that the preoccupation with race has prevented historians from understanding the Jacksonian roots of antislavery politics is made by Feller, "A Brother in Arms." See also Guasco, " 'The Deadly Influence of Negro Capitalists.' "

29. On the political importance of land ownership as a goal for popular radical movements, see Bronstein, *Land Reform and Working Class Experience*, 89. On antislavery Jacksonians, see Earle, *Jacksonian Antislavery*.

30. Gardiner, *The Great Issue*, 21.

31. *Eagle* (Brattleboro, VT), April 17, 1848; *Emancipator* (Boston), August 19, 1846.

32. On the Free Soil Party, see Rayback, *Free Soil*; Silbey, *Party over Section*; Blue, *The Free Soilers*; Mayfield, *Rehearsal for Reconstruction*.

33. *American Freeman* (Milwaukee, WI), August 23, 1848, quoted in Wilentz, *The Rise of American Democracy*, 627.

34. New York *Evening Post*, October 3, 1848.

35. Morton to F. A. Hildreth, August 18, 1849, Marcus Morton Papers, MHS. See also Morton to Seth Whitmarsh, August 21, 1848, Morton Papers. Italics in original. Morton had become one of the first Northern Democrats to be forced to defend his opposition to slavery when Southern senators opposed his nomination as controller of the port of Boston by President Polk.

36. Morton to George Bancroft, December 26, 1845; Morton to Frederick Courgar, January 18, 1852, Morton Papers.

37. Morton to Seth Whitmarsh, August 9, 1848, Morton Papers.

38. Morton to F. A. Hildreth, August 18, 1849, Morton Papers.

39. Morton to Robert Rentoul, April 2, 1852; Morton to John Van Buren, February 7, 1852, Morton Papers.

40. For an alternative perspective, emphasizing the persistence and strength of the Whig and Democrat two-party system in 1848, see Silbey, *Party over Section*.

41. Quoted in Foner, *Free Soil, Free Labor, Free Men*, 153–54.

42. *Boston Post*, August 9, 1848.

43. *Evening Post*, October 3, 1848.

44. *New York Tribune*, November 18, 1848.

45. Morris, *Free Men All*; Finkelman, *An Imperfect Union*.

46. Quotes from Blackett, *Making Freedom*, 36–44.

47. *Pennsylvania Freeman*, October 9, 1851.

48. Finkelman, *An Imperfect Union*, 340.

49. This history is set out in Childers, *The Failure of Popular Sovereignty*. Its supporters saw the original popular sovereignty formula at work in Thomas Jefferson's Northwest Ordinance of 1784, legislation that was, however, superseded by the 1787 ordinance that banned slavery in the Northwest Territories.

50. Johannsen, *Stephen A. Douglas*, 204.

51. On Douglas's understanding of popular sovereignty at the time of the 1850 Compromise, see Huston, *Stephen A. Douglas*; Johannsen, *Stephen A. Douglas*, 283–98.

52. See, for example, Freehling, *The Road to Disunion*, 1:476. For an extremely useful overview of the large literature on the popular sovereignty doctrine, see Childers, "Popular Sovereignty."

53. Niven, *John C. Calhoun*, 306–21.

54. Fehrenbacher, *The Slaveholding Republic*, 266–68.

55. Potter, *The Impending Crisis*, 115–17, argues that the compromise measures were deliberately crafted so that Southerners could claim the measures embodied Calhoun's common-property doctrine while Northerners could (and did) argue that popular sovereignty gave the right to exclude slavery to the settlers. See also Freehling, *The Road to Disunion*, 1:476–82.

56. Johannsen, *Stephen A. Douglas*, 287–90; Holt, *The Rise and Fall of the American Whig Party*, 540–41.

57. Klunder, *Lewis Cass*; and Klunder, "Lewis Cass and Slavery Expansion."

58. The letter appeared in the *Washington Union*, December 30, 1847. Italics in original.

59. Morrison, *Slavery and the American West*, 83; Nevins, *The Ordeal of the Union*, 1:30; Childers, "Popular Sovereignty," 56. For a discussion of public responses to the Nicholson letter and popular sovereignty more generally, see Rayback, *Free Soil*, 116.

60. *Sun* (Pittsfield, MA), October 5, 1848. Southern Whig newspapers reinforced this interpretation for their own partisan ends, arguing that Cass's opposition to slavery extension rendered him unfit to become president. See *Richmond Whig*, August 25, 1848.

61. On the Jacksonian origins of popular sovereignty, see Childers, *The Failure of Popular Sovereignty*; Etcheson, "The Great Principle of Self-Government."

62. Anon., *Papers for the People*, 6.

63. Marshall, *American Progress*, 4.

64. Colton, *The Works of Henry Clay*, 9:467.

65. *Washington Union*, October 15, 1850.

66. *New York Herald*, December 28 1850.

67. Quotes from Holt, *The Rise and Fall of the American Whig Party*, 606.

68. Quoted in Campbell, *The Slave Catchers*, 58.

69. *New York Tribune*, November 21, 1850.

70. Union Safety Committee, *Proceedings*.

71. *Telegraph*, November 13, 1850, quoted in Eggert, "The Impact of the Fugitive Slave Law," 563.

72. *Telegraph*, March 23, 1853, quoted in Eggert, "The Impact of the Fugitive Slave Law," 565.

73. *National Era*, quoted in Blackett, *Making Freedom*, 46–48.

74. Foner, *Gateway to Freedom*, 18. For a survey of free-state public opinion on the Fugitive Slave Act during the 1850s, see Campbell, *The Slave Catchers*.

75. Stewart, "From Moral Suasion to Political Confrontation."

76. *Independent*, February 20, 1851.

77. *Huron Reflector*, November 19, 1850.

78. Quoted in Gara, *The Liberty Line*, 131.

79. Quoted in Richard, *Gentlemen of Property and Standing*, 164.

80. Brown, *Dorothea Dix*, 53.

81. Fisher *Diary*, July 28, September 15 and 18, and October 15, 1855. On the Williamson case, see Brandt, *In the Shadow of the Civil War*; Grow, "Liberty to the Downtrodden," 120–24. This was not a case that arose directly out of the Fugitive Slave Act since Johnson and her children had been brought voluntarily by Wheeler into Pennsylvania;

instead the issue was state comity—the practice of allowing temporary passage or residence for slaves in free states—which was now coming under increasing strain. Nevertheless, as Grow argues, the Williamson case "spoke to the broader controversy over the legal status of fugitives in the North" (121).

82. Fisher, *Address*, 7.

83. *Daily Atlas*, May 16, 1853.

84. Adams, *South-side view of Slavery*, 44.

85. *Boston Daily Advertiser*, December 12, 1854.

86. Nathan Lord to his nephew, March 21, 1846, Nathan Lord Papers, Rauner Special Collections Library, Dartmouth College, Hannover, NH.

87. Nathan Lord, "Is Slavery Right?" undated draft lecture, Lord Papers. The reference to hell is in Crosby, *Eulogy*, 16. On Lord in the context of other Northern proslavery publicists in the antebellum period, see Tise, *Proslavery*, 166–68. A full account of Lord's presidency of Dartmouth is in Lord, *History of Dartmouth College*, 2:252–55, 321–33.

88. Lord, *A Letter to Ministers*, 3. Italics in original.

89. Lord's proslavery views were therefore philosophically very different from O'Sullivan's: the latter argued that the universal principle of equality did not apply to black people; the former simply did not accept that there was any such universal principle. Even after his proslavery conversion, Lord championed the admission of black students at Dartmouth and on at least one occasion attended the ordination of an African American Dartmouth graduate as a minister—the only white man present according to press reports. Crosby, *Eulogy*, 16.

90. In fact, Scott's views on slavery were much closer to those of someone like Fisher. Expressing a general wish that slavery would come to an end, Scott nevertheless claimed that slavery had brought benefits to the enslaved. Scott, *Letter on the Slavery Question*; *Fountain Ledger*, September 3, 1852. Whig newspapers in the South managed to make the case that on the basis of the available evidence, Pierce was a greater danger to slavery expansion than Scott. See *Richmond Whig*, September 15, 1852.

91. Hawthorne, *The Life of Franklin Pierce*, 112. Italics in original.

92. Hawthorne to Henry Wadsworth Longfellow, May 8, 1851, in Woodson, Smith, and Pearson, eds., *Works of Hawthorne*, 16:431.

93. *Alton Telegraph & Democratic Review*, November 22, 1850, quoted in Campbell, *The Slave Catchers*, 56.

94. Lincoln to Joshua F. Speed, August 24, 1855 in CWAL, 2:320.

95. Adams, *Richard Henry Dana*, 270.

96. Parker, *Reminiscences of Rufus Choate*, 472. Italics in original.

97. Choate was not unusual among Webster's Boston allies in throwing his support, however reluctantly, to Buchanan. George T. Curtis and Robert Winthrop are other examples. Curtis went on to write biographies of both Webster and Buchanan.

98. Indicative works exemplifying the trends referred to in this paragraph are Foner, *Free Soil, Free Labor, Free Men*; Holt, *The Political Crisis of the 1850s*; Gienapp, *The Origins of the Republican Party*; May, *Manifest Destiny's Underworld*; May, *Slavery, Race, and Conquest*.

99. Corwin, *Speech of Mr. Corwin of Ohio*, 3.

100. Douglas said this in a debate in the Senate in 1848 in an exchange with Mississippi Senator Henry S. Foote. Johannsen, *Stephen A. Douglas*, 237. Italics in original.

101. Boston *Daily Atlas*, June 16, 1854.

102. *National Era*, May 24, 1849.

103. Quoted in Grow, *"Liberty to the Downtrodden,"* 122.

Chapter Three

1. Cong. Globe, 33rd Cong., 1st Sess., 1209, appendix, 726–29 (1854).

2. *Daily Evening Star*, May 18, 1854.

3. Etheridge was representative of a substantial minority of Upper South slaveholders who feared that slavery extension would destabilize the position of slavery within the Union and reduce the price of slaves, neither of which they, correctly, thought was in their long-term interest. For the background on the Upper South response to the Kansas-Nebraska Act, see Freehling, *The Road to Disunion*, Vol. 1.

4. The phrase "era of good feelings"—an allusion to the supposed period in which partisanship ceased after the War of 1812—was nevertheless used with no apparent irony by some Fillmore-supporting Whig journals. See, for example, the New York *Commercial Advertiser*, cited in the Washington, DC, *Republic*, May 20, 1851; and the Newark *Daily Advertiser*, July 23, 1853.

5. May, *Manifest Destiny's Underworld*; Brown, *Agents of Manifest Destiny*; Franklin, "The Southern Expansionists."

6. Nichols, *Franklin Pierce*, 321–24; Potter, *The Impending Crisis*, 161–62; *New York Herald*, January 24, 1854; *New York Tribune*, January 24, 1854.

7. Holt, *Franklin Pierce*, 79–80.

8. On the passage of the Kansas-Nebraska Act, see Nevins, *Ordeal of the Union*, 2:78–121; Johannsen, ed., *The Letters of Stephen A. Douglas*, 398–413; Johannsen, *The Frontier, the Union*, 77–119; Potter, *The Impending Crisis*, 145–76; Holt, *The Rise and Fall of the American Whig Party*, 804–35; Holt, *Franklin Pierce*, 75–78; Shelden, *Washington Brotherhood*, 96–119; Wunder and Ross, eds., *The Nebraska-Kansas Act*; Nichols, "The Kansas-Nebraska Act."

9. Three of five Democratic congressmen in Illinois, seven of ten from Indiana and eleven of sixteen from Pennsylvania supported the bill. Nine of twenty-one New York Democrats also supported it, as did two of four New Jersey Democrats. Two lone congressmen from New England, Moses McDonald of Maine and Harry Hibbard of New Hampshire, supported the bill. When McDonald returned to his district in the summer recess he was attacked by a mob calling him a "damned doughface," while members of Hibbard's own party hanged him in effigy. Probably wisely, neither sought reelection. All Northern Whigs, and—obviously—the "Independent Democrats" were opposed to the bill. See *Vermont Journal*, July 14, 1854; *Boston Evening Transcript*, August 15, 1854; *New Hampshire Patriot and State Gazette*, May 24, 1854. McDonald's treatment seems to have been considerably harsher than Hibbard's. The latter retained the support of a

large faction of the state's party (possibly a majority), while the Democratic Party in Maine seems to have swung decisively against the Kansas-Nebraska Act and McDonald had few, if any, defenders in his home state. All election data is from Dubin, *Congressional Elections*, cross-checked with newspapers, and supplemented with historical congressional district data from http://cdmaps.polisci.ucla.edu/, a site that reproduces the cartography in Martis, *The Historical Atlas of Congressional Elections*.

10. Lydia Maria Child to Francis George Shaw, January 22, 1854, in Whittier, ed., *Letters of Lydia Maria Child*, 70.

11. New York *Evening Post*, May 30, 1854.

12. Potter, *The Impending Crisis*, 162; *National Era*, January 24, 1854. The "Appeal" was dated January 19. It was reprinted in many newspapers and in the Cong. Globe, 33rd Cong., 1st Sess., 281–82 (1854).

13. *Albany Evening Journal*, May 30, 1854.

14. John Nigley to William Bigler, July 13, 1854, Bigler Papers, Historical Society of Pennsylvania (HSP). Italics in original.

15. Fields, ed., *Life and Letters of Harriet Beecher Stowe*, 211.

16. Johannsen, *The Letters of Stephen A. Douglas*, 451.

17. Stephen A. Douglas to Charles H. Lanphier, August 25, 1854, in Robert W. Johannsen, ed., *The Letters of Stephen A. Douglas*, 327. On the reaction in Illinois to the Kansas-Nebraska Act, see ibid., 447–56.

18. William Penn to Douglas, March 25, 1854, SADP.

19. Johannsen, *The Letters of Stephen A. Douglas*, 442. Comparing Douglas to Judas was a common motif. A committee of Ohio ladies sent Douglas thirty pieces of silver, while a widely circulated anonymous poem attacking the Nebraska Act imagined that even John C. Calhoun, were he still alive, would have disdained the Northern politicians who "betrayed fair freedom with a Judas kiss."

> He would have scorned to own a slave so mean
> As sneaking senators who strive to sell
> For silver pieces, pottage, place, or power,
> The birthright of a nation like our own
> *Nebraska: A Poem, personal and political*, 4.

20. Carwardine, *Evangelicals and Politics*, 234–43.

21. Stephen A. Douglas to Howell Cobb, April 2, 1854, in Johannsen, ed., *The Letters of Stephen A. Douglas*, 300.

22. *Daily Evening Star*, October 9, 1855.

23. *Philadelphia Sun*, September 22, 1855.

24. *St Albans Messenger*, March 2, 1854.

25. *Plain Dealer*, March 3, 1854.

26. *Washington Sentinel*, March 21, 1854.

27. *Cleveland Leader*, October 14, 1854.

28. *Schenectady Cabinet*, October 9, 1855.

29. There were some veterans of the Free-Soil Party of 1848 who remained in Democratic ranks after 1854. There were also Democrats who had fervently supported the Compromise of 1850, were committed to popular sovereignty, and disdained what they saw as the absolutism of the "freedom national" doctrine, who nevertheless left in 1854.

30. Alexander, *A Political History*, 2:211.

31. Anon., *A Plain Statement*, 7.

32. The seven congressmen reelected were William A. Richardson of Illinois; William H. English and Smith Miller of Indiana; George Vail of New Jersey; and Thomas B. Florence, J. Glancey Jones, and Asa Packer of Pennsylvania. None of the nine pro-Nebraska representatives from New York were reelected, nor were any of the four from Ohio. The Democrats suffered their most dramatic losses in New York. On the Democratic losses, see Richards, *The Slave Power*, 190–94; Holt, *The Rise and Fall of the American Whigs*, 836–78; Gienapp, *The Origins of the Republican Party*, 103–66.

33. There was a two-party contest in Michigan in 1854 between the Democrats who united behind the Kansas-Nebraska Act and a new "fusion" coalition, known as the Republicans, consisting of "Anti-Nebraska" Democrats and Whigs. Everywhere else, as Michael F. Holt writes, "the local elections between August 1854 and December 1855 were the most labyrinthine, chaotic, and important off-year contests in all of American political history." Of the 144 Northern congressmen, only 37 were elected as Whigs, although, according to Holt, only 9 won as "straight Whigs, and four of those from Vermont and Maine took such strident antislavery stands that Free-Soilers willingly supported them." *The Rise and Fall of the American Whig Party*, 838, 877.

34. On Pennsylvania and Massachusetts politics in 1854, see Coleman, *The Disruption of Pennsylvania Democracy*; Baum, *The Civil War Party System*; Voss-Hubbard, *Beyond Party*, 111–37. Holt, *The Rise and Fall of the American Whig Party* covers the reaction of Whigs to these election results.

35. *The Star of the North*, August 30, 1855. On the development of nativist politics in the 1850s, see Anbinder, *Nativism and Slavery*; Voss-Hubbard, *Beyond Party*; Holt, "The Politics of Impatience"; Levine, "Conservatism, Nativism, and Slavery"; Gienapp, "Nativism and the Creation of a Republican Majority."

36. Quoted in Voss-Hubbard, *Beyond Party*, 105.

37. *New York Express*, February 9, 1855.

38. *Morning Herald*, August 21, 1854.

39. Henry Phillips to William Bigler, May 28, 1854, Bigler Papers, HSP; Daniel T. Jenks to Buchanan, October 3, 1854, Buchanan Papers, HSP.

40. My best estimate of the Democratic vote share in congressional elections in the free states is that it was around 41 percent in elections to the 34th Congress in 1854–55, compared to about 50 percent in the previous round of elections in 1852–53. This is calculated simply by adding up the votes cast for Democratic candidates, as reported in Dubin, *United States Congressional Elections*, compared to the total number of votes

cast. I have also consulted the statistical appendix in Gienapp, *The Origins of the Republican Party*, and the election results reported in the New York papers. The calculation of popular vote share can only really be expressed as an estimate because of the profusion of party labels, fusion candidates, split-ticket voting, and the drawn-out election calendar, all of which require judgment and sometimes guesswork as well as basic arithmetic.

41. *Plain Dealer*, February 4, 1854.

42. Dorothea Dix to Millard Fillmore, February 11, 1854, in Snyder, ed., *The Lady and the President*, 175. Italics in original. Dix, it should be said, had another reason for resenting the introduction of the Nebraska bill, since it meant that her own project of persuading Congress to appropriate land to endow mental asylums became mired in the politics of slavery. See Brown, *Dorothea Dix*, 201–9.

43. CWAL, 2:272.

44. Quoted in Holt, *The Rise and Fall of the American Whig Party*, 811.

45. Sumner, *Complete Works*, 4:147–48.

46. *Massachusetts Spy*, December 28, 1859.

47. Winthrop to Everett, January 28, February 6 and 24, and April 14, 1854, and Fillmore to Everett, February 8, 1854, Everett Papers, MHS; Gienapp, *The Origins of the Republican Party*, 115.

48. Butler, *A Retrospect of Forty Years*, 261.

49. *New York Courier and Enquirer*, quoted in Boston *Daily Atlas*, July 30, 1855.

50. *New York Courier and Enquirer*, May 29, 1854.

51. James Watson Webb, quoted in Boston *Daily Atlas*, July 30, 1855. The Philadelphia *North American* echoed this sentiment: "True conservatism will not be found palliating Southern aggression, [or] advising submission for the sake of peace." *North American and United States Gazette*, November 3, 1856.

52. Boston *Daily Atlas*, August 18, 1855.

53. *Ohio State Journal*, June 22, 1855.

54. Bushnell, *A Discourse Delivered in the North Church*, 7–9, 18–19.

55. Boston *Daily Atlas*, February 9, 1854.

56. Quoted in Levine, "Conservatism, Nativism, and Slavery," 482.

57. Anon., *An Appeal to the Conservative Masses, North and South*; Magoun, "A Conservative View."

58. Palfrey, *Letter to an Old Whig Neighbor*.

59. Boston *Daily Atlas*, August 18, 1855.

60. Philadelphia *Sun*, quoted in the *Herald of Freedom*, September 22, 1855.

61. *Ohio State Journal*, October 22, 1854.

62. Anbinder, *Nativism and Slavery*, 89.

63. Burlingame, *Oration*, 22.

64. Spooner, *Report of the President of the State Council of Ohio*, 7–12.

65. Quotes from Voss-Hubbard, *Beyond Party*, 132.

66. See Woods, *Emotional and Sectional Conflict*, 124–48.

67. *Weekly Chronicle*, March 2, 1854.

68. On the antebellum crusade against violence and anger, see Kasson, *Rudeness & Civility*; Masur, *Rites of Execution*; Gilje, *The Road to Mobocracy*; Stearns and Stearns, *Anger*.

69. *Daily Union*, June 29, 1854.

70. Douglas, *Speech in Philadelphia, July 4, 1854*.

71. *New York Herald*, June 4, 1854; *New York Tribune*, June 4, 1854; *Plain Dealer*, June 7, 1854. The *New York Herald*, February 9, 1854, provides excerpts from Democratic newspapers supportive of the Nebraska bill, most of which emphasized its conservatism.

72. *National Era*, April 26, 1855.

73. Winthrop, *Algernon Sidney*; *North American Review* 80, no. 166 (January 1855), 21–49.

74. Winthrop, *Memoir*, 205.

75. The reinvention of Cromwell was thanks in part to the widespread republication of Thomas Carlyle's influential *On Heroes*. It was widely reviewed and reprinted in the United States. For a brief discussion of the book's reception, see the *New York Herald*, May 14, 1842.

76. Bancroft, *A History of the United States*, 1:310; Friedlander and Butterfield, eds. *The Diary of Charles Francis Adams*, 4:360. On the image of the English Civil War in the nineteenth-century United States, see Karsten, "Cromwell in America"; Karsten, *Patriot-Heroes*; Taylor, *Thinking America*, 71–78. See also Worden, "The Victorians and Oliver Cromwell."

77. See Young, "English Plebian Culture," 195.

78. Boston *Daily Atlas*, November 20, 1855. Less unkind reviews are quoted in Anbinder, *Nativism and Slavery*, 184.

79. See, for example, Boston *Evening Transcript*, December 30, 1847, which reports a lecture on Cromwell by a Dr. Choules, defending the Lord Protector over his actions at Drogheda.

80. *Emancipator and Republican*, April 12, 1849.

81. *New York Tribune*, August 18, 1855.

82. On the violence in Kansas Territory, see Etcheson, *Bleeding Kansas*; Harrold, *Border War*; Oertel, *Bleeding Borders*; Rawley, *Race & Politics*.

83. The assault in the Senate is described in Shelden, *Washington Brotherhood*, 122; Donald, *Charles Sumner*, 243–60. On the political uses of the Sumner assault, see Sinha, "The Caning of Charles Sumner"; Gienapp, "The Crime Against Sumner"; David, "The Politics of Emasculation"; Puleo, *The Caning*.

84. Lydia Maria Child to Sarah Blake Sturgis Shaw, 1856, in Whittier, ed., *Letters of Lydia Maria Child*, 78–80.

85. Quoted in Gienapp, *The Origins of the Republican Party*, 359.

86. Woods, *Emotional and Sectional Conflict*, 149–60.

87. Ellen Birdseye Wheaton, May 1856, in Gordon, ed., *Diary of Ellen Birdseye Wheaton*, 325–26.

88. Amy Greenberg has argued that there were two competing conceptions of manhood visible in the antebellum period: "martial" manhood, which manifested itself in

the enthusiasm for imperial expansion, and "restrained" manhood, prizing discipline and self-control. These are useful categories, but in practice the language of Northerners in the 1850s oscillated between them. While Greenberg's description of "restrained" manhood most aptly describes the values of many antislavery Northerners, there was also a "martial" violence about the language of resistance to the Slave Power matched by symbolic acts of violence such as the burning of Douglas in effigy and the disruption of pro-Nebraska meetings. Greenberg, *Manifest Manhood*.

89. *Albany Evening Journal*, June 7, 1856.

90. *Plain Dealer*, May 28, 1856.

91. Johannsen, *The Letters of Stephen A. Douglas*, 506; *Plain Dealer*, October 1, 1856. Italics in original.

92. Fisher, *Diary*, May 28, 1856.

93. The fullest examination of the 1856 presidential election is Gienapp, *The Origins of the Republican Party*, 239–448. See also Holt, *The Rise and Fall of the American Whig Party*, 941–61; Nichols, *The Disruption of the American Democracy*, 17–62; Anbinder, *Nativism and Slavery*, 194–245.

94. Gienapp, "Nativism and the Creation of a Republican Majority"; Baum, *The Civil War Party System*; Anbinder, *Nativism and Slavery*.

95. Preston King to Tilden, October 13, 1854, Tilden Papers, NYPL. See also King to Azariah C. Flagg, May 20, 1854, Flagg Papers, Special Collections, Columbia University Library, New York; James S. Wadsworth to Martin Van Buren, August 1, 1856, Van Buren Papers, Library of Congress (LC).

96. Blaine, *Twenty Years of Congress*, 1:117.

97. *Advertiser* (Portland, ME), May 20, 1856.

98. Gideon Welles, "National Affairs during the last 30 years," [1858], Welles Papers, Connecticut Historical Society, Hartford. On Welles, see Niven, *Gideon Welles*.

99. Anon., *Life of Millard Fillmore*, 22.

100. Brown, *Dorothea Dix*, 242.

101. Holt, *The Rise and Fall of the Whig Party*, ch. 22–26; Everett to Trescot, September 12, 1856, Everett Papers, MHS.

102. On Frémont's political career, the best study remains Nevins, *Frémont*. An enjoyable account of Frémont's life, including his elopement with and marriage to Jessie Benton, the beautiful daughter of a Democratic Missouri senator, see Denton, *Passion and Principle*.

103. Dorothea Dix to Millard Fillmore, November 8, 1856, in Snyder, ed. *The Lady and the President*, 264.

104. Holt, *The Rise and Fall of the American Whig Party*, 979; Gienapp, *The Origins of the Republican Party*, 532. On Buchanan, see Klein, *President James Buchanan*; Baker, *James Buchanan*.

105. Lewis Cass was also supported at the convention, receiving five votes on the first ballot, but he was now so venerable that he made Buchanan look like the embodiment of vigorous manhood.

106. The emphasis on "conservatism" in Democratic as well as Republican campaign literature is discussed in an article in *Frank Leslie's Weekly*, October 18, 1856.

107. *New York Herald*, June 10, 1856.

108. *The Press*, August 1, 1857.

109. *Weekly Patriot and Union*, November 19, 1856.

110. Butler, *A Retrospect of Forty Years*, 302.

111. *The Press*, August 24, 1857.

112. Price, *An Appeal for the Union*.

113. Whig Party (U.S.), *The great fraud upon the public credulity*.

114. Choate, *Hon Rufus Choate*.

115. Joseph Cracaft to Stephen A. Douglas, July 4, 1856, SADP.

116. Democratic State Committee (PA), *Address and Correspondence*. Charles R. Buckalew wrote the address.

117. *Dover Gazette*, January 9, 1858.

118. *Dover Gazette*, February 18, 1860.

119. Kendall, ed., *Maria Mitchell*, 56.

120. Democratic State Committee (NY), *Proceedings*.

121. Choate letter in the *Boston Post*, August 12, 1856. The letter was widely reprinted by Buchanan-supporting newspapers. See, for example, *Daily Illinois State Journal*, August 21, 1856. Choate repeated the phrase "the madness of the times" in other addresses in the same year. See his "Speech on the Political Topics now Prominent Before the Country, Delivered at Lowell, Mass., October 28, 1856," in Woods, *The Political Writings of Rufus Choate*, 327.

122. *North American and United States Gazette*, October 30, 1856.

123. Ibid., November 3, 1856.

124. Boston *Daily Atlas*, August 18, 1855.

125. Fish and Hamilton, *Fremont the Conservative Candidate*.

126. *New York Times*, September 27, 1856.

127. Bigelow, *Memoir of Frémont*, 72. The need to maintain a conservative posture in previously Democratic states was made clear by Lincoln's Whig colleague Orville Hickman Browning in a letter to Lyman Trumbull, formerly a Democrat, now a Republican senator from Illinois: "We wish if possible to keep the party in this state under the control of moderate men and conservative influences, and if we do so the future destiny of the state is in our own hands and victory will inevitably crown our exertions. On the other hand, if rash and ultra counsels prevail all is lost." Browning to Trumbull, May 19, 1856, Trumbull Papers, LC.

128. Fermer, *James Gordon Bennett*, 1–2; Pray, *Memoirs of James Gordon Bennett*; Seitz, *The James Gordon Bennetts*.

129. *New York Herald*, May 30, August 15, 18, September 8, 30, 1856. Buchanan's papers contain alarmed correspondence about the likely impact of the *Herald*'s support for Frémont. See, for example, Daniel E. Sickles to James Buchanan, May 24, 1856; George N. Sanders to Buchanan, June 20, 1856; John W. Forney to Buchanan, 29 June, 7, 25 July, 1856, Buchanan Papers, HSP.

130. *Philadelphia Public Ledger*, September 6, 1856; *Pennsylvanian*, October 6, 1856; Allen, *Letter*. Italics in original.

131. Boston *Daily Atlas*, October 2, 1856.

132. *North American and United States Gazette*, March 30, April 30, 1860. Italics in original.

133. *Daily Illinois State Journal*, September 1, 1856. The same article made the case that it was the duty of "every true conservative man" to labor for the principle that "freedom is national" and slavery sectional.

134. See, for example, *Daily Illinois State Journal*, September 24, 1856, which warned that Fillmore's partisans were just as committed to disunion as Buchanan's. Their cry was, "Either Buchanan or Fillmore or revolution."

135. Boston *Daily Atlas*, July 22, 1856.

136. *New York Tribune*, September 22, 1856.

137. Boston *Daily Atlas*, July 23, 1856.

138. May, *The Southern Dream*, 67–71.

139. The *New York Herald* had first declared its support for Cuban annexation as a free state on December 28, 1848. On opposition to the possibility of expansion into the tropics in the context of the crisis over the Mexican territories and the Wilmot Proviso, see Francis P. Blair to Van Buren, July 15, 1850, Van Buren Papers, LC. See also May, *Slavery, Race, and Conquest*, 64. Northern Democrats were very aware of their candidates' vulnerability to charges of radicalism over the Ostend Manifesto. See Richards, *The Slave Power*, 198–99.

140. Everett, *Correspondence on the Proposed Tripartite Convention*, 16. On Everett's role in writing and subsequently publishing what he called his "great Cuban Manifesto," see Mason, *Apostle of Union*.

141. *New York Courier and Enquirer*, October 22, 1856. Italics in original.

142. Barnard, *Letter from the Hon. Daniel D. Barnard*.

143. *New York Herald*, September 11, 1856, February 10, 1854; *Chicago Tribune*, June 16, 1856.

144. *Daily Illinois State Journal*, October 22, 1856; *North American and United States Gazette*, February 2, 1855.

145. *New York Herald*, June 15, 1857. An image of the riot is in *Frank Leslie's Illustrated Newspaper*, June 27, 1857, 57.

146. See, for example, a report in the *New York Herald*, July 10, 1857, of a "sham" riot between two Eleventh Ward gangs who lured the Metropolitans into their midst in order to "entrap the police and give them a good drubbing." More antipolice riots took place on July 12, reported at length in the *Herald*, July 14, 1857.

147. Richardson, "Mayor Fernando Wood"; Richardson, *The New York Police*, 82–110; *New York Times*, April, 16 and 18, May 23, and June 15, 17, and 20, 1857; *New York Tribune*, April 25, 1857; *Harper's Weekly*, March 28, 1857, p. 194, April 15, 1857, p. 258; Walling, *Recollections*.

148. Figures for casualties are from the *New York Herald*, June 3, 1857; the *Boston Daily Advertiser*, June 3, 1857; and the *Daily National Intelligencer*, June 3, 1857.

149. Quotations from Stampp, *America in 1857*, 43.

150. *Frank Leslie's Illustrated Newspaper*, June 20, 1857, 44–45.

151. Stampp, *And the War Came*, 1–12, describes this transition exceptionally well.

Chapter Four

1. Quotes from *Plain Dealer*, November 11, 1855.

2. Lewis G. Pearce to Douglas, February 20, 1852, SADP.

3. *Frank Leslie's Illustrated Newspaper*, September 27, 1856.

4. *Daily Illinois State Journal*, April 20, 1855.

5. On the history of the doctrine of popular sovereignty, see Childers, *The Failure of Popular Sovereignty*.

6. Although often attributed to him, Jefferson probably never said this. See Peterson, *The Jefferson Image*, 79. The phrase "that government is best which governs least, because its people discipline themselves" is in the mission statement of the *United States Magazine and Democratic Review* 1 (1837): 6.

7. *Daily Illinois State Journal*, September 22, 1856.

8. *Canton Transcript*, quoted in *Wooster Republican*, June 15, 1854.

9. *Daily Commercial Register*, October 18, 1854; *Tail Ender*, quoted in *Plain Dealer*, June 14, 1854; *Ohio State Journal*, September 27, 1854; *Cleveland Leader*, October 3, 1854; *Quincy Whig*, October 9, 1854; *Canton Repository*, March 24, 1854; *Cleveland Herald*, March 26, 1854.

10. *Evening Post*, November 23, 1854. Italics in original. As Christopher Childers writes, "Historians have failed to recognize that the labyrinthine negotiations over the meaning of popular sovereignty actually represented the inauguration of a new phase in the debate in which the judiciary would have to determine how the people could exercise their will. Someone would eventually have to decide whether the northern or southern interpretation would prevail." Childers, "Popular Sovereignty," 62. For a similar observation see, Jaffa, *Crisis of the House Divided*, 169.

11. Potter, *The Impending Crisis*, 173. For similar judgments, see Etcheson, *Bleeding Kansas*, 15; Morrison, *Slavery and the American West*, 151.

12. *Albany Evening Journal*, July 24, 1854; Douglas, *Letter*.

13. *Canton Repository*, March 29, 1854; *Weekly Union*, February 22, 1854; *Ohio State Journal*, March 23, 1854; Reemelin, *Life of Charles Reemelin*, 134; *Weekly Chronicle*, March 2, 1854.

14. Salmon P. Chase made these remarks in a speech at an anti-Nebraska meeting in Columbus, Ohio. See *Ohio State Journal*, March 23, 1854.

15. *Cleveland Leader*, September 19, 1854.

16. *Cleveland Plain Dealer*, June 14, 1854.

17. New York *Evening Post*, November 23, 1854.

18. Dix, *Memoirs*, 1:334.

19. Ibid., 207.

20. Dix to James C. Curtis, February 25, 1854 in Dix, *Memoirs*, 1:284.

21. Ibid., 336.

22. Tilden to [illegible], August 26, 1854, Tilden Papers, NYPL.

23. Horatio Seymour to Stephen A. Douglas, April 14, 1854, SADP.

24. Around the same time he clashed with Thomas Morris, an outspoken antislavery Democrat and U.S. senator who later went on to be the vice presidential candidate for the Liberty Party.

25. David Tod to Secretary of State John M. Clayton, January 8, 1850, in Conrad, ed., *In the Hands of Strangers*, 98–101.

26. Butler, *A Retrospect of Forty Years*, 83.

27. *Plain Dealer*, May 28, 1856.

28. W. Y. Roberts to Bigler, February 18, 1856, Bigler Papers, HSP. Roberts was the president of the Topeka Convention and a founder of the Free State Party, which organized at Big Springs, Kansas in 1855. Other Pennsylvania Democrats were also prominent in the free soil movement in Kansas at this time, including George W. Smith and Galusha A. Grow (who was later elected as a Republican congressman and became speaker of the House).

29. W. Y. Roberts to Bigler, February 18, 1856, Bigler Papers.

30. *Plain Dealer*, February 15, 1854.

31. Declaration of members of the Kansas Territorial Legislature, quoted in Etcheson, *Bleeding Kansas*, 63.

32. Etcheson, *Bleeding Kansas*, 71.

33. Hutter, *"God Hath Not Dealt So,"* 4.

34. Bancroft to W. L. Marcy, September 24, 1856 in Howe, ed., *The Life and Letters of George Bancroft*, 2:124. The Kansas-Nebraska Act had initially appalled Bancroft, but in the end he accepted it on the grounds that it would lead, so he thought, to the exclusion of slavery. "These are not my views only; they pervade the Democracy," he wrote by way of explanation.

35. Joseph Cracraft to Stephen A. Douglas, July 4, 1856, SADP.

36. Green C. Bronson to Stephen A. Douglas, February 8, 1854, SADP. Bronson was the candidate of the "hardshell" or "national" faction of the Democratic Party for governor of New York in 1854. He came in a distant fourth, behind the American Party candidate, Daniel Ullmann, the "softshell" Democratic candidate and sitting governor Horatio Seymour, and the winner (by a tiny margin of just 309) Myron H. Clark, a Whig nominated by a Temperance convention. Bronson was consequently much reviled by the majority of New York Democrats as a spoiler.

37. *New York Times*, October 30, 1857. On Cushing, see Belohlavek, *Broken Glass*.

38. John O'Sullivan to Stephen A. Douglas, February 10, 1854, SADP.

39. O'Sullivan quoted in Sampson, *John O'Sullivan*, 223.

40. Campbell, *Negro-mania*, 437–59.

41. For the British Chartist context, see Boston, *British Chartists in America*, 60. An insightful article on Campbell's career is Heath, " 'The producers on the one side, and the capitalists on the other.' "

42. On the tensions between the Biblical and the pseudoscientific theories of polygenesis, see Stanton, *The Leopard's Spots*; Frederickson, *The Black Image in the White Mind*, 71–96; Lurie, *Louis Agassiz*.

43. Seymour, *Speech at Springfield*, 3, 5.

44. Ibid., 7.

45. *Quincy Whig*, November 6, 1854.

46. *New Hampshire Reporter*, February 14, 1854.

47. Burke's article appeared in the *New Hampshire Reporter*, February 14, 1854. Editorial quoted from the same issue; italics in original. Douglas replied in the *New Hampshire Patriot and State Gazette*, February 20, 1854. For reports of the spat between Douglas and Burke, see *Boston Courier* March 2, 1854; *Weekly Union*, February 22, 1854. See also Johannsen, *The Letters of Stephen A. Douglas*, 442–43. Douglas's reply was reprinted as a pamphlet: *Letters of Stephen Douglas, in Reply to the Editor of the State Capitol Reporter*, reprinted in Johannsen, *The Letters of Stephen A. Douglas*, 284–90. Attacks on Burke quoted here appear in the *Weekly Union*, February 22 and March 1, 1854. For background skirmishing between the two over this issue, see Burke to Stephen A. Douglas, January 9, 1854, SADP.

48. Shenton, *Robert John Walker*.

49. Bancroft to Buchanan, February 21, 1857, in Howe, ed., *The Life and Letters of George Bancroft*, 2:126.

50. Quoted in Nevins, *The Ordeal of the Union*, 4:236.

51. Walker to Buchanan, June 28, 1857, in Covode and Train, *The Covode Investigation*, 115.

52. Covode and Train, *The Covode Investigation*, 118.

53. Amos Goodrich to Stephen A. Douglas, June 7, 1858, SADP.

54. *Herald of Freedom*, September 22, October 13, and February 24, 1855.

55. The reelected Lecompton Democrats were Dan Sickles, William B. Maclay, and John Cochrane, from the neighboring first, fifth, and sixth districts of New York, respectively; Thomas B. Florence from the first district in Pennsylvania (Philadelphia) and William H. Dimmick, from Pennsylvania's thirteenth district, running along the state's eastern border with New York; and William E. Niblack from Indiana's first district, centered on Gary. I am very grateful to Andrew Heath for sharing with me research about Florence from his outstanding forthcoming study of Philadelphia in the Civil War Era.

56. *Philadelphia Inquirer*, October 14, 1858; *Springfield Republican*, October 14, 1858. Florence's majority in the first district was slashed to just 493, with his share of the vote falling from 56 to 43 percent in a three-way race. There were other issues at work in the Pennsylvania congressional and state elections in October 1858, principally the effect within the state of an economic slowdown and consequently a revived pressure for a higher tariff on imported manufactured goods, an issue which the Opposition Party, or People's Party, had adopted in addition to Lecompton. See Coleman, *The Disruption of Pennsylvania Democracy*; Collins, "The Democrats Loss of Pennsylvania." For the context of Philadelphia politics, see Dusinberre, *Civil War Issues*.

57. Fisher, *Diary*, October 13, 1858.

58. "The rift in the Democracy [over Lecompton]," writes Michael F. Holt, "had broken the link between the South and the Northern Democratic party that the Republicans

were trying to forge. By erasing the clear line of difference between the parties, Douglas' action vitiated the Republicans' argument that only they could resist the South." Holt, *The Political Crisis*, 206.

59. Fehrenbacher, *The Dred Scott Case*.

60. Taney to J. Mason Campbell, October 2, 1856, Roger Brooke Taney Collection, Johns Hopkins University.

61. Bancroft to James L. Mason, July 24, 1857, in Howe, ed., *The Life and Letters of George Bancroft*, 127–28.

62. *New York Times*, March 9, 1857.

63. Bancroft to Douglas, December 2, 1857 in Howe, *The Life and Letters of George Bancroft*, 128–33.

64. John L. Kierons to Stephen A. Douglas, October 3, 1858, SADP.

65. P. W. Randle to Stephen A. Douglas, July 4, 1858. See also J. J. Harvey to Douglas, July 11; Thomas L. Harris to Douglas, July 7, 1858, SADP.

66. Quoted in Johannsen, *The Letters of Stephen A. Douglas*, 598.

67. McClure, *Old-Time Notes*, 1:255.

68. In late 1849, Forney's election as clerk of the House was blocked, on the twentieth ballot, by Southerners suspicious of his antislavery views. An Illinois postmaster, Isaac R. Diller, was depressed by Foney's defeat and the way in which the Whig press were using it to argue that free-state Democrats were subservient to the South. Northern Democrats, Diller wrote, "have a fearful responsibility before them, in endeavoring to convince the North that they are as true to northern men (Cass and Forney) as southern democrats have always proved themselves in their interests." Diller to Douglas, February 12, 1850, SADP.

69. McClure, *Old-Time Notes*, 255–56.

70. John W. Forney to Cameron, May 25, 1858, Simon Cameron Papers, LC; Coleman, *The Disruption of Pennsylvania Democracy*, 113–14.

71. Forney, *Speech of John W. Forney at Tarrytown*.

72. C. Goepp to Stephen A. Douglas, June 3, 1858, SADP.

73. W. Rice to Bigler, July, 1858; Paul Johnson to Bigler, July 6, 1858; Charles H. Pine to Bigler, June 11, 1858, Bigler Papers, HSP. See also *Illinois State Register*, June 11, 1858, a Douglas paper, which trumpeted Douglas' success in controlling the patronage despite rift with administration.

74. Jonathan H. Bendick to Bigler, April 24, 1858, Bigler Papers.

75. Even in Pennsylvania, however, the vast majority of Democratic voters supported Douglas's line on Lecompton. See Coleman, *The Disruption of Pennsylvania Democracy*; Holt, *Forging a Majority*; Nichols, *The Disruption of American Democracy*, 173. A somewhat different view is offered by Meerse, "The Northern Democratic Party."

76. N. Wright to Bigler, April 27, 1858, Bigler Papers.

77. William D. Furness to Bigler, June 11, 1858, Bigler Papers.

78. J. A. Beans and M. Master to Bigler, March 31, 1859, Bigler Papers.

79. Douglas still had allies within the Northern pro-Lecompton camp, however. The prominent antiwar Democrat Clement L. Vallandigham wrote to Douglas's close

ally Charles H. Lanphier expressing support for Douglas against Lincoln, since the latter "represent[ed] the extreme and dangerous doctrines of what yet remains of the sectional Black Republican movement of 1856." C. L. Vallandigham to Charles H. Lanphier, October 19, 1858, Lanphier Papers, Abraham Lincoln Presidential Library, Springfield, Illinois.

80. George M. Davis to Douglas, December 10, 1857, SADP.

81. Martin Ryerson to Douglas, December 18, 1857, SADP. See also Marshal J. Bacon to Douglas, December 23, 1857 and A. D. Furren to Douglas, December 26, 1857, SADP. Several historians have acknowledged the alignment of the great majority of Democrats with Republicans after 1858 on the core issue of the need to face down Slave Power and to ensure that Kansas was free. For example, Nevins, *The Ordeal of the Union*, 3:250; Wells, *Stephen Douglas*; Holt, *The Political Crisis*, 205–6. Even Eric Foner, in a book arguing for the distinctiveness of Republican ideology, acknowledges "in their devotion to the Union and their bitter opposition to southern domination of the government, Republicans and Douglasites stood close together in 1860." *Free Soil, Free Labor, Free Men*, 307. The implications of this convergence for our understanding of the path to Civil War have rarely been acknowledged, however. An exception is Woods, *Emotional and Sectional Conflict*, 170–80.

82. See Col. T. B. Seanght [?] to Bigler, October 18, 1858, Bigler Papers.

83. Unidentified to Charles H. Lanphier, no date [February 1858], Lanphier Papers.

84. Silas Woodson to Douglas, November 10, 1858, SADP.

85. William H. Kleim, in Cong. Globe, 35th Cong., 2nd Sess., 100–102 (1858), cited in Collins, "The Democrats Loss," 522. Kleim won a special election, called when the sitting congressman, J. Glancy Jones, who had been the administration's floor whip in the Lecompton votes, resigned after losing his race for reelection in the eighth district in October 1858. Jones resigned because Buchanan had given him a plumb patronage post as minister to Austria, typical of the favors that the administration bestowed on those who had shown loyalty during the Lecompton battle.

86. C. Goepp to Douglas, June 3, 1858, SADP. Italics in original.

87. In some contexts, Democrats also used the polygamy issue as a political device, demanding to know why opponents of the Kansas-Nebraska Act were focusing on the morality of slavery in the territories but were not rallying to the same extent over the practice of polygamy, which was "even more repulsive to Anglo Saxon sentiment." *Plain Dealer*, February 20, 1854.

88. Douglas, *Remarks on Kansas, Utah, and the Dred Scott decision*, 13.

89. There was an irony in Lincoln and other Republicans' use of the pejorative term "squatter sovereignty" to refer to Douglas's popular sovereignty, since it was first coined by Calhounites who argued for the national recognition of property rights in slaves. So Lincoln was right about "squatter sovereignty" being generated in South Carolina but for the wrong reason: it was generated there as way of attacking popular sovereignty not in support of it!

90. Foner, *Free Soil, Free Labor, Free Men*, 204.

91. *Campaign Plain Dealer and Popular Sovereignty Advocate*, July 7, 1860. Emphasis in original.

92. Baker, *Speech of Hon. Edward D. Baker*, 10. I am very grateful to Jack Furniss, who spotted this source and kindly sent me a copy.

93. This was an accurate reflection of reality. The historian David Brion Davis points out that the gross domestic product of the United States in 1860 was only about 20 percent above the value of slaves. As investment capital, the value of slaves exceeded by perhaps a billion dollars the total value of all the farms in the slave-holding states. And it was three times the cost of constructing all the nation's railroads. More broadly, economic development in the free states was fueled in multiple ways by the massive profits being made by the export of raw cotton, especially in the 1840s and 1850s—an export industry reliant, of course, on enslaved labor. See Davis, "The Impact of British Abolitionism," 21. See also Davis, *Inhuman Bondage*, 298.

94. Anon., *Grand Mass Meeting of the Democracy of New York!*, 2 .

95. Ibid., 8.

96. Lovejoy, *The True Democracy*, 3.

97. Florence, *Principles of Democracy*, 2, 5–6.

98. E. M. McFarland to Bigler, May 5, 1858, Bigler Papers.

99. J. Cook to Bigler, May 6, 1858, Bigler Papers.

100. Buchanan to Dix, January 13, 1858, John A. Dix Papers, Columbia University, New York.

101. Democratic Party, *Free Soil, Free Speech, Free Men*, 10.

102. J. L. O'Sullivan to Stephen A. Douglas, February 10, 1854, SADP.

103. Evert Duyckinck to George Duyckinck, October 20, 1856, Duyckinck Family Papers, NYPL.

Chapter Five

1. Washington *Constitution*, January 13, 1860.

2. For one episode of violence pitting the free-state against slave-state representatives, see *Baltimore Clipper*, February 9, 1858.

3. Washington *Constitution*, January 13, 1860.

4. *New York Herald*, January 16, 1860.

5. Galbreath, "The Trial of William Bebb."

6. Letter from Corwin replying to an invitation to speak at a political meeting in Kentucky, reprinted in *Daily National Intelligencer*, October 27, 1859.

7. Abbot, *The Republican Party and the South*, 5–13; Foner, *Free Soil, Free Labor, Free Men*, 186–225.

8. On John Brown's politics, the best study is McGlone, *John Brown's War*.

9. *Pittsburgh Post*, October 25, 1859.

10. *Democratic Review* 43 (October 1859): 201–17.

11. *Plain Dealer*, December 15, 1859.

12. Ibid., November 15, 1859.

13. Dorothea Dix to Millard Fillmore, November 21, 1859, in Snyder, ed., *The Lady and the President*, 234.

14. Knupfer, "A Crisis in Conservatism."

15. *Ohio Statesman*, November 4, 1859.

16. Quoted in Knupfer, "A Crisis in Conservatism," 135.

17. Letter from Lydia Maria Child to Henry Alexander Wise, 1859, in Whittier, ed., *Letters of Lydia Maria Child*, 107–8.

18. See, for example, McPherson, *Disorganization and Disunion*.

19. Fisher, *Diary*, May 17, 1860.

20. *North American and United States Gazette*, May 30, September 28, June 4, October 17, June 4, and March 30, 1860.

21. Quoted in Egerton, *Year of Meteors*, 187. See also McKnight, *Mission of Republicans*.

22. This point is made in correspondence between Manton Marble and his friend, the lieutenant governor of Rhode Island Samuel G. Arnold. See, for example, Arnold to Marble, March 20, 1861, Manton Marble Papers, LC.

23. Fisher, *Diary*, October 19, 1860.

24. Potter, *The Impending Crisis*, 478–79. See also Channing, *Crisis of Fear*.

25. Craven, "Coming of the War Between the States," 304–5. The key works referred to here to are Randall, *The Civil War and Reconstruction*, 113; Ramsdell, "The Changing Interpretation of the Civil War"; Ramsdell, "The Natural Limits of Slavery Expansion"; Randall, "The Blundering Generation"; Craven, *The Coming of the Civil War*; Craven, *The Repressible Conflict*; Owsley, "The Fundamental Cause of the Civil War." The phrase "needless war" is associated with the writings of all these scholars but was specifically used by Milton, *The Eve of Conflict*.

26. *New York Herald*, April 14, 1858.

27. *New York Herald*, January 16 and April 5, 1860.

28. *Providence Post*, April 5, 1860.

29. *Providence Evening Press*, February 16, 22, March 12, April 12, 1860; *Constitution*, April 11, 1860. His opponent, Seth Padelford, was an abolitionist who became governor in the 1870s.

30. *Providence Post*, April 5, 1860; *Weekly Union*, April 10, 1860.

31. *North American and United States Gazette*, December 6, 1859. See also *Philadelphia Public Ledger*, May 5, 1860. Rhode Island was, in fact, a dubious model to serve as a precedent for anywhere else since the electorate was so small and the Sprague family retained an extraordinarily effective hold on the politics of the state, notwithstanding the new constitution that had replaced the old colonial charter in the 1840s. Probably no state in the Union other than South Carolina retained such a strong politics of deference, nor was there any other state in which Irish immigrants were as politically marginalized. See Williams and Conley, eds., *The Rhode Island Home Front*; Hoffmann and Hoffmann, *Brotherly Love*.

32. Manton Marble to Samuel G. Arnold, May 1, 1860, Marble Papers.

33. Fisher, *Diary*, November 6, 1860.

34. *Great Union Meeting in Philadelphia; North American and United States Gazette,* December 8, 1859.

35. *New York Observer and Chronicle,* February 10, December 15, 1859. *Official Report of the Great Union Meeting Held at the Academy of Music, New York.*

36. Fisher, *The Law of the Territories,* xxi.

37. Speech of Edward Everett, February 8, 1854, Cong. Globe, 33rd Cong., 1st Sess., appendix, 158. Sumner, *The Landmark of Freedom.*

38. Everett, *Oration Delivered before the City Authorities of Boston,* 28, 48. On the Mount Vernon campaign, see Mason, *Apostle of Union.*

39. Constitutional Union Party, *Address of the National Executive Committee,* 6–7.

40. Ibid., 8.

41. Fisher, *Diary,* June 25 and November 6, 1860.

42. See, for example, C. H. Hampstead to William Bigler, January 19, 1860, Bigler Papers, HSP, referring to Hampstead's successful "coup d'état" against the pro-Douglas Gwin faction of the Democratic Party in California.

43. Fisher, *Diary,* July 10, 1860. Emphasis in original.

44. Douglas and Lincoln's combined share of the free-state vote was 85.2 percent. The Bell and Breckinridge vote in the slave states was 85.1 percent.

45. Charles H. Boone to William Bigler, August 28, 1860, Bigler Papers.

46. C. L. Lamleuton to William Bigler, March 29, 1860, Bigler Papers.

47. Autobiographical Sketch of William Dock, Dock Family Papers, Pennsylvania State Archives, Harrisburg.

48. George Dock to William Bigler, October 8, 1860, Bigler Papers.

49. I. C. Viollet to William Bigler, February 12, 1860, Bigler Papers.

50. Dix, *Memoirs,* 1:342.

51. Buckalew, *Proportional Representation.* Buckalew introduced a bill that would have changed the electoral system: Senate Bill 772, 40th Congress, 3d Session (January 13, 1869).

52. Stampp, *Indiana Politics,* 211.

53. Voorhees, *Speeches,* 49.

54. *The End of the Irrepressible Conflict,* 41, 49.

55. Bigelow, "Some Recollections of Charles O'Conor."

56. Quoted in Finkelman, *An Imperfect Union,* 299.

57. The best analysis of the Lemmon case and its significance is in Finkelman, *An Imperfect Union,* 296–312.

58. *Massachusetts Spy,* December 28, 1859.

59. *The National Crisis,* May 15, 1860.

60. *Boston Post,* March 16, 1859, reprinted in *Wisconsin Patriot,* May 7, 1859.

61. *Boston Post,* March 16, 1859.

62. See, for example, *Campaign Plain Dealer and Popular Sovereignty Advocate,* July 7, 1860.

63. *North American and United States Gazette,* August 31, 1860.

64. *Illinois State Journal*, September 1, 1860; Burlingame, *Abraham Lincoln*, 1:666; Seymour, "'Conservative'—Another Lincoln Pseudonym"; Seymour, "Lincoln: Author of Letters by a Conservative"; Burlingame, ed., *Lincoln's Journalist*, xx.

65. *New York Times*, August 28, 1860.

66. New York Young Men's Republican Union, *Lincoln and Liberty!*, 3.

67. Republican National Committee, *Homesteads*, 1.

68. *New York Tribune*, June 11, 1860.

69. Crenshaw, *The Slave States*, 89–111.

70. Quoted in Tewell, *A Self-Evident Lie*, 127. Italics in original.

71. *The Ruin of the Democratic Party*. See also a newspaper published by the Young Men's Republican Union, *Lincoln and Liberty!*, June 26, 1860. For a summary of the role of the corruption issue in the election, see Mark W. Summers, *The Plundering Generation: Corruption and the Crisis of the Union* (New York: Oxford, 1987), 270–80.

72. On the significance of corruption in Civil War–era politics, see Smith, *The Enemy Within*.

73. Meerse, "Buchanan, Corruption, and the Election of 1860," 124.

74. *New York World*, October 23, 1860, quoted in Burlingame, *Abraham Lincoln*, 2:681.

75. August Belmont to John Forsyth, New York, November 22, 1860, in Belmont, *Letters, Speeches and Addresses*, 23–24.

76. Reemelin, *Life*, 130.

77. Abraham Lincoln [September 16–17, 1859], "Notes for Speech in Kansas and Ohio," Abraham Lincoln Papers, LC.

78. *North American and United States Gazette*, June 4, 1860.

79. For accounts of the 1860 campaign, see Egerton, *Year of Meteors*; Green, *Lincoln and the Election of 1860*; Fite, *The Presidential Campaign of 1860*; Luthin, *The First Lincoln Campaign*; Rawley, *Edwin D. Morgan*, 103–20; Fuller, *The Election of 1860 Reconsidered*. Morgan was the chairman of the Republican National Committee. Luthin suggests that "the cohesive force" within the Republican Party was "not anti-Southern sentiment, but opposition to the Democrats. It was this common antagonism to the dominant political organisation, the eagerness of the 'outs' to get 'in,' that made possible co-operation between the diverse elements who joined forces under the Republican standard." Luthin, *The First Lincoln Campaign*, 220. I think there is something in this, although in practice the two impulses overlapped, since anti-Democratic feeling was driven by the perception that the Democratic Party had become hopelessly corrupted by the South. Foner, *Free Soil, Free Labor, Free Men* remains the most comprehensive account of the blend of antislavery, Protestant evangelicalism, and nationalist sentiment that bound together the Republican Party. On the choices voters made, see Luebke, ed., *Ethnic Voters*; Van Deusen, "Why the Republican Party Came to Power"; Kremm, "Cleveland and the First Lincoln Election"; Carwardine, "Methodists, Politics, and the Coming of the American Civil War"; Carwardine, *Evangelicals and Politics*, 296–307. On the tenor of the campaign and the cultural resonance of the respective parties in Michigan and Pittsburgh, respectively, see Formisano, *The Birth of Mass Political Parties*, and

272 Notes to Chapter 6

Holt, *Forging a Majority*. The relative strength of the Democrats is assessed by Silbey, *A Respectable Minority*, 14–21.

80. *Campaign Plain Dealer and Popular Sovereignty Advocate*, October 17, 1860.

81. Schurz, *Judge Douglas*, 1. See also Blaine, *Political Discussions*, 12.

82. Thomas B. Long to Stephen A. Douglas, September 17, 1860, SADP.

83. *Campaign Plain Dealer and Popular Sovereignty Advocate*, October 13, 27, 1860.

84. Ibid., June 30, October 13, 1860.

85. *An Appeal to the Conservative Men*.

86. W. Brindle to William Bigler, January 23, 1860, Bigler Papers, HSP.

87. Fehrenbacher, *Dred Scott Case*.

88. Greeley, *Recollections*, 389–90.

89. *Wisconsin Patriot*, May 7, 1859.

90. Fisher, *Diary*, February 6, 1857.

91. Fisher, *Diary*, December 13, 1860.

92. Lowell, "The Question of the Hour."

93. C. L. Lamleuton to William Bigler, March 29, 1860, Bigler Papers.

94. Pennsylvania saw by far the biggest increase in Republican vote share between 1856 and 1860, followed by New Jersey, where Lincoln polled 48.1 percent compared to Frémont's 28.5 percent. In Indiana and Illinois, Lincoln just managed to score over 50 percent, whereas Frémont had been stuck at around 40 percent. Without Pennsylvania's 27 electoral votes, Lincoln would still have had a majority but only of 1 (153 votes with 152 needed for a majority). Since no one thought it likely in advance that Lincoln would win the 7 votes from Oregon and California or any of the electoral votes from New Jersey (he won 4 out of 7), and given the closeness of the race in Indiana and Illinois, Pennsylvania was by any measure the crucial state for the Republicans.

95. In the nonseceding states (i.e., the free states plus the four border slave states), Joel Silbey estimates that the Democratic vote averaged 44.7 percent, which, as he notes, was only fractionally lower than the party's average vote between 1840 and 1856. Silbey, *Respectable Minority*, 19.

Chapter Six

1. On the politics of the secession crisis, see McClintock, *Lincoln and the Decision for War*; Holzer, *Lincoln President-Elect*; Denton, *William Henry Seward*; Cooper, "The Critical Signpost." On Northern responses to secession, see Potter, *Lincoln and His Party*; Stampp, *And the War Came*.

2. George Dock to William Bigler, January 25, 1861, Bigler Papers, HSP.

3. A. E. Rogers to Samuel S. Cox, February 26, 1861, Cox Papers, John Hay Library, Brown University. Emphasis in original.

4. Indiana Democratic State Committee, *Facts for the People*, 1.

5. R. M. Lee to William Bigler, February 9, 1861, Bigler Papers, HSP.

6. Theo Williams to Stephen A. Douglas, 1 April, 1861, SADP.

7. On the Democrats' response to secession, see Silbey, *Respectable Minority*, 30–39.

8. Victor Piollet to William Bigler, December 31, 1860, Bigler Papers. On Piollet, see Hazeltine, "Victor E. Piollet."

9. Major Robert Anderson to John A. Dix, March 7, 1861, Dix Papers, Columbia University, New York.

10. Quoted in Steven J. Novak, "Bigler, John," American National Biography Online (February 2000), accessed March 19, 2015, http://www.anb.org/articles/04/04-00102 .html,

11. John Bigler to William Bigler, June 16, 1860, Bigler Papers.

12. De Cordova, *A lecture on war, foreign and civil.*

13. W. S. V. Prentiss to S. S. Cox, January 5, 1861, Cox Papers. Other papers in the collection contain similar sentiments. See, for example, A. E. Rogers to Cox, February 26, 1861, Cox Papers.

14. Victor Piollet to William Bigler, December 31, 1860, Bigler Papers. On Piollet, see Ralph Hazeltine, "Victor E. Piollet."

15. This was the Democrats' perception, but in fact Lincoln was among those Republicans who were willing to support the admission of New Mexico as a slave state as part of a compromise deal. Since the status of slavery in that territory had been determined by popular sovereignty under the terms of the Compromise of 1850, which Lincoln had supported, it was to him an entirely different case from that of Kansas or any other future territory, such as Cuba. Lincoln's willingness to accept New Mexico under the terms of popular sovereignty was later used by George Bancroft as the ultimate evidence of Lincoln's reasonableness in the face of the radicalism of the South. See, for example, a speech given by Bancroft to the Union League of Philadelphia in 1863: Bancroft and Milliken, *The League for the Union*, 17.

16. *Boston Courier*, August 13, 1860.

17. Joseph Burns to Samuel S. Cox, January 8, 1861, Cox Papers.

18. *Cincinnati Israelite*, January 11, 1861. On the editor of the *Israelite*, see Sefton D. Temkin, "Isaac Mayer Wise and the Civil War"; Marcus, *The Americanization of Isaac Mayer Wise.*

19. *Hartford Times*, November 7, 1860.

20. *North American and United States Gazette*, December 31, 1860.

21. *New York Herald*, January 14, 1861; *North American and United States Gazette*, January 18, 1861; Dusinberre, *Civil War Issues in Philadelphia*, 104.

22. *North American and United States Gazette*, January 17, 1861. Macalester also advocated the repeal of personal liberty laws as a gesture of conciliation also advocated by several Democratic state conventions around this time. See Silbey, *Respectable Minority*, 35–36.

23. *New York Tribune*, November 9, 1860. This editorial is generally cited by historians as evidence that Greeley's initial position after Lincoln's election was to support the right of secession, which is true up to a point, but taken as a whole, the piece makes a far more nuanced case than is often suggested.

24. August Belmont to John Forsyth, New York, 22 November 1860, in Belmont, *Letters, Speeches and Addresses*, 23–24.

25. George Dock to William Bigler, January 25, 1861, Bigler Papers. Italics in original.

26. Joseph Burns to Samuel S. Cox, January 8, 1861, Cox Papers.

27. John James to William Bigler, January 18, 1861, Bigler Papers.

28. Quotations from Temkin, "Isaac Mayer Wise and the Civil War," 166.

29. Samuel Culver to William Bigler, February 11, 1861, Bigler Papers.

30. Edmund Burke to Thomas Richie, February 14, 1850, Burke Papers, Manuscripts Division, LC.

31. W. H. Miller to Stephen A. Douglas, March 14, 1861, SADP.

32. Theo Williams to Stephen A. Douglas, April 1, 1861, SADP.

33. John McCook to Stephen A. Douglas, February 15, 1861, SADP.

34. A. Boyd Hamilton to Bigler, December 31, 1860, Bigler Papers.

35. A Cincinnati newspaper quoted in Paludan, "American Civil War Considered," 1018.

36. Evidence for the hardening of attitudes toward the South before Sumter among Democrats can be seen in the correspondence of S. S. Cox and Stephen A. Douglas, and was noted in the *Illinois Daily Register*, February 12, 1861. Fisher also seems to have hardened his stance between his January 1 article in the *North American* and the beginning of April.

37. Philip S. Paludan has shown that a complete explanation of the Northern response to secession must take into account the importance of the concept of law and order. Paludan, "The American Civil War Considered." See also Bernstein, *The New York City Draft Riots*, 125–60.

38. *New York Herald*, February 2, 1861.

39. *New York Commercial Advertiser*, excerpted in the New London, Connecticut, *Daily Chronicle*, May 16, 1861.

40. Caleb S. Woodhull to Peter Erben Jr., March 22, 1861, Miscellaneous Manuscripts, Astor Place Riot, NYHS.

41. Henry Ward Bellows to "my dear friend" [Cyrus Bartol?], February 13, 1861, Bellows Papers, MHS. Italics in original.

42. Henry W. Bellows to Cyrus Bartol, January 8, 1861, Bellows Papers.

43. Cyrus Bartol to Henry W. Bellows, April 16, 1861, Bellows Papers.

44. Buckingham, *Message of His Excellency William A. Buckingham*, 17–20; Walter Q. Gresham to Tillie Gresham, April 28, 1861, Gresham Papers, LC.

45. Henry W. Bellows to Cyrus Bartol, December 12, 1860, Bellows Papers.

46. CWAL, 4:267–69; *New York Times*, March 5, 1861.

47. *New York Times*, March 5, 1861.

48. *Commercial Advertiser* (New York), March 5, 1861. The newspaper's Washington correspondent also claimed that the address was "warmly" received by Buchanan, Cox, "and others of the Democratic Party." Similar sentiments were expressed in the *New York Herald*, March 5, 1861; the *New York World*, March 5, 1861; the *Philadelphia Inquirer*, March 5, 1861; and the *Plain Dealer*, March 7, 1861.

49. *New York Times*, March 5, 1861.

50. Amazingly, a similar fate befell a Stars and Stripes outside the White House just three months later. On that occasion, Lincoln himself tugged at the halyard to draw the flag through a hole at the top of a tent; he pulled so hard that it ripped, with two upper

stripes and three of the stars separated from the rest. A clerk in the War Department, Benjamin French, recorded the incident. "I felt a sorrow that I cannot describe, at seeing the torn flag. It seemed to me an omen of ill luck. My only consolation was observing the determined energy with which the President pulled away at the halliards—as if he said, in his mind, "It has got to go up whether or no." And I thought, "Well, let what reverses may come, he will meet them with the same energy, and bring us out of the war, if with a tattered flag, still it will all be there!" *New York Times*, March 5, 1861; French, *Witness to the Young Republic*, 362.

51. Dix, *Memoirs*, 342.

52. Howland, ed., *Letters of a family*, 69.

53. Elizabeth Cady Stanton to William Henry Seward, September 19, 1861, in Blatch and Stanton, eds., *Elizabeth Cady Stanton*, 89.

54. James Buchanan to Lewis S. Coryell, September 18, 1861, Coryell Papers, HSP.

55. *Concord Monitor*, May 23, 1861.

56. Johannsen, *Stephen A. Douglas*, 864, 866; *Illinois State Journal*, April 26, 1861.

57. Alfred Clapp to Stephen A. Douglas, April 15, 1861, SADP. Italics in original.

58. McClernand and Dickinson quoted in Silbey, *A Respectable Minority*, 55–56.

59. Silbey, *A Respectable Minority*, argues that the defection of the War Democrats was an elite affair. I am not sure it was quite as simple as that. Undoubtedly most voters who had supported Democrats in 1860 continued to do so, but election results indicate how susceptible voters were to the nature of the campaign, the candidates, and the coalitions built in support of them. In Ohio, for example, election results in 1862 and 1863 indicate that perhaps as many as a half of all 1860 Democrat voters did not support the regular Democratic ticket. But the rest supported a Union ticket, headed (in 1863) by John Brough, who was a Democrat, so in their own minds they were not necessarily departing from the old party fold at all. See *Wooster Republican*, July 2, 1863; *Plain Dealer*, May 14, 1863 for evidence of the struggle over the identity of the Democratic Party in that state. Clearly this is a tricky subject, and of all the terminology still in use among historians of Civil War politics the one with the least clarity is "War Democrat." In *A Respectable Minority*, Silbey uses it to describe the Democrats who acted with the Lincoln administration, including those appointed to important political or military roles like Edwin M. Stanton, John A. Dix, John W. Forney, Benjamin F. Butler, and Andrew Johnson. Christopher Dell, in *Lincoln and the War Democrats*, uses the term much more broadly to describe the wing of the party that supported the principle of military subjugation of the Confederacy. See also Weber, *Copperheads*. This confusion among historians may simply reflect the confusion of contemporaries. There is certainly scattered evidence that the experience of war shifted ingrained partisan loyalties. For example, Joseph T. Glatthaar describes an Ohio family in which the eldest son's service in a black regiment helped to transform the racial views of his father. Having previously damned all abolitionists and Lincoln supporters as traitors, the father apparently became so convinced of the rightness of emancipation that he secured election to the state legislature as a Unionist. Glatthaar, "Duty, Country, Race, and Party."

60. Silbey, *Respectable Minority*, 43–51.

61. Joseph Ristine to Daniel Voorhees, June 20, 1861, Carrington Family Papers, Manuscripts and Archives, Yale University Library.

62. On the creation of Union parties in the free states in 1861, see Smith, *No Party Now*, 36–44.

63. Ibid., 41–42; Porter, *Ohio Politics*, 88; Neely, *The Divided Union*, 38.

64. S. G. Arnold to Manton Marble, April 7, 1861, Marble Papers, LC.

65. *Philadelphia Inquirer*, April 25, 1861; Philadelphia, *The Press*, July 13, 1861. Evidence from newspapers suggests that there were similar committees of public safety in dozens of other places in the free states, including Pittsburgh, Trenton, and Cincinnati, although most were in the border slave states and in the Confederacy.

66. Charles Eliot Norton to Henry W. Bellows, August 25, 1861, Bellows Papers.

67. Samuel G. Arnold to Manton Marble, April 7, 1861, Marble Papers.

68. Samuel G. Arnold to Manton Marble, March 20, 7 April, 1861, Marble Papers.

69. Samuel G. Arnold to Manton Marble, April 21, 1861, Marble Papers.

70. *New York Herald*, December 5, 1861.

71. *Allen County Democrat*, September 14, 1861.

72. Benjamin F. Potts to Samuel S. Cox, June 30, 1861, Cox Papers. Italics in original.

73. Cook and Knox, eds., *The Public Record Including Speeches*, 42.

74. It helped that in the factionalized world of the New York Democracy, Seymour had steered a middle course. He had not been a Free-Soiler in 1848 but had been a Softshell in the early 1850s, supporting the bolting Free-Soilers' readmission into the Democratic fold against the hardline Hardshell opposition of people like Daniel Dickinson. And then, having supported the Kansas-Nebraska Act, he followed Douglas's opposition to the Lecompton Constitution and strongly campaigned for Douglas in the 1860 election. Seymour's 1862 campaign also benefitted from the support of the still-extant Constitutional Union Party in New York State, as well as with the at least tacit support of moderate Republicans. See Cook and Knox, eds., *The Public Record Including Speeches*; Smith, *No Party Now*, 59–61; Furniss, "To Save the Union 'in Behalf of Conservative Men.'"

75. *New York Herald*, October 26, 1862.

76. *The Independent*, October 10, 1861.

77. Henry W. Bellows to Eliza H. Schuyler, August 9, 1861, Bellows Papers.

78. Charles Eliot Norton to Henry W. Bellows, August 25, 1861, Bellows Papers.

79. Bellows, *Historical Sketch of the Union League Club*, 5.

80. Bellows, *Unconditional Loyalty*, 2.

81. Parton, *General Butler in New Orleans*, 257.

82. Dix, *Memoirs*, 91.

83. Frederickson, *The Inner Civil War*.

84. On Northern racism, see Berwanger, *The Frontier against Slavery*; Litwack, *North of Slavery*.

85. Annie Adams Fields Diary, July 28, 1863, in Howe, ed., *Memories of a Hostess*, 14.

86. Voorhees, *Speeches*, 40.

87. Fisher, *Diary*, January 2, 1860.

88. *New York Herald*, December 12, 1861.

89. *New York Tribune,* December 11, 1861.

90. A faction of Democrats, including, most prominently, Clement L. Vallandigham, had objected very strongly.

91. Charles Eliot Norton to Henry W. Bellows, August 25, 1861, Bellows Papers.

92. Norton, "The Advantages of Defeat," 361.

93. Charles Eliot Norton to Henry W. Bellows, August 25, 1861, Bellows Papers.

94. *New York Herald,* December 12, 1861.

95. Bellows, *The Valley of Decision,* 7.

96. Furness, *Our Duty as Conservatives,* 6–7.

97. McClellan's "Harrison's Landing Letter" to Lincoln, written after his defeat in the Seven Days Battles, is the exemplar of this approach. See McClellan to Lincoln, July 7, 1862, in Sears, *Civil War Papers of George B. McClellan,* 334.

98. Caton, *The Position and Policy of the Democratic Party.*

99. *Ohio Statesman,* September 25, 1862.

100. Cook and Knox, eds., *The Public Record Including Speeches,* 55.

101. *New York World,* November 8, 1862.

102. *New York World,* September 26, 1862.

103. Though there were between 20,000 and 50,000 thousand slaves in areas under Union occupation—including the South Carolina Sea Islands, parts of Arkansas, and the Shenandoah Valley—who were liberated immediately on January 1, 1863. See *New York Times,* January 8, 1863; Guelzo, *Lincoln's Emancipation Proclamation,* 107–8.

104. See, for example, *Albany Evening Journal,* January 1, 1863.

105. *New York Herald,* January 1, 1863. For a sense of the continuing importance of the image of the Haitian Revolution, see Clavin, *Toussaint Louverture and the American Civil War.*

106. Fisher, *Diary,* November 28, 1862; *North American and United States Gazette,* November 29, 1862 and October 3, 1862.

107. Gutjahr, *Charles Hodge;* Carwardine, "The Politics of Charles Hodge," 288; Torbett, *Theology and Slavery.*

108. Carwardine, "The Politics of Charles Hodge," 253, 256.

109. Quoted in Noll, *Charles Hodge,* 1.

110. Hodge, "The War," 152.

111. *North American and United States Gazette,* November 10, 1862.

112. *Harpers' Weekly,* November 15, 1862.

113. *North American and United States Gazette,* November 10, 1862.

114. The resolutions of a faction of Democrats in Illinois in October 1863 captured the Jacksonian pro-emancipation position especially well. They resolved, first, that following "the immortal Jackson" they favored "plain Government, void of pomp"; second, that they were in favor of "confiscation by the Federal authorities of all property owned by rebels against the Constitution and laws of the land, *slaves not excepted*" (italics in original); and, third, that they were "opposed to the political or social equality of the white and black races" and favored racial separation and the "colonization of the black race at the earliest practical period." Reported in the *Washington Reporter,* October 14, 1863.

115. Bowen, ed., *A Frenchman in Lincoln's America*, 1:125.

116. Dix, *Memoirs*, 116.

117. Quoted in Brown, *Dix*, 315.

118. Wharton, *Speech*, 1.

119. Quoted in Silbey, *Respectable Minority*, 49.

120. Ingersoll, *Civil War Speeches*, 329. See also, Greenberg, "Charles Ingersoll"; Cowden, *"Heaven Will Frown."*

Chapter Seven

1. The evidence of a one-time confidante that Forrest supplied funds to buy tickets for anti-Macready demonstrators to attend the Astor Place Opera House is extremely plausible. See "Secret History of the Astor Place Riot with Glimpses of the Forrest Divorce Case, by Andrew Stevens," Astor Place Riot Scrap Book, Charles P. Daly Papers, NYPL. The claims were published in various newspapers after Stevens fell out with Forrest. On the Forrest divorce trial, see Baker, *Sentiment and Celebrity*, 115–75. By the end of the 1850s, Forrest was suffering ill health. He retired from the stage for a couple of seasons but was forced to reenter the limelight largely in order to pay his ex-wife's increasingly large alimony bills. See, Moody, *Edwin Forrest*, 325–40.

2. *Washington Chronicle*, May 11, 1862; Payne, *Brutus*, 49–50.

3. Stillé, *How a Free People Conduct a Long War*, 2.

4. Cox, *Eight Years in Congress*, 188.

5. Biddle, *The Alliance With the Negro*, 2–4.

6. On Forrest's sympathetic attitude to the Confederacy, see Edwin Forrest to John T. Ford, August 8, 1864, Ford Papers, LC.

7. Edwin B. Forrest to James Lawson, June 11, 1861, Edwin Forrest Collection, University of Pennsylvania Library, Philadelphia.

8. Quoted in Moody, *Edwin Forrest*, 347.

9. A. H. Stockly to Thomas F. Bayard, September 9, 1864, Bayard Papers, LC.

10. *Sullivan Democrat*, October 13, 1863.

11. *Daily State Sentinel*, April 13, 1861.

12. *"The Patriot and Scholar" Address of the Hon C. L. Vallandigham to the Students of the University of Michigan*, November 14, 1863, reprinted in the *Detroit Free Press* with an accompanying report of the meeting, reproduced in the *Philadelphia Age*, November 23, 1863.

13. *Daily National Intelligencer*, June 20, 1863.

14. Democratic Party, *Proceedings of the Nob Mountain Meeting*, 18.

15. John Dodson Stiles to Lewis S. Coryell, July 1, 1862, Coryell Papers, HSP.

16. John Brewster to Samuel S. Cox, May 13, 1862, Cox Papers, Brown University.

17. Charles J. Biddle to Charles L. Stillé, March 24, 1863, Biddle Collection, HSP.

18. Two nuanced studies of wartime opposition are Sandow, *Deserter Country*; Warshauer, *Connecticut in the American Civil War*. Other work tends either to see antiwar dissent as as much of a treasonous threat as Republicans did at the time, or, in contrast, to downplay its political potency. An example of the former is Weber, *Copperheads*. Ex-

amples of the latter are Klement, *The Copperheads in the Middle West*; Klement, *Limits of Dissent*; Klement, *Dark Lanterns*.

19. Sandow, "Damnable Treason," 51.

20. *Columbia Democrat*, 11 April, 1863, 20 August, 1864, quoted in Sandow, "Damnable Treason," 51.

21. *New York World*, October 22, 1863.

22. Richards, *Sir Henry Irving*, 367.

23. Moore and Frost, *The Reign of Terror*.

24. *Clearfield Republican*, August 17, 1864.

25. Leading Pennsylvania Democrats, for example, appear to have been genuinely convinced that George W. Woodward was the rightful winner of the 1863 gubernatorial election with a majority of over 100,000, and that half of the Union Party members of congress from Pennsylvania were elected fraudulently. See John Bell Robinson to Pennsylvania Democratic State Committee, January 12, 1864, Biddle Collection; George W. Woodward, *An Address*, 1.

26. [Philadelphia] *Daily Age*, October 24, 1863.

27. James Potts to Charles J. Biddle, October 28, 1863, Biddle Collection; [Philadelphia] *Daily Age*, October 24, 1863.

28. [Philadelphia] *Daily Age*, October 24, 1863.

29. Charles J. Biddle to Lewis S. Coryell, April 21, 1862, Coryell Papers.

30. Charles J. Biddle to J. Breden, August 20, 1863, Biddle Collection.

31. James Potts to Charles J. Biddle, October 28, 1863, Biddle Collection. On Union Leagues, see Smith, *No Party Now*, 68–70; Lawson, *Patriot Fires*, 89. For the declarations of Union Leagues in favor of "loyalty" and for evidence that Biddle had some justification for criticizing their clandestine character, see *The Loyal National League*. The Union Leagues Biddle was concerned about were popular organizations that were sometimes connected to, but were separate from, the metropolitan, elite Union clubs that were founded in Boston, Philadelphia, and New York at the same time. Henry Bellows, inevitably, was a founding member of the New York Union League Club. On these clubs, see Smith, *No Party Now*, 73–75; Lawson, *Patriot Fires*, 98–128.

32. See H. L. Wayland to Manton Marble, October 13, 1862; Samuel L. M. Barlow to Manton Marble, June 15, 1862, Marble Papers.

33. Manton M. Marble to William C. Bryant, undated draft [July 1862?], Marble Papers.

34. J. McClintock to Manton M. Marble, September 22, 1862. This was the day that Lincoln signed the preliminary Emancipation Proclamation, though presumably McClintock did not know that when he wrote the letter.

35. *New York World*, July 3, August 21, 1863.

36. Elizabeth Stoddard to Manton Marble, undated [May 1864?], undated [1863], May 12, 1863; undated [July, 1863]; undated [May 1864], Marble Papers.

37. Samuel G. Arnold to Manton M. Marble, September 4, 1862, Marble Papers.

38. Samuel G. Arnold to Manton M. Marble, October 24, 1862, Marble Papers.

39. Draft of letter to the editors of the *Evening Post*, February 7, 1863, Tilden Papers, NYPL.

40. Bigelow, *The Life of Samuel J. Tilden*, 1:173.

41. Manton M. Marble to Hon. James W. Wall, March 30, 1864, Marble Papers.

42. Ingersoll, *Personal Liberty and Martial Law*, 4.

43. [Philadelphia] *Daily Age*, November 25, 1863.

44. W. H. Winder to Charles J. Biddle, January 4, 1863, Biddle Collection.

45. W. J. Woodward to Lewis S. Coryell, April 6, 1863, Coryell Papers.

46. *Weekly Union*, April 7, 1863.

47. Nathaniel Hawthorne, "Chiefly About War Matters," *Atlantic Monthly*, July 1862. On this fascinating, funny article by Hawthorne, see Wachtell, *War No More*.

48. New Jersey Democratic State Central Committee, *Address of the New Jersey Democratic State Central Committee to the Voters of the State*.

49. *Boston Courier*, July 26, 1863. Manton Marble wrote long pieces drawing on British history and English legal precedent to condemn the Emancipation Proclamation and compare Lincoln to Charles I. *New York World*, August 30, October 28, November 2, 5, December 27, 1862, May 23, 1864.

50. Morse, *An Argument on the Ethical Position of Slavery*.

51. Dartmouth College Trustees, *Proceedings*. On Lord's resignation, see Lord, *Nathan Lord*. The Dartmouth College special collections also contain copies of two excellent BA dissertations on the subject by Chesley A. Homan and Steven M. Kirsch.

52. *Boston Courier*, November 26, 1862, April 15, May 28, 1863; *The Congregationalist*, 22 May, July 17, 1863. Clippings from these newspapers are included in the Nathan Lord Papers, Rauner Special Collections Library, Dartmouth College.

53. Nathan Lord, letter of resignation, July 24, 1863, Lord Papers.

54. Morse, *An Argument on the Ethical Position of Slavery*, 1863, 2.

55. John McGaffey to Samuel S. Cox, January 10, 1863, Cox Papers.

56. *Hartford Times*, January 20, 1863.

57. Ibid., February 17, 1863.

58. *Cincinnati Enquirer*, excerpted in the *Clearfield Republican*, August 17, 1864.

59. CWAL, 8:451. On the politics of Lincoln's letter, see Smith, *No Party Now*, 112–14.

60. *Elk County Advocate*, August 27, 1864

61. See John Murray Forbes, "By a Conservative who believes in Abolition as a Military Necessity," Broadsides Collection, Houghton Library, Harvard University. See also *Boston Daily Advertiser*, September 27, 1864; *New York Evening Post*, September 21, 1864; *Chicago Tribune*, October 12, 1864.

62. Mansfield, *The Issues and Duties of the Day*. A Presbyterian minister from New York assured his congregation that there was no point in wasting time talking about the Emancipation Proclamation because "the bondsmen would have snatched their freedom" anyway. Hitchcock, *Thanksgiving for Victories*, 3.

63. William E. Chandler to Montgomery Blair, November 20, 1863, Blair Family Papers, LC. Italics in original.

64. Silbey, *A Respectable Minority*, 68–70.

65. See, for example, G. S. Millard to Luke F. Cozens, June 30, 1863, Marble Papers.

66. Cyrus Hall McCormick to Manton Marble, August 17, 1864, Marble Papers.

67. Henry J. Raymond to Lincoln, August 22, 1864, Lincoln Papers. See also Henry J. Raymond to Simon Cameron, August 19 and August 21, 1864, Cameron Papers, LC; Schuyler Colfax to Edwin M. Stanton, August 29, 1864, Stanton Papers, LC.

68. Caton, *The Position and Policy*, 30–31.

69. Harris, "Conservative Unionists"; Winthrop, *Memoir*, 228–29, 252–53.

70. On the prospects of a presidential nomination, see S. Ellsworth to Fillmore, April 29, 1864; John R. Johnston to Fillmore, June 4, 1864; Dorothea Dix to Fillmore, June 12; Fillmore to J. R. Riddle, July 5, 1864; Hiram Ketchum to Fillmore, July 22, 1864; Democratic Committee of Iowa to Fillmore, July 28, 1864; John Bell Robinson to Fillmore, July 30, 1864; John Stuart to Fillmore, August 6, 1864; A. B. Norton to Fillmore, August 6, 1864, all in Fillmore Papers, Buffalo and Erie County Historical Society. On Fillmore's anxious political predicament, especially after the Emancipation Proclamation, see Millard Fillmore to Ephraim Hutchens, February 9, 1863; R. F. Stevens to Millard Fillmore, August 5, 1863; Leslie Combs to Fillmore, August 7, 1863, Millard Fillmore to Ellen McClellan, March 24, 1864; S. Ellsworth to Fillmore, April 4, 15, 29, 1864, Fillmore Papers.

71. Dix was pressed to run for various offices by Democrats and Republicans as well as Conservative Unionists. See Dix to Edwards Pierrepont, July 24, September 17, 1862, John A. Dix Collection, Syracuse University Library; Dix to Catherine M. Dix, October 22, 1863, Dix Papers, Columbia University Library.

72. Martin Ryerson to Simon Cameron, September 10, 1864, Cameron Papers, LC.

73. *Boston Courier*, September 12, 1864.

74. Winthrop, *Great Speech*; McClellan to Robert C. Winthrop Jr., October 22, 1864, Winthrop Family Papers, MHS. See also Winthrop, *Speech at the Ratification Meeting*. For a similar Whiggish pro-McClellan pitch, see Anon., *A Political Conservative Circular*.

75. Severance, ed. *Millard Fillmore Papers*, 86–87.

76. For another former Whig argument for McClellan, see Anon., *A Political Conservative Circular*. In addition, there is plenty of scattered evidence of habitual Democrats voting for Lincoln in 1864. See, for example, Michael T. Gibbons to William H. Seward, September 27, 1864, Seward Papers, LC.

77. *New York Herald*, October 18, 1864. The Union Party was also very assiduous at playing up its Jacksonian roots, including stressing the antislavery achievements of Democrats in the past. Andrew Johnson's presence on the ballot was hugely helpful in reinforcing this message. See Smith, *No Party Now*, 135–38.

78. *New York Times*, November 5, 1864.

79. Fisher, *Diary*, October 26, 1864.

80. *Washington Reporter*, February 24, 1864.

81. *Columbus Crisis*, November 30, 1864.

82. Dix, *Memoirs*, 116.

83. Fisher, *Diary*, April 5, 1865.

84. *New York Times*, April 18, 1865.

85. Goldfield, *America Aflame*, 1; Hummel, *Emancipating Slaves, Enslaving Free Men*, 359; McPherson, "The Civil War and the Transformation of America," 5.

86. Beard and Beard, *Rise of American Civilization*, 2:52–121.

87. Frederickson, *The Inner Civil War*; Lawson, *Patriot Fires*; Menand, *The Metaphysical Club*; Bellows, *Unconditional Loyalty*; Whitman, *Complete Prose Works*, 314.

88. McPherson, "The Civil War and the Transformation of America," 5.

89. Richardson, *The Greatest Nation of the Earth*.

90. On the impact of the war on fiscal policy, from the origins of the state's capacity to tax-and-spend to the beginning of the Republic, see Edling, *A Hercules in the Cradle*. For a contrasting argument that stresses the transformative impact of the Civil War on the functions and scope of the federal government, see, Bensel *Yankee Leviathan*. See also Balogh *A Government Out of Sight*, which argues that although the federal government operated in a very different way from its bureaucratic twentieth-century successor, it nevertheless performed vital functions. In his forthcoming PhD dissertation, Jack Furniss of the University of Virginia makes a powerful case that state governments played a far more important role in the Northern war effort than has generally been recognized.

91. Richardson, *West from Appomattox*, 28.

92. Brown, *Dorothea Dix*, 320–21.

93. Ibid.

94. CWAL, 8:333.

95. For Lincoln's views on slavery, see Foner, *The Fiery Trial*, which makes a case for Lincoln's gradual moral growth; Carwardine, *Lincoln*, which stresses the influence of evangelical ideas and political pragmatism; Donald, *Lincoln*, which portrays him as a man of consistency, driven by events; and Frederickson, *Big Enough To Be Inconsistent*, which allows space for the development of Lincoln's racial views in wartime, while making a powerful case for his essential consistency.

96. Wills, *Lincoln at Gettysburg*.

97. On contemporary reaction to the Gettysburg Address, see Boritt, *The Gettysburg Gospel*, esp. 137–52.

98. The implications of Pettit's provocative phrase are explored in Tewell, *A Self-Evident Lie*.

99. Ross, "Lincoln and the Ethics of Emancipation."

100. Although in some important respects the interpretation outlined in this book differs from that offered by James Oakes in *Freedom National*, I share Oakes's dissatisfaction with a narrative of transforming Northern war aims.

101. Schmeller, *Invisible Sovereign*, argues persuasively that the concept of public opinion was crucial to the development of the antislavery movement. I would add that, more broadly, a consciousness of public opinion—including debating what it was and how it was constituted—was intrinsic to the invocation of "conservatism," which gained meaning not just through appeal to timeless verities or historical continuity but to the imagined collective common sense of "the public."

102. Oakes argues that by quarantining slavery Republicans fully intended that it would die of its own internal contradictions even without the war that triggered military emancipation. Oakes sees Lincoln as emblematic of this consistent Republican antislavery purpose, stressing not his moral growth but the radicalism of his consistently anti-

slavery views. I am less persuaded that this is true of Lincoln, and in general I think Oakes's analysis works well for radical Republicans but less well, in my reading of the evidence, for the majority of Northerners. See Oakes, *Freedom National*; Oakes, *The Radical and the Republican*; Oakes, *The Scorpion's Sting*. For a similar interpretation of Lincoln, see Striner, *Father Abraham*. Where I differ most from Oakes is over his depiction of a bifurcated Northern polity in which Republicans were driven by the moral purpose of ending slavery while Democrats were trapped in a morally blind attachment merely to nation. The calculus of political choices that Northerners made was rarely so straightforward; compromises and evasions are always more possible than we might like to think.

103. Gallagher, *The Union War*, 2. While I strongly endorse the broad outlines of Gallagher's argument, I have placed much more emphasis on the ways in which a dislike of slavery and a determination to preserve the Union as the last, best hope of Earth were intertwined, indeed mutually interdependent, moral goals.

104. Norton, "The Advantages of Defeat."

105. Higginson, *Harvard Memorial Biographies*, 1:19, 192, 84.

106. Guyatt, *Providence and the Invention of the United States*; Grant, *North Over South*; Bellah, *The Broken Covenant*; Moorhead, *American Apocalypse*; Paludan, "Religion in the American Civil War."

107. Ross, "Lincoln and the Ethics of Emancipation," 390. Italics in original.

108. Jonathan W. White's study of Union soldiers reveals men torn between their anxiety about the implications of emancipation and their understanding that slavery, as the prime cause of the rebellion, was impossible to protect. One soldier, Mack Ewing, exemplified, I suspect, the views of many other Northerners. Complaining that the conflict had become "a niger [sic] war instead of a union war," he was nevertheless willing to help free the slaves so long as there was no prospect of them being considered his equal." White, *Emancipation, the Union Army, and the Reelection of Abraham Lincoln*, 121, 104, 69–97. Chandra Manning makes a similar point in her study of the views of Union soldiers. She argues that "white Union troops continued to separate the institution of slavery from the more complicated question of black rights. . . . Ending slavery was one thing, but caring for or about black Americans was something else altogether." Manning, *What This Cruel War Was Over*, 78.

109. "Reconstruction," *Atlantic Monthly*, April 1865, 544.

Conclusion

1. *Frank Leslie's Illustrated Newspaper*, October 25, 1873.

2. *North American and United States Gazette*, May 26, 1875. Italics in original.

3. Callcott, *History in the United States*; Ross, "Historical Consciousness in Nineteenth-Century America"; Kammen, *A Season of Youth*.

4. Buckley, ed., *Did You Ever See a Dream Walking?*, ix.

5. Beecher, *The American Rebellion*, 160.

6. Schurz, *Speeches*, 1:5–8.

7. Perry, *Boats Against the Current*, 48.

8. *United States Magazine and Democratic Review* 6, no. 23 (November 1839): 426–30.

9. Democratic Party, *Proceedings of the Nob Mountain Meeting,* 17.

10. *New York World,* December 17, 1867.

11. Draft of Speech, 1867, Edmund Burke Papers, LC.

12. [Philadelphia] *Daily Age,* July 1, 1864.

13. John A. Dix to Edwards Pierrepont, July 13, 1866, Dix Collection, Syracuse University Library.

14. *North American and United States Gazette,* September 5, 1865.

15. Tulloch, "Changing British Attitudes."

16. Bryce, *American Commonwealth,* 1:339–40. Portes, *Fascination and Misgivings,* 174. On the conservative turn in public attitudes toward the United States after the Civil War, see Körner, Miller, and Smith, eds., *America Imagined.*

17. The continued threat of instability is a major theme of two recent studies of Reconstruction: Summers, *The Ordeal of the Reunion;* Downs, *After Appomattox.*

18. Fisher, *Diary,* April 11, 1865.

19. "Annual Report of the Union League Club of New York, 1865," 77.

20. Quoted in Turner, *The Liberal Education of Charles Eliot Norton,* 166.

21. *Rhode Island Press,* July 8, 1871.

Bibliography

Primary Sources

MANUSCRIPT COLLECTIONS

Baltimore, MD
    The Winston Tabb Center for Rare Books, Manuscripts, and Archives,
        Johns Hopkins University
      Francis Lieber Papers
      Roger Brooke Taney Collection
Boston, MA
    Massachusetts Historical Society (MHS)
      Henry W. Bellows Papers
      Edward Everett Papers
      Marcus Morton Papers
      Winthrop Family Papers
Buffalo, NY
    Buffalo and Erie County Historical Society
      Millard Fillmore Papers
Cambridge, MA
    Houghton Library, Harvard University
      Broadsides Collection
      Dorothea Dix Papers
Chicago, IL
    Chicago History Museum
      Stephen A. Douglas Papers
    Special Collections Research Center, University of Chicago
      Stephen A. Douglas Papers (SADP)
Harrisburg, PA
    Pennsylvania State Archives
      Dock Family Papers
Hartford, CT
    Connecticut Historical Society
      Gideon Welles Papers
Hannover, NH
    Rauner Special Collections Library, Dartmouth College
      Nathan Lord Papers
New Haven, CT
    Manuscripts and Archives, Sterling Memorial Library, Yale University
      Carrington Family Papers

New York, NY
  New York Public Library (NYPL)
    Charles P. Daly Papers
    Duyckinck Family Papers
    Samuel J. Tilden Papers
    Gideon Welles Papers
  Rare Book and Manuscript Library, Columbia University
    John A. Dix Papers
    Azariah C. Flagg Papers
  New-York Historical Society (NYHS)
    Miscellaneous Manuscripts, Astor Place Riot
    Seventh Regiment Archives
    Horatio Seymour Papers
    Edward N. Tailer Diaries
Philadelphia, PA
  Historical Society of Pennsylvania (HSP)
    Charles J. Biddle Collection
    William Bigler Papers
    James Buchanan Papers
    Lewis S. Coryell Papers
  Kislak Center for Special Collections, Rare Books and Manuscripts,
      University of Pennsylvania Library
    Edwin Forrest Collection
Providence, RI
  John Hay Library, Brown University
    S. S. Cox Papers
Rochester, NY
  Department of Rare Books and Special Collections,
      University of Rochester Library
    William H. Seward Papers
Syracuse, NY
  Syracuse University Library
    John A. Dix Collection
Springfield, IL
  Abraham Lincoln Presidential Library
    Charles H. Lanphier Papers
Washington, DC
  Manuscripts Division, Library of Congress (LC)
    Thomas F. Bayard Papers
    Blair Family Papers
    Edmund Burke Papers
    Simon Cameron Papers
    Hamilton Fish Papers

John Thompson Ford Papers

Horace Greeley Papers

Walter Quintin Gresham Papers

Abraham Lincoln Papers

Manton Marble Papers

Edwin McMasters Stanton Papers

Lyman Trumbull Papers

Martin Van Buren Papers

Gideon Welles Papers

David Ames Wells Papers

Wilmington, DE

Historical Society of Delaware

Scott Manuscripts

Wilmington Debating Society Minutes, 1863

PRINTED PRIMARY SOURCES

Adams, Charles Francis. *Richard Henry Dana*. 2 vols. Boston: Houghton, Mifflin, 1891.

Adams, Nehemiah. *A South-side View of Slavery, or, Three Months at the South in 1854*. Boston: T. R. Marvin, 1854.

Allen, Thomas G. *Letter from Thomas G. Allen to Col. Thomas B. Florence, Representative in the XXXIVth Congress from the First Congressional District, Pennsylvania*. Philadelphia, 1856.

An Appeal to the Conservative Men of All Parties: The Presidential Question. New York, 1860. https://archive.org/details/appealtoconservaoonp___.

Anon. *An Appeal to the Conservative Masses, North and South: To End Agitation For or Against Slavery, by Decided Action Now*. Lancaster, PA, 1856.

Anon. *The Boston Slave Riot and Trial of Anthony Burns*. Boston: Fetridge, 1854.

Anon. *The End of the Irrepressible Conflict by a Merchant of Philadelphia*. Philadelphia: King & Baird, 1860.

Anon., *Grand Mass Meeting of the Democracy of New York!* [At Tammany Hall, March 4, 1858]. New York, 1858.

Anon. *Life of Millard Fillmore*. New York: R. M. De Witt, 1856.

Anon. *Nebraska: A Poem, personal and political*. Boston: John P. Jewett & Co., 1854.

Anon. *Papers for the People*. New York: Offices of the Jefferson Union, 1852.

Anon. *A Plain Statement Addressed to Honest Democrats by one of the People*. Boston: John P. Jewett, 1856.

Anon. *A Political Conservative Circular, from an "Old Line Webster Whig" of Forty Years VOTING experience, in support of constitutional freedom and sound CONSERVATIVE principles; with reasons for opposing the RE-ELECTION of Abraham Lincoln, for his gross violation of both spirit and provisions of the same*. Boston, 1864.

Anon. *A rejoinder to "The replies from England, etc. to certain statements circulated in this country respecting Mr. Macready."* New York: Stringer & Townsend, 1849.

Bacon, Ezekiel. *Recollections of Fifty Years Since: With glances at the present aspects and future prospects of the age and the times: a lecture delivered before the Young Men's Association of the city of Utica, February 2, 1843.* Utica, NY: R. W. Roberts, 1843.

Baker, Edward D. *Speech of Hon. Edward D. Baker, US Senator from Oregon, delivered at a Republican Mass Meeting, held at the American Theatre in the City of San Francisco on Friday Evening, October 26th, 1860.* San Francisco: Republican State Central Committee of California, Campaign Document No. 15, 1860.

Bancroft, George. *A History of the United States, from the Discovery of the American Continent.* 10 vols. Boston: Little, Brown, 1854–78.

Bancroft, George, and James Milliken. *The League for the Union: Speeches of the Hon. George Bancroft and James Milliken, Esq.* Philadelphia: William S. & Alfred Marten, 1863.

Barnard, Daniel D. *Letter from the Hon. Daniel D. Barnard: Addressed to James A. Hamilton Esq., On the Political Condition of the Country, and the State of Parties, and in Favor of Millard Fillmore for President.* Albany, NY: J. Munsell, 1856.

Basler, Roy P., ed. *The Collected Works of Abraham Lincoln.* 9 vols. New Brunswick, NJ: Rutgers University Press, 1953.

Bearse, Austin. *Reminiscences of Fugitive-Slave Law Days in Boston.* Boston: W. Richardson, 1880.

Beecher, Henry Ward. *The American Rebellion: Report of the Speeches of the Rev Henry Ward Beecher, delivered at Public Meetings in Manchester, Glasgow, Edinburgh, Liverpool, and London; and at the Farewell Breakfasts in London, Liverpool and Manchester.* Manchester: Union and Emancipation Society, 1864.

Bellows, Henry W. *Historical Sketch of the Union League Club of New York.* New York: Union League Club, 1879.

———. *A Sermon, occasioned by the late riot in New York, preached in the Church of the Divine Unity, on Sunday, May 13, 1849.* New York: C. S. Francis, 1849.

———. *The Valley of Decision: a plea for unbroken fealty on the part of the loyal states to the Constitution and the Union, despite the offences of the rebel states: a discourse given on occasion of the National Fast, Sept. 26, 1861, in All Souls' Church.* New York: H.B. Price, 1861.

———. "Cities and Parks: With Special Reference to the New York Central Park." *Atlantic Monthly* 7 (April 1861): 416–29.

———. *Unconditional Loyalty.* New York: Anson D. Randolph, 1863.

Belmont, August. *Letters, Speeches and Addresses of August Belmont.* New York: Privately printed, 1890.

Biddle, Charles J. *The Alliance With the Negro: Speech of Charles J. Biddle of Pennsylvania delivered in the House of Representatives of the United States, March 6, 1862.* Washington, DC, 1862.

Bigelow, John. *The Life of Samuel J. Tilden.* 2 vols. New York: Harper & Brothers, 1896.

———. *Memoir of the life and public services of John Charles Frémont: Including an account of his explorations, discoveries and adventures on five successive expeditions across the North American continent; voluminous selections from his private and public correspondence; his defence, before the court martial, and full reports of his principal speeches in the Senate of the United States.* Cincinnati: Derby & Jackson, 1856.

———. "Some Recollections of Charles O'Conor." *Century Magazine* 29 (March 1885): 725–36.

Blaine, James G. *Political Discussions: Legislative, Diplomatic and Popular, 1856–1886.* Norwich, CT: Henry Bill, 1887.

———. *Twenty Years of Congress: From Lincoln to Garfield.* 2 vols. Norwich, CT: Henry Bill, 1884.

Blatch, Harriot Stanton, and Theodore Stanton, eds. *Elizabeth Cady Stanton, As Revealed in Her Letters, Diary and Reminiscences.* Vol. 2. New York: Harper & Brothers, 1922.

Bowen, Ralph H., ed. *A Frenchman in Lincoln's America.* 2 vols. Chicago: R.R. Donnelley & Sons, 1974.

Brace, Charles Loring. *The Dangerous Classes of New York and Twenty Years Work Among Them.* New York: Wynkoop & Hallenbeck, 1872.

Bryce, James. *The American Commonwealth.* 2 vols. London: Macmillan, 1888.

Buckalew, Charles R. *Proportional Representation.* Philadelphia: J. Campbell & Son, 1872.

Buckingham, William A. *Message of His Excellency William A. Buckingham, Governor of Connecticut, to the Legislature of the State, May Session, 1860.* New Haven, CT: Carrington & Hotchkiss, 1860.

Burke, Edmund. *A Philosophical Enquiry into the Origin of Our Ideas of the Sublime and the Beautiful.* Edited by Adam Phillips. New York: Oxford University Press, 1990.

Burlingame, Anson. *Oration by Hon. Anson Burlingame, Delivered at Salem, July 4, 1854.* Salem, MA, 1854.

Burlingame, Michael, ed., *Lincoln's Journalist: John Hay's Anonymous Writings for the Press, 1860–1864.* Carbondale, IL: Southern Illinois University Press, 1998.

Bushnell, Horace. *A Discourse Delivered in the North Church, Hartford, on the annual state fast, April 14, 1854.* Hartford, CT: E. Hunt & Son, 1854.

Butler, William Allen. *A Retrospect of Forty Years, 1825–1865.* New York: Charles Scribner, 1911.

Campbell, John. *Negro-mania: being an Examination of the Falsely Assumed Equality of the Various Races of Men.* Philadelphia: Campbell & Power, 1852.

Carlyle, Thomas. *On Heroes, Hero-Worship and the Heroic in History.* London: James Fraser, 1841.

Caton, J. D. *The Position and Policy of the Democratic Party.* Albany, [1862?].

Chadwick, John White, ed. *A Life for Liberty: Anti-Slavery and Other Letters of Sallie Holley.* New York: G.P. Putnam's Sons, 1899.

Chaney, Ednah Dow, ed. *Louisa May Alcott: Her Life, Letters, and Journals.* Boston: Robert Bros, 1889.

Child, Lydia Maria. *Letters of Lydia Maria Child with a Biographical Introduction by John G. Whittier and Appendix by Wendell Phillips.* Boston: Houghton, Mifflin, 1883.

Choate, Rufus. *Hon Rufus Choate on the Presidential Question.* Boston, 1856.

Clarke, James Freeman. *Anti-Slavery Days: A Sketch of the Struggle Which Ended in the Abolition of Slavery in the United States.* New York: R. Worthington, 1888.

Clay, Henry. *Speech of Henry Clay, delivered at the Great Barbeque at Lexington, (Kentucky), June 9, 1842.* Sing Sing, NY: E.G. Sutherland, 1842.

Colton, Calvin. *The Works of Henry Clay: Comprising His Life, Correspondence and Speeches.* 10 vols. New York: G.P. Putnam, 1904.

Conrad, Robert Edgar, ed. *In the Hands of Strangers: Readings on Foreign and Domestic Slave Trading and the Crisis of the Union.* University Park: Pennsylvania State University Press, 2001.

Constitutional Union Party, National Committee. *Address of the National Executive Committee of the National Union Party to the People of the United States.* Washington, DC: W.H. Moore, 1860.

Cook, Thomas M., and Thomas W. Knox, eds. *The Public Record Including Speeches, Messages, Proclamation, Official Correspondence, and Other Public Utterances of Horatio Seymour.* New York: I.W. England, 1868.

Cooper, James Fennimore. *The American Democrat; or, hints on the social and civic relations of the United States of America.* Cooperstown, NY: H. & E. Phinney, 1838.

Corwin, Thomas. *Speech of Mr. Corwin of Ohio, on the Mexican War, Delivered in the Senate of the United States, February 11, 1847.* Cincinnati: Stevenson, Looker & Todd, Office of the Atlas, 1847.

Cox, Samuel S. *Eight years in Congress, from 1857–1865. Memoir and speeches. By Samuel S. Cox.* New York, D. Appleton, 1865.

Covode, John, and Charles Russell Train. *The Covode Investigation: Report of the Select Committee on Alleged Corruptions in Government.* Washington, DC: Government Printing Office, 1860.

Crosby, Alpheus. *Eulogy Commemorative of the Life and Character of Nathan Lord.* Hanover, NH: A.B. Parker, 1871.

Curtis, George Ticknor. *History of the origin, formation, and adoption of the Constitution of the United States, with notices of its principal framers.* New York: Harper & Row, 1854.

———. *The True Uses of American Revolutionary History: An Oration delivered before the authorities of the City of Boston, on Monday the fifth of July, 1841, being the day set apart for the celebration of the Sixty-Fifth Anniversary of American Independence.* Boston: John H. Eastburn, 1841.

Dartmouth College Trustees. *Proceedings of the Trustees of Dartmouth College, July 24, 1863, Upon the Resolutions of the Merrimack County Conference of Congregational Churches, in reference to the President of said College, passed at their session, June 23 and 24, 1863.* Concord, NH: McFarland & Jenks, 1863.

Day, Timothy C. *The Democratic party as it was and as it is! Speech of Hon. Timothy C. Day, of Ohio, in the House of Representatives, April 23, 1856.* Washington, DC: n. p., 1856.

De Cordova, R. J. *A lecture on war, foreign and civil, and the blessings of union and peace, delivered by R.J. De Cordova, Esq., in the Temple Emanuel, New York, on Saturday, December 8th, 1860.* New York: M. Ellinger, 1860.

Democratic Party (NY). *Free Soil, Free Speech, Free Men: Proceedings of the Democratic Republican State Convention at Syracuse, July 24, 1856: the Address and Resolutions, with the List of Delegates*. Albany, New York, 1856.

Democratic Party (PA). *Proceedings of the Nob Mountain Meeting held in Columbia County, Pa on the last three days of August, 1865*. Philadelphia: McLaughlin Brothers, 1865.

Democratic State Committee (NY). *Proceedings and Address of the Democratic State Convention held at Syracuse*. Albany, NY, 1856.

Democratic State Committee (PA). *Address and Correspondence of the Democratic State Committee of Pennsylvania*. Philadelphia: B. Franklin Jackson, 1856

Dewey, Mary E., ed. *Life and Letters of Catherine M. Sedgwick*. New York: Harpers, 1871.

Dix, John A. *Memoirs of John Adams Dix*. 2 vols. Edited by Morgan Dix. New York: Harper Bros., 1883.

Douglas, Stephen A. *Letter of Stephen Douglas, in Reply to the Editor of the State Capitol Reporter, Concord, NH*. Washington, DC, 1854.

———. *Remarks of the Hon. Stephen A. Douglas, on Kansas, Utah, and the Dred Scott decision. Delivered at Springfield, Illinois, June 12th, 1857*. Chicago, 1857.

———. *Speech of Senator Douglas, at the Democratic Celebration of the Anniversary of American Freedom, in Independence Square, Philadelphia, July 4, 1854*. Philadelphia, 1854.

Eisenschiml, Otto, ed. *Vermont General: the Unusual War Experiences of Edward Hastings Ripley, 1862–1865*. New York: Devin-Adair, 1960.

Everett, Edward. *Correspondence on the Proposed Tripartite Convention Relative to Cuba*. Boston: Little, Brown, 1853.

———. *Oration Delivered before the City Authorities of Boston, on the Fourth of July, 1860*. Boston: Rand & Avery, 1860.

———. *Stability and Progress. Remarks made on the 4th of July, 1853, in Faneuil Hall*. Boston, 1853.

———. *The Works of Daniel Webster*. 6 vols. Boston: Little, Brown, 1853.

Fields, Annie, ed. *Life and Letters of Harriet Beecher Stowe*. Boston: Houghton, Mifflin, 1897.

Fish, Hamilton, and James A. Hamilton. *Fremont the Conservative Candidate: Correspondence between Hon. Hamilton Fish and Hon James A. Hamilton*. New York, 1856.

Fisher, Sidney George. *Address Delivered before the Montgomery County Agricultural Society*. Philadelphia: J.B. Chandler, 1858.

———. *The Law of the Territories*. Philadelphia: C. Sherman and Son, 1869.

Florence, Thomas B. *The Principles of Democracy: Speech of the Hon. Thomas B. Florence of Penn. Delivered in the House of Representatives of the United States, Thursday April 12, 1860*. Washington, DC, 1860.

Forney, John W. *Speech of John W. Forney at Tarrytown, West Chester County, New York, on Thursday, September 2d, 1858*. n.p., [1858?].

Foster, George G., and Thomas Dunn English. *The French Revolution of 1848: Its causes, actors, events and influences*. Philadelphia: G.B. Zieber, 1848.

French, Benjamin Brown. *Witness to the Young Republic: A Yankee's Journal, 1828–1870*. Edited by John J. McDonough and Donald B. Cole. Hanover, NH: University Press of New England, 2002.

Friedlander, Marc, and L. H. Butterfield, eds. *The Diary of Charles Francis Adams.* 6 vols. Cambridge, MA: Harvard University Press, 1968.

Furness, W. H. *Our Duty as Conservatives.* Philadelphia: C. Sherman & Son, 1860.

Gardiner, Oliver C. *The Great Issue. Or, The Three Presidential Candidates, Being a Brief Historical Sketch of the Free Soil Question in the United States, From the Congresses of 1774 and '87 to the Present Time.* New York: W.C. Bryant, 1848.

Gordon, Donald, ed. *The Diary of Ellen Birdseye Wheaton.* Boston: Privately published, 1923.

Great Union Meeting in Philadelphia, December 7, 1859: Fanaticism Rebuked. Philadelphia: Crissy & Markley, 1859.

Greeley, Horace. *Recollections of a Busy Life.* New York: J.B. Ford, 1868.

Guelzo, Allen. *Lincoln's Emancipation Proclamation: The End of Slavery in America.* New York: Simon & Schuster, 2006.

Harlow, Alvin F. *Old Bowery Days: The Chronicles of a Famous Street.* New York: D. Appleton, 1931.

Hawthorne, Nathaniel. *The Life of Franklin Pierce.* Boston: Ticknor, Reed and Fields, 1852.

Headley, Joel T. *Pen and Pencil Sketches of the Great Riots.* New York: F.B. Treat, 1882.

Higginson, Thomas Wentworth. *Harvard Memorial Biographies.* 2 vols. Cambridge, MA: Sever and Francis, 1866.

Hitchcock, Roswell D. *Thanksgiving for Victories.* New York, 1864.

Hodge, Charles. "The War." *Biblical Repository and Princeton Review* 35 (Jan 1863): 152–55.

Howe, Mark A. DeWolfe. *Memories of a Hostess: A Chronicle of Eminent Friendships.* Boston: Atlantic Monthly Press, 1922.

Howe, Mark A. DeWolfe, ed. *The Life and Letters of George Bancroft.* 2 vols. New York: Scribner's, 1908.

Howland, Eliza Woolsey, ed. *Letters of a family during the war for the Union, 1861–1865.* New Haven, CT: Tuttle, Morehouse and Taylor, 1889.

Hutter, Rev. E. W. *"God Hath Not Dealt So with any Nation": A Discourse preached in St Matthew's Lutheran Church.* Philadelphia, F. Pierson, 1858.

Indiana Democratic State Central Committee. *Facts for the People.* Indianapolis, 1862.

Ingersoll, Charles. *Civil War Speeches.* Philadelphia, 1865. Library Company of Philadelphia (LCP).

Ingersoll, Edward. *Personal Liberty and Martial Law.* Philadelphia, 1862.

James, William. *A Full and Correct Account of the Military Occurrences of the Late War Between Great Britain and the United States of America.* London, 1818.

Johannsen, Robert W., ed. *The Letters of Stephen A. Douglas.* Urbana: University of Illinois Press, 1961.

Kendall, Phebe Mitchell, ed. *Maria Mitchell: Life, Letters, and Journals.* Boston: Lee & Shepard, 1896.

Lord, John King. *History of Dartmouth College.* 2 vols. Cambridge, MA: John Wilson & Son, 1891.

———. *Nathan Lord, D.D.* Concord: New Hampshire Historical Society, 1900.

Lord, Nathan. *The Improvement of the present state of things, A discourse to the students of Dartmouth College, November 1852.* Hanover, NH: Dartmouth Press, 1852.

———. *A Letter to Ministers of the Gospel of All Denominations, on Slavery. By a Northern Presbyter.* Boston: Little, Brown, 1854.

Lovejoy, Joseph C. *The True Democracy: A Speech Delivered at East Cambridge, September 29, 1856.* Boston, 1856.

Lowell, James Russell. *The Early Poems of James Russell Lowell, Including the Biglow Papers.* New York: A. L. Burt, 1900.

———. "The Question of the Hour." *Atlantic Monthly* 7 (1861): 120–21.

Loyal National League. *The Loyal National League.* New York, 1863.

Lucid, Robert F., ed. *The Journal of Richard Henry Dana.* 3 vols. Cambridge, MA: Harvard University Press, 1968.

Macready, William Charles. *The Replies from England etc., to certain statements circulated in this country respecting Mr. Macready.* New York: Stringer & Townsend, 1849.

Magoun, George F. "A Conservative View of the Nebraska Question." *New Englander and Yale Review* 12 (1854): 536

Mansfield Edward. *The Issues and Duties of the Day.* Cincinnati: Caleb Clark, 1864.

Marshall, Edward C. *American Progress, Judge Douglas, the Presidency: Speech of Mr Marshall of California in the House of Representatives.* Washington, DC: Congressional Printing Office, 1852.

McClure, Alexander K. *Old-Time Notes of Pennsylvania: a connected & chronological record of the commercial, industrial & educational advancement of Pennsylvania, & the inner history of all political movements since the adoption of the constitution of 1838.* 2 vols. Philadelphia: John C. Winston, 1905.

McKnight, Robert. *Mission of Republicans; Sectionalism of Modern Democratic Party. Speech of Robert McKnight of Penn., delivered in the House of Representatives, April 24, 1860.* New York: Republican National Committee, 1860.

McPherson, Edward. *Disorganization and Disunion: Speech of Hon. Edward McPherson of Pennsylvania: Delivered in the House of Representatives, February 24, 1860.* Washington, DC: Buell & Blanchard, 1860.

Moore, H. N., and John Frost. *The Reign of Terror: Historically and Biographically Treated, Being a Compendium of the French Revolution from its Commencement to the Fall of Robespierre. To which is added the Revolutions in France, from 1830 to 1851 by John Frost.* Philadelphia: J.B. Perry, 1851.

Morley, John. *On Compromise.* London: Macmillan, 1898.

Morse, Samuel F. B. *An Argument on the Ethical Position of Slavery in the social system, and its relation to the politics of the day.* New York: Society for the Diffusion of Political Knowledge, 1863.

Moses, Montrose J. *The Fabulous Forrest: The Record of an American Actor.* Boston: Little, Brown, 1929.

Moses, Montrose, and John Mason Brown, eds. *The American Theatre as Seen by Its Critics.* New York: W.W. Norton, 1934.

Nevins, Allan, ed. *The Diary of Phillip Hone.* 2 vols. New York: Dodd, Mead, 1927.

Nevins, Allan, and Milton Halsey Thomas, eds. *The Diary of George Templeton Strong.* 4 vols. New York: Macmillan, 1952.

New Jersey Democratic State Central Committee. *Address of the New Jersey Democratic State Central Committee to the Voters of the State.* Trenton: n.p., 1862.

New York Young Men's Republican Union. *Lincoln and Liberty!* Tract No. 2. New York: Young Men's Republican Union of the City of New York, June 26, 1860.

——. *Lincoln and Liberty!* Tract No. 3. New York: Young Men's Republican Union of the City of New York, July 3, 1860.

Norton, Charles Eliot. "The Advantages of Defeat." *Atlantic Monthly* 8 (September 1861): 363–64.

Official Report of the Great Union Meeting Held at the Academy of Music, New York, December 19, 1859. New York: Davies & Kent, 1859.

Palfrey, John Gorham. *Letter to an Old Whig Neighbor on the Approaching State Election.* Boston: Cosby, Nichols, 1855.

Parker, Edward Griffin. *Reminiscences of Rufus Choate: The Great American Advocate.* New York: Mason Brothers, 1860.

Parton, James. *General Butler in New Orleans: History of the Administration of the Department of the Gulf in the Year 1862.* New York: Mason Brothers, 1864.

Payne, John Howard. *Brutus, or, the fall of Tarquin: a tragedy in five acts by John Howard Payne; with the stage business, cast of characters, costumes, relative positions, etc.* New York: William Taylor, [1853?].

Porte, Joel, ed. *Ralph Waldo Emerson: Essays and Lectures.* New York: Library of America, 1983.

Price, Eli. *An Appeal for the Union by a Philadelphia Whig.* Philadelphia, 1856.

Ranney, H. M. *Account of the terrific and fatal riot at the New York Astor Place Opera House, on the night of May 10th, 1849; with the quarrels of Forrest and Macready, including all the causes which led to that awful tragedy! etc.* New York, 1849.

Rantoul, Robert, Charles G. Loring, and George T. Curtis. *Trial of Thomas Sims on an Issue of Personal Liberty.* Boston, 1851.

Reemelin, Karl. *Life of Charles Reemelin, in German: Carl Gustav Rumelin, From 1814–1892.* Cincinnati, OH: Weier & Daiker, 1892.

Republican National Committee. *Homesteads: The Republicans and Settlers against Democrats and Monopoly.* New York, Republican National Committee, 1860.

Republican Congressional Committee, 1857–1859. *The Ruin of the Democratic Party: Reports of the Covode and Other Committees.* Washington, DC: Republican Congressional Committee, 1860.

Schurz, Carl. *Judge Douglas: The Bill of Indictment. Speech of Carl Schurz, of Wisconsin, at the Cooper Union Institute, New York, September 13, 1860.* New York: Tribune, 1860.

——. *Speeches, correspondence and political papers of Carl Schurz.* Selected and edited by Frederic Bancroft on behalf of the Carl Schurz Memorial Committee. 6 vols. New York: G.P. Putnam's Sons, 1913.

Scott, Winfield. *Letter on the Slavery Question.* Washington, DC, 1852.

Scoville, Joseph. *The Old Merchants of New York City*. 2 vols. New York, 1863–66.

Sears, Stephen B., ed. *The Civil War Papers of George B. McClellan*. New York: Ticknor & Fields, 1989.

Severance, Frank H., ed. *Millard Fillmore Papers*. Vol. 2. Buffalo, NY: Buffalo Historical Society, 1907.

Seymour, Horatio. *Speech of Horatio Seymour at Springfield, Mass., July 4th, 1856*. Springfield, MA: Argus, 1856.

Snyder, Charles M., ed. *The Lady and the President: The Letters of Dorothea Dix & Millard Fillmore*. Lexington: University Press of Kentucky, 1975.

Spooner, Thomas. *Report of the President of the State Council of Ohio, June 5, 1855*. Cincinnati, OH: C. Clarke, 1855.

Stevens, Charles. *Anthony Burns: A Narrative*. Boston: J.P. Jewett, 1856.

Stillé, Charles J. *How a Free People Conduct a Long War*. New York: Loyal Publication Society, 1863.

Sumner, Charles. *Charles Sumner: His Complete Works*. Edited and with an introduction by George Frisbie Hoar. 20 vols. Boston: Lee & Shepherd, 1900.

———. *The Landmark of Freedom: Speech of Hon. Charles Sumner, against the repeal of the Missouri prohibition of slavery north of 36°30' In the Senate, February 21, 1854*. Washington, DC: Congressional Globe Office, 1854.

Tocqueville, Alexis de. *Democracy in America*. Edited by Arthur Goldhammer. New York: Library of America, 2004.

Toynbee, William, ed. *The Diaries of William Charles Macready*. 2 vols. New York: G.P. Putnam's Sons, 1912.

Union Safety Committee of New Haven. *The Proceedings of the Union meeting: held at Brewster's Hall, December 24, 1850*. New Haven, CR: W. H. Stanley, 1851.

Voorhees, Daniel W. *Speeches of Daniel W. Voorhees of Indiana, Embracing his most prominent forensic, political, occasional and literary addresses*. Cincinnati, OH: R. Clarke, 1875.

Wainwright, Nicholas B., ed. *A Philadelphia Perspective: The Diary of Sidney George Fisher, 1834–1871*. Philadelphia: Historical Society of Pennsylvania, 1967.

Walling, George W. *Recollections of a New York Chief of Police*. New York: Caxton Book Concern, 1887.

Wharton, G. M. *Speech of G. M. Wharton at the Mass Meeting held at West Chester, Pa., Oct. 27, 1864*. Philadelphia, 1864.

Whichter, Stephen E., and Robert E. Spillar, eds. *The Early Lectures of Ralph Waldo Emerson*. Vol. 1, *1833–1836*. Cambridge, MA: Harvard University Press, 1959.

Whig Party (US). *The great fraud upon the public credulity in the organization of the Republican party upon the ruins of the "Whig party": an address to the old-line Whigs of the Union*. Washington, DC: Union Office, 1856.

Whitman, Walt. *Complete Prose Works*. Philadelphia: David McKay, 1892.

Whitney, Thomas R. *A defence of the American policy, as opposed to the encroachments of foreign influence, and especially to the interference of the papacy in the political interests and affairs of the United States*. New York: De Witt & Davenport, 1856.

Whittier, John G., ed. *Letters of Lydia Maria Child.* Boston, MA: Houghton, Mifflin, 1883.

Winthrop, Robert C. *Algernon Sidney. A Lecture delivered before the Boston Mercantile Library Association, Dec. 21, 1853.* Boston: Mercantile Library Association, 1854.

———. *Great Speech of Robert C. Winthrop, at New London, Conn., October 18. The Principles and Interests of the Republican party against the Union. The Election of McClellan the Only Hope for Union and Peace.* Democratic Campaign document, no. 23. New York, 1864.

———. *Robert C. Winthrop: A Memoir.* Boston: Little, Brown, 1897.

———. *Speech at the Great Ratification Meeting in Union Square, New York, September 17, 1864.* Democratic Campaign Document no. 9. New York, 1864.

Woods, Thomas E. Jr. *The Political Writings of Rufus Choate.* Washington, DC: Regnery, 2002.

Woodson, Thomas, L. Neal Smith, and Norman Holmes Pearson, eds. *The Centenary Edition of the Works of Nathaniel Hawthorne.* Vol. 16, *1843–1853.* Columbus: Ohio State University Press, 1985.

Robinson, John Bell. *An Address to the "People" of the Several Sovereign States of the United States on the Frauds Committed on their Elective Franchise, under Official Orders, and the Danger of the People being Reduced to Mere Serfs to a Tyrant Despot, Under the Pretext of Negro Freedom, Military Necessity, Union, and Liberty.* Philadelphia, 1864.

NEWSPAPERS AND PERIODICALS

Connecticut
Constitution (Middletown)
Daily Chronicle (New London)
Hartford Times
New Englander and Yale Review (New Haven)
Weekly Chronicle (New London)

District of Columbia
Congressional Globe
Constitution
Daily Evening Star
Daily National Intelligencer
Daily Union
National Era
Republic
Washington Chronicle
Washington Union

Illinois
Chicago Tribune
Daily Illinois State Journal (Springfield)
Illinois State Register (Springfield)
Quincy Whig (IL)

Indiana
Daily State Sentinel (Indianapolis)
Fountain Ledger (Covington)
Sullivan Democrat

Kansas
Herald of Freedom (Lawrence)

Maine
Weekly Advertiser (Portland)

Maryland
Baltimore Clipper

Massachusetts
Atlantic Monthly (Boston)
Boston Courier
Boston Daily Advertiser
Boston Daily Traveller
Boston Evening Transcript
Boston Post
Boston Recorder
Daily Atlas (Boston)

Emancipator (Boston)
Emancipator and Republican (Boston)
Liberator (Boston)
Massachusetts Spy (Worcester)
Nantucket Inquirer
North American Review (Boston)
Springfield Republican
Sun (Pittsfield)

Michigan
Detroit Free Press

Missouri
Daily Missouri Republican (St Louis)

New Hampshire
Concord Monitor
Dover Gazette
New Hampshire Patriot and State Gazette (Concord)

New Hampshire Reporter (Concord)
Weekly Union (Manchester)

New Jersey
Biblical Repertory and Princeton Review

Daily Advertiser (Newark)

New York
Albany Evening Journal
American Whig Review [alternatively known as *American Review: A Whig Journal*]
Brooklyn Daily Eagle
Christian Inquirer
Clarion (New York)

Commercial Advertiser (New York)
Congregationalist (New York)
Frank Leslie's Illustrated Newspaper (New York)
Harpers' Weekly (New York)
Home Journal (New York)
Huron Reflector

Independent (New York)
Irish-American (New York)
Literary Messenger (New York)
National Crisis (New York)
New York Courier and Enquirer
New York Evening Post (New York)
New York Express
New York Herald
New York Ledger
New York Observer and Chronicle

New York Reformer (Watertown, NY)
New York Times
New York Tribune
New York World
Schenectady Cabinet
Trumpet and Universalist Magazine
  (New York)
United States Magazine and Democratic
  Review [alternatively known as
  Democratic Review]

Ohio

Allen County Democrat
Campaign Plain Dealer and Popular
  Sovereignty Advocate (Cleveland)
Canton Repository
Canton Transcript
Cincinnati Israelite
Cleveland Herald
Cleveland Leader

Columbus Crisis
Daily Commercial Register (Sandusky)
Ohio State Journal (Columbus)
Ohio Statesman (Columbus)
Plain Dealer (Cleveland)
Tail Ender (Cleveland)
Wooster Republican
Zanesville Courier

Pennsylvania

Clearfield Republican
Elk County Advocate (Ridgeway)
Morning Herald (Harrisburg)
North American and United States Gazette
  [alternatively known as *North*
  American] (Philadelphia)
Patriot (Harrisburg)
Pennsylvania Freeman (Philadelphia)
Pennsylvanian (Philadelphia)
The Daily Age (Philadelphia)

Philadelphia Inquirer
Philadelphia Public Ledger
Philadelphia Sun
Pittsburgh Post
Press (Philadelphia)
Star of the North (Bloomsburg)
Telegraph (Harrisburg)
Washington Reporter
Weekly Patriot and Union (Harrisburg)

Rhode Island

Providence Evening Press
Providence Post

Rhode Island Press (Providence)

Vermont

Eagle (Brattleboro)
St. Albans Messenger
Vermont Journal (Windsor)

Vermont Patriot (Brattleboro)
Washington Sentinel

Virginia
Richmond Whig

Wisconsin
American Freeman (Milwaukee)
Wisconsin Patriot (Madison)

London, England
Reynolds's News

Secondary Sources

Abbot, Richard H. *The Republican Party and the South, 1855–1877: The First Southern Strategy*. Chapel Hill: University of North Carolina Press, 1986.

Adams, Peter. *The Bowery Boys: Street Corner Radicals and the Politics of Rebellion*. Westport, CT: Praeger, 2005.

Adorno, Theodor W., Elise Frenkel-Brunswik, Daniel J. Levinson, and R. Nevitt Sanford. *The Authoritarian Personality*. New York: Harper & Brothers, 1950.

Alexander, D. S. *A Political History of the State of New York*. 3 vols. New York: Henry Holt, 1906.

Allitt, Patrick. *The Conservatives: Ideas and Personalities throughout American History*. New Haven, CT: Yale University Press, 2009.

Anbinder, Tyler. *Five Points: The 19th-Century New York City Neighborhood that Invented Tap Dance, Stole Elections, and Became the World's Most Notorious Slum*. New York: Simon & Schuster, 2001.

———. *Nativism and Slavery: The Northern Know Nothings and the Politics of the 1850s*. New York: Oxford University Press, 1992.

Appleby, Joyce. *Capitalism and a New Social Order: The Republican Vision of the 1790s*. New York: New York University Press, 1984.

———. "Republicanism and Ideology." *American Quarterly* 37, no. 4 (Fall 1985): 461–73.

Applegate, Debby. *The Most Famous Man in America: The Biography of Henry Ward Beecher*. New York: Doubleday, 2006.

Arac, Jonathan. "The Politics of the Scarlett Letter." In *Ideology and Classic American Literature*, edited by Sacvan Bercovitch and Myra Jehlen, 247–66. Cambridge: Cambridge University Press, 1986.

Ashworth, John. *"Agrarians" and "Aristocrats": Party Political Ideology in the United States, 1837–1846*. London: Royal Historical Society, 1983.

———. *Slavery, Capitalism, and Politics in the Antebellum Republic*. 2 vols. New York: Cambridge University Press, 1995–2007.

Ayers, Edward L. *In the Presence of Mine Enemies: The Civil War in the Heart of America, 1859–1863*. New York: Norton, 2003.

———. *What Caused the Civil War? Reflections on the South and Southern History.* New York: Norton, 2005.

Baker, Jean H. *Affairs of Party: The Political Culture of the Northern Democrats in the Mid-Nineteenth Century.* Ithaca, NY: Cornell University Press, 1983.

———. *James Buchanan.* New York: Henry Holt, 2004.

Baker, Thomas N. *Sentiment and Celebrity: Nathaniel Parker Willis and the Trials of Literary Fame.* New York: Oxford University Press, 1999.

Balogh, Brian. *A Government Out of Sight: The Mystery of National Authority in Nineteenth-Century America.* New York: Cambridge University Press, 2009.

Barnes, L. Diane, Brian Schoen and Frank Towers, eds., *The Old South's Modern Worlds: Slavery, Region and Nation in the Age of Progress.* New York: Oxford Univerrsity Press, 2011.

Baughn, William A. "Bullets and Ballots: The Election Day Riots of 1855." *Bulletin of the Historical and Philosophical Society of Ohio* 21 (1963): 267–72.

Baum, Dale. *The Civil War Party System: The Case of Massachusetts, 1848–1876.* Chapel Hill: University of North Carolina Press, 1984

Beard, Charles A., and Mary R. Beard. *The Rise of American Civilization.* 2 vols. New York: Macmillan, 1927.

Beckert, Sven. *The Monied Metropolis: New York City and the Consolidation of the American Bourgeoisie, 1850–1896.* New York: Cambridge University Press, 2007.

Bellah, Robert. *The Broken Covenant: American Civil Religion in a Time of Trial.* New York: Seabury, 1975.

Belohlavek, John M. *Broken Glass: Caleb Cushing and the Shattering of the Union.* Kent, OH: Kent State University Press, 2005.

Bensel, Richard F. *Yankee Leviathan: The Origins of Central State Authority in the United States, 1859–1877.* New York: Cambridge University Press, 1991.

Bernstein, Iver. *The New York City Draft Riots: Their Significance for American Society and Politics in the Age of the Civil War.* New York: Oxford University Press, 1990.

Berthold, Dennis. "Class Acts: The Astor Place Riots and Melville's 'The Two Temples.'" *American Literature* 71, no. 3 (1999): 429–61.

Berwanger, Eugene H. *The Frontier against Slavery: Western Anti-Negro Prejudice and the Slavery Extension Controversy.* Urbana: University of Illinois Press, 1967.

Blackett, R. J. M. *Making Freedom: The Underground Railroad and the Politics of Slavery.* Chapel Hill: University of North Carolina Press, 2013.

Blodgett, Geoffrey. "Landscape Architecture as Conservative Reform." *Journal of American History* 62 (March 1976): 869–89.

Blue, Frederick J. *The Free Soilers: Third Party Politics, 1848–54.* Urbana: University of Illinois Press, 1973.

———. *No Taint of Compromise: Crusaders in Antislavery Politics.* Baton Rouge: Louisiana State University Press, 2005.

———. *Salmon P. Chase: A Life in Politics.* Kent, Ohio: Kent State University Press, 1987.

Boritt, Gabor. *The Gettysburg Gospel: The Lincoln Speech Nobody Knows.* New York: Simon & Schuster, 2006.

Boston, Ray. *British Chartists in America, 1839–1900.* New York: Rowman & Littlefield, 1971.

Brandt, Nat. *In the Shadow of the Civil War: Passmore Williamson and the Rescue of Jane Johnson.* Columbia: University of South Carolina Press, 2007.

Brasher, Thomas L. *Whitman as Editor of the Brooklyn Daily Eagle.* Detroit: Wayne State University Press, 1971.

Bristol, Michael D. *Shakespeare's America, America's Shakespeare.* London: Routledge, 1990.

Brock, W. R. *Conflict and Transformation: The United States, 1844–1877.* New York: Penguin, 1973.

Bronstein, Jamie. *Land Reform and Working Class Experience in Britain and the United States, 1800–1862.* Stanford, CA: Stanford University Press, 1999.

Brooks, Corey M. *Liberty Power: Antislavery Third Parties and the Transformation of American Politics.* Chicago: University of Chicago Press, 2016.

Brown, Charles H. *Agents of Manifest Destiny: The Lives and Times of the Filibusters.* Chapel Hill: University of North Carolina Press, 1980.

Brown, Thomas J. *Dorothea Dix: New England Reformer.* Cambridge, MA: Harvard University Press, 1998.

Bruce, Dickson D. Jr. *The Rhetoric of Conservatism: The Virginia Convention of 1829–30 and the Conservative Tradition in the South.* San Marino, CA: Huntingdon Library, 1982.

Buckley, Peter G. "To the Opera House: Culture and Society in New York City, 1820–1860." PhD diss., SUNY Stony Brook, 1984.

Buckley, William F., ed. *Did You Ever See a Dream Walking? American Conservative Thought in the Twentieth Century.* New York: Bobbs-Merrill, 1970.

Burlingame, Michael. *Abraham Lincoln: A Life.* 2 vols. Baltimore: Johns Hopkins University Press, 2008.

Burrows, Edwin G., and Mike Wallace. *Gotham: A History of New York City to 1898.* New York: Oxford University Press, 1999.

Burstein, Andrew. "The Political Character of Sympathy." *Journal of the Early Republic* 21, no. 4 (Winter 2001): 601–23.

Callcott, George H. *History in the United States, 1800–1860: Its Practice and Purpose.* Baltimore: Johns Hopkins University Press, 1970.

Campbell, Stanley W. *The Slave Catchers. Enforcement of the Fugitive Slave Law, 1850–1860.* Chapel Hill: University of North Carolina Press, 1970.

Carens, Joseph H. "Compromises in Politics." In *Compromise in Ethics, Law, and Politics,* edited by J. Roland Pennock and John W. Chapman, 123–41. New York: New York University Press, 1979.

Cartelli, Thomas. *Repositioning Shakespeare: National Formations, Postcolonial Appropriations.* London: Routledge, 1999.

Carwardine, Richard J. *Evangelicals and Politics in Antebellum America.* New Haven: Yale University Press, 1993.

———. *Lincoln: A Life of Purpose and Power*. New York: W.W. Norton, 2006.

———. "Methodists, Politics, and the Coming of the American Civil War." *Church History* 69 (2000): 578–609.

———. "The Politics of Charles Hodge in Nineteenth-Century Context." In *Charles Hodge Revisited: A Critical Appraisal of His Life and Work*, edited by James Moorhead and John Stewart, 247–98. Grand Rapids, MI: Eerdmans, 2002.

Channing, Steven A. *Crisis of Fear: Secession in South Carolina*. New York: Simon & Schuster, 1970.

Cheever, Susan. *American Bloomsbury: Louisa May Alcott, Ralph Waldo Emerson, Margaret Fuller, Nathaniel Hawthorne, and Henry David Thoreau: Their Lives, Their Loves, Their Works*. New York: Simon & Schuster, 2006.

Childers, Christopher. *The Failure of Popular Sovereignty: Slavery, Manifest Destiny, and the Radicalization of Southern Politics*. Lawrence: University Press of Kansas, 2012.

———. "Popular Sovereignty: A Historiographical Essay." *Civil War History* 57, no. 1 (March 2011): 48–70.

Clark, Christopher. "After 1848: The European Revolution in Government." *Transactions of the Royal Historical Society* 22 (2012): 171–97.

Clark, Michael D. *Coherent Variety: The Idea of Diversity in British and American Conservative Thought*. Westport, CT: Greenwood, 1983.

Clavin, Matthew J. *Toussaint Louverture and the American Civil War: The Promise and Peril of a Second Haitian Revolution*. Philadelphia: University of Pennsylvania Press, 2010.

Cleves, Rachel Hope. *The Reign of Terror in America: Visions of Violence from Anti-Jacobinism to Antislavery*. New York: Cambridge University Press, 2012.

Cliff, Nigel. *The Shakespeare Riots: Revenge, Drama, and Death in Nineteenth-Century America*. New York: Random House, 2007.

Cohen, Patricia Cline. *The Murder of Helen Jewett*. New York: Alfred A. Knopf, 1998.

Coleman, John F. *The Disruption of the Pennsylvania Democracy*. Harrisburg: Pennsylvania Historical and Museum Commission, 1975.

Collins, Bruce. "The Democrats Loss of Pennsylvania in 1858." *Pennsylvania Magazine of History and Biography* 109, no. 4 (October 1985): 499–536.

Collison, Gary L. "The Boston Vigilance Committee: A Reconsideration." *Historical Journal of Massachusetts* 12 (June 1984): 104–16.

———. *Shadrach Minkins: From Fugitive Slave to Citizen*. Cambridge, MA: Harvard University Press, 1997.

Conley, Patrick T. *Democracy in Decline: Rhode Island's Constitutional Development, 1776–1841*. Providence: Rhode Island Historical Society, 1977.

Connelly, James F. *The Visit of Archbishop Gaetano Bedini to the United States of America*. Rome: Università Gregoriana, 1960.

Cooper, William J., Jr. "The Critical Signpost on the Journey toward Secession." *Journal of Southern History* 77, no. 1 (February 2011): 3–16.

Cover, Robert M. *Justice Accused: Antislavery and the Judicial Process*. New Haven, CT: Yale University Press, 1975.

Cowden, Joanna D. *"Heaven Will Frown on Such a Cause as This": Six Who Opposed Lincoln's War*. Lanham, MD: University Press of America, 2001.

Craig, David, and James Thompson, eds. *Languages of Politics in Nineteenth-Century Britain*. Basingstoke, UK: Palgrave, 2013.

Craven, Avery O. *The Coming of the Civil War*. Chicago: University of Chicago Press, 1957.

———. "Coming of the War Between the States: An Interpretation." *Journal of Southern History* 2, no. 3 (1936): 303–22.

———. *The Repressible Conflict, 1830–1861*. Baton Rouge: Louisiana State University Press, 1939.

Crenshaw, Ollinger. *The Slave States in the Presidential Election of 1860*. Baltimore: Johns Hopkins University Press, 1945.

Cunliffe, Marcus. *Chattel Slavery and Wage Slavery: The Anglo-American Context 1830–1860*. Athens: University of Georgia Press, 1979.

Current, Richard N. *Daniel Webster and the Rise of National Conservatism*. Boston: Little Brown, 1955.

Dalzell, Robert F. Jr. *Daniel Webster and the Trial of American Nationalism, 1843–1852*. Boston: Houghton Mifflin, 1973.

David, James Corbett. "The Politics of Emasculation: The Caning of Charles Sumner and Elite Ideologies of Manhood in the Mid-Nineteenth-Century United States." *Gender & History* 19, no. 2 (2007): 324–45.

Davis, David Brion. "The Impact of British Abolitionism on American Sectionalism." In *In the Shadow of Freedom: The Politics of Slavery in the National Capital*, edited by Paul Finkelman and Donald R. Kennon, 19–35. Athens: Ohio University Press, 2011.

———. *Inhuman Bondage: the Rise and Fall of Slavery in the New World*. New York: Oxford University Press, 2006.

Dell, Christopher. *Lincoln and the War Democrats: The Grand Erosion of Conservative Tradition*. Cranbury, NJ: Farleigh Dickinson University Press, 1975.

Dennison, George M. *The Dorr War: Republicanism on Trial, 1831–1861*. Lexington: University Press of Kentucky, 1976.

Denton, Lawrence M. *William Henry Seward and the Secession Crisis: The Effort to Prevent Civil War*. Jefferson, NC: McFarland, 2009.

Denton, Sally. *Passion and Principle: John and Jessie Frémont, the Couple Whose Power, Politics, and Love Shaped Nineteenth-Century America*. New York: Bloomsbury, 2007.

Diggins, John Patrick. *The Lost Soul of American Politics: Virtue, Self-Interest, and the Foundations of Liberalism*. Chicago: University of Chicago Press, 1984.

Dizikes, John. *Opera in America: A Cultural History*. New Haven: Yale University Press, 1993.

Donald, David Herbert. *Charles Sumner and the Coming of the Civil War*. New York: Alfred A. Knopf, 1967.

———. *Lincoln*. New York: Simon & Schuster, 1995.

Downer, Alan S. *The Eminent Tragedian: William Charles Macready*. Cambridge, MA: Harvard University Press, 1966.

Downs, Gregory P. *After Appomattox: Military Occupation and the Ends of War*. Cambridge, MA: Harvard University Press, 2015.

———. "The Mexicanization of American Politics: The United States' Transnational Path from Civil War to Stabilization." *American Historical Review* 117, no. 2 (April 2012): 387–409.

Dubin, Michael J. *United States Congressional Elections, 1788–1997: The Official Results of the Elections of the 1st through 105th Congresses*. Jefferson, NC: McFarland, 1998.

Dunn, Charles W., and J. David Woodward. *The Conservative Tradition in America*. rev. ed. Lanham, MD: Rowman & Littlefield, 2003.

Dusinberre, William. *Civil War Issues in Philadelphia 1856–1865*. Philadelphia: University of Pennsylvania Press, 1965.

Earle, Jonathan. *Jacksonian Antislavery and the Politics of Free Soil, 1824–1854*. Chapel Hill: University of North Carolina Press, 2004.

Edling, Max M. *A Hercules in the Cradle: War, Money, and the American State, 1783–1867*. Chicago: University of Chicago Press, 2014.

Egerton, Douglas R. *Year of Meteors: Stephen Douglas, Abraham Lincoln, and the Election That Brought on the Civil War*. New York: Bloomsbury, 2010.

Eggert, Gerald G. "The Impact of the Fugitive Slave Law on Harrisburg: A Case Study." *Pennsylvania Magazine of History and Biography* 109, no. 4 (1985): 537–569.

Etcheson, Nicole. *Bleeding Kansas: Contested Liberty in the Civil War Era*. Lawrence: University Press of Kansas, 2004.

———. "The Great Principle of Self-Government: Popular Sovereignty and Bleeding Kansas." *Kansas History: A Journal of the Central Plains* 27 (Spring/Summer 2004): 14–29.

Ethington, Philip. *The Public City: The Political Construction of Urban Life in San Francisco, 1850–1900*. Berkeley: University of California Press, 1994.

Eustace, Nicole. *Passion Is the Gale: Emotion, Power, and the Coming of the American Revolution*. Chapel Hill: University of North Carolina Press, 2008.

Evelev, John. "*The Contrast*: The Problem of Theatricality and Political and Social Crisis in Postrevolutionary America." *Early American Literature* 31, no. 1 (1996): 74–97.

———. *Tolerable Entertainment: Herman Melville and Professionalism in Antebellum New York*. Amherst: University of Massachusetts Press, 2006.

Eyal, Yonatan. *The Young America Movement and the Transformation of the Democratic Party, 1828–1861*. New York: Cambridge University Press, 2012.

Fehrenbacher, Don E. *The Dred Scott Case: Its Significance in American Law and Politics*. New York: Oxford University Press, 1978.

———. *The Slaveholding Republic: An Account of the United States Government's Relations to Slavery*. New York: Oxford University Press, 2001.

Feller, Daniel. "A Brother in Arms: Benjamin Tappan and the Antislavery Democracy." *Journal of American History* 88, no. 1 (June 2001): 48–74.

Fermer, Douglas. *James Gordon Bennett and the New York Herald: A Study of Editorial Opinion in the Civil War Era, 1854–1867*. New York: St. Martin's, 1986.

Finkelman, Paul. *An Imperfect Union: Slavery, Federalism, and Comity*. Union, NJ: Lawbook Exchange, 2000.

Fite, Emerson D. *The Presidential Campaign of 1860*. New York: Macmillan, 1911.

Fleche, Andre M. *The Revolution of 1861: The American Civil War in the Age of Nationalist Conflict*. Chapel Hill: University of North Carolina Press, 2012.

Foner, Eric. *The Fiery Trial: Abraham Lincoln and American Slavery*. New York: W.W. Norton, 2012.

———. *Free Soil, Free Labor, Free Men: The Ideology of the Republican Party before the Civil War*. New York: Oxford University Press, 1970.

———. *Gateway to Freedom: The Hidden History of America's Fugitive Slaves*. New York: W.W. Norton, 2015.

———. *Politics and Ideology in the Age of the Civil War*. New York: Oxford University Press, 1980.

Formisano, Ronald P. *The Birth of Mass Political Parties: Michigan, 1827–1861*. Princeton: Princeton University Press, 1971.

———. "The Concept of Political Culture." *Journal of Interdisciplinary History* 31, no. 3 (2001) 393–426.

———. "The 'Party Period' Revisited." *Journal of American History* 86, no. 1 (June 1999): 93–120.

Foster, George G., and Thomas Dunn English. *The French Revolution of 1848: Its causes, actors, events and influences*. Philadelphia: G.B. Zieber, 1848.

Foulkes, Richard. *Performing Shakespeare in the Age of Empire*. Cambridge: Cambridge University Press, 2002.

Franklin, John Hope. "The Southern Expansionists of 1846." *Journal of Southern History* 25, no. 3 (1959): 323–38.

Frederickson, George M. *Big Enough To Be Inconsistent: Abraham Lincoln Confronts Slavery and Race*. Cambridge, MA: Harvard University Press, 2008.

———. *The Black Image in the White Mind: The Debate on Afro-American Character and Destiny, 1817–1914*. New York: Harper & Row, 1971.

———. *The Inner Civil War: Northern Intellectuals and the Crisis of the Union*. Urbana: University of Illinois Press, 1965.

Freehling, William W. *The Road to Disunion*. Vol. 1: *Secessionists at Bay, 1776–1854*. New York: Oxford University Press, 1990.

———. *The Road to Disunion*. Vol. 2: *Secessionists Triumphant, 1854–1961*. New York: Oxford University Press, 2007.

———. *The South vs. The South: How Anti-Confederate Southerners Shaped the Course of the Civil War*. New York: Oxford University Press, 2001.

Freeman, Joanne B. "The Culture of Politics: The Politics of Culture." *Journal of Policy History* 16, no. 2 (2004): 137–43.

Fritz, Christian G. *American Sovereigns: The People and America's Constitutional Tradition before the Civil War*. New York: Cambridge University Press, 2008.

Furniss, Jack. "To Save the Union 'in Behalf of Conservative Men': Horatio Seymour and the Democratic Vision of the Union War." In *New Perspectives on the Union War*, edited by Gary W. Gallagher and Elizabeth R. Varon. New York: Fordham University Press, forthcoming.

Furstenberg, François. *In the Name of the Father: Washington's Legacy, Slavery, and the Making of a Nation*. New York: Penguin, 2006.

Galbreath, C. B. "The Trial of William Bebb." *Ohio History Journal* 36, no. 1 (1927): 48–61.

Gallagher, Gary. *The Union War*. Cambridge, MA: Harvard University Press, 2011.

Gallman, J. Matthew. *Defining Duty in the Civil War: Personal Choice, Popular Culture, and the Union Home Front*. Chapel Hill: University of North Carolina Press, 2015.

Gara, Larry. *The Liberty Line: The Legend of the Underground Railroad*. Lexington: University Press of Kentucky, 1961.

Gemme, Paola. *Domesticating Foreign Struggles: The Italian Risorgimento and Antebellum American Identity*. Athens: University of Georgia Press, 2005.

Gendzel, Glen. "Political Culture: Genealogy of a Concept." *Journal of Interdisciplinary History* 28, no. 2 (1997): 225–50.

Genovese, Eugene D. *The Political Economy of Slavery: Studies in the Economy and Society of the Slave South*. New York: Vintage, 1967.

———. *The Slaveholders' Dilemma: Freedom and Progress in Southern Conservative Thought, 1820–1860*. Columbia: University of South Carolina Press, 1992.

———. *The Southern Tradition: The Achievement and Limitations of an American Conservatism*. Cambridge, MA: Harvard University Press, 1994.

Gettleman, Marvin E. *The Dorr Rebellion: A Study in American Radicalism, 1833–1849*. New York: Random House, 1973.

Gienapp, William E. "The Crime Against Sumner: The Caning of Charles Sumner and the Rise of the Republican Party." *Civil War History* 25, no. 3 (1979): 218–45.

———. "Nativism and the Creation of a Republican Majority in the North before the Civil War." *Journal of American History* 72, no. 3 (1985): 529–59.

———. *The Origins of the Republican Party, 1852–1856*. New York: Oxford University Press, 1987.

Gilje, Paul A. *The Road to Mobocracy: Popular Disorder in New York City, 1763–1834*. Chapel Hill: University of North Carolina Press, 1987.

Glatthaar, Joseph. "Duty, Country, Race, and Party: The Evans Family of Ohio." In *The War Was You and Me: Civilians in the American Civil War*, edited by Joan E. Cashin, 332–57. Princeton, NJ: Princeton University Press, 2002.

Glickstein, Jonathan A. *Concepts of Free Labor in Antebellum America*. New Haven, CT: Yale University Press, 1991.

Goldfield, David R. *America Aflame: How the Civil War Created a Nation*. New York: Bloomsbury, 2011.

Grant, Susan-Mary. *North Over South: Northern Nationalism and American Identity in the Antebellum Era*. Lawrence: University of Kansas Press, 2000.

Green, Michael S. *Lincoln and the Election of 1860*. Carbondale: Southern Illinois University Press, 2011.

Greenberg, Amy S. *Manifest Manhood and the Antebellum American Empire*. New York: Cambridge University Press, 2005.

Greenberg, Iwin F. "Charles Ingersoll: The Aristocrat as Copperhead." *Pennsylvania Magazine of History and Biography* 93, no. 2 (1969): 190–217.

Grimsted, David. *American Mobbing: 1828–1861: Toward Civil War*. New York: Oxford University Press, 1998.

———. *Melodrama Unveiled: American Theater and Culture, 1800–1850*. Chicago: University of Chicago Press, 1968.

Grodzins, Dean. "Constitution or No Constitution, Law or No Law: The Boston Vigilance Committees, 1841–1861." In *Massachusetts and the Civil War: The Commonwealth and National Disunion*, edited by Matthew Mason, Katheryn P. Viens, and Conrad Edick Wright, 47–73. Amherst: University of Massachusetts Press, 2015.

Gross, Neil, Thomas Medvetz, and Rupert Russell. "The Contemporary American Conservative Movement." *Annual Review of Sociology* 37 (2011): 325–54.

Grow, Matthew J. *"Liberty to the Downtrodden" Thomas L. Kane, Romantic Reformer*. New Haven, CT: Yale University Press, 2009.

Guasco, Suzanne Cooper. " 'The Deadly Influence of Negro Capitalists': Southern Yeomen and Resistance to the Expansion of Slavery in Illinois." *Civil War History* 47, no. 1 (March 2001): 7–29.

Gutjahr, Paul C. *Charles Hodge: Guardian of American Orthodoxy*. New York: Oxford University Press, 2011.

Guyatt, Nicholas. *Providence and the Invention of the United States, 1607–1876*. New York: Cambridge University Press, 2007.

Hadley, Elaine. *Melodramatic Tactics: Theatricalized Dissent in the English Marketplace, 1800–1885*. Stanford, CA: Stanford University Press, 1995.

Hahn, Steven. *The Political Worlds of Slavery and Freedom*. Cambridge, MA: Harvard University Press, 2009.

Haidt, Jonathan. *The Righteous Mind: Why Good People Are Divided by Politics and Religion*. New York: Pantheon, 2012.

Haltunnen, Karen. *Murder Most Foul: The Killer and the American Gothic Imagination*. Cambridge, MA: Harvard University Press, 1998.

Hamilton, Holman. *Prologue to Conflict: The Crisis and Compromise of 1850*. Lexington: University Press of Kentucky, 1964.

Handlin, Lillian. *George Bancroft: The Intellectual as Democrat*. New York: Harper & Row, 1984.

Harris, William C. "Conservative Unionists and the Presidential Election of 1864." *Civil War History* 38, no. 4 (1992): 298–318.

Harrold, Stanley. *Border War: Fighting over Slavery before the Civil War*. Chapel Hill: University of North Carolina Press, 2010.

Hartz, Louis. *The Liberal Tradition in America: An Interpretation of American Political Thought since the Civil War*. New York: Harcourt, 1955.

Hawkins, Angus. *Victorian Political Culture: "Habits of Hearts and Minds."* Oxford: Oxford University Press, 2015.

Haynes, Sam W. *Unfinished Revolution: The Early American Republic in a British World.* Charlottesville: University of Virginia Press, 2010.

Hazeltine, Ralph. "Victor E. Piollet: Portrait of a Country Politician." *Pennsylvania History* 40, no. 1 (1973): 1–20.

Heath, Andrew. "'The producers on the one side, and the capitalists on the other': Labor Reform, Slavery, and the Career of a Transatlantic Radical." *American Nineteenth Century History* 13, no. 2 (2012): 199–227.

Hersinger, Rodney. *Seduced, Abandoned, and Reborn: Visions of Youth in Middle Class America, 1780–1850.* Philadelphia: University of Pennsylvania Press, 2005.

Higham, John. *From Boundlessness to Consolidation: The Transformation of American Culture, 1848–1860.* Ann Arbor, MI: William L. Clements Library, 1969.

Hoffmann, Charles G., and Tess Hoffmann. *Brotherly Love: Murder and the Politics of Prejudice in Nineteenth-Century Rhode Island.* Amherst: University of Massachusetts Press, 1998.

Holt, Michael F. "An Elusive Synthesis: Northern Politics during the Civil War." In *Writing the Civil War: The Quest to Understand,* edited by James M. McPherson and William J. Cooper, 112–34. Columbia: South Carolina University Press, 1998.

———. *Franklin Pierce.* New York: Times Books, 2010.

———. *Forging a Majority: The Formation of the Republican Party in Pittsburgh.* New Haven, CT: Yale University Press, 1969.

———. *The Political Crisis of the 1850s.* New York: Wiley, 1979.

———. "The Politics of Impatience: The Origins of Know Nothingism." *Journal of American History* 60, no. 2 (1973): 309–31.

———. *The Rise and Fall of the American Whig Party: Jacksonian Politics and the Onset of the Civil War.* New York: Oxford University Press, 1999.

Holzer, Harold. *Lincoln President-Elect: Abraham Lincoln and the Great Secession Winter, 1860–1861.* New York: W.W. Norton, 2008.

Honeck, Mischa. *We Are the Revolutionists: German-Speaking Immigrants and American Abolitionists after 1848.* Athens: University of Georgia Press, 2011.

Horsman, Reginald. *Race and Manifest Destiny: The Origins of American Racial Anglo-Saxonism.* Cambridge, MA: Harvard University Press, 1981.

Howe, Daniel Walker. *The Political Culture of the American Whigs.* Chicago: University of Chicago Press, 1979.

———. *Unitarian Conscience: Harvard Moral Philosophy, 1805–1861.* Cambridge, MA: Harvard University Press, 1970.

———. "Victorian Culture in America." In *Victorian America,* edited by Daniel Walker Howe, 1–19. Philadelphia: University of Pennsylvania Press, 1976.

———. *What Hath God Wrought: The Transformation of America, 1815–1848.* New York: Oxford University Press, 2007.

Hummel, Jeffrey Rogers. *Emancipating Slaves, Enslaving Free Men: A History of the American Civil War.* Chicago: Open Court, 1996.

Jacobs, Meg, and Julian E. Zelizer. "The Democratic Experiment: New Directions in American Political History." In *The Democratic Experiment: New Directions in American Political History*, edited by Meg Jacobs, William J. Novak, and Julian E. Zelizer, 1–19. Princeton, NJ: Princeton University Press, 2003.

Jaffa, Harry V. *Crisis of the House Divided: An Interpretation of the Issues in the Lincoln-Douglas Debates*. Garden City, NJ: Doubleday, 1959.

Johannsen, Robert Walker. *The Frontier, the Union, and Stephen A. Douglas*. Urbana: University of Illinois Press, 1989.

———. *Stephen A. Douglas*. New York: Oxford University Press, 1973.

Johnson, Michael P. *Toward a Patriarchal Republic: The Secession of Georgia*. Baton Rouge: Louisiana State University Press, 1977.

Jost, John T., and Orsolya Hunyady. "Antecedents and Consequences of System-Justifying Ideologies." *Current Directions in Psychological Science* 14, no. 5 (2005): 260–65.

Joyce, Patrick. *Democratic Subjects: The Self and the Social in Nineteenth-Century England*. Cambride: Cambridge University Press, 1994.

Kammen, Michael. *A Season of Youth: The American Revolution and the Historical Imagination*. New York: Knopf, 1978.

Karsten, Peter. "Cromwell in America." In *Images of Oliver Cromwell: Essays for and by Roger Howell*, edited by R. C. Richardson, 207–29. Manchester, UK: Manchester University Press, 1993.

———. *Patriot-Heroes in England and America: Changing Political Cultures, 1650–1950*. Madison: University of Wisconsin Press, 1978.

Kasson, John. *Rudeness & Civility: Manners in Nineteenth-Century Urban America*. New York: Hill & Wang, 1990.

Katz, Jonathan. *Resistance at Christiana*. New York: Crowell, 1974.

Katz, Philip M. *From Appomattox to Montmartre: Americans and the Paris Commune*. Cambridge, MA: Harvard University Press, 1998.

Kendall, Willmoore, and George W. Carey. "Towards a Definition of 'Conservatism.'" *Journal of Politics* 26, no. 2 (May 1964): 406–22.

Kirk, Russell. *The Conservative Mind: From Burke to Eliot*. Chicago: Regenery, 1985.

Kirkpatrick, Jennet. *Uncivil Disobedience: Studies in Violence and Democratic Politics*. Princeton, NJ: Princeton University Press, 2008.

Klein, Philip S. *President James Buchanan: A Biography*. Philadelphia: University of Pennsylvania Press, 1962.

Klement, Frank L. *The Copperheads in the Middle West*. Chicago: University of Chicago Press, 1960.

———. *Dark Lanterns: Secret Political Societies, Conspiracies, and Treason Trials in the Civil War*. Baton Rouge: Louisiana University Press, 1984.

———. *The Limits of Dissent: Clement L. Vallandigham and the Civil War*. Lexington: University Press of Kentucky, 1970.

Kloppenberg, James T. "The Virtues of Liberalism: Christianity, Republicanism, and Ethics in Early American Political Discourse." *Journal of American History* 74, no. 1 (June 1987): 9–33.

Klunder, Willard Carl. *Lewis Cass and the Politics of Moderation*. Kent, OH: Kent State University Press, 1996.

———. "Lewis Cass and Slavery Expansion: 'The Father of Popular Sovereignty' and Ideological Infanticide." *Civil War History* 32, no. 4 (1986): 293–317.

Knupfer, Peter. "A Crisis in Conservatism: Northern Unionism and the Harpers Ferry Raid." In *His Soul Goes Marching On: Responses to John Brown and the Harpers Ferry Raid*, edited by Paul Finkelman, 119–48. Charlottesville: University of Virginia Press, 1995.

———. *The Union as It Is: Constitutional Unionism and Sectional Compromise, 1787–1861*. Chapel Hill: University of North Carolina Press, 1991.

Kohl, Lawrence Frederick. *The Politics of Individualism: Parties and the American Character in the Jacksonian Era*. New York: Oxford University Press, 1989.

Koselleck, Reinhart. *Critique and Crisis: Enlightenment and the Pathogenesis of Modern Society*. Cambridge, MA: MIT Press, 1988.

Kremm, Thomas W. "Cleveland and the First Lincoln Election: The Ethnic Response to Nativism." *Journal of Interdisciplinary History* 8, no. 1 (1977): 69–86.

Ladd, Jonathan McDonald, and Gabriel S. Lenz. "Reassessing the Role of Anxiety in Vote Choice." *Political Psychology* 29, no. 2 (April 2008): 275–96.

Landis, Michael Todd. *Northern Men with Southern Principles: The Democratic Party and the Sectional Crisis*. Ithaca, NY: Cornell University Press, 2014.

Lasser, Carol. "Voyeuristic Abolitionism: Sex, Gender, and the Transformation of Antislavery Rhetoric." *Journal of the Early Republic* 28, no. 1 (Spring 2008): 83–114.

Lawson, Melinda. *Patriot Fires: Forging a New American Nationalism in the Civil War Era North*. Lawrence: University of Kansas Press, 2002.

Lehning, James R. *The Melodramatic Thread: Spectacle and Political Culture in Modern France*. Bloomington: Indiana University Press, 2007.

Levine, Bruce. "Conservatism, Nativism, and Slavery: Thomas R. Whitney and the Origins of the Know-Nothing Party." *Journal of American History* 88, no. 2 (2001): 455–88.

———. *Spirit of 1848: German Immigrants, Labor Conflict, and the Coming of the Civil War*. Urbana: University of Illinois Press, 1992.

Levine, Lawrence W. "William Shakespeare and the American People: A Study in Cultural Transformation." *American Historical Review* 89, no. 1 (1984): 34–66.

Litwack, Leon F. *North of Slavery: The Negro in the Free States, 1790–1860*. Chicago: University of Chicago Press, 1961.

Lubert, Steven. *Fugitive Justice: Runaways, Rescuers, and Slavery on Trial*. Cambridge, MA: Harvard University Press, 2010.

Luebke, Frederick C., ed. *Ethnic Voters and the Election of Lincoln*. Lincoln: University of Nebraska Press, 1971.

Lurie, Edward. *Louis Agassiz: A Life in Science*. Chicago: University of Chicago Press, 1960.

Luthin, Reinhard H. *The First Lincoln Campaign*. Cambridge, MA: Harvard University Press, 1944.

Lynch, William. "Antislavery Tendencies of the Democratic Party in the Northwest, 1848–1850." *Mississippi Valley Historical Review* 11 (December 1924): 319–31.

Macaig, Drew. *Edmund Burke in America: The Contested Career of the Father of Modern Conservatism.* Ithaca, NY: Cornell University Press, 2013.

Mach, Andrew. "'The Name of Freeman is Better Than Jesuit': Anti-Catholicism, Republican Ideology, and Cincinnati Political Culture, 1853–1854." *Ohio Valley History* 15, no. 4 (Winter 2015): 3–21.

Mach, Thomas S. *"Gentleman George" Hunt Pendleton: Party Politics and Ideological Identity in Nineteenth-Century America.* Kent, OH: Kent State University Press, 2007.

Mallett, Mark E. "'The Game of Politics': Edwin Forrest and the Jacksonian Democrats." *Journal of American Drama and Theater* 5 (1993): 31–46.

Maltz, Earl M. *Fugitive Slave on Trial: The Anthony Burns Case and Abolitionist Outrage.* Lawrence: University Press of Kansas, 2010.

Manning, Chandra. *What This Cruel War Was Over: Soldiers, Slavery, and the Civil War.* New York: Random House, 2007.

Marcus, George E. *The Sentimental Citizen: Emotion in Democratic Politics.* University Park: Pennsylvania State University Press, 2002.

Marcus, Jacob Rader. *The Americanization of Isaac Mayer Wise.* Cincinnati: Author, 1931.

Martin, Scott C. "Interpreting 'Metamora': Nationalism, Theater, and Jacksonian Indian Policy." *Journal of the Early Republic* 19, no. 1 (1999): 73–101.

Martis, Kenneth C. *The Historical Atlas of the United States Congressional Districts: 1789–1983.* New York: Macmillan, 1989.

Mason, Matthew. *Apostle of Union: A Political Biography of Edward Everett.* Chapel Hill: University of North Carolina Press, 2016.

Masur, Louis P. *Rites of Execution: Capital Punishment and the Transformation of American Culture, 1776–1865.* New York: Oxford University Press, 1989.

May, Robert E. *Manifest Destiny's Underworld: Filibustering in Antebellum America.* Chapel Hill: University of North Carolina Press, 2002.

———. *Slavery, Race, and Conquest in the Tropics: Lincoln, Douglas, and the Future of Latin America.* New York: Cambridge University Press, 2013.

———. *The Southern Dream of a Caribbean Empire, 1854–1861.* Gainesville: University Press of Florida, 2002.

Mayfield, John. *Rehearsal for Reconstruction: Free Soil and the Politics of Anti-slavery.* Port Washington, NY: Kennikat Press, 1980.

McClintock, Russell. *Lincoln and the Decision for War: The Northern Response to Secession.* Chapel Hill: University of North Carolina Press, 2008.

McConachie, Bruce A. "New York Operagoing, 1825–50: Creating an Elite Social Ritual." *American Music* 6, no. 2 (1988): 181–92.

———. "The Theater of Edwin Forrest and Jacksonian Hero Worship." In *When They Weren't Doing Shakespeare: Essays on Nineteenth-Century British and American Theatre,* edited by Judith L. Fisher and Stephen Watt, 3–18. Athens: University of Georgia Press, 1989.

―――. "'The Theatre of the Mob': Apocalyptic Melodrama and Pre-industrial Riots in Antebellum New York." In *Theater for Working Class Audiences in the United States, 1830–1890*, edited by Bruce A. McConachie and Daniel Friedman, 17–46. Westport, CT: Greenwood Press, 1985.

McCormick, Richard L. "The Party Period and Public Policy: An Exploratory Hypothesis." *Journal of American History* 66, no. 2 (September 1979): 281–83.

McCoy, Colin. "Jackson Men in the Party of Lincoln." In *Politics and Culture of the Civil War Era: Essays in Honor of Robert W. Johannsen*, edited by Daniel McDonough and Kenneth W. Noe, 178–98. Selinsgrove, PA: Susquehana University Press, 2006.

McCoy, Drew R. *The Elusive Republic: Political Economy in Jeffersonian America*. Chapel Hill: University of North Carolina Press, 1980.

McGlone, Robert E. *John Brown's War Against Slavery*. New York: Cambridge University Press, 2009.

McLoughlin, William G. *The Meaning of Henry Ward Beecher: An Essay in the Shifting Values of Mid-Victorian America, 1840–1870*. New York: Knopf, 1970.

McPherson, James M. *Battle Cry of Freedom: The Civil War Era*. New York: Oxford University Press, 1988.

―――. "The Civil War and the Transformation of America." In *In the Cause of Liberty: How the Civil War Redefined American Ideals*, edited by William J. Cooper Jr. and John M. McCardell Jr., 1–8. Baton Rouge: Louisiana State University Press, 2009.

McWilliam, Rohan. "Melodrama and the Historians." *Radical History Review* 78 (2000): 57–84.

Meerse, David E. "Buchanan, Corruption, and the Election of 1860." *Civil War History* 12, no. 2 (1966): 116–31.

―――. "The Northern Democratic Party and the Congressional Elections of 1858." In *Beyond the Civil War Synthesis: Political Essays of the Civil War Era*, edited by Robert P. Swierenga, 79–97. Westport, CT: Greenwood Press, 1975.

Melish, Joanne Pope. *Disowning Slavery: Gradual Emancipation and "Race" in New England, 1780–1860*. Ithaca, NY: Cornell University Press, 1998.

Menand, Louis. *The Metaphysical Club: A Story of Ideas in America*. New York: Farrar, Straus & Giroux, 2001.

Meyers, Marvin. *The Jacksonian Persuasion: Politics and Belief*. Stanford, CA: Stanford University Press, 1957.

Miller, Edwin Haviland. *Salem Is My Dwelling Place: A Life of Nathaniel Hawthorne*. Iowa City: University of Iowa Press, 1991.

Miller, Kerby A. *Emigrants and Exiles: Ireland and the Irish Exodus to North America*. New York: Oxford University Press, 1985.

Milton, George Fort. *The Eve of Conflict: Stephen A. Douglas and the Needless War*. Boston: Houghton Mifflin, 1934.

Mitchell, Stewart. *Horatio Seymour of New York*. Cambridge, MA: Harvard University Press, 1938.

Moody, Richard. *The Astor Place Riot*. Bloomington: Indiana University Press, 1958.

———. *Edwin Forrest, First Star of the American Stage*. New York: Knopf, 1960.

Moorhead, James H. *American Apocalypse: Yankee and Protestants and the Civil War, 1860–1869*. New Haven, CT: Yale University Press, 1978.

Morris, Thomas D. *Free Men All: The Personal Liberty Laws of the North, 1780–1861*. Baltimore: Johns Hopkins University Press, 1974.

Morrison, Chaplain W. *Democratic Politics and Sectionalism: The Wilmot Proviso Controversy*. Chapel Hill: University of North Carolina Press, 1967.

Morrison, Michael A. "American Reactions to European Revolutions, 1848–1852." *Civil War History* 49 (June 2003): 111–32.

———. *Slavery and the American West: The Eclipse of Manifest Destiny and the Coming of the Civil War*. Chapel Hill: University of North Carolina Press, 1997.

Murrin, John M. "A Roof without Walls: The Dilemma of American National Identity." In *Beyond Confederation: Origins of the Constitution and American National Identity*, edited by Richard R. Beeman, Stephen Botein, and Edward Carlos Carter, 333–48. Chapel Hill: University of North Carolina Press, 1987.

Nakamura, Masahiro. *Visions of Order in William Gilmore Simms: Southern Conservatism and the Other American Romance*. Columbia: University of South Carolina Press, 2009.

Neely, Mark E. *The Divided Union: Party Conflict in the Civil War North*. Cambridge, MA: Harvard University Press, 2002.

Neuman, W. Russell, Michael L. Spezio, and Todd L. Belt, eds. *The Affect Effect: Dynamics of Emotion in Political Thinking and Behavior*. Chicago: University of Chicago Press, 2007.

Nevins, Allan. *Frémont: Pathmarker of the West*. New York: Appleton, 1939.

———. *The Ordeal of the Union*. 8 vols: Vol. 1, *Fruits of Manifest Destiny, 1847–1852*; Vol. 2, *A House Dividing, 1852–1857*; Vol. 3, *Douglas, Buchanan, and Party Chaos, 1857–1859*; Vol. 4, *Prologue to Civil War, 1859–1861*; Vol. 5, *The Improvised War, 1861–1862*; Vol. 6, *War Becomes Revolution, 1862–1863*; Vol. 7, *The Organized War, 1863–1864*; Vol. 8, *The Organized War to Victory, 1864–1865*. New York: Charles Scribner's Sons, 1947–71.

Newman, Richard S. *Freedom's Prophet: Bishop Richard Allen, the AME Church, and the Black Founding Fathers*. New York: New York University Press, 2008.

———. *The Transformation of American Abolitionism: Fighting Slavery in the Early Republic*. Chapel Hill: University of North Carolina Press, 2002.

Nichols, Roy F. *The Disruption of the American Democracy*. New York: Macmillan, 1948.

———. *Franklin Pierce: Young Hickory of the Granite Hills*. Philadelphia: University of Pennsylvania Press, 1958.

———. "The Kansas-Nebraska Act: A Century of Historiography." *Mississippi Valley Historical Review* 43, no. 2 (September 1956): 187–212.

Niven, John. *Gideon Welles: Lincoln's Secretary of the Navy*. New York: Oxford University Press, 1973.

———. *John C. Calhoun and the Price of Union: A Biography*. Baton Rouge: Louisiana State University Press, 1988.

Noll, Mark A. *Charles Hodge: The Way of Life*. New York: Paulist Press, 1987.

Nye, Russel B. *Society and Culture in America, 1830–1860*. New York: Harper & Row, 1974.

Oakes, James. *Freedom National: The Destruction of Slavery in the United States, 1861–1865*. New York: W. W. Norton, 2013.

———. "The Political Significance of Slave Resistance." *History Workshop Journal* 22, no. 1 (Autumn 1986): 89–107.

———. *The Radical and the Republican: Frederick Douglass, Abraham Lincoln, and the Triumph of Antislavery Politics*. New York: W.W. Norton, 2007.

———. *The Scorpion's Sting: Antislavery and the Coming of the Civil War*. New York: W.W. Norton, 2014.

O'Brien, Michael. *Conjectures of Order: Intellectual Life in the American South, 1810–1860*. 2 vols. Chapel Hill: University of North Carolina Press, 2004.

———. "Conservative Thought in the Old South." Review of *The Slaveholders' Dilemma: Freedom and Progress in Southern Conservative Thought, 1820–1860* by Eugene D. Genovese. *Comparative Studies in Society and History* 14, no. 3 (July 1992): 566–76.

Oertel, Kristen Tegtmeier. *Bleeding Borders: Race, Gender, and Violence in Pre-Civil War Kansas*. Baton Rouge: Louisiana State University Press, 2009.

Owsley, Frank L. "The Fundamental Cause of the Civil War: Egocentric Sectionalism." In *The South: Old and New Frontiers: Selected Essays of Frank Lawrence Owsley*, edited by Harriet Chappell Owsley. Athens: University of Georgia Press, 1969.

Paludan, Philip S. "The American Civil War Considered as a Crisis of Law and Order." *American Historical Review* 77, no. 4 (1972): 1013–34.

———. "Religion in the American Civil War." In *Religion and the American Civil War*, edited by Randall M. Miller, Harry S. Stout, and Charles Regan Wilson, 21–42. New York: Oxford University Press, 1998.

Parish, Peter J. "Confidence and Anxiety in Victorian America." In *The North and the Nation in the Era of the Civil War*, edited by Adam I. P. Smith and Susan-Mary Grant, 1–22. New York: Fordham University Press, 2003.

———. "The Distinctiveness of American Nationalism." In *The North and the Nation in the Era of the Civil War*, 57–70.

Parrington, Vernon Louis. *Main Currents in American Thought: An Interpretation from the Beginnings to 1920*. 2 vols. Boston: Harcourt Brace & World, 1927–30.

Paulus, Sarah Bishcoff. "America's Long Eulogy for Compromise: Henry Clay and American Politics, 1854–58." *Journal of the Civil War Era* 4, no. 1 (March 2014): 28–52.

Pease, Jane H., and William H. Pease. "Confrontation and Abolition in the 1850s." *Journal of American History* 58, no. 4 (1972): 923–37.

Perry, Lewis. *Boats Against the Current: American Culture Between Revolution and Modernity, 1820–1860*. New York: Oxford University Press, 1993.

Pessen, Edward. "How Different from Each Other Were the Antebellum North and South?" *The American Historical Review* 85, no. 5 (1980): 1119–49.

Peterson, Merrill. *The Jefferson Image in the American Mind*. Oxford: Oxford University Press, 1960.

Porter, George H. *Ohio Politics in the Civil War*. New York: Macmillan, 1911.

Portes, Jacques. *Fascination and Misgivings: The United States in French Public Opinion, 1870–1914*. Translated by Elborg Forster. Cambridge: Cambridge University Press, 2000.

Potter, David Morris. *The Impending Crisis: America before the Civil War, 1848–1861*. Completed and edited by Don E. Fehrenbacher. New York: Harper & Row, 1976.

———. *Lincoln and His Party in the Secession Crisis*. New Haven, CT: Yale University Press, 1942.

———. "The Literature on the Background of the Civil War." In *The South and the Sectional Conflict*, 87–150. Baton Rouge: Louisiana State University Press, 1968.

Pray, Isaac C. *Memoirs of James Gordon Bennett and His Times*. New York: Stringer & Townsend, 1855.

Puleo, Stephen. *The Caning: The Assault That Drove America to Civil War*. Yardley, PA: Westholme, 2012.

Quarles, Benjamin. *Black Abolitionists*. New York: Oxford University Press, 1969.

Quigley, David. *Second Founding: New York City, Reconstruction, and the Making of American Democracy*. New York: Hill & Wang, 2004.

Quitt, Martin H. *Stephen A. Douglas and Antebellum Democracy*. New York: Cambridge University Press, 2012.

Rael, Patrick. *Eighty-Eight Years: The Long Death of Slavery in the United States, 1777–1865*. Athens: University of Georgia Press, 2015.

Randall, James G. "The Blundering Generation." *Mississippi Valley Historical Review* 27, no. 1 (1940): 3–28.

Ramsdell, Charles W. "The Changing Interpretation of the Civil War." *Journal of Southern History* 3, no. 1 (1937): 3–27.

———. "The Natural Limits of Slavery Expansion." *Mississippi Valley Historical Review* 16, no. 2 (1929): 151–71.

Randall, James G. *The Civil War and Reconstruction*. Boston: D.C. Heath, 1937.

Rawley, James A. *Edwin D. Morgan, 1811–1883: A Merchant in Politics*. New York: Columbia University Press, 1955.

———. *Race & Politics: "Bleeding Kansas" and the Coming of the Civil War*. Lincoln: University of Nebraska Press, 1969.

Rayback, Joseph G. *Free Soil: The Election of 1848*. Lexington: University of Kentucky Press, 1970.

Reddy, William M. *The Navigation of Feeling: A Framework for the History of Emotions*. New York: Cambridge University Press, 2001.

Reisen, Harriet. *Louisa May Alcott: The Woman behind* Little Women. New York: Picador, 2009.

Remini, Robert V. *At the Edge of the Precipice: Henry Clay and the Compromise That Saved the Union*. New York: Basic Books, 2010.

Renda, Lex. *Running on the Record: Civil War Era Politics in New Hampshire*. Charlottesville: University of Virginia Press, 1997.

Reynolds, David S. *John Brown, Abolitionist: The Man Who Killed Slavery, Sparked the Civil War, and Seeded Civil Rights*. New York: Knopf, 2005.

———. *Walt Whitman's America: A Cultural Biography*. New York: Knopf, 1995.

Reynolds, Larry J. *European Revolutions and the American Literary Renaissance*. New Haven, CT: Yale University Press, 1988.

Richards, Jeffrey. *Sir Henry Irving: A Victorian Actor and His World*. London: Bloomsbury, 2005.

Richards, Leonard L. *Gentlemen of Property and Standing: Anti-Abolition Mobs in Jacksonian America*. New York: Oxford University Press, 1971.

———. *The Slave Power: The Free North and Southern Domination, 1780–1860*. Baton Rouge: Louisiana State University Press, 2000.

Richardson, Heather Cox. *The Greatest Nation of the Earth: Republican Economic Policies during the Civil War*. Cambridge, MA: Harvard University Press, 1997.

———. *West from Appomattox: The Reconstruction of America after the Civil War*. New Haven, CT: Yale University Press, 2007.

Richardson, James F. "Mayor Fernando Wood and the New York Police Force, 1855–57." *New York Historical Society Quarterly* 50 (January 1966): 5–40.

———. *The New York Police: Colonial Times to 1901*. New York: Oxford University Press, 1970.

Riley, Glenda. *Divorce: An American Tradition*. New York: Oxford University Press, 1991.

Roberts, Timothy Mason. *Distant Revolutions: 1848 and the Challenge to American Exceptionalism*. Charlottesville: University of Virginia Press, 2009.

Robin, Corey. *Fear: The History of a Political Idea*. New York: Oxford University Press, 2006.

———. *The Reactionary Mind*. New York: Oxford University Press, 2011.

Rodger, Gillian. "Class Politics and Theater Law in New York City." *American Music* 20, no. 4 (2002): 381–98.

Rodgers, Daniel T. "Republicanism: The Career of a Concept." *Journal of American History* 79, no. 1 (June 1992): 11–38.

Rodgers, Thomas E. "Liberty, Will, and Violence: The Political Ideology of the Democrats of West-Central Indiana during the Civil War." *Indiana Magazine of History* 92, no. 2 (June, 1996): 133–59.

Roediger, David. *The Wages of Whiteness: Race and the Making of the American Working Class*. New York: Verso, 1991.

Rohrs, Richard C. "American Critics of the French Revolution of 1848." *Journal of the Early Republic* 14, no. 3 (Autumn 1994): 359–77.

Roitman, Janet L. *Anti-Crisis*. Durham, NC: Duke University Press, 2013.

Rose, Anne C. *Victorian America and the Civil War*. New York: Cambridge University Press, 1994.

Rosenzweig, Roy, and Elizabeth Blackmar. *The Park and the People: A History of Central Park*. Ithaca, NY: Cornell University Press, 1992.

Ross, Dorothy. "'Are We a Nation?': The Conjuncture of Nationhood and Race in the United States, 1850–1876." *Modern Intellectual History* 2, no. 3 (November 2005): 327–60.

———. "Historical Consciousness in Nineteenth-Century America." *American Historical Review* 89, no. 4 (October 1984): 909–28.

———. "Lincoln and the Ethics of Emancipation: Universalism, Nationalism, Exceptionalism." *Journal of American History* 96, no. 2 (2009): 379–99.

Rossiter, Clinton. *Conservatism in America: The Thankless Persuasion*. New York: Random House, 1955.

Roth, Randolph. *American Homicide*. Cambridge, MA: Harvard University Press, 2012.

Rugemer, Edward Bartlett. *The Problem of Emancipation: The Caribbean Roots of the American Civil War*. Baton Rouge: Louisiana State University Press, 2008.

Russel, Robert R. "What Was the Compromise of 1850?" *Journal of Southern History* 22, no. 3 (August 1956): 292–309.

Ryan, Mary P. *Civic Wars: Democracy and Public Life in the American City During the Nineteenth Century*. Berkeley: University of California Press, 1997.

Salafia, Matthew. *Slavery's Borderland: Freedom and Bondage along the Ohio River*. Philadelphia: University of Pennsylvania Press, 2013.

Sampson, Robert D. *John L. O'Sullivan and His Times*. Kent, OH: Kent State University Press, 2003.

Sandow, Robert M. "Damnable Treason or Party Organs? Democratic Secret Societies in Pennsylvania." In *This Distracted and Anarchical People: New Answers for Old Questions about the Civil War–Era North*, edited by Andrew L. Slap and Michael Thomas Smith, 42–59. New York: Fordham University Press, 2013.

———. *Deserter Country: Civil War Opposition in the Pennsylvania Appalachians*. New York: Fordham University Press, 2009.

Saxton, Alexander. *The Rise and Fall of the White Republic: Class Politics and Mass Culture in Nineteenth-Century America*. New York: Verso, 1990.

Schmeller, Mark G. *Invisible Sovereign: Imagining Public Opinion from the Revolution to Reconstruction*. Baltimore: Johns Hopkins University Press, 2016.

Schmitt, Jeffrey M. "The Antislavery Judge Reconsidered." *Law and History Review* 29, no. 3 (August 2011): 797–834.

Scobey, David M. *Empire City: The Making and Meaning of the New York City Landscape*. Philadelphia: Temple University Press, 2002.

Seitz, Don C. *The James Gordon Bennetts, Father and Son, Proprietors of the New York Herald*. Indianapolis: Bobbs, Merrill, 1928.

Seymour, Glenn H. "'Conservative'—Another Lincoln Pseudonym." *Journal of the Illinois State Historical Society* 29, no. 2 (July 1936): 135–50.

———. "Lincoln: Author of Letters by a Conservative." *Bulletin of the Abraham Lincoln Association* 50 (December 1937): 8–9.

Shalhope, Robert E. "Republicanism and Early American Historiography." *William and Mary Quarterly* 39, no. 2 (April 1982): 334–56.

———. "Toward a Republican Synthesis: The Emergence of an Understanding of Republicanism in American Historiography." *William and Mary Quarterly* 29, no. 1 (January 1972): 49–80.

Shattuck, Charles Harlen. *Shakespeare on the American Stage*. Washington, DC: Folger Shakespeare Library, 1976.

Shelden, Rachel. *Washington Brotherhood: Politics, Social Life and the Coming of the American Civil War*. Chapel Hill: University of North Carolina Press, 2013.

Shenton, James P. *Robert John Walker: A Politician from Jackson to Lincoln*. New York: Columbia University Press, 1961.

Silbey, Joel H. *The American Political Nation, 1838–1893*. Stanford, CA: Stanford University Press, 1991.

———. *The Partisan Imperative: The Dynamics of American Politics before the Civil War*. New York: Oxford University Press, 1985.

———. *Party over Section: The Rough and Ready Presidential Election of 1848*. Lawrence: University Press of Kansas, 2009.

———. *A Respectable Minority: The Democratic Party in the Civil War Era, 1860–1868*. New York: Norton, 1977.

Sim, David. *A Union Forever: The Irish Question and U.S. Foreign Relations in the Victorian Age*. Ithaca, NY: Cornell University Press, 2013.

Sinha, Manisha. "The Caning of Charles Sumner: Slavery, Race, and Ideology in the Age of the Civil War." *Journal of the Early Republic* 23, no. 2 (2003): 233–62.

———. *The Slave's Cause: A History of Abolitionism*. New Haven, CT: Yale University Press, 2016.

Slap, Andrew L., and Michael Thomas Smith, eds. *This Distracted and Anarchical People: New Answers for Old Questions about the Civil War–Era North*. New York: Fordham University Press, 2013.

Slaughter, Thomas P. *Bloody Dawn: The Christiana Riot and Racial Violence in the Antebellum North*. New York: Oxford University Press, 1991.

Smith, Adam I. P. *No Party Now: Politics in the Civil War North*. New York: Oxford University Press, 2006.

Smith, David G. *On the Edge of Freedom: The Fugitive Slave Issue in South Central Pennsylvania, 1820–1870*. New York: Fordham University Press, 2013.

Smith, Michael Thomas. *The Enemy Within: Fears of Corruption in the Civil War North*. Charlottesville: University of Virginia Press, 2011.

Smith, Rogers M. *Civic Ideals: Conflicting Visions of Citizenship in U.S. History*. New Haven, CT: Yale University Press, 1998.

Spann, Edward K. *The New Metropolis: New York City, 1840–1857*. New York: Columbia University Press, 1981.

Spencer, Donald S. *Louis Kossuth and Young America: A Study of Sectionalism and Foreign Policy, 1848–1852*. Columbia: Missouri University Press, 1977.

Srebnick, Amy Gilman. *The Mysterious Death of Mary Rogers: Sex and Culture in Nineteenth-Century New York*. New York: Oxford University Press, 1995.

Stampp, Kenneth M. *America in 1857: A Nation on the Brink*. New York: Oxford University Press, 1990.

———. "The Concept of Perpetual Union." In *The Imperiled Union: Essays on the Background of the Civil War*, 3–36. New York: Oxford University Press, 1980.

———. *Indiana Politics during the Civil War*. Indianapolis: Indiana Historical Bureau, 1949.

———. "The Irrepressible Conflict." In *The Imperiled Union: Essays on the Background of the Civil War*, 191–245. New York: Oxford University Press, 1980.

———. *And the War Came: The North and the Secession Crisis*. Baton Rouge: Louisiana State University Press, 1950.

Stanton, William Ragan. *The Leopard's Spots: Scientific Attitudes toward Race in America, 1815–1859*. Chicago: University of Chicago Press, 1960.

Stauffer, John. *The Black Hearts of Men: Radical Abolitionists and the Transformation of Race*. Cambridge: Harvard University Press, 2002.

Stearns, Carol Zisowitz, and Peter N. Stearns. *Anger: The Struggle for Emotional Control in America's History*. Chicago: University of Chicago Press, 1987.

Stearns, Peter N., and Jan Lewis, eds. *An Emotional History of the United States*. New York: New York University Press, 1998.

Stewart, James Brewer. *Abolitionist Politics and the Coming of the Civil War*. Amherst: University of Massachusetts Press, 2008.

———. "The Emergence of Racial Modernity and the Rise of the White North, 1790–1840." *Journal of the Early Republic* 18, no. 2 (Summer 1998): 181–217.

———. "From Moral Suasion to Political Confrontation: American Abolitionists and the Problem of Resistance." In *Passages to Freedom: The Underground Railroad in History and Memory*, edited by David W. Blight, 76–83. Washington, DC: Smithsonian Books, 2004.

Striner, Richard. *Father Abraham: Lincoln's Relentless Struggle to End Slavery*. New York: Oxford University Press, 2006.

Sturgess, Kim C. *Shakespeare and the American Nation*. Cambridge: Cambridge University Press, 2004.

Summers, Mark W. *A Dangerous Stir: Fear, Paranoia, and the Making of Reconstruction*. Chapel Hill: University of North Carolina Press, 2009.

———. *The Ordeal of the Reunion: A New History of Reconstruction*. Chapel Hill: University of North Carolina Press, 2014.

———. *The Plundering Generation: Corruption and the Crisis of the Union*. New York: Oxford, 1987.

Swann, Charles. *Nathaniel Hawthorne: Tradition and Revolution*. Cambridge: Cambridge University Press, 1991.

Tamarkin, Elisa. *Anglophilia: Deference, Devotion, and Antebellum America*. Chicago: University of Chicago Press, 2004.

Tate, Adam L. *Conservatism and Southern Intellectuals 1789–1861: Liberty, Tradition and the Good Society*. Columbia: University of Missouri Press, 2005.

Taylor, Andrew. *Thinking America: New England Intellectuals and the Varieties of American Identity*. Lebanon, NH: University of New Hampshire Press, 2000.

Teague, Frances N. *Shakespeare and the American Popular Stage*. Cambridge: Cambridge University Press, 2006.

Temkin, Sefton D. "Isaac Mayer Wise and the Civil War." In *Jews and the Civil War: A Reader*, edited by Jonathan D. Sarna and Adam Mendelsohn, 161–80. New York: New York University Press, 2010.

Tewell, Jeremy J. *A Self-Evident Lie: Southern Slavery and the Threat to American Freedom*. Kent, OH: Kent State University Press, 2013.

Tise, Larry E. *Proslavery: A History of Defense of Slavery in America, 1701–1840*. Athens: University of Georgia Press, 1990.

Torbett, David. *Theology and Slavery: Charles Hodge and Horace Bushnell*. Macon, GA: Mercer University Press, 2006.

Towers, Frank. "Partisans, New History, and Modernization: The Historiography of the Civil War's Causes, 1861–2011." *Journal of the Civil War Era* 1, no. 2 (2011): 237–64.

Tuchinsky, Adam-Max. " 'The Bourgeoisie Will Fall and Fall Forever': The New-York Tribune, the 1848 French Revolution, and American Social Democratic Discourse." *Journal of American History* 92, no. 2 (2005): 470–97.

Tulloch, H. A. "Changing British Attitudes towards the United States in the 1880s." *Historical Journal* 20, no. 4 (1977): 825–40.

Turner, James. *The Liberal Education of Charles Eliot Norton*. Baltimore: Johns Hopkins University Press, 199.

VanDette, Emily. " 'It Should Be a Family Thing': Family, Nation, and Republicanism in Catharine Maria Sedgwick's *A New-England Tale* and *The Linwoods*." *American Transcendental Quarterly* 19, no. 1 (March 2005): 51–74.

Van Deusen, Glyndon G. "Why the Republican Party Came to Power." In *The Crisis of the Union, 1860–1861*, edited by George Harmon Knoles, 3–20. Baton Rouge: Louisiana State University Press, 1965.

Varon, Elizabeth R. *Disunion! The Coming of the American Civil War, 1789–1859*. Chapel Hill: University of North Carolina Press, 2008.

Von Frank, Albert J. *The Trials of Anthony Burns: Freedom and Slavery in Emerson's Boston*. Cambridge, MA: Harvard University Press, 1998.

Voss-Hubbard, Mark. *Beyond Party: Cultures of Antipartisanship in Northern Politics before the Civil War*. Baltimore: Johns Hopkins University Press, 2002.

Wachtell, Cynthia. *War No More: The Antiwar Impulse in American Literature, 1861–1914*. Baton Rouge: Louisiana State University Press, 2010.

Warshauer, Matthew. *Connecticut in the American Civil War*. Middletown, CT: Wesleyan University Press, 2011.

———. "Copperheads in Connecticut: A Peace Movement that Threatened the Union." In *This Distracted and Anarchical People: New Answers for Old Questions about the Civil War Era North*, edited by Andrew L. Slap and Michael Thomas Smith, 60–80. New York: Fordham University Press, 2013.

Waugh, John C. *On the Brink of Civil War: The Compromise of 1850 and How It Changed the Course of American History*. Wilmington, DE: Rowman & Littlefield, 2003.

Weber, Jennifer L. *Copperheads: The Rise and Fall of Lincoln's Opponents in the North*. New York: Oxford University Press, 2006.

Wells, Damon. *Stephen Douglas: The Last Years, 1857–1861*. Austin: University of Texas Press, 1971.

Welter, Rush. *The Mind of America, 1820–1860*. New York: Columbia University Press, 1975.

White, Jonathan W. *Emancipation, the Union Army, and the Reelection of Abraham Lincoln*. Baton Rouge: Louisiana State University Press, 2014.

Widmer, Edward. *Young America: The Flowering of Democracy in New York City*. New York: Oxford University Press, 1998.

Wiecek, William. "Popular Sovereignty in the Dorr War: Conservative Counterblast." *Rhode Island History* 32 (1973): 35–51.

———. *Sources of Antislavery Constitutionalism in America, 1760–1848*. Ithaca, NY: Cornell University Press, 1977.

Wilentz, Sean. *Chants Democratic: New York City and the Rise of the American Working Class, 1788–1850*. New York: Oxford University Press, 1984.

———. "Jeffersonian Democracy and the Origins of Political Antislavery in the United States: The Missouri Crisis Revisited." *Journal of the Historical Society* 4, no. 3 (2004): 375–401.

———. *The Rise of American Democracy: Jefferson to Lincoln*. New York: W.W. Norton, 2005.

———. "Slavery, Antislavery, and Jacksonian Democracy." In *The Market Revolution in America: Social, Political and Religious Expressions, 1800–1880*, edited by Melvyn Stokes and Stephen Conway, 202–23. Charlottesville: University Press of Virginia, 1996.

Williams, Frank J., and Patrick T. Conley, eds. *The Rhode Island Home Front in the Civil War*. Nashua, NH: Taos Press, 2013.

Williams, Mary Floyd. *History of the San Francisco Committee of Vigilance of 1851: A Study of Social Control on the California Frontier in the Days of the Gold Rush*. Berkeley: University of California Press, 1921.

Wills, Gary. *Lincoln at Gettysburg: The Words That Remade America*. New York: Simon & Schuster, 1992.

Wilson, Carol. *Freedom at Risk: The Kidnapping of Free Blacks in America, 1780–1865*. Lexington: University of Kentucky Press, 1994.

Wineapple, Brenda. *Hawthorne: A Life*. New York: Knopf, 2003.

Woods, Michael E. *Emotional and Sectional Conflict in the Antebellum United States*. New York: Cambridge University Press, 2014.

Worden, Blair. "The Victorians and Oliver Cromwell." In *History, Religion, and Culture: British Intellectual History, 1750–1950*, edited by Stefan Collini, Richard Whatmore, and Brian Young, 112–35. Cambridge: Cambridge University Press, 2000.

Wunder, John R., and Joann M. Ross, eds. *The Nebraska-Kansas Act of 1854*. Lincoln: University of Nebraska Press, 2008.

Yokota, Kariann Akemi. *Unbecoming British: How Revolutionary America Became a Postcolonial Nation*. New York: Oxford University Press, 2014.

Young, Alfred. "English Plebian Culture and 18th-Century American Radicalism." In *The Origins of Anglo-American Radicalism*, edited by Margaret C. Jacob and James R. Jacob, 185–212. London: Humanities Press, 1984.

Zelinsky, Wilbur. *Nation into State: The Shifting Symbolic Foundations of American Nationalism*. Chapel Hill: University of North Carolina Press, 1988.

Index

Wadsworth, James S., 94, 107, 206

Walker, Robert J., 113–15

Walker, William, 137

Walsh, Mike, 26, 40, 147

War of 1812, 51, 57, 128

Washington, George, 29, 31, 116, 143

Washington Chronicle, 198

Webb, James Watson, 36–38, 59, 77, 81, 131

Webster, Daniel, 9, 19, 32, 44, 45, 56, 57, 75, 82, 109, 142, 229

Weed, Thurlow, 103

Welles, Gideon, 88

Wheeler, John H., 60

Whiggery (political tradition), 10–12, 32–33, 36–40, 46, 55, 61–62, 77–79, 93, 127, 189, 196, 204, 227–28

Whig Party, 12, 17, 19, 35, 56–58, 62, 64, 69–70, 74–76, 90–93, 135, 142. *See also* Whiggery (political tradition)

Whitman, Walt, 11, 35, 36, 41, 217

Whitney, Thomas R., 29

Wide-Awakes, 177

Williams, Theo, 166

Williamson, Passmore, 60–61, 66

Wills, Gary, 219

Wilmot, David, 49–50. *See also* Wilmot Proviso

Wilmot Proviso, 53–54, 71, 105

Winthrop, John, 82

Winthrop, Robert C., 82–83, 119, 183, 212

Wisconsin, 74

Wise, Isaac Mayer, 169, 171–72

Wood, Fernando, 98, 127

Woodhull, Caleb S., 30, 35, 36, 48, 184, 189, 246 (n. 16), 248 (n. 64)

Woods, Michael E., 81

Woodward, George W., 207

Wright, Silas, 73, 88, 105

Young America, 103

CPSIA information can be obtained
at www.ICGtesting.com
Printed in the USA
LVHW091313220321
682094LV00008B/216